C000109299

The Doctor's Life Support

Maintaining Christian Vitality

Edited by
Muriel Crouch and Ronald Winton

Published for ICMDA
International Christian Medical and Dental Association
by
CHRISTIAN MEDICAL FELLOWSHIP
LONDON

Published for ICDMA by
Christian Medical Fellowship
157 Waterloo Road, London SEI 8XN

First Edition
in quarterly booklets
First published 1986

Second Edition
in a single volume
First published July 1994

ISBN 0-906747-30-9

Version of the Bible used

Unless otherwise indicated, quotations are taken from the:

RSV Revised Standard Version (C) 1946, 1952, 1971, 1973 by the Division of
Christian Education of the National Council of Churches of Christ in the United
States of America.

Other versions used are:

AV   Authorised (King James) Version

GNB   Good News Bible. (C) American Bible Society 1966, 1971, 1976. Published
by The Bible Societies and Collins.

JBP   J B Phillips' translation. (C) Geoffrey Bles Ltd.

LB   The Living Bible. (C) Tyndale House Publishers.

NEB   New English Bible. (C) the Delegates of the Oxford University Press and
the Syndics of the Cambridge University Press 1961, 1970.

NIV   New International Version. (C) 1973, 1978, 1984, New York International
Bible Society.

Cover Photo & Design: Gavin Williams Associates, London

Printed in Great Britain by
Stanley L. Hunt (Printers) Ltd, Midland Road, Rushden, Northamptonshire

Contents

Preface

The years immediately after qualification can be a testing time for the Christian doctor. Unfamiliar surroundings, unpreparedness for unexpected demands, the fatigue of overwork, the strain of life and death decisions, and unaccustomed spiritual isolation all take their toll. Disillusionment with the life and work of the Junior Hospital Doctor, a sense of inadequacy and the fear of being unable to 'cope' conspire to sap his spiritual vitality, while lack of time deprives him of the very chance he needs to recharge his spiritual batteries.

Many have won through in God's strength to fulfil their Christian calling in professional life; some fall by the way, jettisoning their faith, while others, suffering from spiritual inanition and preoccupied with other things, lose their vision and their first love and are lost to active Christian witness in their chosen professional sphere. It is for this reason that this book has been compiled. Intended primarily for those in the first year after qualification, it may yet appeal to many others in more senior positions both within and without the hospital service.

Contributions, with two exceptions, are from doctors who have themselves experienced the exigencies and opportunities of the early years. The list of contributors gives their specialties and professional status at the time of writing. Since the pressures on junior doctors are universal, half of the readings come from the United Kingdom and half from other parts of the world. Since terminology may sometimes be unfamiliar to the reader, a glossary has been included at the end of the book.

Each reading is intended to give one thought from the Word of God, relevant to the reader's situation and short enough to be retained in his mind all day. Readings are not designed to replace more comprehensive Bible study.

The work originally appeared as four booklets, each covering a quarter of the year. The need to reprint further copies has given the opportunity to make a number of changes, the most important being the decision to issue it in its new form in one volume. We hope that this will find ready acceptance by those who use these readings regularly. Opportunity has also been taken to correct a number of errors in the biblical references in the text, to replace two or three of the original readings by others that seemed more relevant to the rapidly changing circumstances of our times, and to include a brief index of themes for the benefit of those who look for help in particular situations. The readings for the Easter period have also been re-arranged and these have been placed, as before, between the readings for March and April.

Thanks are due to the many contributors who have given time and thought to the project. Their sincere hope and prayer is that the readings will prove helpful to many hard pressed doctors and the means of strengthening their faith and vitality, and deepening their love for the Lord Jesus Christ whose we are and whom we serve.

Muriel Crouch & Ronald R Winton
Editors

Index of Themes

Ambition
Feb 20; Mar 11, 23; Apr 15; Jul 2; Sep 13; Oct 5

Beatitudes
Jun 14-23; Dec 10-17

Cost of Discipleship
Feb 13-15; Aug 31

Easter
Between March and April readings

Friendship, Sex and Morality
Feb 25; Apr 11, 12; Jun 5, 6; Jul 29; Nov 12-15; Dec 18

Good Friday
After March readings

The Good Shepherd
Jan 9-10; Feb 9; Mar 9; Apr 9-10; May 9-10; Jun 9-10; Jul 9-10; Aug 9; Sep 9; Oct 9-10; Nov 9-10; Dec 30-31

Guidance
Jan 19; Mar 4; May 9-10, 12-17; Aug 1; Oct 31; Nov 1

Hopeless patients
Jan 25, 27; Feb 24, 26, 27; Apr 20; May 29; Jul 4

Money and possessions
Feb 20; Mar 6, 23; Apr 2, 18; Jul 15; Aug 2; Sep 11; Oct 1

Physical Stress
Jan 2, 20; Feb 5, 11; Mar 25; Apr 8; Jun 24; Aug 4, 17; Oct 18

Spiritual resources
Jan 4; Feb 2; Mar 1, 18; May 8; Jun 1; Jun 25; Aug 5, 6; Oct 16

The Way
3rd reading of each month

Introduction

The Daily Watch

Be still, and know that I am God. Psalm 46:10

We all need a time each day to meet with our Creator, the eternal God, in whom we live and move and have our being (Acts 17:28). Each day we need to be still before him, even if only for a brief time.

Long ago a great Christian leader, Augustine of Hippo, summed up our need to know God: 'Thou has made us for thyself and our souls are restless until they find their rest in thee'.

The Lord Jesus, Son of God though we know him to be, needed time to be with his Father in the days when he walked this earth as a man amongst us. He prayed often: sometimes just where he was; sometimes after withdrawing into a quiet place in the hills or in the wilderness, to be alone with God.

Most people would say that the best time to meet with God in this way is first thing in the morning, and that the best place is where we are alone. This is fine, but both of these 'bests' can be virtually impossible. Doctors, especially those working in hospital, are very often masters neither of their time nor of the place where they must be. It can be fatuous to tell them that they must take time every morning to be alone with God. All sorts of situations can rule this out.

That is one of the main reasons why this little book of daily readings has been prepared. There is almost always some time — an unpredictable time — when a short pause comes in the doctor's day. The little book comes out of the doctor's pocket, and something is there to read and think about in a reasonably short time — something of God's truth in the Scriptures related to the doctor's need, personal and professional. And there is an opportunity, however brief, to be still before God, that short time each day when the Spirit of God will lead you into the presence of the Most High.

> Whoso has felt the Spirit of the Highest
> Cannot confound nor doubt Him nor deny:
> Yea, with one voice, O world, tho' thou deniest,
> Stand thou on that side, for on this am I.
>
> F W H Meyer, St Paul

January 1 (New Year's Day)

New Leaf or New Life? New Year or new 'You'?

The steadfast love of the Lord never ceases, his mercies never come to an end: they are new every morning; great is thy faithfulness. Lamentations 3:22-24

The New Year is traditionally regarded as a time for a new start, a herald of better things, the chance to turn over 'a new leaf'. For most of us it is not so much a question of how many and what resolutions we make, but how long any of them will last! The New Year is littered with shattered good intentions. At no time is the weakness and helplessness of our fallen human nature so revealed as on January lst.

Some of us may be starting the year with high hopes, laudable ambitions and exciting dreams, not only of professional success but of fruitful Christian service. Others perhaps face the New Year with foreboding. Maybe our cherished hopes have not materialised, we are disillusioned with our professional progress or with the quality of our spiritual lives; we can't see the way forward and there are seemingly insoluble problems in our circumstances or relationships.

But, thank God, the coming year depends not on our resolutions but on God's reliability, not on our moods and misgivings but on God's continuing mercies (La 3:22-25). He offers not merely help to turn over a new leaf, but the gift of a new life. God may not change our circumstances but he can and indeed is changing us into his likeness by his Spirit as he daily renews our inner nature (2 Cor 3:18; 4:16).

We may not be able to see far ahead, but we may be sure that he has planned the way for us, for 'we are his workmanship created in Christ Jesus for good works, which God prepared beforehand, that we should walk in them' (Eph 2:10).

But we have a part to play; we are commanded to 'put on the new nature, created after the likeness of God in true righteousness and holiness' (Eph 4:24), 'to be renewed in the spirit of your minds' (Eph 4:23), 'to be transformed by the renewal of your mind' (Rom 12:2). We can enter the New Year with confidence and assurance.

> Keep thou my feet, I do not ask to see
> The distant scene, one step enough for me.
>
> J H Newman

Further reading: The references in context. Rev 21:1-7.

MC

January 2

Pressed above Measure

'Then came a man called Jairus... and... knelt before him, pleading for his help... Jesus went off with him, followed by a large crowd jostling at his elbow. Among them was a woman who had had a haemorrhage for twelve years.' Mark 5:22-25 (JBP)

Interrupted on the way to one patient by the urgent need of another, incessantly distracted, constantly in demand, jostled, hampered, harassed, tired — a description of my day? No, a day in the life of the Lord Jesus Christ. His response was willing, attentive, gracious, healing: in a word, loving. 'This woman touched his cloak... At once, Jesus knew intuitively that power had gone out of him... But he said to her "Daughter, it is your faith that has healed you. Go... in peace and be free from your trouble."'

What is my response to similar pressure? Resentful, curt, irritable, hurtful — loving myself more than my patients and more than my Lord? I forget that nothing happens to me without his consent. He has permitted each exasperating 'phone call and every extra booking in the clinic. Each irritation is a chance for me to show his control, not my own lack of it.

My life should be so full of his Holy Spirit that when I am jostled, his love overflows and brings healing and calm. Too often, it is self-love which spills out and brings discord.

> Lord Jesus, like all your other patients, I need healing. I confess that I have a short temper and a hasty tongue. Among all the jostlings of today, please help me to keep in touch with you, so that your power, peace and patience fill my heart and spill over into our work together.

Further reading: Mk 5:22-34.

JG

January 3

The Way (1) — The Way of God

'This is the way, walk in it.' Isaiah 30:21

Sir William Osler, the famous physician of years gone by, whose name was a legend in his own day, once wrote a little book called 'A Way of Life'. It was the text of an address he gave to Yale University undergraduates in 1913. It would sound rather old-fashioned to a student audience today. But it nevertheless contained a good deal of homely yet shrewdly realistic advice intended for students but still very much to the point for a wider audience.

Osler saw dedication to medicine as a way of life, and he followed that way consistently and effectively. To some extent at least, it needs also to be a way of life for every good doctor. But there is more to life than medicine.

Following Christ is another way, a greater way. And it goes well with medicine, as indeed Osler acknowledged. In its earliest days Christianity was called The Way (Acts 9:2; 18:25-26; 19:9,23; 24:14,22). It was the Way of the Lord, the Way of God — a concept already familiar from the Hebrew scriptures (eg 2 Sam 22:31; Ps 27:11; Ps 37:5). That is what Isaiah was talking about when he said: 'This is the way, walk in it'. It is a way by which to live, a way in which to walk, a way to bring us to God. It is The Way. The prophet Jeremiah spells it out a little more fully:

> This is what the Lord says:
> 'Stand at the crossroads and look;
>   ask for the ancient paths,
> ask where the good way is, and walk in it,
>   and you will find rest for your souls'

Jer 6:16 NIV

> Lord, make your way plain before my feet, and grant
> me the grace to walk in it faithfully and consistently.

Further reading: The passages cited in the text are all worth looking up.

RRW

January 4

A Token for Good

Show me a sign of thy favour. Psalm 86:17

There are barren times in the lives of all of us, when we long for God to reveal himself afresh, and show his hand. Maybe the pressures of work have drained us, or isolation from the Christian fellowship and worship we once knew has taken its toll. Bible reading has gone 'stale', and prayer seems to get nowhere. In fact, we have almost lost the appetite for either. It is then that we long for God 'to do something'.

But God does not reveal himself on demand. The requests of the Pharisees and Herod for signs and miracles evoked no response from Jesus except 'No sign shall be given...' (Mt 12:38-39; Lk 23:8-9). In both cases they asked for the wrong reasons. We, too, sometimes want God to manifest himself, or give his gifts for a wrong reason, to assure ourselves or perhaps others of our spirituality. But our faith is too precious in the sight of God for him to accede to our request for a sign of his favour, by sending us exalted feelings or reassuring experiences, pleasant and uplifting as they may be (1 Pet 1:7).

But nevertheless God knows our weakness. He understands the dark tunnel with no light at the end, and has promised that we shall never be tempted beyond our strength (1 Cor 10:13). He will give us a 'token for good' just when we need it, but often not in the way we expect or would choose. Elijah would have recognised God's presence had he manifested it in wind, earthquake or fire. Instead he came in 'a still small voice' (1 Ki 19:11-12). He will reveal himself, often in little ways — the split-second timing that is more than coincidence, a bad mistake averted, an unexpected turn of events, the gratitude of a patient for a trivial kindness, or the hint of unexpected fruit from a word of witness long forgotten. The Lord of hosts is with us (Ps 46:11) and will give us the 'token' we need, in his own time and way. But — watch for it!

> When the way is dark and I cannot see
> Through the mist of his wise design
> Through the darkness wide, he is by my side
> With a touch of his hand on mine.
>
> There are times when tired of the toilsome round
> That for ways of the world I pine,
> But he drags me back to the upward track
> With a touch of his hand on mine.

Further reading: 1 Pet 1:3-9. Ps 121.

MC

January 5

Running Ahead

'Father,' Jesus said, 'If you will, take this cup of suffering away from me. Not my will, however, but your will be done.' Luke 22:42 (GNB)

A blank wall, a closed door. All the plans and preparations had gone smoothly — and then suddenly almost at the climax, and far too late to find an alternative, the way is blocked. Hopes are dashed, excitement drained, expectations unfulfilled. Why, Lord? You knew what was coming — why did I get so far along the road before this happened?

I try to find another route — and every way is barred: no way forward, no way around the obstacle. What am I meant to do now, Lord? Wait. There is no alternative now. At last, I am thrown back onto God. I have rushed ahead again — frequently pausing to mention the overall idea to God, but never really asking him, or listening and waiting for his plan. Rather, I only ask for confirmation of my own plans — please, God, this is what I'd like to do.

Every day I make decisions — some I make alone, some after consulting others. As I learn more, I expect to assume more responsibility. This includes making increasingly far-reaching decisions and acting upon them alone. This is entirely right, and the path to professional maturity. In personal decisions too, including spiritual ones, I must aim at maturity.

Self-determination, however, is not the maturity I seek. To forget that I am not my own, and to do as I please, is not the way that Jesus took. Worse, having once given myself to God, to begin little by little to isolate from him decisions affecting my life, while deceiving myself that he is really still in charge, only leads to distancing myself from him. And so, the sudden shock of disappointment, and the awful realisation of the true state of things. I am glad of the pain too, though, for it reassures me of God's great love for me — that he will not let me stray too far.

> Forth in thy name, O Lord, I go
>   My daily labour to pursue;
> Thee, only thee, resolved to know,
>   In all I think or speak or do.
>
> Thee may I set at my right hand
>   Whose eyes my inmost substance see;
> And labour on at thy command
>   And offer all my works to thee.

Charles Wesley

Further reading: Nu 22:12-14, 22-34. Is 30:21.

PIMA

January 6

Gifts of Nature and of Grace

Well done, good and faithful servant; you have been faithful over a little, I will set you over much; enter into the joy of your master. Matthew 25:21

There is a tendency to interpret this parable of the talents in terms of our natural abilities and earthly endowments, and certainly the Christian doctor should seek to use his God-given talents to the glory of his master. Doctors are high flyers, and the competition for places these days ensures that most have personal qualities of intellect and skill, even if at times we wonder if this is really true! However, we must not forget that although God has given us these talents for the relief of medical needs of others, there are other gifts that are not inherited by nature, nor acquired by training, which are needed if our work is to bear eternal fruit.

Churches often look up to doctors, who can easily find themselves in positions of leadership. But being a doctor does not automatically fit us for the leadership we are often asked to assume in spiritual circles. How often is our prayer, 'Where, Lord, can I use my talents to their greatest advantage?' Paul in the first four chapters of his first letter to the Corinthians reminds his hearers that his message to them was preached in weakness, and not with the persuasive oratory that was his natural gift (1 Cor 2:4) but 'in demonstration of the Spirit and of power'. Although he was one of the greatest intellects of the day, he did not himself use a flashy demonstration of that intellect to convert the world — he would not have succeeded. In 1 Corinthians 13:1-3 Paul points out that natural gifts and goodness will never produce spiritual results.

What God wants is ourselves. He will then supply spiritual talents appropriate to the work to which he calls us. These spiritual gifts may well dovetail with our natural abilities. He will probably in his wisdom and providence use our medical training and talents, though not necessarily so. It is only after doing the work God has called us to, whether that involves our medical training or not, that we shall hear our Lord's 'well done, good and faithful servant'.

> Our heavenly Father, forgive us for the self-centredness which seeks to fit your work round our natural gifts. Help us to see that you require nothing less than our total commitment to your will and to seek those spiritual qualities you can use in the furtherance of your kingdom in whatever secular sphere you place us.

Further reading: Mt 25:14-30. Ro 12:1-18.

TAG

January 7

Attitudes

Your attitude should be the same as that of Christ Jesus. Philippians 2:5 (NIV)

'I've got to look good on Prof's ward round today!'
> *Do nothing out of selfish ambition ...*
'I'm going to talk to him afterwards about his Senior House Officer post, I really am the best applicant!'
> *... or vain conceit,*
'Oh don't bother me now, nurse, can't you see I'm very busy?'
> *but in humility ...*
'No, I'm not going to do it, anyway, it's not my job, I am a doctor!'
> *... consider others better than yourselves.*

'I just hope he doesn't make a fuss again about that old bed-blocker!' (one who occupies a much needed bed).

Look not only to your own interests ...,

'It would look good if I could get her transferred before next week!'
... but also to the interests of others.

Now read Philippians 2:3-11 (NIV) and ask yourself:

Am I motivated by selfish ambition?
Am I conceited?
Is my work always more important than that of others?
Am I prepared to be a servant?
Who matters most? Me or my patients?

Thank you Lord that you humbled yourself — even to death on a cross — for me. Help me to humble myself for you.

DCM

January 8

Worry

Do not ask anxiously ... your heavenly Father knows ... Matthew 6:31-32 (NEB)

The child brought up in a well-provided home with normal security is not anxious about tomorrow's needs because he has complete confidence in his parents' will and ability to provide as they always have done. Unless the parents have, through negligence or through circumstances beyond their control, failed to make provision, the child's attitude is unquestioning.

When does worry begin? It begins when we become more mature, realise our place in time and start to look into the future and see our parents' limitations. But our heavenly Father has no such limitations apart from those we impose on him. Worry is always concerned with tomorrow and its tomorrows. Most of us can cope with today, even if it is agonisingly difficult. But a vista of endless tomorrows may be too much to bear. Jesus says that we must use our energy in promoting the kingdom of God: the human material needs can and must be left to the Father's care.

It is for the heathen to consume their nervous energy in worrying about the future. Our heavenly Father knows we have need of all these things, and he has no limitations. He is master of circumstances.

To worry is not to trust; to trust is not to worry. 'Do not be anxious about tomorrow; tomorrow will look after itself. Each day has troubles enough of its own' (Mt 6:34 NEB).

How God will lead
Throughout the year
We cannot tell –
But this is sure, all will be well
And every need supplied
With Christ
As Guide.

R E Cleeve

Further reading: 1 Kings 17:1-16. Psalm 121

HMW

January 9

Sheep and Shepherding

We are his people, and the sheep of his pasture. Psalm 100:3

There is a unique relationship between a shepherd and his own flock; he knows their names and their idiosyncrasies, their needs and their wilfulness. He watches, tends, leads and disciplines them. They are his responsibility and his chief concern. His own livelihood depends on their wellbeing, so what affects them affects him. If they stray he must seek them, if they roll on their backs he must help them up, if they are attacked he must drive away the aggressor. His life is sheep-centred and a good flock will be shepherd-centred, for they will know his voice among all others. A self-willed flock will be led away from his influence by their own foolish waywardness, but then quickly learn the bleakness and lostness of life without him.

In a world that has gone astray, everyone turning to his own way, what a need there is for a return to the Good Shepherd — to hear his voice, to know him and to follow him! We are reminded in each surgery or clinic and on all our rounds that the consequences of self-will are destructive, bringing physical as well as emotional and spiritual disaster. A sense of purposelessness pervades our society. Yet even those who admit to the existence of God may make no attempt to follow him. He may be regarded as a shepherd among other possible leaders and sometimes promoted to the Shepherd, yet still without recognition as to how he gave his life to save us from straying and longs to become personal Saviour and guide. We each need to tune in to his voice in a daily act of personal commitment and obedience. Only so does he become my Shepherd.

As I have reflected on Psalm 23 while following the Shepherd over the years, as well as in writing these notes, two authors have provided particular insight and inspiration. Ian Barclay's little book 'He is everything to me' deserves a reprint (Falcon Press, 1972). Philip Keller's selection of shepherding books is still available: 'A shepherd looks at Psalm 23' and its companion volume 'A shepherd looks at the Good Shepherd' (both published by Pickering & Inglis) and 'Lessons from a sheepdog' (Hodder & Stoughton, 1984). David would have enjoyed them!

Further reading: Ps 23. Is 53:4-6.

JG

January 10

My Shepherd (1)

The Lord is my shepherd. Psalm 23:1

My dictionary holds ten associations for the word 'lord'. Including its use as a verb, they all indicate one in a position of authority who commands respect. A shepherd is simply defined as one who tends his sheep, either literally (as a sheep-herd) or metaphorically (as a pastor). The one is a mighty potentate, the other a practical care-giver. At the start of this psalm, then, we have an immediate contrast: the creator and controller of heaven and earth is given a name which identifies him with the down-to-earth task of shepherding.

David knew all about the selfless devotion needed to be a good shepherd for he had been one himself. Constantly watching and counting, out at all hours and in all weathers, pursuing, rescuing, tending and protecting — a shepherd's life is far from idyllic: it may even involve the literal laying down of physical as well as personal life on behalf of the sheep. From such a lifestyle he had been promoted to kingship — a lord in his own right. Yet some of his other psalms tell us how aware he was that, even from the throne, he had behaved as foolishly as one of his old flock. He had turned to his own way and run into hazards of his own making and then cried in desperation to the Lord to rescue him. Here, it comes as a shaft of light to realise that this same mighty, conceivably estranged, Lord is willing to act as a shepherd to him — and not just 'a' shepherd but 'my' shepherd. The same concern for his individual sheep that David had shown to his flock was now being shown to him. The power, majesty and authority rightly indicated in his title 'Lord' are matched by the unfailing concern and practical love of the shepherd. His longing to bring back the wanderer would lead him, as history would unfold, to lay down his life for the sheep.

Doctors are sometimes accused of lording it over others, jostling with each other and trampling on their patients. It is good to be reminded that the Lord regards us as so many sheep! This restores focus and humility. To some he may give tasks as leaders of the flock or even under-shepherds. Harassed housemen, busy GPs or unit administrators may see themselves in this light and identify with the burden of a shepherd's life. The Lord is in absolute authority and, whether shepherding or shepherded, my cries for help and deliverance will be heard, whatever the crisis or challenge. The human equivalents of helpless lambs or stubborn old rams who fill our lives are equally precious to him. He hears their pitiful cries and knows their conflicts as well as the problems they bring to others. In his lordship he could enforce his will, but as shepherd he is strong but gentle and expects me, as his follower, to be the same.

Whether dealing with absentees from the clinic or aggressors on committee, the authoritarian attitude which may arise so readily must be tempered by the recollection of the ways of a shepherd with his sheep, putting aside all self-interest and seeking to be patient, yet pursuing — just as the Good Shepherd is in dealing with me.

The King of love my Shepherd is, whose goodness faileth never.

H W Baker

Further reading: Jn 10:11-18.

JG

January 11

Paul and Physical Handicap

By the grace of God I am what I am. 1 Corinthians 15:10

According to an ancient tradition, the Apostle Paul was 'an ugly little man'. Ancient traditions vary in their authenticity, but nothing in Paul's own letters or in the record of his travelling companion Luke contradicts this tradition. Much fits in with it.

Paul (2 Cor 10:10-11 NIV) quotes his critics in Corinth as saying, 'His letters are weighty and forceful, but in person he is unimpressive and his speaking amounts to nothing'. He firmly refutes any idea that his letters are just words, but neither here nor elsewhere does he make any attempt to contradict what is said about his personal appearance and speaking.

On the nature of Paul's 'thorn in the flesh' (2 Cor 12:7), about which he is not specific (one has to try to read between the lines), one of the most widely held theories is that it was an eye affliction, which may well have marred his facial appearance. He acknowledges (Gal 4:13-15) that a bodily ailment made him a trial to the Galatians, and he is grateful for the way in which they received him: 'you did not scorn or despise me,... if possible, you would have plucked out your eyes and given them to me'.

When Paul and Barnabas came to Lystra (Acts 14:8-18), and set the cripple walking, the people said they were gods. Because Paul was the chief speaker, they called him Hermes, the messenger of the gods. But it is not difficult to infer which of the two was the taller and more impressive in appearance, for it was Barnabas whom they called Zeus, the chief of the gods.

When Paul came to Athens, at first he failed to make an impression on at least some of the philosophers, who saw him only as 'this babbler' (Acts 17:18). Some later changed their minds.

There can be little doubt that Paul was small and outwardly unimpressive. Yet, by the grace of God, he was foremost among that little band of people who turned the world upside down. He had intellect, learning, courage, endurance, humility without weakness and loyalty to those to whom he ministered. Above all he had a deep unswerving devotion to Christ, on whose indwelling presence he depended. If the ancient tradition is accurate, may God give us more such ugly little men!

> Ay, for this Paul, a scorn and a reviling,
>   Weak as you know him and the wretch you see –
> Even in these eyes shall ye behold His smiling,
>   Strength in infirmities and Christ in me.

FWH Meyer, St Paul

Further reading: Look up the references.

RRW

January 12

God's Limits (1) — The Limits of Provision

Man shall not live by bread alone. Matthew 4:4

The first thing that Jesus did when he felt his hour had come to begin his ministry was to submit himself in humility to the baptism of repentance at the hands of his cousin, John the Baptist. It was then that he received his first commendation from his Father: 'Thou art my beloved son; with thee I am well pleased' (Lk 3:22). After that he was led out into the wilderness to consider the methods his Father wanted him to adopt. The Tempter was at hand.

After forty days of fasting, Jesus is hungry. He needs food, and the first temptation is to turn stones into bread. Nothing wrong about that, is there? 'God is your provider, you need never be hungry, only believe that he can provide for you; where God guides, he provides.'

Jesus rejects the suggestion. He quotes the Scripture: 'Man shall not live by bread alone'. He declines to cast his Father in the role of Material Provider. Could it be that it was that same spirit of renunciation which had led him

19

to seek baptism, renouncing his divine exemption which he could have claimed, and was it that same spirit which had earned him his Father's audible approval?

How do we, in the light of this first temptation of Jesus, interpret the Father's love and care? Do we present him as one whose duty it is to provide, forgetting that Jesus himself, in his human form, had to go without an answer to the problem of hunger and bodily discomfort? 'Foxes have holes, and birds of the air have nests,' he said, 'but the Son of man has nowhere to lay his head' (Mt 8:20). It is true that he pointed to the Father's provision for the birds and the lilies of the field. But in the wisdom of God there are limits. Perhaps we must learn the affirmation of the prophet: 'Though the fig tree does not blossom, nor fruit be on the vines, the produce of the olive fail and the fields yield no food...yet I will rejoice in the Lord, I will rejoice in the God of my salvation' (Hab 3:17-18).

> Lord, help me to know and to accept what it means to say:
> 'Man shall not live by bread alone, but by every word that
> proceeds from the mouth of God'.

Further reading: Mt 4:1-4. De 8:1-6.

EPF

January 13

God's Limits (2) — The Limits of Protection

You shall not tempt the Lord your God. Matthew 4:7

The second temptation which assails Jesus is more subtle (Mt 4:5-6). It comes as he is transported to the pinnacle of the temple (whether in body or in mind does not matter): 'Throw yourself down, you won't hurt yourself. God will send his angels to look after you, lest you strike your foot against a stone'. It is both more subtle and more devilish. The Tempter seems perversely to take his cue from the response of Jesus to the first temptation: to show that he too can quote Scripture (Ps 91:11-12).

Jesus as firmly as before rejects the concept of God as Protector. There are certain natural consequences of every action or situation, and it is not God's responsibility to ensure that the natural forces of gravity, wind, flood, earthquakes or micro-organisms are miraculously suspended to ensure that someone is not harmed. Jesus himself, the healer, the stiller of storms, is one who knows what it is to be tired and to suffer pain, who goes willingly to the cross rather than claim God's protection as a right (Mt 26:53). His disciples don't understand. Peter goes so far as to rebuke him for the very idea, bringing upon himself Jesus' strong censure: 'Get behind me, Satan!' (Mt 16:23). He takes his three most intimate associates up the mountain to meet the Father, to learn that God can be his Father without necessarily being his protector from physical harm. Perhaps it was this that earned for Jesus his second audible approbation from God: 'This is my beloved Son, with whom I am well pleased; listen to him'.

How in the light of this second temptation do we interpret the Father's love and care? Do we present him as one whose duty it is to protect us, forgetting that Jesus himself, in his human form, had to go without an answer to the problem of pain? Perhaps we should learn to base our faith not so much on God's power to alter our material environment as on his willingness to live with us through it.

> Lord, help me to know you are with me in all circumstances.
> Help me not to forget you when things go well.
> Help me not to doubt you when things go badly.
> Help me to know that nothing can separate me from your love.

Further reading: Matthew 4:1-7. Romans 8:28-39.

EPF

January 14

God's Limits (3) — The Limits of Promotion

You shall worship the Lord your God and him only shall you serve.
Matthew 4:10

The third temptation offered to Jesus is the boldest. Satan comes right into the open with a naked and direct bid for power. He brings to Jesus' mind's eye all the kingdoms of the world and the glory of them: 'All these I will give you, if you will fall down and worship me' (Mt 4:9).

Jesus does not need the devil's patronage to exercise his rightful authority. 'Begone, Satan,' he says, 'for it is written, "You shall worship the Lord your God and him only shall you serve".' It is not the devil or anybody else, but God alone, who is to be worshipped. In the loneliest depths of his sufferings (Jn 12:27-28) Jesus is to be constrained to say to his Father: 'Now is my soul troubled. And what shall I say, "Father, save me from this hour"? No, for this purpose I have come to this hour. Father, glorify thy name.' And the third commendation comes from the Father: 'I have glorified it, and I will glorify it again'. For the third time, how do we interpret the Father's love and care? Do we present him as one whose duty it is to promote our interests, forgetting that Jesus himself, in his human form, had to go without an answer to the problem of rejection, so that he was to come to say: 'My God, my God, why hast thou forsaken me?' (Mt 27:46).

21

And what of God's glory? And of ours? Perhaps we have risen high in our profession, we have made lots of money and are distinguished academically. We go to all the important congresses and professional conferences. We have walked in company with the devil up to our own high mountain. We have listened to his proposals without even recognising who our companion is. Have we been given the grace, have we sought the grace to say 'Father, glorify thy name', even when we know that such glorification may be costly to ourselves?

> Lord Jesus, help us always to hear your voice saying, as you
> said to your first disciples, and as you say to us in the closed
> security of the upper rooms of our lives, 'As the Father has
> sent me, even so I send you'.

Further reading: Mt 4:1-11. Lk 4:1-15.

EPF

January 15

Certainty

... that you may know the certainty of the things you have been taught.
Luke 1:4

There is nothing more certain in life than its uncertainty, and medicine is not exempt. No matter what we think may happen today, there is no guarantee that it will. The issues of the day are by no means solely in our hands. Other people and other events play their part. We may even be facing a specific choice with far- reaching consequences and find ourselves in a dilemma of indecision.

Professionally we are trained to pause and ponder. While we may diagnose thyrotoxicosis on the basis of a formula, we still face the patient with unique reactions and needs. No two patients are alike, and few 'keep to the book'. Supposedly precise laboratory tests can have startling standard deviations, and diagnosis or treatment often has to be tentative and empirical.

The basis of Luke's good news, however, is that there are some things of which we may be sure. God is a certainty — not as a vague concept, but as a Person. Luke's evidence was provided by eye witnesses (v2), his story is irrefutable history, the birth of Jesus Christ in the days of Herod the king (v5).

The house owner may feel pride as he sees the title deeds of his property, even if it be but a fleeting glimpse before they reside with the Building Society! Luke's Gospel forms the title deeds of the Christian faith, and these we can retain for ourselves.

Dr Luke should appeal to the scientifically minded. He was a research worker: 'having investigated from their source all things accurately' (v3), he proceeded to 'write them up' (vv1,3). He then left it to the reader to assess the reliability of the record. This certainty is not an abstraction but can be verified in an intensely personal way. The onus is on the reader and the responsibility is his.

'Choice is one of the root ideas in the word "believe", and this element of responsibility and commitment is the key to "the obedience of faith" which is the heart of Christian discipleship!' (Os Guinness).

> Lord, it is easy to believe my doubts, and doubt my beliefs.
> I am tempted to trust only the things I can see and handle,
> yet your word says that these are temporary, whereas the
> things I cannot see are eternal. Grant that I may be so certain
> of your unchanging faithfulness that I may not fear the
> uncertainties of life.

Further reading: Ps 46. Jn 20:30,31. Eph 1:15-23.

DEBP

January 16

Intake & Output

So you too, my friends, must be obedient...You must work out your own salvation in fear and trembling; for it is God who works in you, inspiring both the will and the deed, for his own chosen purpose. Philippians 2:12-13 (NEB)

God works within us but it is not a passive experience. We experience God's working in us through new desires, through a new sensitivity to human need, even through visions of opportunities for service to be seized. These thoughts are not enough, they must be put into practice, we must obey the stirrings of the Spirit within us. It is only thus that God can use us as channels for his love, as ambassadors to the world. No wonder Paul regards this as a great and serious matter to be approached with 'fear and trembling'. We have only one life on earth, we must seek God's will for that life with reverence, care and obedience.

Our wills are wayward, we must pray for obedience. Remember what it cost Christ to be obedient unto death; his followers failed him at this time when they could have helped him most. Our spiritual awareness is dull, and we must be careful not to neglect the Spirit within us or stifle him by active disregard.

Everyday life is proving ground. Today as we work with colleagues, as we meet our patients, as we live with our friends or families, let us expect God to suggest actions to us, and let us try to put these thoughts into practice.

> Breathe on me, breath of God;
>   Fill me with life anew,
> That I may love what thou dost love,
> And do what thou wouldst do.

Edwin Hatch

Further reading: Jn 14:21-24, 15:14. Ja 2:14-18,26

JEL-J

January 17

Pray Continually

Be joyful always; pray continually, give thanks in all circumstances. 1 Thessalonians 5:16-18 (NIV)

Jesus told his disciples that they should always pray and not give up. Lk 18:1 NIV.

How much space does prayer occupy in our lives? An old manual suggested four stages in our prayer life:

1. 'Morning by morning, O Lord, you hear my voice; morning by morning I lay my requests before you and wait in expectation' (Ps 5:3 NIV).

2. 'Evening, morning and noon I cry out in distress, and he hears my voice' (Ps 55:17 NIV).

3. 'Seven times a day I praise you for your righteous laws' (Ps 119:164 NIV).

4. 'Pray continually' (1 Thess 5:17 NIV).

Prayer dominated the life of our Lord, and the lives of all the great men of the Bible and Church history. Perhaps we might feel that to pray continually is just for spiritual giants, but that is not so. Paul told all the Thessalonian Christians, 'Pray continually...for this is God's will for you in Christ Jesus'. God wants us all to know this dimension. What does it entail? We need of course a disciplined prayer structure, with set times (whenever possible) to begin and end the day with God. It will mean being up early enough to be undisturbed.

Between these times we are working, travelling, eating, socialising and so on. I was early advised to make my car a sanctuary. This has proved a blessing. Do you pray before checking a patient? I used to pray before intravenous injections, lumbar punctures and paracenteses. It helped. What about prayer regarding problems and relationships? Nehemiah practised this. When the king asked, 'What is it you want?', he said, 'I prayed to God...and I answered the king' (Neh 2:4-5 NIV).

At other times prayer is not verbal but simply an attitude of trust and an awareness that God is with us. Even while concentrating hard on our work the sense of his presence remains. Praying continually is just walking with God throughout the day, taking him into all our activities and relationships.

Lord, teach us to pray.

Further reading: Ex 33:11-17.

CDA

January 18

Tunnel Vision

Seeing they do not see ... Matthew 13:13. Open his eyes that he may see ... 2 Kings 6:17

'Is there a doctor present, please?' I gave a familiar glance at my wife as I left my breakfast half-eaten to respond to the call blaring through the conference centre loudspeakers. One of the organisers drew me aside and told me that a lady known to have numerous spiritual problems had gone into a hypnotic trance; and although several brothers had been praying over her for half an hour, she was still totally blank. They were pretty sure this was an occult problem, but would I just take a look?

I do so, and it was immediately clear that the lady was *in extremis*, and indeed one touch was enough to tell that she was in fact dead and had been for some little time. The coroner's report later informed me that she had died from a subarachnoid haemorrhage.

On another occasion I accompanied one of the leaders of my local church on a visit to see an Indian girl, who had been heavily involved in occult practices and whose father had contacted us, desperate for help, as the girl's mental condition was rapidly deteriorating. When we arrived, she was in a very agitated state. She could hardly speak. Her face was period-ically contorted by violent grimaces, and she was throwing her arms into bizarre postures and freezing in these strange positions for several minutes at a time. She had already been seen by the family doctor earlier that same day, and I would readily have agreed with his opinion that this girl was having an acute psychotic episode and was in urgent need of hos-pitalisation. However, my companion, after asking a few questions of the parents, was sure that this was a case of demonic possession. After a word of explanation to the family, he gently prayed over her and spoke to the demonic power in the name of Jesus.

If I had not personally witnessed the transformation that took place, I would have had difficulty in believing it. Five minutes later that girl was sitting normally and able to hold a rational conversation as we shared the way of salvation with her.

How true it is that we only see what we look for and how essential that we continually ask God to remove the prejudices that so easily keep us from seeing situations as they really are from his perspective.

> The meek will he guide in judgment
>
> (Ps 25:9 AV)
>
> Lord Jesus, you have clearly taught us that we are to 'judge with right judgment'. Help me, I pray, in ever-increasing measure to do just that.

Further reading: Acts 14:8-10. Gn 41:37-39.

TGS

January 19

When God Calls

'Son, go and work in the vineyard today.' He answered, 'I go, sir', but did not go. Matthew 21:28,30

In these days when many are drifting into a career, and many voices are clamouring for our attention, it is easy to miss God's call. It comes like a wind, invisible, purposeful and refreshing, that blows on a man's life; it comes like a fire, warm, melting and glowing, that burns in a man's heart; it comes like a lover, winsome, magnetic and compelling, that beckons a man to follow.

But the wind may be resisted. You can shelter from it behind excuses or procrastination. You can anchor yourself to prejudices and false priorities. You can sail into it and pretend that this was the direction the wind guided you. You can say, 'I cannot tell whence it cometh (is it really God who is calling me?), or whither it goeth' (where is he leading me?)!

The fire may be extinguished. Neglect will do it. Ignore the call, and the fire will go out. Pouring on the cold water of fear will do it — fear of the future, of insecurity, the fear of other people's opinion. Scattering the coals will do it (avoiding the fellowship of other Christians and going your own way).

The Lover may be grieved. A weak, half-hearted insincere reply is enough to grieve the heart of this 'Lover of men'. The son in the parable said, ' I have heard your call, I'm going to work in your vineyard'. But one job led to another and he never went. How easy it is to hear the call clearly in our student days! But then one thing leads to another and we find ourselves settling down with the call unanswered.

> Father, help me not to resist the Spirit when his wind blows on my life, not to quench him when his fire burns in my heart and not to grieve him when his love beckons me to follow.

Further reading: Mt 21:28-32. Je 20:9. Lk 5:27-28.

KM

January 20

Day off that never was!

He said to them: 'Come away by yourselves to a lonely place, and rest awhile!' For many were coming and going, and they had no leisure even to eat. Mark 6:31

No leisure! How well we understand that phrase when so often we lose our half-day, or our plans for an evening out are spoiled by crises. But the Lord was watchful of his disciples' needs and arranged for them to have a day off. But read what happened (Mk 6:31-56)!

It seems that the only time that they had to themselves was during the row across the lake. The rest of the day was spent with the crowds who had pursued Jesus round the shore; and when the precious hours had gone, there were still 5,000 mouths to feed. Can you sense their disappointment and frustration? What was Jesus trying to teach them? Was it that brisk physical exercise could be reinvigorating? That being in a different environment was stimulating? That though they could not get away from finding work for him, his work is itself refreshing? That it was better to share what they had — be it their precious free time or their iron rations — than to keep it to themselves? That even though the day seemed to be ending in frustration and exhaustion, he was still able to dispel fear and fatigue? If these were the lessons he wanted to each them they seem to have missed the point: 'they did not understand' (v52).

He is no less watchful of our needs than he was of theirs. He is interested in the amount of off-duty we have, and how we spend it. He understands the tiredness and the disappointments because he has experienced them himself. If things do not work out just as we have planned, it does not mean that he has forgotten or that his plans have gone wrong. As Lord of our lives he is Lord also of our leisure. He wants to share our off-duty as well as our days on call. He wants to show us that he can meet our need, and the need of others through us. He can still work miracles in his disciples' time off — if they spend it with him.

> Lord Jesus, please teach me how I ought to spend my off-duty, whether alone or in a crowd, in activity or in rest. And when I lose my leisure time through no fault of my own, may I know your companionship, your creativity and your renewal.

Further reading: Mk 6:31-56.

JG

January 21

The Divine Surgeon (1)

I wound and I heal. Deuteronomy 32:39

One of the many titles full of meaning that we give to our Lord is the Great Physician. Certainly as we reflect upon the varied aspects of Christ's ministry, we can only conclude that the title is a most appropriate one.

But not only is he the Great Physician, he is also the Model Physician. We can readily identify with the Model in terms of compassion, love, patience or understanding. However, in terms of medical functions how do we view the Model? I think few would perceive him as a pathologist or oto-laryngologist or radiologist. More likely we would identify him in the role of diagnostician or psychiatrist or family physician.

Recently, as I have been considering my own perceptions of Christ in relation to this question, I have been thinking about his role as surgeon. That verse in the Song of Moses has focused my attention in this regard. There God says, 'I wound and I heal'. To me, this suggests that God takes an active surgical role in the healing process. Wounding, the surgical incision, is painful, but it leads to ultimate healing. God's objective in the life of each believer is to make each one into the image of Christ. Surely our own desire should be to be confirmed to the likeness of Christ — to be more like him in every way.

Did you ever consider that part of this process may require surgical inter-vention? Let me suggest a few areas where the Divine Surgeon may operate.

Firstly, consider the incision and drainage of an abscess. We know that the rationale of this procedure is to let the foul pus and dead matter be released from the body, so that the whole organism will not become infected and toxic. How often we need the Divine Surgeon to open the abscesses of pride or hate or jealousy, so that we can become free of their infective and toxic potentials. Such an incision is often very painful, and the convalescent period may be prolonged; but gradually the wound heals, and health blooms. 'I wound and I heal.'

> Merciful Lord, when we feel the sharpness of your surgery
> in our lives and in ourselves, knowing that it is for our own
> good, help us to remember that always you wound and you
> heal.

Further reading: Heb 12:3-14.

ROS

January 22

The Divine Surgeon (2)

God is at work in you, both to will and to work for his good pleasure. Philippians 2:13

As we contemplate the work of the Divine Surgeon in us, we can think also of the field of orthopaedic surgery. One of the main objectives in this area of specialisation is to help the patient walk more naturally and easily and to restore muscle balance. Often a series of interventions is required before a normal gait is possible. The Christian life is a walk — or a race if you wish — but so often we stumble and fall. We limp, we are poorly balanced. So the Divine Surgeon intervenes, again and again, to correct and repair our deformities and imbalances, so that we may walk more easily in the footsteps of Christ and run more successfully the race that is set before us.

Fashioning us into the image of Christ must involve plastic surgery at times. Balms and oils may help in the process, but warts and ugly lumps require surgical removal. So the plastic Surgeon takes up the scalpel, fashioning us into the image of Christ.

Some operations are performed not only for the health and comfort of the patient, but also for the sake of the life and health of another. Consider a Caesarean section, for example. Without this intervention both the mother and baby would most likely perish. Some of our pain may well be for the sake of the very lives of others. The Divine Surgeon operates with our best interests in view, as well as those of others who are close to us.

> Help us, Lord, to rejoice in the fact that we are your
> workmanship, created in Christ Jesus for good works,
> which you prepared beforehand, that we should walk in
> them.

Further reading: Phil 2:12-18. Eph 2:1-10.

ROS

January 23

The Divine Surgeon (3)

Humble yourselves therefore under the mighty hand of God, that in due time he may exalt you. 1 Peter 5:6

The question of consent is always an important one before any surgery is performed. The patient should place himself, with faith, into the hands of his surgeon, whom he trusts implicitly. Christ will never force his handiwork upon us. He asks us to place ourselves willingly, with implicit trust, in his hands. He only operates for our good. It is difficult for any surgeon to explain to a layman all the intricacies and implications of any operation about to be performed. So we must trust Christ with the sequelae of any intervention, knowing that his promise is 'I wound and I heal'.

Conversely, not every request that we make for surgery will necessarily be granted. Paul had a foreign body — a thorn — that he wished removed. He made a formal request on three occasions, but surgery was denied. How disappointed he must have been, perhaps even doubting the Surgeon's judgment. But in the end he realised that the decision was for his overall good. We must remember that God is working in us and with us, in the ways that God considers best, to make us into the image of Christ — the Perfect Man.

My thinking in this area has been largely triggered by a recent personal experience which has been quite painful — not physically, but in my heart and soul and spirit. In this experience I have been tempted to blame the pain on a number of sources — the Devil, unfortunate circumstances, people who are against me, people whom I don't like, bad luck, etc, etc. Perhaps at this time you are passing through a painful experience. May I ask whom or what you consider to be the cause of your pain?

In my own case, after considerable reflection, I suddenly realised it was God who was working in me — the Divine Surgeon operating. This awareness brought great relief to my heart and mind. As the surgery concluded, just to be sure, I asked the Surgeon to remove his gloves. As he did so, I saw in his palms the marks of Calvary. It was, indeed, he; the One who had passed through the great pain of Calvary, but had triumphed in Resurrection. I knew then that he understood, more than I ever could, the meaning of pain and healing. As he took off his mask I looked into his beautiful, understanding face and heard him gently say 'I wound and I heal'.

Leave to his sovereign sway
   To choose and to command:
So shalt thou wondering own his way
   How wise, how strong his hand.

John Wesley
(translated from the German of Paul Gerhardt)

Further reading: Rom 8:28-30. 2 Cor 3:18, 5:17.

ROS

January 24

Talking with People

A word aptly spoken is like apples of gold in settings of silver. Proverbs 25:11 (NIV)

'The doctor tells me nothing,' people sometimes say. That may not always be completely true, but it can be the impression which is left. The onus is on the doctor to work at it.

The secret of it seems to be to talk with people. This is better than just talking to people. And it is infinitely better than talking at people. Talking with people involves listening to them. If we listen to them, they are much more likely to listen to us — really listen and take it in.

Jesus sometimes talked to people when he was teaching, but even then we have it on record that he checked up on what they understood (Mt 13:51). He even talked at certain people who warranted it, people like the scribes and Pharisees. But when people were in need, he talked with them. His encounter with the Canaanite woman who was anxious about her daughter, and his meeting with Peter after the Resurrection are beautiful examples — and he got through to them.

As these and many others of Jesus' encounters with people show, communication is a two-way business. It takes time, of course. But if people who are talked to or talked at don't take it in anyway, then the whole exercise is a waste of time. Talking with people saves time in the long run. This goes along with the fact that there is 'a time to keep silence and a time to speak' (Ec 3:7). For further practical tips on the subject, consult Solomon: 'a man of knowledge uses words with restraint', (Pr 17:27 NIV); 'he who answers before listening — that is his folly and shame', (Pr 18:13 NIV); 'the tongue that brings healing is a tree of life', (Pr 15:4).

> Lord, give me the tongue that brings healing and the grace
> to be a good listener.

Further reading: Mt 15:21-28. Mk 7:24-30. Jn 21:15-19.

RRW

31

January 25

Where Truth and Love Meet

Speaking the truth in love ... Ephesians 4:15

There are times when doctors have to tell patients very difficult things. It is never easy to tell anyone that he or she has an incurable disease, but it is sometimes necessary. In these circumstances we need to pay special attention to the words of the apostle Paul: we must speak the truth in love. The patient should be aware that we are for him or her as a person as we explain the situation. People with incurable diseases should know that we shall do all we can to ease the pain and suffering of their remaining days. The love we show must be, not just in words, but in deed and in truth (1 Jn 3:18).

The same rule applies as we talk to the relatives and close friends of patients. We must show to them that we care about the sorrow that they feel when they know that someone near and dear to them has not long to live. They may be able to see, from our actions as well as our words, that we have the highest interests of the patient at heart. It is important that the relatives know just what we have said to the patient, and how we have said it. Nobody, least of all someone with an incurable disease, likes to be told something different by the various members of the team caring for him. If the medication the patient is to receive will have any side-effects (such as loss of hair with cytotoxic drugs), the patient should be gently warned in advance that this will happen. A leukaemia patient who took pride in the appearance of her hair was shocked when a nurse asked casually, 'Has your hair fallen out yet?' We must speak the truth in love, with kindness and sympathy towards all concerned.

> Lord, there are times when it is not easy to tell people the truth about themselves and their illnesses. We need your wisdom and grace in a special way at such times. Help us always to speak the truth in love, just as you do to us. Grant that your love may be seen in all our words and actions, so that people will be drawn to you.

Further reading: 1 John 3:13-24.

JWMcM

January 26

Waiting

There was a man ... waiting ... and the Holy Spirit was upon him. Luke 2:25 (NIV)

You do not need to be a London commuter to realise that hurry and impatience characterise our society. Food must be 'instant', so that even the art of unpacking the prepacked is a source of frustrating delay. Public transport puts speed at a premium.

Although hasty work is no longer regarded as a virtue in medicine, the trait still shows itself in the profession. The pendulum has now swung from the extreme of surgeons still 'Assistants' in their fifties, to young people in a hurry for the top in their twenties. The forbidding bottleneck for good registrar posts in a hospital career means greater pressure to publish, to attract attention and gain the support of the influential. Everything must contribute to that end, serving a predetermined objective. Do we still feel the wonder and privilege that is part of the study of medicine? Saturday mornings in hospitals used to be times of departmental meetings, and an occasion for leisured discussion. Nowadays, even large teaching hospitals have corridors that are forbiddingly quiet.

Simeon spent a lifetime of study. No doubt he experienced disappointments. He may have had youthful ambitions, but he had lived long enough to prove that ambition fulfilled can be as empty as ambition frustrated. Yet of one thing he was sure — that a Deliverer would come to the Jews who would also enlighten a darkened Gentile world. He was sure of God's word and its literal fulfilment. This certainty gave him a confidence which, in turn, bred patience. He could afford to wait. It may be significant, especially in a frenetic peripatetic world such as ours, that Simeon did his waiting 'in Jerusalem'. God's other watcher, Anna, 'never left the temple'.

Waiting often means staying put. The distant grass may appear greener, but our first duty must be to wait on God where we are.

> I thought there would be far-off scenes
> the challenge of lost souls till thou did'st show
> in seas of sameness ordinary folk I passed
> In blind familiarity — more lost
> than those whom distance still enhances.

Ruthe Spinnanger

Simeon, the visionary, was no softie. He saw, in advance, the offence of Christ's cross. When he experienced the truth of God's promise, he, in turn, kept true to God's word.

Further reading: Lk 2:25-32. Ps 27:8-14. Ps 62:5-8.

DEBP

January 27

Hope and No Hope

Brothers, we do not want you to be ignorant about those who fall asleep, or to grieve like the rest of men, who have no hope. 1 Thessalonians 4:13 (NIV)

When my predecessor as Editor of the Medical Journal of Australia died, he left two instructions about his funeral service. One was that I should give the address. The other was that the service should conclude with the Hallelujah Chorus. The first of these was for me not only a great honour but a great joy, for all the sadness of his passing. I had worked closely with him for ten years, and he, who was many years my senior, had treated me like a younger brother. He was by no means a sanctimonious man, for he loved life. Nor was he a noisily religious man. But I had come to know him as a man of deep and thoughtful Christian faith. In that respect the bond between us had strengthened, especially in his later years, when his thoughts had turned more and more to Christ and his redeeming love. I was able to tell of that when I spoke at the funeral service. And his second instruction brought the triumphant sound of the Hallelujah Chorus as witness. He was one of those of whom it can be said with glad sincerity and with no false piety; 'Blessed are the dead who die in the Lord' (Rev 14:13).

But Paul does not hide the other, darker side of the picture. One of the loveliest pieces of music that I know is Sibelius' *The Swan of Tuonela*, music that is utterly beautiful and utterly sad. It tells of the swan in Norse mythology which moves for ever around a lake in the world of the dead, carolling a mournful song. The cor anglais sings this song with heart-breaking sweetness and melancholy. It is a song in which there is no hope. It tells of those who are without hope and without God in the world (Eph 2:12).

Do we value enough the hope that we have?
And do we care enough about those who have no such hope?

Thank you, Lord God, for the sure and certain hope we have in Christ. Help us to care more about those who have no such hope.

Further reading: 1 Th 4:13-18.

RRW

January 28

Salt

Have salt in yourselves ... Mark 9:50

Jesus said to his disciples, 'You are the salt of the earth' (Mt 5:13). But doctors say, 'Shake the salt habit'. What can we draw medically and spiritually from this apparent contradiction? Matthew recorded no irrelevant statements of Jesus and we may safely assume that Jesus is saying something important. Knowing that $NaC1$ is as necessary to the bodily milieu now as it was then, we can believe that he took into account its commonness as well as its absolute necessity. Salt has always been used as a preservative, preventing decay both of the living and of the dead. Yet, it is possible to have too much salt. We are told that seagulls do drink sea water; but not too much, because kidneys fall far behind in their salt clearance when faced with continuous overdosage.

Can we as Christians then take a lesson from our own bodies? If we have an over-abundance of saltness, we must dispense it. Merely to absorb it will damage us and make us fruitless. The Dead Sea is so called because it allows of no life within its waters. Constantly receiving, it never gives out and accumulates salt sufficient to destroy all plant and animal life with which it is in contact. If, on the other hand, we allow our inward preservative — even Christ himself — to help to heal the wounds of others, our saltiness will permeate society round us with the saving grace of our Lord Jesus Christ. If we lose our saltness we become useless (Mt 5:13). If we fail to pass on what we have, we destroy ourselves and others.

> 'With all your offerings, you shall offer salt.'
>
> Lv 2:13

> Dear Lord, please preserve in us your saltiness and savour, and let us in turn be willing and able to shake some salt on others, preserving the sweetness of those who know you, and attracting to you those who do not. It is in your name and for your sake we pray.

Further reading: Mt 5:13. Lk 14:34-35.

DEW

January 29

Love in Action

We love, because he first loved us. 1 John 4:19

The following story was published years ago — where and when I quite forget. But I cut out the piece from the paper and kept it. The other day I opened a book and found the clipping. When I read it again, it moved me and challenged me as it must have done when I decided to keep the clipping. Now I pass it on for it has much to tell us all.

A Korean student was battered to death by eleven teenagers in an American city four years ago. The death penalty was invoked until the parents of the boy wrote these words to the District Attorney:

> 'Our family has met together and we have decided to
> petition that the most generous treatment possible
> with the laws of your government be given to those
> who have committed this criminal action...In order
> to give evidence of our sincere hope contained in
> this petition, we have decided to save money to
> start a fund to be used for the religious, educational,
> vocational and social guidance of the boys when they
> are released...We have dared to express our hope with
> a spirit received from the Gospel of our Saviour
> Jesus Christ who died for our sins.'
>
> Help us, Lord, to forgive others as you have forgiven us.

Further reading: Mt 18:21-22. 1 Jn 4:19-21.

RRW

January 30

Security

God is our refuge and strength. Psalm 46:1

When speaking to patients in Thailand about Christ, it wasn't easy to know where to begin. But they all had one clear need — almost a heart cry: they had no one and nothing upon which they could permanently depend. They expected and resigned themselves to change and decay. The thought of God as refuge excited them. And by the time I had finished speaking to them about God as refuge, the thought excited me too!

Have you had days that were a real struggle — when you have felt there was no one to hang on to? Maybe things were going badly wrong in human relationships — someone you trusted and relied on had let you down. You felt uncertain of yourself and of the world in general. Perhaps you began to have doubts about your ability to do things. Your faith may have crumbled, and God, instead of being real, had become a big question mark. When we are in an uncertainty like this, we become tired of 'relative' things, and we want a few 'absolutes' to hang on to.

God tells us frequently in scripture that he is our 'absolute'. He is our refuge, our rock, the one we can hang on to. He will not change, and he will not let us down. Today may be a thoroughly bad day. You may have been up a lot last night. You may be running a low grade fever that nobody wants to know about. Today one of your favourite patients may die. Today's post may bring you bad news. But today, God will not change. At no moment of today will he stop being good, kind, holy, forgiving and watchful. He won't take a break, or lose interest in you, or wander off somewhere. You can hold on to him, and you must hold on to him for dear life.

God loves you very much, and he is wise. He knows that you will hold tighter when you are in real need, uncertainty or sorrow. Perhaps that is why he is letting you have a 'bad day'. You are much safer holding on to him even when you feel wretched than letting go of him when you feel happy! And — don't forget — he has hold of you!

> The soul that on Jesus has leaned for repose
> He will not, he will not, desert to its foes;
> That soul, though all hell should endeavour to shake
> He'll never, no never, no never forsake.

> Rippon's Collection

> Dear Lord, I want to hold on to you today whatever
> happens. Thank you that you don't change, and that
> you are my refuge now and for ever.

Further reading: Ps 46. Ps 121. 1 Pet 1:3-9.

JT

January 31

Body Life

Now you are the body of Christ and individually members of it. 1 Corinthians 12:27

'No man is an island...' So run the all-too-familiar words of John Donne. But the fact remains that far too many Christian doctors are islands separated from the spiritual mainland by a vast sea of time-consuming clinical duties, research projects or hospital committees. Or to change the metaphor to a more medical (and indeed biblical) one, we are like limbs that have become detached from the body. And who more than doctors should be aware of the dangers of that?

Only a few weeks ago, I was talking with a senior colleague when the subject of Christianity came up (as it quite often does, if you pray for sensitive use of such opportunities). 'Well actually I would call myself a believer', he said, 'although as the years have gone by my belief has had less and less to do with formal church activity'.

Whatever he was a believer in, his statement certainly shows that it was not in the God who is the Lord of the Church, and who has commanded us 'not to give up meeting together, as some are doing' (Heb 10:25 GNB).

A widely experienced evangelist told me last week that he felt that the local church where Christians come together for worship and ministry should have more priority in the individual believer's life than any other social factor.

I have had jobs in three very different parts of the United Kingdom since qualifying. On arrival at each locality, as I have been driving round to find the hospital, the first thing that I have looked for en route, is a place to have fellowship with God's people. It's more important than a supermarket, a launderette, a hairdresser or even a good 'local' — vital though these may also prove to be for some of us!

I remember the thrill of driving through the town where I did my first house job. Almost the first thing I noticed was a brightly coloured building with a six-foot high sign and the fish painted on it. God's people meet here, I thought. Although at that moment I did not know a soul in that county, I knew that I would very soon have many brothers and sisters there. And praise God I did!

Of course there are rare occasions when spiritual isolation is forced upon us. But this is not the norm, and every Christian doctor who is able should be found involved in the fellowship of a local church on Sunday. For, as one well-known Christian consultant psychiatrist has put it, 'even the witch-doctor must be a member of the tribe'.

Further reading: 1 Cor 12:12-27. Eph 2:19-22, 4:4-16.

TGS

February 1

Living your Faith

What good is it, my brothers, if a man claims to have faith but has no deeds? Can such faith save him?. . . Show me your faith without deeds, and I will show you my faith by what I do. James 2:14,18 (NIV)

We communicate our faith by speech and action. While working in a hospital does give opportunities to testify in words, most of the time we show our Christianity by what we do and how we do it. I once asked an experienced ward sister what she thought were the qualities of a good nurse. She gave me her opinion and then added the names of three nurses to illustrate what she meant; they were all Christians!

A well-to-do Hindu, who had become a Christian, told how this had come about. It was in a mission hospital in North India where he had been a patient. He had not been influenced by a sermon or a tract, but simply because 'I saw Christ walking through the wards', he said. Jesus said 'Let your light shine before men, that they may see your good deeds and praise your Father in heaven' (Mt 5:16 NIV).

It has been a great encouragement to me over the years to see this light shining in the lives of Christian housemen, nurses, physios and ward maids in my own unit. 'Faith by itself, if it is not accompanied by action, is dead' (Jas 2:17 NIV).

> May the mind of Christ my Saviour
> > Live in me from day to day,
> By his love and power controlling
> > All I do and say.
>
> May the peace of God my Father
> > Rule my life in everything,
> That I may be calm to comfort
> > Sick and sorrowing.

Kate B Wilkinson

Further reading: Lk 10:27-37.

CDA

February 2

First Night

When you walk through fire you shall not be burned, and the flame shall not consume you. Isaiah 43:2

I remember my first night on call as a houseman as if it were only yesterday. All the excitement and triumph of passing finals, the celebration and euphoria of it all, seemed far away, and now there was only the hard reality of being in a place far from home, where I knew no one apart from the few members of staff to whom I had been introduced that morning. I was the only doctor on site responsible for the care of some 30-40 medical patients, many of whom were desperately sick. And although I knew that help was easily available at the end of a telephone line from my senior house officer, that did little to alleviate for me the rather sickening feeling that you get when you've just been thrown in the deep end of a pool and you've only just learned to swim. I slipped out of the ward during a brief lull in the storm, rang some friends back in London, told them how I felt and asked them to pray. They did — and their prayers must have been answered in the affirmative, as I came through the night alive, even if with very little sleep.

Looking back on it, I see that part of the problem was that, although highly taught in theoretical textbook material, I was very ill-prepared in fact to face the concrete reality of house-jobs. I think things could have been much less traumatic if I had been more gently initiated and previously warned about the predictable problems.

I hope that things are a little better for you if this is your first day, but if (as you read this) you are finding things too much for you, then I suggest two practical lines of action.

1. Do as I did, and share your feelings with a Christian friend — in person if you are fortunate enough to have someone understanding close at hand — or over the phone if not. Knowing that someone is sharing your burden is a great help.

2. Try to see your present situation in the light of God's will and future plan for you. It is very unlikely that the Lord has brought you through your five years of medical training in order to let you go under completely at this stage and sink without trace. The river, even though it be deep, will not overwhelm you. So, like Joshua, 'be strong and of good courage'. God will not fail you.

> Lord, among the pressures of work and deprivation of sleep
> I may face tonight, help me to keep close to you and trust

you to bring me through. Cause me to grow in ability and confidence as the weeks pass, yet remain humble in doing so.

Further reading: Is 43:1-4. 1 Sa 23:16. Rom 5:1-5.

TGS

February 3

The Way (2) — The Master of the Way

Jesus said 'Therefore go ... And surely I will be with you always to the very end of the age'. Matthew 28:19-20 (NIV)

Members of an expedition setting out on a tough journey are fortunate indeed if they have a good medical officer who, in addition to declaring them fit before they start, goes with them on the way. For those whose feet are set on The Way, Jesus Christ, the Great Physician, is just that. He is there not only to declare them fit for the journey and to be with them as they travel, but also to be their Leader over ground which he has already travelled. He is in every respect the master of the Way.

As we grow to know the Master, we need to remember certain things about him.

> *He is God:* he is described as 'the visible expression of the invisible God' (Col 1:15 JBP).

> *He is Man:* he knows and understands all the temptations and problems of our life (Heb 2:14-18; 4:14-16).

> *He is Saviour:* he loved us and gave himself for us (Jn 10:11; Gal 2:20).

> *He is the coming Judge* (2 Tim 4:1) and the One towards whose glory the whole creation moves (Phil 2:9-11; Eph 1:20-23; Col 1:15-20).

And yet he calls those who follow him friends (Jn 15:14-15) and brothers (Heb 2:11).

It is no wonder that Paul said: 'I consider everything a loss compared to the surpassing greatness of knowing Christ Jesus my Lord' (Phil 3:8).

> Most merciful redeemer, Friend and Brother,
> May I know you more clearly, Love you more dearly,
> Follow you more nearly, Day by day.

Richard of Chichester

Further reading: The references quoted are all worth looking up.

RRW

February 4

Light

Jesus said: 'I am the light of the world; he who follows me will not walk in darkness, but will have the light of life'. John 8:12

I can almost guarantee that, sometime today, you will need a good light. There is nothing more annoying than to smile cheerfully at a patient, ask her to open her mouth wide and say 'Ahh', and then find that the torch which you have produced with a flourish from your pocket, doesn't work! Her throat may be inflamed or healthy, the back of her tongue may or may not have cancer. But if you can't see it you won't know.

Light shows things up for what they are, and this is one of the most compelling of our Lord's meanings when he describes himself as light. At the beginning of John's gospel (Jn 1:5) we read: 'The light shines in the darkness, and the darkness has not overcome it'. Of course darkness has never overcome light — it never could. But it is good to be reminded of the fact. Just as an inflamed swelling and deviated uvula will flash into prominence the moment your torch works, so the Holy Spirit will stir your life with the reminder of something which you ought (or ought not) to have done. But remember, in Christ, diagnosis and cure follow hard on each other's heels. As you remember the fault, admit it to him, ask his forgiveness, and do anything specific which is needed to put it right. To live like this, keeping short accounts with God, is to respond to his light. It is, in fact, to 'walk in the light'. To live like this is to have light and life, and to avoid the misery, pitfalls, and timewaste of walking in darkness.

There is a second, very important, area of meaning. Jesus wants to use you today, as his light (Mt 5:14-16). In contrast with your own position, you will meet many people today who prefer darkness (Jn 3:19) — though they would never put it like that!. They would rather not know the uncomfortable truth. But Jesus plans to shine into their hearts and lives. Please make sure your battery and bulb are working well — and be ready. Show people today, by the way you treat them, that Jesus loves them. If they ask you why you are like this, tell them. Words spoken about Jesus to those who really want to know are a very powerful, very accurate and well focused light.

> Thank you, Lord Jesus, that you are light. Keep me on the right track today, shine in the dark places of my heart and help me to show your light to other people.

Further reading: 1 Jn 1:1-10. 2 Cor 4:1-7.

JT

February 5

Bottom of the Pile

Have this mind among yourselves, which is yours in Christ Jesus, who, though he was in the form of God, did not count equality with God a thing to be grasped, but emptied himself, taking the form of a servant, being born in the likeness of men. Philippians 2:5-7

The final common pathway is an idea beloved of physiologists and a practical reality to the houseman, who finds he is the administrative cornerstone of his firm. If he fails to inform theatre or the bloodbank that their services will be needed, if he keeps Casualty waiting, or fails to persuade X-ray to part with vital films for the ward round — or, worse, does not return them afterwards — he can call down upon his head the wrath of almost every group of hospital staff. Often their irritation is justified, and then there is no cause to complain. But sometimes it feels as if they are taking the opportunity to hand out abuse simply because they know the houseman cannot answer back. Resentment can easily build up if after five or six years of training — towards the end of which the student has achieved some seniority and respect, culminating in the excitement and satisfaction of passing Finals and at last becoming a doctor — he begins work only to find himself a glorified technician — not a clinician, but a 'dog's body', an unappreciated organiser of trivia, and the target of everyone's bad temper. Disillusionment and depression are not far away, and it is not unusual during these early days for a houseman to be so frustrated as to wonder why he took up medicine at all.

It is a relief to realise that at times the complaints are not directed personally at the houseman, though he may be the recipient. In a hospital, the demands on people's expertise, emotions and energy sometimes become excessive, and they take it out on the person who is nearest and least able to hit back.

More importantly, though, there is a parallel with how Jesus must have felt. He deliberately chose a menial lifestyle, and endured regular and unjustified abuse. The houseman is the most junior and least experienced member of a medical team, but Jesus was God — far above any humanly authoritative figure. And he endured it with and for love. And we have the mind of Christ.

> Teach us, good Lord, to serve thee as though deservest;
> to give and not to count the cost; to fight and not to
> heed the wounds; to toil and not to seek for rest; to
> labour and not to ask for any reward save that of
> knowing that we do thy will.

Ignatius Loyola

Further reading: Col 3:12-14. 1 Pet 1:18-24. Ps 43.

PIMA

February 6

'I have begun, so I will finish'*

He who began a good work in you will carry it on to completion until the day of Christ Jesus. Philippians 1:6 (NIV)

During one's year as a house officer, it is easy to feel that one's Christian faith will not survive. The pressures can be such that the necessary discipline of Christian living becomes squeezed out of daily life. But God's word reassures us that our salvation depends ultimately on him and not on us.

It was he who began the good work in us, his Holy Spirit who opened our eyes to our sin and need of a Saviour, calling us to repent and believe on the Lord Jesus Christ (Jn 6:37). He indwells us and will work in us that which is pleasing in his sight, equipping us for his service (Eph 2:8-10). We may wander from the pathway, but in his mercy he brings us back. His hold on us is greater than our hold on him.

Certainly it is our responsibility to co-operate with him in his gracious work. We may delay the fulfilment of his purposes, we may, by our selfwill, even miss his work, and he will bring it to completion however long it takes and however costly the process. In 'the day of Jesus Christ' the final reckoning will be made, and on that day not one of his sheep will be lost.

> What from Christ that soul shall sever
>   Bound by everlasting hands?
> Once in him, in him for ever,
>   Thus the eternal covenant stands.

John Kent

Further reading: Jn 10:22-30. 1 Pet 1:3-9. Heb 13:20-21.

JHCM

* words familiar to British television viewers

February 7

Praise that is Costly

I will bless the Lord at all times; his praise shall continually be in my mouth. Psalm 34:1

After a hard day it is very easy for us to forget the many biblical injunctions to praise God. Hebrews 13:15 talks about a 'sacrifice of praise', and there is a sense in which through the tensions and fatigue of the day, any effort to praise God is a sacrifice. Though we may not share all the sufferings of Job, we often find praise an effort.

A few Sundays ago, I went to church in a bad mood, tired because the children had been awkward. I was having problems with a housing transaction, and a paper I had been trying to write that week had proved very difficult. I found I couldn't join in the singing before the service, nor pray, until the minister, as if aware of my mental turmoil, challenged me to 'render a sacrifice of praise'. I accepted the challenge, and following prayer I found a real release in praise. The tensions went, and that night I slept better than I had for a week.

We don't have to sing at the top of our voices to praise God. Try reading Psalms 104, 107 or 145 to lift your thoughts from your immediate concerns. The Westminster Confession reminds us that the chief end of man is to glorify God, and although our lives can be a silent witness, he delights in our audible praise. Practise praising God when everything goes wrong! 'I will not offer burnt offerings to the Lord my God which cost me nothing' (2 Sam 24:24).

> I'm happy when everything happens to please,
> But happiness comes and goes;
> While the heart that is stayed on Jesus the Saviour
> Ever with joy o'erflows.
> Happiness happens, but joy abides
> In the heart that is stayed on Jesus.

H H Lemmel*

> Heavenly Father, forgive us for our lack of desire to praise you as we ought. Subdue our anxieties and help us to remember your daily mercies to us; turn our minds to you and let our ordered lives confess the beauty of your peace.

Further reading: Ps 107 & 145. Phil 4:4-6.

TAG

* Reproduced by permission National Christian Education Council.

February 8

The Inner Nature

Therefore, having this ministry ... we do not lose heart ... What we preach is not ourselves, but Jesus Christ as Lord, with ourselves as your servants for Jesus' sake ... But we have this treasure in earthen vessels, to show that the transcendent power belongs to God and not to us ... Though our outer nature is wasting away, our inner nature is being renewed every day. 2 Corinthians 4:1,5,7,16

Paul's constant preoccupation is with the work of God in the heart of the believer. As doctors our constant and proper preoccupation is with what he refers to as the outer nature, this body which begins to deteriorate so early in its biological history. This preoccupation can easily induce in us a despondency. No matter how successful our treatment may be, no matter what marvels of surgery may be performed, the body is inexorably wasting away. Two-year survival, ten, twenty, what's the difference? It will soon be gone.

But this outer man, which we examine and explore in a hundred ways with hand and eye, needle, scope and imaging, is not to be written off as of no account. Only while it serves the owner can he pursue this pilgrimage, this quest. It alone affords him the opportunity to receive new life for that inner man which through an eternity must fire his resurrected body. It is on the basis of 'things done in the body' that we shall be judged. The marvel is that for the Christian the winter of senility and the dark night of death are not the end of the road — rather they are the beginning of the best of all. Then, that inner man which by God's Spirit has been nurtured within the believer will be clothed again with an incorruptible body, perfectly fitted to take up that new life in the presence of God where Christ the perfect man has already gone.

Hear then Paul's word of encouragement:

> We do not lose heart... We look not to the things that
> are seen but to the things that are unseen; for the things
> that are seen are transient, but the things that are
> unseen are eternal.

2 Cor 4:1,18

Further reading: 2 Cor 4:1-18.

AMB

February 9

My Shepherd (2)

I shall not want. Psalm 23:1

There are lots of things that I want: to be ready for the ward-round, to climb the ladder, to keep my temper, to take a half-day, to have a lot of friends, to get out of the rat race and to have a bigger car. Oh! yes, and to be a better witness. It is untrue to say that I don't want anything. Our error is to equate wants with needs, but this is a toddler attitude. David's more mature concept is of unlimited provision available rather than any imperiousness of appetite: I shall not want for anything rather than not wish for anything. 'I shall lack nothing' (NIV).

The Good Shepherd has endless resources (Phil 4:19). He also has great career plans (Jn 10:27). He is totally aware of our practical needs (Mt 6:25, 32). He cares about all our needs (Jas 1:4).

In the technological society the waiting is taken out of wanting: whether a cup of coffee, a biochemical profile or a trans-continental 'phone-in, we only have to press the right buttons and the deed is done. Not so with the shepherding. To watch a flock of sheep is to see the conflict between each sheep's longing for its own way and the shepherd's intention for them all. They may become bewildered, panic or make a dash for freedom, unaware that he is trying to lead them to better pastures or safe shelter. How much easier for all concerned when they have learned to fall in with his plans! The pursuit of a wisp of dry moorland grass is a very small ambition, and it is sheer folly to bleat after that when more verdant pastures are waiting. Learning to trust and obey does involve waiting — for us, learning to wait upon God.

Doctors are often impatient by nature. The pressures of over-work and of life-threatening crises mingled with the subservience of patients and high expectations of other team members, can lead to an arrogant and hasty approach to others, conducive neither to good patient care nor to a good team spirit. Tests of patience come in many guises: the intrusive 'phone-call, the opportunist consultation ('while you're here, doctor'), the blocked drip or the over-booked clinic — we each have our own last straw. In time, we may learn to use each as an opportunity to run to the Shepherd, choosing to stay close to him rather than running wildly out of control. Then we shall have daily exercises in seeing how he can, and does, lead towards calmer waters. Then a more cohesive spirit will invade the team, patients will perceive a more restful attitude and we shall learn that when requests are made according to his will, he really does supply. I shall not want.

I nothing lack if I am his and he is mine for ever.

H W Baker

Further reading: Phil 4:6-19.

JG

February 10

Living at Peace

If possible, so far as it depends on you, live peaceably with all. Romans 12:18

Very nice, too, but what about people who really get on our nerves? Most of us could compile a little list — people we have to live with or work with, perhaps in hospital, like that bossy ward sister, that critical or (worse still) patronising administrator, that impossible senior surgeon (ugh!), that inept junior. They'd none of them be missed, as it says in *The Mikado*. But Paul says we should live at peace with them — so far as it depends on us, or as much as lies in us (AV). His qualification is interesting and provides the sort of 'back door' we like to have (but not abuse). Paul probably needed it himself sometimes. He was a very positive person.

Moreover, there are occasions when peace at any price is not good enough. Those occasions will not be when our own personal pride or dignity is affronted. The Lord Jesus did not care about that sort of thing. Nor should we. But it may be right and necessary to fight when the interests of another person are at stake — a patient for whom we have responsibility, a vulnerable junior member of staff, someone who is the victim of malicious gossip.

Even here, of course, there are ways and ways of doing it. The soft manner (Pr 15:1) can be more effective than the cutting comment that gives us malicious pleasure. Love is always part of the requirement. Jeremy Taylor said three centuries ago, 'It is no great matter to live lovingly with good-natured, with humble and meek persons; but he that can do so with the forward, with the wilful, and the ignorant, with the peevish and perverse, he only hath true charity'. Happily, as C S Lewis says, loving our neighbours does not necessarily mean thinking them nice. There are much better approaches, such as William Law's advice: 'There is nothing that makes us love a man so much as praying for him'. And just another thought: could it possibly be that other people find it difficult to live peaceably with us?

> Give to me, Lord, the grace to be patient as you were patient; that I may bear with the faults of others, and strive at all times to root out my own.

Further reading: Rom 12:14-21.

RRW

February 11

No Time to Eat

There were many people coming and going, and Jesus and his disciples didn't even have time to eat. Mark 6:31 (GNB)

Does this sound familiar? Perhaps it reminds you of a busy casualty or outpatient department, with too many patients and not enough staff. It might remind you of such a crowd in a third-world country, with not enough doctors to handle adequately all the people clamouring for medical attention. You have seen the reproachful looks they give you when you take time off for something to eat, knowing that this will mean a longer wait for them. But you know that you need to eat to keep going. 'Does anyone really care about me?' you wonder, and feel tempted to indulge in a little self-pity.

Yes. Someone cares! What's more, he understands from experience what it is like. The Lord Jesus knew what it was like to have so many people seeking his help that he and his disciples just didn't have enough time to sit down and enjoy a decent meal. They needed to 'get away from it all', and even there the crowds followed them, and there were more demands on their time and energy.

Is this your experience today? Then remember that the Lord Jesus does understand; it's an experience that he has been through. Wherever you may be as you read these words, lift your heart to him in prayer and ask his help for today.

> Lord, I thank you that you know from experience what it is like to have so many people clamouring for your help that you did not even have time to eat. Lord, you know what today holds. Give me your grace to cope with whatever tasks and experience today holds for me.

Further reading: Heb 4:14-16.

JWMcM

February 12

Discipleship (1) — Following — How far?

He said to them all, 'if any man would come after me, let him deny himself and take up his cross daily and follow me'. Luke 9:23

These words came at a crucial time in the experience of the disciples. Their initial response to the magnetism of Jesus had progressed to a deep personal devotion. They had returned from a tour of evangelism, when they had been given special powers of healing and exorcism, and they wanted to share their exultation with Jesus. Then came his question in verse 18 as to who he really was. Peter spoke for them all when he expressed their conviction that he was the Christ, the Son of God.

It was at this point that he took them into his close confidence. To be a disciple would not just be a success story. He began to unfold what the future held for him — swift rejection and a cruel death, followed by the resurrection. To follow him would lead them the same way and would mean identification with him in it all. However little they understood it at the time, the words, 'If any man would come after me' in this context meant a committal for life, for a wonderful purpose it is true, but at great cost. Christ needed these men to take up his cause there and then, however costly, that they might be his representatives after his ascension. Christ's words come with equal force and authority to us as his disciples today. To commit ourselves to following him is no insurance against calamity nor any easy perspective, both in the long term and in the daily round and common task that await us today. And the reward of following? Then as now it is constant fellowship with him. 'Because he is at my right hand, I shall not be moved' (Ps 16:8), for he has promised: 'Be assured, I am with you always, to the end of time' (Mt 28:20 NEB).

> O Lord, when thou givest to thy servants to endeavour
> any great matter, grant us also to know that it is not the
> beginning, but the continuing of the same unto the end,
> until it be thoroughly finished, which yieldeth the true
> glory; through him who for the finishing of thy work laid
> down his life, our redeemer, Jesus Christ.
>
> Sir Francis Drake

Further reading: Lk 9:18-26, 57-62.

GNG

February 13

Discipleship (2) — Denying myself — how much?

He said to them all, 'If any man would come after me, let him deny himself and take up his cross daily and follow me'. Luke 9:23

Our Lord in his pattern for discipleship lays down two explicit conditions, the first of which we consider today: 'If any man would come after me, let him deny himself'. Phillips' translation gives the words more emphasis still: 'he must give up all right to himself'. There is no escape from this obligation to those who are committed to follow Jesus Christ.

It is easy to think of self-discipline simply in terms of the more socially unacceptable sins, and to overlook indiscipline in our personal habits and thinking. Yet we are told to 'lay aside every weight and the sin which clings so closely' (Heb 12:1). We all too readily accept and condone our own shortcomings as an inevitable part of human nature. The mite in someone else's eye is much more obvious than the beam in my own, and I tolerate and excuse in myself what I condemn in others. Self-denial we often see in the traditional terms of alcohol, tobacco and questionable amusements, but it goes far deeper. Is it not true that many of our ambitions, desires, choices, leisure activities and decisions are centred in ourselves and our own selfish interests? The result is a boastful self-confidence like that of Peter the day before our Lord's crucifixion, to be followed by just as catastrophic a fall — a denial not of ourselves but of our Lord.

Jesus gave us the pattern of self-denial. 'He humbled himself and became obedient unto death' (Phil 2:8). And the reward of denying ourselves? 'Whoever loses his life for my sake, he will save it' (Lk 9:24).

> Measure thy life by loss and not by gain
> Not by the wine drunk but by the wine poured forth.
> For love's strength standeth in love's sacrifice
> And he who suffers most has most to give.

Further reading: Lk 14:25-33.

GNG

February 14

Discipleship (3) — A Cross is for Crucifixion

He said to them all, 'If any man would come after me, let him deny himself and take up his cross daily and follow me'. Luke 9:23

'Let him take up his cross daily.' This further command can only be fulfilled by one who has accepted yesterday's condition of discipleship: 'Let him deny himself'. There is no discipleship without the cross, and throughout the New Testament it is clear that death is the pre-requisite of life. 'Unless a grain of wheat falls into the earth and dies, it remains alone; but if it dies, it bears much fruit' (Jn 12:24). It is obvious that the disciples who first heard these words had little idea of the shame and suffering that the cross would mean to their Master and themselves. Before the end of their lives they had come to understand their Master's words to the full.

Jesus said that the cross must be taken up. This means that it is not imposed upon us, but something that we voluntarily take up. And it must be taken up daily. It is a temptation to us, who have become 'conformable to his death', to come down from the cross — as it was to him at Calvary. The cross has been for so long the symbol of the Christian faith that its real significance has often been forgotten. Yet our Lord's words have clear meaning for disciples everywhere and in every age. To some, to take up the cross means physical death. To all, it means living a 'dying life' — we are to 'present our bodies a living sacrifice...which is our spiritual worship' (Rom 12:1).

Campbell Morgan summarises the meaning of cross-bearing: (i) refusal to compromise with sin, (ii) bearing the consequences of sin in others, (iii) the uttermost of compassion. And the reward of crucifixion? That I may know him and the power of his resurrection! (Phil 3:10).

> O cross that liftest up my head
> I dare not ask to fly from thee;
> I lay in dust life's glory dead,
> And from the ground there blossoms red
> Life that shall endless be.

George Matheson

Further reading: Phil 3:7-14.

GNG

February 15

Blindness of Heart

I counsel you to buy from me ... salve to anoint your eyes, that you may see. Revelation 3:18

The poet, Robert Burns, sitting one day in church, saw a louse climbing up the back of a lady's bonnet. The lady was unaware of the louse's presence. In a subsequent piece of verse Burns apostrophized the louse in good round Scottish dialect, berating it for its impudent intrusion on 'sae fine a lady'. Then, mindful of the lady's unawareness, he concluded:

> O wad som Pow'r the giftie gie us
> To see oursels as others see us!
> It wad frae monie a blunder free us
> An' foolish notion:
> What airs in dress an' gait wad lea'e us,
> An' ev'n Devotion!

That lowly but ambitious louse — that ridiculous Pediculus — has long since gone its way. But the poet's thought remains. Unfortunately the gift 'to see oursels as others see us' is one that few of us naturally possess. One reason for this is perhaps essentially practical: unless I have eyes in the back of my neck, I cannot easily see the louse on the back of my bonnet. And I may be reluctant to look in the mirror. The louse, however, will be there just the same.

Reluctance to look in the mirror of truth, or to remember what we see there, is a tragic form of voluntary blindness. God holds up the mirror of his Word to us, so that we may see our blemishes and come to him to get them put right. It is foolish then to be voluntarily blind, like the person who 'observes himself and goes away and at once forgets what he is like' (Jas 1:24). We are then in the pathetic state of the lukewarm church at Laodicea, which did not know that it was 'wretched, pitiable, poor, blind and naked' (Rev 3:17).

God loves his people too much to want us to be like that and offers a remedy, a salve to put on our spiritual eyes so that we may see, and so know what is wrong with us. He can then deal with it firmly but in love. We are only fooling ourselves if we think that he will ignore it. Beware the louse on the back of your bonnet. Whether or not others see it, God does.

> Deliver me, Lord, from blindness of heart, and so quicken
> my conscience that I may see myself as you see me.

Further reading: Jas 1:22-25. Rev 3:14-22.

RRW

February 16

The Stands are Full

With all these witnesses to faith around us like a cloud, we must run with resolution the race for which we are entered. Hebrews 12:1 (NEB)

Today you must run another lap in the race of life. Maybe you're tired and dreading to run. Or perhaps you are discouraged or depressed and wonder how you can ever manage to put one foot in front of the other. Or perhaps you feel that you are running in a dry desert, alone, where no one cares or sees, unheralded and unsung.

Well, it's not like that. Actually you are running in a great stadium. The stands are filled to capacity with thousands of onlookers (a cloud of witnesses); and believe it or not, they are all cheering for you.

Take a quiet look at some in the stands — men and women who have run before, with success, because of their faith. There's Moses — remember the Red Sea, and Abraham — remember Isaac and the ram. And there's Joseph — remember the prison, and Rahab — the wall, and David — Goliath, and Daniel — the lions, and Paul — the prison, and Luther — the door, and Livingstone — Africa, and Elliot — the Aucas.

Look carefully, you may see some from your family, your church or your medical colleagues there. You are not running alone, in a desert or a vacuum.

Finally, look carefully again. In a special place, apart from all the other thousands, sits One who has also run before and conquered. In his hands are nailprints. His brow is scarred. He was tested in all points like you, but never sinned. He endured the cross and despised the shame. He is vitally interested in you and your race. He is encouraging you on.

So think of him...; that will help you not to lose heart and grow faint (Heb 12:3).

> Well I know your trouble, O my servant true,
> You are very weary, I was weary too;
> But this toil shall make you someday all mine own,
> And the end of sorrow shall be near my throne.

J M Neale

Further reading: Heb 11:1-12:3. Phil 3:12-14.

ROS

February 17

Righteous Anger... or is it? (1)

But God said to Jonah, 'Do you do well to be angry?' Jonah 4:9

A few weeks ago I became demonstrably angry with two patients in as many days (very unusual for me!), but both of these incidents taught me some valuable lessons.

I was angry with the first patient before I had even set eyes on him! It was a weekend, and I was requested to do a home visit way out in the countryside many miles from the town in which I practise. For weeks I had been trying to convince the other partners that we should have all outlying patients removed from our list, and nothing had been done about it; and now, here was yet another such patient who couldn't get to the surgery.

I was fuming through every mile of the narrow country lanes; and when I finally reached the village, I had no map of the area and twice had to stop in the biting January wind to ask for further directions. When I eventually found the house, I was in no fit state to have compassion on the sick! A cursory history and examination was followed by a strong recommendation that since the patient was so seriously ill he should change his doctor to someone more local. This was greeted with considerable hostility, as well it might for, unknown to me, he had been a patient of the practice for 22 years before recently moving out of town. I quickly stifled his objections, however, by telling him I had only his best interests at heart. But even as I said it, the Spirit of God pricked my conscience saying, 'Really it's your own best interests you have at heart. You are resentful that you had to drive such a long way and you will be late for lunch.'

My righteous indignation was exposed for what it actually was — self-centredness — and it had led to hypocrisy and lying to a patient.

> Lord, save us from the prejudice that makes up its mind before knowing the facts, and the hypocrisy that blames other people and 'takes it out' on them when the fault is really our own. Give me more of the selfless love of Jesus that gives others the benefit of the doubt and meets their need at whatever inconvenience to myself.

Further reading: Jo 4:1-11.

TGS

February 18

Righteous Anger... or is it? (2)

A soft answer turneth away wrath, but a harsh word stirs up anger.
Proverbs 15:1

The mother of the second patient had the misfortune to ask for a home visit on a very busy Monday morning. My surgery had finished one and a quarter hours late, and there were twice as many visits as normal to be done. I already knew this particular Indian family to be a hypochondriacal bunch, and after examining the boy at home I found no abnormality to explain his rather vague symptoms. As I was about to explain that I thought nothing serious was wrong, the boy began to recite some further symptomatology in my right ear while the mother commenced firing into my left. I felt really angry with the pair of them and curtly told them I did not consider the visit necessary, and if she wanted the boy seen again she could bring him down to the surgery. Almost as an after thought I gave them a form for a blood count 'just to prove that there is nothing wrong with him' and then walked out. Imagine my embarrassment when the result came back showing a grossly elevated sedimentation rate! My anger had almost led to a missed diagnosis.

Although scripture indeed says 'Be angry but do not sin...' (Eph 4:26), I suspect that 99% of the times when we are angry we are actually sinning too! Certainly we never read of the Lord Jesus losing his temper. In the much misrepresented incident of the cleansing of the temple it is clearly stated that Jesus made the whip of cords himself. This must have taken some time, and Christ's action was therefore premeditated, planned and thought out, and not a sudden burst of anger as is often suggested.

Never is there any hint of anger expressed by Jesus towards those who came to him for his healing, and we would do well to follow his example in our relationships with patients. 'Love is not easily angered' (1 Cor 13:5 AV). So if we are, it is a sure indicator that we need to know more of God's love shed abroad in our hearts.

> Lord, show me what it really is that makes me angry and convict me of sin every time that it is my self-interest and not your glory at stake. Make me more tolerant of others than of myself and help me to discern the real need that may lurk behind a barrage of whining complaints.

Further reading: Jn 2:13-17. 1 Cor 13:4-7.

TGS

February 19

Biblical Case Histories: Moses Aphasia

Moses said to the Lord, 'I am slow of speech and tongue'. Exodus 4:10 (NIV)

A debilitating condition, which any one of us is liable to develop from time to time, is Moses aphasia. This was the affliction which Moses produced when God told him: 'I am sending you to Pharaoh to bring my people the Israelites out of Egypt'.

Moses was obviously scared stiff. The phobia was on him — Pharaoh-phobia. He tried delaying tactics — questions, questions, questions. God had all the answers.

Then the unhappy man had what he must have thought was a brilliant idea. He played his trump card:

Moses said to the Lord, 'O Lord, I have never been eloquent, neither in the past nor since you have spoken to your servant. I am slow of speech and tongue'.

Then came the Lord's reply, and Moses must have wished that his alleged aphasia (we may call it that) had been complete and that he had not said what he had said. He had really put his foot in his mouth.

The Lord said to him, 'Who gave man his mouth? Who makes him deaf or dumb? Who gives him sight or makes him blind? Is it not I, the Lord? Now go; I will help you speak and will teach you what to say'.

But Moses said (he must have had Pharaoh-phobia badly), 'O Lord, please send someone else to do it'.

Then the Lord's anger burned against Moses and he said, 'What about your brother, Aaron the Levite? I know he can speak well...You shall speak to him and put words in his mouth; I will help both of you speak and will teach you what to do'.

The defences were now down for Moses. His aphasia was swept aside. His Pharaoh-phobia was swallowed up in a new confidence in a God infinitely greater than Pharaoh. Moses went out to become one of the greatest leaders in history.

If we are suddenly smitten with Moses aphasia in some challenging situation, it is as well to remember what our Lord said to his disciples when they were faced with the prospect of very daunting threats (Lk 12:12): 'the Holy Spirit will teach you in that very hour what you ought to say'.

> Blessed Spirit of God, teach my mind, touch my heart and loosen my tongue, that I may speak the truth faithfully and in love.

Further reading: Ex 3 & 4.   **RRW**

February 20

Numbering our Days

So teach us to number our days that we may get a heart of wisdom. Psalm 90:12

Youth is a most vital time of life. Goals and decisions are made then which affect the whole future. Changes can be made later, but are harder, and statistically much less likely to happen.

First, we can lose so much by default, especially as a senior medical student or a young doctor. The demands of the job, or study, the irregularity of the hours and the resulting chronic fatigue at times, all tend to disrupt regular devotional life and worship and cause spiritual and social isolation.

Against this background, the young resident may become easy prey to temptations common to man, such as sexual laxity, making money the main goal, and power through the pride of professional prestige. Also, there is the particular onslaught of the behaviourist world, now waiting to grasp the mind or at least weaken the faith of the isolated and overworked.

I have been saddened over the years to see the number of keen Christian medical students who, by the time they reach their place of influence for Christ, have fallen prey to these various temptations, especially money making. They may not have renounced their faith, but they have forfeited most of their usefulness as active Christian doctors whose life and quality of care draw people including patients towards the Lord.

Secondly, I have been saddened by those who, perhaps because its super-structure was second-hand, have renounced their faith. Someone recently said to me: 'I'll come to Christ in my time'. Unfortunately we may become so entangled that we can't find the way back just when we want to do so. I would implore all young Christian doctors and students reading this to maintain a total commitment to Christ, keep up a devotional life, and have regular prayer and discussion with an older Christian through this difficult period of life when the whole direction of the future is almost certainly laid.

> Lord, so teach me to number my days that I may get a heart
> of wisdom.

Further reading: Ps 90:12. Heb 12:15-17.

DAB

February 21

Grateful Shade

He bore our sins in his body on the tree. 1 Peter 2:24

'He that betaketh him to a good tree has good shade' wrote Ralph Waldo Emerson in 1866. And all through the toilsome history of our race mankind has sought relief and strengthening in the shade of trees that were not only good but great, having shade that was both deep and farspread. Two such were the tree of Cos, the plane tree under which the great Greek physician, Hippocrates, is said to have gathered his pupils to teach them, and the tree of Calvary, on which the Lord Jesus was lifted up to die.

Some years ago the President of the Australian Medical Association, Sir Angus Murray, referring to the tree of Cos, wrote, 'The grateful shade of this tree on the tiny sunbaked island in the Aegean Sea spread far beyond any confines of which Hippocrates and his pupils knew or even dreamt'. He was thinking, of course, of the Hippocratic tradition, which has influenced Medicine for good, both clinically and ethically, over the succeeding centuries.

Those who raised the rough wooden cross on the Hill of the Skull would not have thought of it as a tree. To Rome it was a gibbet. But it was a tree to Peter (Acts 5:30, 10:39) and to Paul (Acts 13:29). Among the Jews, after execution by stoning, a body was sometimes hung on a tree and was regarded as accursed (Gal 3:13, Dt 21:22-23). It was ultimate shame. Yet for the joy that was set before him Jesus endured the Cross, despising the shame (Heb 12:2). He bore our sins in his body on the tree, that we might die to sin and live to righteousness.

We in medicine may well be thankful for the grateful shade of the tree of Cos. But the shadow of the tree of Calvary calls for infinite gratitude as it stretches backwards and forwards, far into eternity, giving grateful healing shade to all who will come into its shelter. It is the tree of life. How often do we say 'thank you' for it — not only with our lips but in our lives?

> Beneath the cross of Jesus
> I fain would take my stand,
> The shadow of a mighty rock
> Within a weary land.

Elizabeth Clephane

Further reading: 1 Pet 2:20-25.

RRW

February 22

Highways to Zion

Blessed are the men whose strength is in thee, in whose heart are the highways to Zion. Psalm 84:5

In the United States, freeways are often named for the city in which they terminate. This is reasonable, for the destination of the road is of primary importance to travellers. A highway derives its value from its ability to help people reach their destination. Not only the size of the entryway and width of road are important, Jesus warned, but whether the road leads to destruction or to life. Korah's sons, who gave us Psalm 84, wrote of highways that are available to each of us, heavenly highways that take us to Zion. Pilgrims along the psalmist's heavenly highway will one day appear before God. The destination is secure.

But it is not only the destination that is important; how our time is spent on the trip is also of some value. As the highway of Psalm 84 passed through an uninviting, sorrowful valley, it brought abundant blessing. Travellers on the heavenly highway need never be alone. God offers companionship to all who pass this way, and this companionship gives comfort. 'Even though I walk through the valley of the shadow of death', Kind David wrote, 'I fear no evil; for thou art with me; thy rod and thy staff, they comfort me' (Ps 23:4).

Just what are these 'highways to Zion'? We can equate them with the timeline of our life and relate that to the New Testament injunctions to 'walk worthy' and 'walk circumspectly'. But I am not sure that this is what Korah's sons had in mind when they wrote the 84th Psalm. They wrote of highways in an individual's heart, and they associated this with having strength in God. Ours is not a pitiful pilgrimage to get to God; we are on a joyful journey with him.

Someday, I shall live with God. That destination is secure. But even now, as I live on earth, I share personally with him day by day. Within my heart, I have highways of communication with him, and he has supply routes to provide for me. Whether at home or in a foreign land, my task is simply to keep the highways open.

Further reading: Ps 84:5-7. Mt 7:13-14. Heb 11:1-16.

PRF

February 23

Being there for Others

But a Samaritan, as he journeyed, came to where he was; and when he saw him, he had compassion, and went to him ... Luke 10:33-34

In the story of the good Samaritan, which Jesus told, the first two people who came down the road where the traveller had been beaten up were a priest and a Levite. They came down to the place, they saw the man, and they avoided him. The Samaritan came to the place, he saw the man, and he went to him. He came not just to the place, but to the man. He involved himself in the man and his need.

Emil Brunner has described love as 'being there for others'. The Samaritan showed love. He was there, really there, for the man in need. That is the pattern. Being really 'there'. It is basic to real care, whether medical or otherwise.

Once I wrote something along these lines in an article in a missionary magazine. Some time later, out of the blue, a letter came to me from an Australian nurse working in a missionary situation. She wrote: 'I would like you to know that your recent article...was a help to me — in particular the idea of love being there for others. It came just as I was finding it hard to love someone I was living with, but to "be there for her" was possible. It works!'

This underlines the practical nature of love. It does not depend on feelings, though compassion and understanding go with it. It does not depend on liking. Some people are difficult to like. Aren't we all difficult to like sometimes? How could God possibly like us all the time? Yet he loves us. The Son of God loved us and gave himself for us. 'Beloved', writes the Apostle John (1 Jn 4:11), 'if God so loved us, we also ought to love one another'. In a pungent comment on Emil Brunner's description of love as 'being there for others', John V Taylor (in his book *The Primal Vision*) says: 'The failure of so many "professional" Christians has been that they are "not all there"'.

> Help us, Lord, to understand the meaning and the impli-
> cations in everyday life of 'being there for others'. Help us
> to be willing in the daily round to be there for others. Help
> us to love as you have loved us.

Further reading: Luke 10:25-37.

RRW

February 24

Hope for the Best

Set your hope fully upon the grace that is coming to you at the revelation of Jesus Christ ... Always be prepared to make a defence to anyone who calls you to give account for the hope that is in you, yet do it with gentleness and reverence. 1 Peter 1:13b, 3:15

Shortly after completing my medical school training, I cared for a premature infant with dysplastic kidneys and end-stage renal failure. She was too small for then-available dialysis or transplantation therapy, and supportive care was maximised. Aware that her renal function was inadequate to support growth and that there was no more than a miniscule chance for recovery, I sent her home from the hospital with her parents saying, 'We'll hope for the best'. It was then that God pierced my heart with Peter's words. Viewing this young patient's life, had I focused my hope on too temporal a goal? Had I cheated the parents by failing to direct them to a hope that transcends death?

Peter is straightforward in directing us to place our expectation completely on the ultimate revelation of grace as our current age draws to a close. At the end of his second epistle, Peter makes it clear that the day of the Lord will come. Certainly, this day will usher in an age of righteousness where sickness and sorrow will not exist. Hope focused on this promised provision will not be disappointed. Lesser objects of our hope (as seen in 3 Jn 14) can be accepted, but should always be seen as secondary to our guaranteed Blessed Hope.

If, as Christian physicians, we have accepted God's provision of a perfect hope, do we dare hide it selfishly from our patients and their families? Certainly not! God is patiently delaying our ultimate salvation (cf 2 Pet 3:9), because he desires others to come to him. We face a great opportunity! As we deal with individuals in humanly hopeless situations, we can direct them to the Source of a hope that goes far beyond the limits of our medical care.

Yes, I think I failed to offer my patient's family all that was available to them. God has given me a hope that goes beyond healthy kidneys. Each of us must fix our hope properly and then, with gentleness and reverence, offer to our patients God's hope of eternal salvation.

> Lord, fill our minds and hearts with your words of hope:
> 'Now may the God of hope fill you with all joy and peace
> in believing, so that by the power of the Holy Spirit
> you may abound in hope'.

Rom 15:13

Further reading: Mt 12:15-21. Ti 2:11-3:8. Heb 11:13-16. 1 Pet 1:3-9. Col 4:5-6.

PRF

February 25

U-Turns and Strait Gates

Therefore, my beloved brethren, be steadfast, immovable, always abounding in the work of the Lord, knowing that in the Lord your labour is not in vain. Consider him, so that you may not grow weary or faint-hearted. 1 Corinthians 15:58. Hebrews 12:3

The leading article in the April 16 1984 issue of the magazine *MacLeans* was entitled 'Life with Less Sex'. I was fascinated to learn from it that Germaine Greer, author of *The Female Eunuch*, in a new book has publicly reversed many of her previous stands. To quote the Sunday Times, 'The High Priestess of Sex does a U-Turn'.

Referring to her first boom, which appeared in 1970, *MacLeans* states: 'In her passioned analysis Greer argued that a patriarchal cult had castrated women by perverting their energies into impotent femininity. She argued that women might break through the crippling stereotype by casting off the shackles of marriage, family and sexual repression. The most radical feminists argued for nothing less than an end to the traditional family and an outright rejection of society's most sacred institutions: marriage, motherhood and religion.'

Now fifteen years later, Greer is apparently 'a disillusioned warrior, in full retreat from her former battle'. She warns 'that sex has become a social gesture as trivial as a handshake'. She now contends that the permissive Western world is sliding towards extinction and that contraceptive technology, instead of liberating women, has turned them into courtesans who risk their health and fertility for constant sex.

This is certainly an amazing U-Turn.

It seems clear to me that in this world of chameleons, there is an ever-increasing urgency for Christian physicians, both individually and collectively, to announce and demonstrate, as did their Master, that there is an eternal, unchanging, God-given, happy way; that marital fidelity, the joys of motherhood and family closeness are clearly taught in the Scriptures, as are the beauty and sanctity of sexual relations.

> Lord, help us to keep life in perspective — your perspective. Amid the confused, help us to be clear; amid the chameleons, help us to be constant; amid those that announce extinction, help us to tell of hope in Jesus Christ — the same yesterday, today and forever.

Further reading: Heb 12:1-3.

ROS

February 26

Just to Watch

'Could you not watch with me one hour?' Matthew 26:40

Jesus Christ was about to die. He knew that within a few hours he would be tried, flogged, crucified, and would die.

His reactions were those of dying people — to withdraw from the crowd, to have with him only his closest friends, and then just a final few. The last inner conflict was alone.

Patients do this. They withdraw from outsiders to close friends, to the inner family and finally to themselves, alone as they contemplate and prepare for their dying. We are often included as doctors in that final group, but feel just as helpless as family. What do we do? Jesus left us in no doubt as to his expectations of our role: 'Couldn't you watch with me for one hour?'

He asked them to be there, to watch and pray. He wanted them there: not as expert witnesses; not for protection; not for warmth or even consolation; not as Job's comforters. He wanted them to 'watch'. 'Couldn't you watch with me for one hour?'

To watch is to be awake — to be alert to the needs of the hour; to be with the person; just to be there.

In dying, the dying person needs us there, just for comfort, just to watch. We don't have to do anything, just to watch with them.

We do so often feel embarrassed and out of place. We don't know what to do. We seem to want to do something, to say something. This is not necessary. It is our presence, not our performance, that is needed.

> Lord, grant me the understanding to know when what is wanted is just to watch. And grant then the patience and the love just to watch.

Further reading: Mt 26:36-46.

LS

February 27

We See Jesus

We see Jesus... Hebrews 2:9

Yesterday I admitted an eighteen-year-old girl unconscious from a severe head injury. The Casualty Sister took me aside and said she had been on duty eighteen months previously when a brother and sister from the same family had been killed in another car accident. I went to speak to the parents with some trepidation, and found two middle-aged people, not hysterically weeping, though obviously distraught, but quiet and in control of themselves. They thanked me for coming to talk to them.

What could I say to such people? I felt helpless, and yet I longed somehow to be able to comfort them. They are old enough to be my own parents, and their intimate experience of suffering is far greater than my short exposure to other people's grief.

How would I cope with such an experience, myself? Our humanist society believes that there is ample evidence that no loving God exists — or, if he does, then he must be impotent. Doesn't this incident support their view? Yet Sunday by Sunday, I stand shoulder to shoulder with other Christians and say I believe in God, the Father Almighty.

The letter to the Hebrews — written to people who were in danger of giving up their faith — has the answer: we see Jesus, who for a little while was made lower than the angels, crowned with glory and honour because of the suffering of death, so that by the grace of God he might taste death for everyone. For it was fitting that he, for whom and by whom all things exist, in bringing many sons to glory, should make the pioneer of their salvation perfect through suffering (Heb 2:9-10).

God does not answer the 'why?' — just as the 'why?' of Job was not answered. The point at issue is rather the real nature of God. Seeing Jesus, we know that God is both wholly good and wholly loving. Faith trusts that, and accepts the inevitable tension that remains this side of heaven.

Further reading: Hab 3:17-18. Ps 73. Heb 2:9-18.

PIMA

February 28

Fantasy or Reality

The things that are seen are transient, but the things that are unseen are eternal. 2 Corinthians 4:18

I have recently been reading a most thought-provoking book by Malcolm Muggeridge entitled *Christ and the Media*. His thesis is that the media, especially television, encourage us to live in a world of fantasy. He states*:

> 'The prevailing impression I have come to have of the contemporary scene is of an ever-widening chasm between the fantasy in terms of which the media induce us to live, and the reality of our existence as made in the image of God, as sojourners in time whose true habitat is eternity. The fantasy is all-encompassing; awareness of reality requires the seeing eye which comes to those born again again in Christ. It is like coming to after an anaesthetic; the mists lift, consciousness returns, everything in the world is more beautiful than ever it was, because related to a reality beyond the world — every thought clearer, love deeper, joy more abounding, hope more certain. Who could hesitate, confronted with this choice between an old fantasy and a newly discovered reality?'

As affluent Canadian physicians we find it easy to live in the fantasy world of materialism, forgetting that the things which one sees — our medical instruments, our incomes, our work places, homes and clubs — are temporal, and failing to remember that things which are not seen — relationships to others, love, concern — are eternal.

This fantasy of affluence, where good, comfort, shelter and energy are in abundance, can easily blind us to the realities of the Third World, where tens of millions are hungry, homeless, deprived or starving.

Even within the context of our Christian Medical and Dental Society we may be living in fantasy. Our symbols are the cross (self-sacrifice towards God and others) and the towel and basin (humble service to others). Do these really represent our personal daily actions and attitudes, as well as those of our local Chapter? Are we deluded with the fantasy that all is well with our peers, especially our Christian peers, or are we aware of and sensitive to depression, frustration and bewilderment among them as well as a tendency to succumb to the current climate of sinful materialism?

At the conclusion of the book John Stott writes*:

> 'Let us keep hearing the alarm bell that Malcolm has been so faithfully ringing so loudly. I shall never forget the

contrast that he's been drawing between fantasy and reality. I am going to take with me his words: 'Stay with the reality of Christ. Lash yourself to the reality of Christ, like sailors in a stormy sea'. I have a fresh determination to do even that in this fantasy world in which we live!'

Deliver me, Lord, from the fantasy world of materialism, and show me in my life the things that are real. Then grant me the grace to live accordingly.

Further reading: 2 Cor 4:16-18. Heb 11:13-16.

ROS

February 29

Living Mirrors

We Christians have no veil over our faces; we can be mirrors that brightly reflect the glory of the Lord. And as the Spirit of the Lord works within us, we become more and more like him. 2 Corinthians 3:18 (LB)

The most amazing thing in this life is that God wants us to reflect him. But how can we sinners reflect his holiness and glory? Like a mirror, which has no light of its own. It can only reflect light when it faces light. Similarly, man can only reflect God's glory when he keeps a right relation with Jesus. He is the light of this world. The more we obey him the more his Spirit works in us to make us like him. Let us daily invite him into every area of our life to enable us to reflect him.

My uncle Daniel A was a professional photographer. Whenever I visited his studio, I knew that unless he was shooting a portrait, I could find him in the darkroom. The hours he spent there made the difference between a mediocre picture and a superior one. The picture had been taken in the studio, where the subject was impressed upon the sensitive film the instant it was exposed to light. But that was just the beginning. The film had to undergo the careful process of development, which required darkness, the right temperature, special chemicals and time. Only through this procedure could the impression on the film be brought out and printed.

Similarly, at the moment of salvation, a permanent impression of the Saviour is made in our heart. But it takes a life time for the beauty of Christ's character to be brought out in us. For Christ's image to be developed we must willingly accept God's chastening through life's hardship and trials. This 'dark room' discipline will assure a spiritual portrait of Christ's likeness in our lives.

Richard Wurmbrandt, a Romanian pastor, was put in prison for many years. Because of his faith and love to Jesus he had to suffer. In the same dirty prison, a young atheist was really attracted by the pastor's life as he gave English lessons from the life of Christ. Impressed by the personality of Jesus, the young communist asked who Jesus was. The pastor answered: 'So many love Jesus and want to follow him. If you really want to know who Jesus is, I can humbly say that Jesus is like me, because I follow him'. 'If Jesus is like you, I also want to love and follow him.' The pastor's life reflected Christ, so others were attracted to Jesus, even in the dark prison full of misery.

In the medical field, we often face suffering and meet people in need. What a great privilege to become mirrors reflecting God's love to them. A close relation with Jesus enables us to do this.

> Lord, make me your instrument as a living mirror to shine
> in the dark places of the human heart.

Further reading: Mt 5:14-16. Phil 2:15-16. 1 Thes 1:6.

JA

March 1

Doctor, be Still: God is There

Teacher, don't you care if we drown? Mark 4:38 (NIV)

That is what the disciples said to Jesus in the middle of a storm on the lake of Galilee. And plenty of us have said the same sort of thing in the middle of one of life's storms. 'God, do you know, or don't you know, what is going on?' The storm, the problem, the pain, may be in our personal lives, in the lives of those near to us, in the lives and crises of patients, in the lives of people far away caught in famine or war or disaster. 'God', we say, 'do you know, or don't you know, what is going on?'

When the squall hit the disciples' boat crossing the lake, Jesus was asleep. The disciples panicked and woke him. 'Teacher, don't you care?' they said. Of course he cared. He dealt with the problem and then — sadly and quietly, no doubt — said, 'Where is your faith?'

It was not just a minor problem. Among the men were fishermen who knew the lake and its moods. Luke's account tells us they were in great danger. So it can be with the things that trouble us. They may be very real problems that threaten to destroy lives, to wreck personalities or to tear families apart. They can completely throw us. That great 17th century minister and saint, Samuel Rutherford, when he lost his wife and two little daughters, wrote: 'It is, I know, hard to keep sight of God in a storm'. But his faith stood the test, and he was the stronger and the more effective in his ministry because of the experience.

What we so easily forget is that, in the Galilee storm, Jesus was in the boat. Yes, he was sleeping. But he was there, in the same situation, sharing the danger. The sleeping bit was irrelevant. He was neither unaware nor indifferent nor uncaring. He was there.

So it is today. He is there. We must never forget it; the sleeping bit is irrelevant. Long ago, the Psalmist knew: '... he who keeps you will not slumber. Behold, he who keeps Israel will neither slumber nor sleep' (Ps 121:3-4).

Our God is a sharing God. He does know what is going on. He does care. He is there in the middle of our storms.

> Gracious Lord, you know the storms and problems of our lives. You have shared our human life and know it. Help us to know and to trust that you still share with us in everything. And that you are always there.

Further reading: Mk 4:35-41. Lk 8:22-25. Heb 2:10-15, 4:15-16.

RRW

March 2

Casual Conversation

Let your conversation be always full of grace, seasoned with salt, so that you may know how to answer everyone. Colossians 4:6 (NIV)

We are speaking here with non-Christians. Grace carries the idea of attractiveness and generosity. It gives the listener a feeling that the speaker is eager to know and is interested in him.

Grace is a relationship at the heart of which is a readiness to give freely. And the gift I have to offer is myself — my listening, my understanding, my sensitive response, my practical wisdom. So many today in conversation have no empathy. They do not want to get alongside and help. They don't even look you in the face.

It is a good adage that no patient should leave a doctor without feeling better for the interview: in other words, he has got something out of it, and he knows he has a friend.

But grace isn't all. Words need to be seasoned with salt. Seasoning makes food appetising, so that you enjoy eating it and want more. How does this apply to the Christian in medicine? Firstly, I'm sure, by the use of homely words and simple illustrations. We must never slip into the lazy habit of silencing a confused patient with obscure jargon. Secondly, humour and imagination make the patient feel relaxed by dispelling his fears that the doctor is unapproachable. But thirdly, there is bound to be a freshness and vitality of speech in one who daily lives in the Spirit and walks by the Spirit of truth. The Spirit of Jesus Christ constantly 'makes all things new', and with him there is hope unquenchable.

Jesus Christ is, of course, our great example of One who, throughout his ministry, spoke words which were invariably gracious and salty. And that is how we ought to answer everyone.

> Lord, you have given us lips to praise you and proclaim your truth. We ask that we may never use them to bring shame to your Name, nor to hurt or offend our fellow men. Grant that by our conversation, we may always comfort and strengthen others and point them to you who alone can meet every need.

Further reading: Jn 6:63-69.

CGS

March 3

The Way (3) — The Unseen Guide on the Way

All who are led by the Spirit of God are sons of God. Romans 8:14

When our Lord was near the end of his earthly life, he told his disciples that he was going away, but that he would ask the Father to send 'another Counsellor', to be with them for ever (Jn 14:16). This was the Holy Spirit, the Spirit of God, the Spirit of truth, who would guide them into all truth (Jn 16:13).

This gracious guide, who goes with us on the way, has been described like this: 'The Holy Spirit is God in action: God as he works directly with human personalities. He is God in contact with me, confronting me, and if I am a Christian, living in me. He has personal dealings with me, so that I know that he is He, as Christ spoke of Him, not It, a vague influence from God. He is in this sense a person — not a separate being from the Father and the Son, but God in one of His three relationships with human personality' (H M Cundy).

The Holy Spirit convicts us of sin, reveals Christ the Saviour to us and makes the redeeming work of Christ effective in us. He makes Christ real to us with his power to transform our lives. He teaches us the truth, especially through the Scriptures, which he has inspired. Through him God's love has been poured into our hearts. He can make us like Christ.

The Holy Spirit's role as Counsellor should appeal to medical people, most of whom have a counselling role to fill. The fact that we know how difficult it can be to get through to people, and how sadly often they fail to act on counselling given, should stir us to listen to God's Spirit. It is a tremendous privilege, and should be a great joy, to have him as Counsellor. We are urged not to grieve him (Eph 4:30) or to quench him (1 Thes 5:19). It certainly makes little sense to have a Guide and then to take scant notice of what he tells us. That way lies disaster.

> Breathe on me, Breath of God;
>   Fill me with life anew,
> That I may love what thou dost love,
>   And do what thou wouldst do.

Edwin Hatch

Further reading: Jn 14:15-27, 16:7-15.

RRW

March 4

Good Plans

For I know the plans I have for you, says the Lord, plans for welfare and not for evil, to give you a future and a hope. Jeremiah 29:11

God, through a letter written by Jeremiah the prophet, gave explicit instructions to Hebrew captives exiled in Babylon. He instructed them regarding family relationships, contacts with their community, and false leaders. He then focused their thoughts on the future to keep them pressing on through adversity. We too, as we undergo long and arduous years of medical training, need to heed God's reminder through it all. Three points in the Lord's declaration recorded above can encourage us.

First, there is preparation. Through all of our difficulties and distractions during our training year, God knows his plans and is prepared to implement them. God does not get distracted. He is not forgetful. He knows what he has in store for us and will not be caught unaware as history unfolds. Based on his overview of the big picture, he can lead us step by step. And based on our confidence in him, we can have assurance that he does know what he has planned and what he is doing. Thus, we can follow him step by step.

Second, God's plans for us are profitable. God is not merely using us as puppets in a cosmic drama. He wants us to benefit. He is working for our welfare. He wants the best for us. Even in the difficult times we can rest in the knowledge that he is actually bringing good for us.

Third, God's plans are practical. Right now, his plans are useful to us. Whether we are in a time of peace and blessing or in a time of pain and bewilderment, there is a practical value in God's plans — they give us hope. We can realise that no matter how good or bad things are now, they will get better. We need not lose heart amid difficulty. Captives in a strange land, Jeremiah's countrymen could look for and plan for a better future. And now, as pilgrims on a passing planet, we can plan for better days ahead. God's plans for our future give us hopeful optimism today.

Through our training and into our practice, we can be assured that God knows his plans and is prepared to bring them to pass. We can see his plans as good and profitable for us, and we can have practical hope in the future that God has planned for us. That's great, but the distractions of professional life still threaten us. God will not forget his plans; neither should we! We must remember our 'first love' and continue to follow the God who will, step by step, unveil his plans before us.

Let us also lay aside every weight, and the sin which
clings so closely, and let us run with perseverance
the race that is set before us.

Heb 12:1

Further reading: Je 29. Pr 3:5-6. Gal 1:6.

PRF

March 5

Keep your ears Open

Speak, Lord, for your servant is listening. 1 Samuel 3:9 (GNB)

As we spend time alone with God each day, reading the scriptures,
praying or just waiting silently in his presence, I believe that we should
always do so with the expectancy that God will speak to us. Of course, it
is not every day that we shall hear his voice speaking directly about the
major issues in our lives, but how important it is that we should be
listening when he does!

One morning I was reading in Genesis 40. The final verse which reads, 'Yet
the chief butler did not remember Joseph, but forgot him', seemed to be
emblazoned on the page in letters of fire, and I distinctly heard the Holy
Spirit say in my heart 'Remember that! You will soon need to!'

A few days later I was at a Christian Medical Fellowship conference in
London. One of my fellow local general practice trainees was also present,
and we soon started chatting. 'Did you know that Dr Snook's practice is
looking for a new partner and they have already made out a short-list?'
'No, I knew nothing about it,' I murmured quietly, but inside my mind
was racing.

I had written to that very practice only a few months before, having heard
a rumour that one of the partners was going to retire. I had a reply saying
that the rumour was not true and that they had no vacancies. On hearing
that they actually had, I felt hurt and angry, and it was obviously the sort
of situation that could lead to weeks or even years of resentment. Then the
Holy Spirit spoke again, 'The chief butler did not remember Joseph but
forgot him'. That word from God was just like soothing oil on a fresh
wound. As I thought about Joseph's reaction in his situation, my anger
evaporated. 'God meant it for good' was Joseph's conclusion and instantly
the voice of the tempter was silenced. The entire internal conflict had only
taken a matter of seconds, and I was able to carry on the conversation as if
nothing had happened.

But suppose I had not been listening to God that week? The outcome might have been very different. Let us not short-change God — or ourselves — of the incalculable benefits of spending time in absorbing his word.

Further reading: Gn 45:5-8, 50:15-21. Ps 32, 119:129-135.

TGS

(Subsequent unforeseen events revealed that God had a still better future for this contributor. Ed)

March 6

Two Sides of the Coin

God richly furnishes us with everything to enjoy. 1 Timothy 6:17. You cannot serve both God and money. Matthew 6:24 (GNB)

A senior consultant said recently that the sudden acquisition of money is the greatest curse to the junior hospital doctor of the West. Some might disagree, since money is one of God's many gifts. Perhaps he was thinking not so much of what we do with money as of what money may do with us. The love of money is a hazard to all Christians, and as a profession we are more exposed to it than many. Which of us is not aware of the pleasure in the time spent in working out our expenses claims and legitimate (or not so legitimate) ways of avoiding taxes? Insidiously money pre-occupies more and more of our thinking. The Bible warns us it attacks our heart's love (Mt 6:21), deceives us and distorts our judgments and chokes our fruitfulness (Mt 13:22 NIV). It alters our valuation of people (Jas 2:1-5,9), makes fools of godly men (Lk 12:20-21), and can destroy our soul (1 Tim 6:9). 'Riches corrupt everybody who is in the least corruptible' (*The Golden Cow*, John White).

So — don't set your heart on it (Ps 62:10), don't trust it or become dependent on it (1 Tim 6:17). Don't accumulate it unnecessarily (Ec 5:11,13), or imagine that it will make you either happy (Ec 5:10) or important (1 Tim 6:17).

What then is the use of it? Money, though a ruthless master, is a useful servant, and a potential blessing. It can lead us to a thankful trust in the Giver. It is a means of serving God and helping to meet the world's need. It is an outlet for practising the fruit of the Spirit which is goodness. It enable us to express a generous and liberal heartedness and furnishes a way to lay up treasure in heaven (1 Tim 6:18-19).

> Lord, I know that every gift that comes from you is perfect.
> Keep me from ever using any of your gifts to my own or
> any other's hurt, or to your dishonour. Take what you have
> given me and use it for your glory and for the sole purpose
> of making your love and truth known.

Further reading: Lk 12:15-21. Mt 6:19-21.

MC

March 7

Who are we Working For?

Whatever you do, whether in word or deed, do it all in the name of the Lord Jesus, giving thanks to God the Father through him. Colossians 3:17 NIV.

Whatever you do, work at it with all your heart, as working for the Lord, not for men, since you know that you will receive an inheritance from the Lord as a reward. It is the Lord Christ you are serving (Colossians 3:23-24 NIV).

The King will reply, 'I tell you the truth, whatever you did for one of the least of these brothers of mine, you did for me' (Matthew 25:40 NIV).

A pop song of half a century ago had the intriguing title, 'It ain't what you do, it's the way that you do it'. In other words, our motives are more important than the things we do. What is the force driving us? For Paul it was the love of Christ. It is true we work for the National Health Service, our chief and the patients, but for the Christian 'It is the Lord Christ you are serving'. This new orientation does a number of things. It makes our job come alive, so that even the most drab of chores is meaningful. A sense of purpose comes to each day as we live it and give it to him, and we discover that we do our work with the sense of being in the presence of God. It means that our hospital life is just as much spiritual service as what we call our 'Christian work'. The division into the secular and the spiritual is artificial.

The little booklet, *The Practice of the Presence of God*, deals with this idea and how it worked out in the life of a godly monk who served the monastery by overseeing the kitchen. Brother Lawrence found he could serve God here by living and working in his presence at all times. We find him worshipping more in the kitchen than in the cathedral; he could pray with another:

> Lord of all pots and pans and things...
> Make me a saint by getting meals
> And washing up the plates.

Further reading: 1 Thes 4:1-12.

CDA

March 8

The Workaholic

'Martha, Martha,' the Lord answered, 'you are worried and upset about many things, but only one thing in needed'. Luke 10:41-42 (NIV)

Putting it into modern terms, Martha was an obsessive-compulsive personality. She invited the Lord and his men to her home for dinner, and because she loved them deeply, she wanted it to be a dinner they would never forget. Nothing less than a seven course meal would do!

Obsessive-compulsive people are like that. Their motto is: If a thing is worth doing it is worth doing well'. That motto has murdered as many people as it has motivated. It's not enough to serve a meal when company comes; it has to be a banquet. Cleaning the house will not satisfy; the house must be scoured. People who buy into that slogan not only help their neighbour on the Jericho road, they determine to start a Jericho road missionary society and attend all the meetings.

Now, busyness is not bad. That was not Martha's problem. What did draw mild rebuke from the Lord was the sour spirit that the busyness produced. Luke tells us that Martha was 'cumbered' with her serving, and Jesus could tell from her tone of voice that Martha was 'anxious and troubled about many things'. That is the test of whether or not we are too busy. What does our activity do to our spirits? Whenever our activity puts a cankersore on our souls, then we have overextended ourselves. The trouble with obsessive-compulsive personalities is not that they are constantly doing more than other people. The trouble is that it sometimes affects their attitudes. They do their good deeds with a bad spirit.

> Drop thy still dews of quietness,
> Till all our strivings cease;
> Take from our souls the strain and stress,
> And let our ordered lives confess
> The beauty of thy peace.

J G Whittier

Further reading: Mt 6:25-34.

HWR

March 9

My Shepherd (3)

He makes me lie down in green pastures. He leads me beside the still waters. Psalm 23:2

He makes me lie down... After two nights up, what bliss! It is a very different matter if I am struck down by a virus, a heart attack or a lorry. Surely, he did not do this? Patients sometimes say to us that they can have no faith in God who allows such disasters, even if he did not engineer them. Is this my reaction, too?

A long train journey recently gave opportunity to look at hundreds of sheep over a period of hours. By far the majority were on their feet, foraging for good, constantly on the move. Those lying down were chewing the cud or watching and feeding their lambs. These tended to be in the meadows, not on the mountain sides, where the search for fodder seemed endless. Sheep are too nervous to drink from rushing streams and need quiet waters for refreshment. For David, the shepherd, the intended analogy must have been that of satiation, rumination and recreation, all shown by sheep at rest. The spiritual parallels could be a cessation of other activities to enjoy the sense of the Shepherd's ample provision for us, spending time with him and with others to mull over his goodness and guidance. To hand on to the next generation the distillation of the good things that he has provided in turn strengthens them and encourages their growth. The picture may simply convey times of relaxation, enjoying tranquil reflection or, for the young in heart, more frolicsome activities.

Yet it may be that for some the Shepherd has to 'make' them lie down — to put them either temporarily or permanently 'out to grass' — if, in the full spate of a busy life, this need is ignored. It is possible to act out our own need to be needed by keeping up ceaseless activity while fondly assuming that we are following his lead. Certainly, when on earth, our Lord went about doing good, with hectic days and prayerful nights, having compassion on those who seemed so harassed and helpless, like sheep without a shepherd. We can easily overlook the fact that this pattern applied only to the last three years of his life and to a very small part of the world. He had to accept physical and geographical limitations and so must we. Among all the acts of healing, he must have taken many long walks with his disciples and many *al fresco* conversations and meals. It was not all 'go'. Many of us feel terribly guilty about taking a break, using up all our annual leave or enjoying a relaxing hobby. The Shepherd actually encourages times of peace and quiet. Better to follow his lead voluntarily than be forced by illness or accident, sometimes self-imposed, to step aside.

Come ye yourselves apart and rest awhile,
    Weary, I know it, of the press and throng;
Wipe from your brow the sweat and dust of toil,
    And in my quiet strength again be strong.

E H Bickersteth

Further reading: Mt 11:28-30. Mk 6:30-32. Ps 37:1-7.

JG

March 10

My Shepherd (3 cont'd)

He leads me beside still waters. Psalm 23:2

Clearly, each of us must discern what is our Shepherd-given task and do it
with our might. Some have easier terrain to traverse than others, but we
are never as trapped by circumstances as we imagine. The real question is
whether he is in control, or whether a pattern has been set without further
reference to him. It is essential that some regular time is found for
reflection in his presence and rumination on his guidance if faith is to be
fresh rather than formal. He may suggest delegation, better planning,
even saying 'No' to some cherished (or even charitable) activity, taken on
without his blessing. If we do not make this time for him, he may have no
choice but to make it for himself, even through crises of our own creation.
For some of our patients, an unwelcome period of lying down may be one
when they start seeking spiritual guidance for the first time. If, from our
own experience, we are sensitive to this possibility, we shall more readily
tune in to their deeper needs and lead them toward the living water so
essential now for our own survival. If instead we convey a sense of
turbulence and roughness, with no inner tranquillity, all our other
activities on their behalf will leave them as harassed and helpless as before
and with their healing incomplete. The choice is ours, and we take it each
day. How we need the Shepherd's leading.

Where streams of living water flow
    My ransomed soul he leadeth,
And, where the verdant pastures grow,
    With food celestial feedeth.

H W Baker

Further reading: Jn 4:10,14. Jn 7:37-39.

JG

March 11

Reach for the Sky — Laudable Ambition

Do you not know that in a race all the runners compete, but only one receives the prize? So run that you may obtain it... I do not run aimlessly.
1 Corinthians 9:24-26

'Shall I work for a higher qualification?' is a question most doctors ask at some time. For some the answer is straightforward. They have known the path ahead since student days, and nothing deflects them from it. For others it is a real battle to find the answer as the arguments for and against go to and fro.

The Christian doctor has a two-fold obligation: towards God, and towards the people he is going to serve. And because he is responsible for the use of the talents God has lent to him, he knows that he must discover, develop and use them to the glory of God and the benefit of his fellow men. While, on the one hand, we are told not to rate ourselves too highly (Rom 12:3), on the other we are encouraged to 'aim high' and strive for the mastery (1 Cor 9:25 AV). In the Christian sense striving for the top is not due to pride or a desire for recognition, but stems from a genuine conviction that — thanks to the genes, chromosomes, heredity and all that — we have been entrusted with certain advantages and privileges, and are duty bound to use them. We must therefore make an objective assessment of our gifts and capabilities. We may discover unsuspected skills — in surgery, teaching or personal relations. It all comes from God and should all go back to God.

Those called to serve God abroad should not underestimate the professional demands they are likely to face, and face alone, with no available second opinion. Study to show yourself a 'good workman' (2 Tim 2:15), as much experienced and as well qualified as possible, perhaps working 'all out' for the higher qualification, the little extra that may make all the difference between life and death for a missionary colleague, or between success or failure in some other demanding situation.

> Help me to put you first, Lord, in everything. In the matter ... which has been on my mind for some time, help me to think clearly and seek your will honestly. Help me to decide, and give me the courage to do what is right.

Further reading: Rom 12:1-7.

SGB

March 12

What is Man?

What is man? Psalm 8:4

Doctors are people — human beings — who look after patients, also human beings. We are men and women looking after other men and women. So this question 'What is man?' is one of vital interest for us. What kind of beings are we and our patients? What does it mean to be human?

Followers of different philosophies have given very different answers to this question. The Humanist teaches that man is the highest being in the universe, and that he has evolved as the result of the random movement of atoms and molecules. This philosophy is widespread in Western countries. Man, as the highest being in the universe, is his own saviour. God is non-existent, or irrelevant to man and his concerns.

Those who hold this teaching often fail to see the fundamental contradiction involved in it. If man is simply the end result of material particles in motion, what reason have we for believing that thought is valid? None at all: we have simply proved by human reason that human reason is invalid, which of course is nonsense.

The Bible answer is totally different. Man is a creature made in the image of God: we are told this in the very first chapter of the Bible. Man's special position and dignity spring from this fundamental fact. 'The image of God' is seen particularly in those human characteristics of thought, ability to speak and reason which distinguish man from the animal creation. Man is more than matter in motion. Human thought processes are not just the result of particles in motion: they reflect God's wisdom. (This does not mean, of course, that the brain does not have a function in this: we all know a person's ability to think is affected by certain drugs, such as alcohol, and by certain diseases.) But we believe that reason has a certain validity, and is not just the end result of random movement.

The New Testament shows us an even greater truth. God has revealed himself to man as Man: the Man Christ Jesus. The Lord Jesus Christ is both fully God and fully Man: he has a fully divine and a fully human nature in one Person. God has entered the world of man in Christ, and we now see the glory of God in the face of Christ.

> Lord, I thank you for making man in your image and I thank you for making me. I thank you most of all for the Lord Jesus, who is God come as man for our salvation. Help me, as I move among my patients today, to remember that

they, like me, are creatures made in your image, and to treat them accordingly.

Further reading: Ps 8. 2 Cor 4:3-6.

JWMcM

March 13

Man: The Image of God

Then God said, 'Let us make man in our image, after our likeness...' So God created man in his own image, in the image of God he created him; male and female he created them. Genesis 1:26-27

What does the 'image of God' mean for man? We cannot answer this question fully in this brief meditation, but here are three things it does include.

1. It means that communication is possible between God and man, and between man and his fellow men and women. God has spoken to us through his Word: both the incarnate Word, the Lord Jesus Christ, and the written Word, the Bible. Communication is likewise possible between human beings, because we have been made in God's image.

2. It is possible for man to experience communion or fellowship with God, and with other people (1 Jn 1:1-4).

The coming of sin into the world has spoiled both of these areas.

3. It has, however, highlighted the fact that we can receive comfort from God, and pass it on to others (see 2 Cor 1:3-7). Remember that in Bible usage, to comfort is to strengthen and encourage as well as to give consolation.

What does the 'image of God' NOT mean? Again it is impossible to give a full answer, but here are three areas it does not include.

1. It does not mean omnipresence. God is present in all places at all times. We can only be in one place at any given time.

2. It does not mean omnipotence. God is Almighty or all-powerful: he can do all that he has purposed to do. We are not: there are many things that hinder us from doing much that we would like to do.

3. It does not mean omniscience. God knows all things. We do not, and we are foolish to let our patients think we do. In fact, the more we know, the more we realise how much we do not know. We need to remind ourselves often of this fact, to rest thankfully in the knowledge that God does indeed know everything, and to remind ourselves that there is nothing which we can hide from him.

Lord, I thank you that you are all-pervading, all powerful and all-knowing, and yet that you can communicate with me, have fellowship with me and strengthen and help me today. Help me *today* to live in the conscious enjoyment of what it means to be your child, made in your image, and redeemed by you.

Further reading: Gn 1:26-28. 1 Cor 2:7-14.

JWMcM

March 14

Old Age

... Man goes to his eternal home. Ecclesiastes 12:5

The first seven verses of the 12th chapter of the book Ecclesiastes contain one of the greatest poetic descriptions of old age in all literature. If you have a Bible handy, take time to read through these verses now. Some of the allusions are not easy to grasp, as modern man does not think quite so readily in pictures as people did 3,000 years ago, but the overall picture of senile tremor, degenerative joint disease, cataracts, deafness and the general slowing down of metabolism is quite clear. Death comes as the final scene in the drama: man goes to his eternal home, the dust returns to the earth as it was, and the spirit returns to God who gave it.

What happens at death? 1 Thessalonians 5:23 and Hebrews 4:12 indicate that man is a tri-unity of spirit, soul and body. What happens at death? Think for a moment of what happened when the Lord Jesus died on the cross. His body was laid in the grave. (It did not, however, decay.) His soul went to Paradise (Lk 23:43), the happy part of Hades or Sheol, the unseen world (Acts 2:31). He committed his spirit into the hands of his father (Lk 23:46). You will see the similarity of language with that of Ecclesiastes (see also Ec 9:10). Death can be described as entering the gates of Sheol or Hades (Is 38:10).

These gates into man's eternal home are everlasting gates (Ps 24:7-10). In most of the Old Testament death is painted in gloomy colours: even in the New Testament it is called 'the last enemy' (1 Cor 15:26). But the Lord Jesus told Peter that the 'gates of Hades' would not prevail against his Church (Mt 16:18). The King of Glory has entered those gates, and risen from the dead: he now has the keys of death and Hades (Rev 1:18). So the Christian can face death with confidence, knowing that the Lord has himself been through the gates of death, by his death on the cross for us.

Lord Jesus, as I care for older folk who are drawing near to the end of their lives, give me the patience and understanding I need. Give me sympathy and compassion. Help me to care for these folk as I would like others to care for my parents, or for myself as I grow old.

Further reading: Ec 12:1-8.

JWMcM

March 15

A Good Finish

The time of my departure has come... 2 Timothy 4:6

A few days ago I stood at the graveside of a man of 87 years, a Christian whom I had known since childhood. He was a humble, godly man with a good testimony at work, at home and in the church. He died from carcinoma of the prostate, with bone secondaries. A few days before he died he said to a Christian nurse in the Nursing Home where he was: 'I'm on the home straight of the last lap to the finishing post, and it's a winning post!' He was not himself a man who took an interest in horse-racing, but anyone who has lived all his life in Australia knows something about it, and it is no wonder that he used this illustration as he drew near to the end of his life.

I do not imagine that the apostle Paul often frequented the athletic contests which were such a feature of Hellenic life. But as he lived all his life in a society in which they were part of the general culture, it is not surprising that he used illustrations taken from athletics. We find this in what was almost certainly his last letter, the one we know as 2nd Timothy. Paul was facing death: not death from illness, but death by execution. He uses a variety of pictures in 2 Timothy 4:6-8. The first is that of the drink-offering, poured out on the altar: the second is that of the ship at the wharf, about to set out to sea. Then follow two metaphors from athletics: 'I have fought the good fight, I have finished the race'. The first picture is that of the wrestler, the second that of the runner. The next clause gives us the meaning of these two expressions: 'I have kept the faith'. Then comes the picture of the final ceremony of the games, when the *stephanos* or garland of victory was placed on the head of the victors. Paul looks forward to the time when the Lord, the righteous Judge, will give to him that crown, and not to him only, but to all those who have loved his appearing. My old friend, whose funeral I recently attended, will surely share in that reward.

As we run the race of life, and fight the warfare of life, it is good, from time to time, to think about how it will end. There are many things in a doctor's life which can distract the mind from the goal in view, and many who have fallen by the wayside in the race. Let us beware.

Lord, help me to run the race of life, looking to you, the Author and Finisher of faith, so that when the closing days of life come, I can look forward to death with the calm assurance that I have fought the good fight, run the race, and kept the faith, in your strength.

Further reading: 2 Tim 4:1-8.

JWMcM

March 16

After Death

It was appointed for man to die once, and after that comes judgment...
Hebrews 9:27

The idea of *karma* and reincarnation is one which is deeply embedded in many religions with theirs roots in Southern and Eastern Asia. It is one of the fundamental doctrines of Hinduism and of the different religions which have sprung up from it, such as Theosophy and Buddhism. The Hare Krishna people have propagated it widely in many western countries in recent years.

Briefly, the teaching is this. During its residence in a body, a soul does good and bad deeds: from the good deeds it accumulates merit, from the bad deeds it accumulates sin. At death, the soul passes into another body, of a kind determined by the ratio of accumulated merit and sin. If the soul has accumulated much merit, it will have a good birth, such as a man of the upper class, or a cow, or a monkey; if sin predominates, it will have a bad birth, such as a dog, or a pig or a woman. All misfortune of any kind is seen as the consequence of sin, often in a previous existence. There are some variations in the teaching, but this is the general picture. Salvation is seen as final deliverance from the cycle of endless births and rebirths in different bodies to be absorbed into deity, as a river is absorbed in the sea.

We need to understand very clearly that this is not what the Bible teaches. A man dies once, and then stands before God's judgment seat. The new birth is not the soul passing into a new body, but a spiritual change which takes place when a person puts his or her trust in the Lord Jesus Christ as Saviour, and receives from him the gift of eternal life. Christian doctors who work in cultures where the idea of *karma* is widespread — and this is now true of the West as well as the East — need to be very clear in their own understanding of the teaching of the Bible on this issue, so that, as opportunity occurs, they can share it with those with whom they come in contact.

Lord, I thank you for your Word, the Bible, I thank you for

what it shows me about yourself, and about myself. I pray now for each patient with whom you are going to bring me into contact today. Many of them may know nothing of the wonderful truths revealed in your Word. Give me opportunities to share with others the things you have given me the privilege of knowing.

Further reading: 2 Cor 5:1-10.

JWMcM

March 17

Opportunity

Seek the Lord while he may be found. Isaiah 55:6

Late one night, when I was a house surgeon at a city hospital, Mrs P was admitted to the medical ward in congestive heart failure. She was in her early sixties, very breathless, and also very apprehensive. She progressed only slowly in subsequent days, and was obviously very worried about her prognosis.

I stopped to talk to her one day, and she asked about her chances. I said 'We all like to hang on to a little bit of this life, but I believe in more to come'. She was both interested and surprised that I, as a doctor, should believe in the spiritual realm. I discussed my faith.

Her immediate response was: 'I'm not cut out to be a believer. Anyway, isn't it rather presumptuous to believe?' 'Christ obviously meant himself to be taken seriously,' I replied.

A week later I paused in the ward to talk to her on the Saturday morning of my weekend off. She asked me what I did to become a Christian. I explained: 'There was nothing magic — I came to the point of surrender to Christ, and now I seek to follow his will'.

Came the reply: 'Don't you think it's a coward's way out at my age?' 'Not if you are truly repentant' I said. 'The dying thief on the cross could not have been nearer his end, and he was "accepted"'.

'Couldn't I follow in a sort of way?' she said. 'Very vague, isn't it?' I replied.

I left for my weekend off. When I came back on the Monday morning the other house surgeon on the ward said: 'Oh, a patient of yours died suddenly at 8.30pm last night'. It was Mrs P.

As I saw the cold, lifeless body lying in the post-mortem room later that day, I couldn't help thinking of our conversations and wondering what she had done with Christ in that last 36 hours. Death had come, with sudden finality, as a thief in the night and ushered her into eternity. Post-mortem examination showed a myocardial infarction, which the ECG had not picked up, and death was due to ventricular fibrillation.

> Help me, Lord, to be ready always to give an account of my faith, and to share it with others.

Further reading: Pr 29:1. Is 55:6-7. 2 Tim 2:24-26.

DAB

March 18

Out of the Depths

He was in the world, and the world was made by him, and the world knew him not. He came unto his own, and his own received him not. John 1:10-11 (AV)

Lord, today I have had no time with you alone. I have longed all day for a break, just to come back to you and tell you that I love you above all else. But this was not to be. I had a whole day's work to get through: fifteen list admissions, twenty patients on the wards and none of them altogether well, scores of forms to complete, many for 'serum rhubarb' (a favourite investigation) and, as well, I was on call at night for all medical wards and all emergencies. The 'bleep' continually interrupted my flow of work. I have never been so reluctantly indispensable in all my life — and never so exhausted.

My patience was wearing thin, Lord — I cut short the fat gentleman who was telling me about all his aches and pains — I walked straight past the bed of that elderly lady dying of pneumonia, whose eyes were dulled with incomprehension, staring at the mad world passing by — I couldn't bring myself to stop: I felt so tired within. Tears welled into my eyes: what a failure of a day! Have I not failed you, my sweet Lord, repeatedly, today? Have I not walked straight past you without a loving word of comfort? But I must disappear before colleagues see my tears.

A comforting arm came around my shoulders and she, my senior house officer, simply whispered: 'Don't worry. We've all been through this.' I cried with tears of relief. Your words to St Paul came back to me: 'My power is strongest when you are weak. My grace is all you need' (2 Cor 12:9 GNB).

> Be it unto me, Lord, according to your word.
>
> Lk 1:38

Further reading: 1 Cor 1:26-29. Heb 4:14-15.

L-MN

March 19

When Silence is Golden

A gossip betrays a confidence, but a trustworthy man keeps a secret.
Proverbs 11:13 (NIV)

This verse is a clear precept for everyday medical practice. Indeed, the confidential relationship between doctor and patient is a time-honoured principle. The ancient Hippocratic Oath says: 'Whatever, in connection with my professional practice, or not in connection with it, I see or hear in the life of men, which ought not to be spoken of abroad, I will not divulge, as reckoning that all such should be kept secret'. Its modern counterpart, the World Medical Association's Declaration of Geneva, says: 'I will respect the secrets which are confided to me, even after the patient has died'.

There are many good reasons for this restraint. Basically it is essential to an honourable and effective professional relationship. On a purely practical level, if confidentiality is not assured, the patient may withhold sensitive information that is needed for sound diagnosis and management. It certainly belongs to a proper attitude of respect for the feelings, the welfare and sometimes the reputation of someone who has come to the doctor for help — an attitude which a Christian will acknowledge as part of a genuine caring relationship.

In today's world, respect for confidentiality can produce dilemmas for both doctor and patient. Sometimes the law very properly overrules, as in the compulsory notification of certain infectious diseases. Community interest may make it untenable, as when, for example, a patient's disability (colour blindness, epileptic fits and so on) may in certain occupations endanger other people. The doctor's conscience can then be greatly troubled. An answer to such a dilemma will usually (and indeed should) involve talking it out with the patient and getting his co- operation. A good deal will then depend upon whether the patient respects and trusts the doctor and knows that he has a good reputation for normally observing confidentiality. Otherwise we may well find the patient's relatives and friends echoing another piece of Solomon's wisdom: 'A gossip betrays a confidence; so avoid a man who talks too much' (Pr 20:19 NIV). As a pragmatic postscript, we may well remember that 'even a fool is thought wise if he keeps silent and discerning if he holds his tongue' (Pr 17:28 NIV).

> Grant me, Lord, the wisdom and the respect for other people's needs that will enable me to know when and how to keep silent.

Further reading: Browse through the book of Proverbs and note how often there is advice on when to speak and when to keep silent.

RRW

March 20

Christ in Me

...we have the mind of Christ. 1 Corinthians 2:16

Who has not had the experience of getting annoyed with patients? Perhaps impatient at their non-compliance, their failure to modify their health-damaging life-style, their lack of punctuality, their failure to consider one's time off, or the unexpected demands at the end of a long day...or night.

Mark 6 records events in an extremely busy day in the life of Jesus. So many people demanded his attention that there was not time to eat. Does that sound familiar? Concerned for his tired disciples, Jesus ordered them into a boat to find a quiet place. However, the people saw where the boat was heading and ran ahead. As the boat approached the beach, the disciples were once again faced by a large crowd clamouring for attention.

It is Jesus's response to this crowd that challenges me. Moved with compassion, he immediately began to minister to them, setting aside his own weariness. Paul exhorts us to have the same mind or attitude that Jesus had (Phil 2:5). Do I show love and compassion to my patients as Jesus did at that beach scene? The dictionary defines compassion as 'sympathy with the distress and suffering of another'. No, in my natural self it is not in me to do this. However, elsewhere Paul affirms that I may have the mind of Christ within me (1 Cor 2:16). Christ lives in me. The Holy Spirit imparts to me the very life and mind of Christ himself. Paul could say, 'I have been crucified with Christ and I no longer live, but Christ lives in me' (Gal 2:20 NIV). There I find the answer to my problem. I surrender myself to him, reckoning my own natural, selfish nature dead, crucified with him. I allow him to live his life through me, and as he does this I am able to show his love and compassion to others. I see patients and love them as he did, even at those difficult times, at the end of a long day or in the middle of a cold, wet winter night. 'For God has poured out his love into our hearts by the Holy Spirit, whom he has given us' (Rom 5:5 NIV).

'You are a chosen people, a royal priesthood, a holy nation, a people belonging to God, so that you may fully and completely proclaim the virtues and excellence of him (Jesus) who called you out of darkness into his wonderful light' (1 Pet 2:9).

> Thank you, Lord Jesus, for your indwelling presence. Grant that your understanding and love might be shown through me to all I meet today.

Further reading: Mk 6:45-56. 1 Cor 2:14-16.

PV

March 21

Doubts

The devil said to him, 'If you are the Son of God...' Luke 4:3

The first test that our Lord had to face in the wilderness was the temptation to doubt. Satan opened the contest with the insinuation that Christ might be basing his ministry on a false assumption.

Since faith is the vital link between man and God, it is the place where the enemy is most likely to attack. Is our belief and our life work after all based only on an illusion? But to be tempted is not to fall.

Doubts are nourished by the incessant questions 'How?' and 'Why?'. It is imperative to remember that science cannot prove or disprove spiritual realities. It rightly asks the question 'How?' But the things of the Spirit belong to an altogether different dimension and require a different approach. The victory lies not in the search for intellectually satisfying answers to all problems but in drawing close to God and asking him to speak to us through his word. Our Lord did not argue with the devil, he relied on the authority of scripture.

Doubts that take the form of questioning the wisdom of God's activity or even his existence inevitably disrupt our relationship with him and can lead to arrogant disbelief. On the other hand, a measure of perplexity about certain aspects of Christian truth promotes a spirit of searching and can lead to further understanding and the strengthening of our faith, whereas a glib and purely superficial assertion of certainty may indicate only sterile complacency.

What we do with our doubts is of vital consequence. Faltering faith is most readily strengthened by 'looking to Jesus the pioneer and perfecter of our faith' (Heb 12:2). Peter seeing the waves and beginning to sink cried 'Lord save me' (Mt 14:30). His security lay in focusing his attention on Jesus rather than on his precarious position.

Further reading: Compare 2 Tim 2:23 and Tit 3:9 with Jn 16:13-14 and Eph 1:15-23

DPB

March 22

We have heard for ourselves

They said to the woman, 'We no longer believe just because of what yo said: now we have heard for ourselves, and we know that this man reall is the Saviour of the world'. John 4:42 (NIV)

This verse comes at the end of the account of the encounter of Jesus Chris with the Samaritan woman. Because of her faith she had told many in he town about Jesus which is the Christ. As a result many believed (Jn 4:39) I also came to the Lord Jesus Christ because someone told me about him. believed and was joyful. I trusted the testimony of someone else because i appeared true. I had no reason to doubt its sincerity. I read about it in th Bible and know that it is true. The Holy Spirit also witnessed to my spiri that Christ is Lord. That was the beginning of my faith.

However, we cannot go on in our Christian life sustained by th testimonies of others. We need to come to the One who is the very fountai of life. We need to be sustained by the One who has given us the gift o faith.

The Samaritan men were good examples. At first they had believe because of the testimony of a woman, but now they had come to know Jesus Christ personally. It was a direct encounter with him. It was a firs hand experience, and they no longer relied on the word of another.

We need to know the Lord Jesus Christ in a real and personal way. W need to be able to experience his presence in every facet of our living — i our work, in our home, in our recreation and holiday.

There is a growing dependence today on professional people in ever walk of life. Many depend heavily on their doctor. Christians tend to rel on their pastors or ministers, who are indeed very godly people and hav been a great gift to the churches. But many Christians have grown so use to having them to sustain their Christian lives that they have forgotten th very One who is the Giver of life, Jesus Christ himself. We need to relear how to come to him and to be able to have a personal relationship wit him.

> Jesus, our only joy be thou
>   As thou our prize wilt be;
> In thee be all our glory now,
>   And through eternity.

Bernard of Clairvaux

Further reading: Jn 4:1-30, 39-42.

S-KT

March 23

Work — A Part of Life

Whatever your task, work heartily, as serving the Lord and not man.
Colossians 3:23

Work is an important part of life and features prominently in affluent societies. For some the reason for working is solely to earn a living and support a family. Others become obsessed with accumulating money and possession, achieving fame and status, or wielding power and authority over others. A few may work solely to occupy their time or pursue some interest, or even to keep themselves away from less congenial circumstances. But many doctors embark on their chosen career with a sense of vocation and are motivated by a desire to honour God in serving people.

But the pressures of work can be overwhelming. Sadly the writer has seen colleagues and friends who started well drawn, sometimes unwittingly, into the 'rat-race' of an achievement orientated society. Their booming practices have robbed them of all their time, their physical health, their family life, and, for some of them, their spiritual vitality as well. Some have slipped back in their Christian lives having, like Demas, loved this present world (2 Tim 4:10). Work has taken the place of God as a first priority. It has become their idol. They have forgotten, too, that God in his wisdom has also designed leisure for our refreshment and renewal (Ex 23:12), and above all the opportunity to replenish our spiritual resources by time spent in his presence.

Sometimes our workload is beyond our control, but it is all too easy to undertake voluntarily, or perhaps for the wrong reasons, more than we can possibly accomplish satisfactorily.

Our only safeguard against allowing work to become an end in itself is to remember that even in our secular work we serve the Lord Jesus Christ and that whatever we do should be done as to the Lord and not to man (Col 3:23-24).

> Lord, help me to work hard for you. In the pressures that come my way, as they surely must, help me to know your strength and grace. Remind me that my work is a means of bringing glory to you, and keep me from allowing my work to become my idol.

Further reading: 1 Cor 3:11-16, 10:31.

OMY

March 24

Then he will Answer

Then you shall call, and the Lord will answer; you shall cry, and he will say, Here I am. Isaiah 58:9

Ruth, the refugees' teacher, slipped into the room. She had come to pray with me. It was early in the day, and the afternoon heat of the Thailand-Laos hill country was still to come. Racked with high fever for five days, I had learnt to dread the afternoon's 40°C heat, and its labour of constant sponging to stave off the indignity of delirium.

Chris had driven off to the regional town, to organise my transport home via Bangkok. The chance of success seemed slight. Fire had swept through Nan days before. Communication with Bangkok was difficult, and local plane services were booked up well ahead. With suspected typhoid, and the enteric phase to come, it was likely that any delay would ground me in hospital at Nan or Bangkok, extending the separation from my family in Australia by weeks.

I was depressed at the prospect, and anxious about my much-loved elder medical colleague at the refugee clinic, whom I had planned to take back to Sydney for surgical exploration of a bowel mass. Clearly, that would be impossible now.

As Ruth started to pray, she recapitulated the promises in Isaiah 58:8-9 and answered the anguish in my heart.

Soon there were the sounds of the Land Rover returning, and Chris was at the door. Against the odds, he had been able to book a flight connection through a friend's pedal radio. Transit home was an ordeal, but I was buoyed up at every step by timely support: the Tear Fund representative who helped me in Bangkok, the airline official who pushed me, near-fainting, aboard the plane and the businessman in the next seat who 'talked me down' all the way home to Sydney.

My colleague was transported to Chieng-Mai, where she had the surgery she required, before returning to the UK. Her operation was performed by a specialist friend who happened to be visiting Chieng-Mai when she arrived there.

Sometimes the Lord allows his servants to reach an extremity of concern so that they can experience the power of his rescue when it comes, as surely it will. Even though we ourselves may be too weak or burdened to pray for help, intercessory prayer is 'powerful and effective' (Jas 5:16 NIV). Always 'our help is in the name of the Lord' (Ps 124:8). So always we should pray in John Donne's words:

O Lord, never suffer us to think that we can stand by
ourselves, and not need thee.

Further reading: Is 58: 6-12.

GS

March 25

Pray for your Hospital

*Seek the welfare of the city where I have sent you into exile, and pray to
the Lord on its behalf, for in its welfare you will find your welfare.
Jeremiah 29:7*

My first house-job seemed unreasonably demanding. My Chief began
operating at 9am. By that he meant that the patient was on the table,
doped and draped, and he with his scalpel poised... Woe betide if he were
kept waiting.

My last round began at 11pm with the night sister. I was lucky if it was
over by 12. Then there were the night calls... 14 major emergencies in my
first 5 nights! For the first 6 weeks I didn't leave the hospital. At the end of
that time I felt more like a prisoner doing hard labour than a recently
qualified doctor.

It is at times like this that daily prayer and Bible study so easily get
crowded out. Faith is in danger of withering and dying from malnutrition.
Of course the answer lies in a loving, live Christian fellowship, but this is
not always available. It is then that the words of Jeremiah to those in
captivity in his day become so practical: 'Pray for the welfare of the city'...
the hospital... the medical unit where you are right now. The blessing that
comes from your prayers for those around you will assuredly spill over to
yourself too.

> Lord and master, I so readily forget you when I'm so busy.
> Forgive me, I pray. May your love and peace pervade the
> unit where I work. May I reflect the love you have shown to
> me, onto my patients, and to those with whom I work.

Further reading: Gn 39:1-6, 20-23.

JHEB

March 26

God doesn't make Junk

By the grace of God I am what I am. 1 Corinthians 15:10

It was certainly an unusual piece of graffiti, and I wondered who had thought it up. Graffiti are usually provocative, often querulous and sometimes unprintable. But this one had a special quality. 'God made me and he doesn't make junk', it said with an air almost of defiance. Certainly it breathed confidence. And the joy of it was that the confidence was not self-confidence but God-confidence.

As a condensed piece of theology (with something of a medical slant) it covered by implication a lot of ground. It applied to God's original creation and to his new creation. In a fair expansion of this thought, the unknown graffiti writer was saying: 'God made me in his image (Gn 1:26-27; Jas 3:9). I am fearfully and wonderfully made (Ps 139:14 AV). In Christ I am a new creation (Rom 8:29). And it is solely "by the grace of God that I am what I am".'

It is well if we can with the same joyful humble confidence also say: 'God made me and he doesn't make junk', and go on to sing with Charles Wesley:

> Finish, then, thy new creation;
>   Pure and spotless let us be;
> Let us see thy great salvation,
>   Perfectly restored in thee.
> Changed from glory into glory,
>   Till in heaven we take our place,
> Till we cast our crowns before thee,
>   Lost in wonder, love and praise.

Further reading: All the references quoted are worth looking up in their context.

RRW

March 27

Photophobia

This is the verdict: Light has come into the world but men loved darkness instead of light because their deeds were evil. Everyone who does evil hates the light, and will not come into the light for fear that his deeds will be exposed. John 3:19-20 (NIV)

Jesus blames unbelief on moral defection. As cockroaches scurry for darkness when a light is turned on, men reject Christ because they do not want their lifestyle exposed for what it really is. Too often we're like the smoker who explains 'I read so much about how cigarette smoking leads to cancer, I gave up reading'.

Are there other reasons for unbelief? Perhaps there are. Sometimes the light doesn't shine brightly. What a person learns about Christ may have been taught in the context of other beliefs that are now rejected as absurd. The mind may not be willing to sort through these false beliefs to keep the true God. We toss out the gift with the wrapping paper. At other times a student may be ambushed by philosophers who start without God, reasoning him out of existence. When the student cannot answer the arguments, he may give up God. Francis Bacon understood the danger when he wrote: 'A little philosophy inclineth a man's mind to atheism'. Granted that many factors contribute to unbelief, what about Jesus' assertion that our unbelief springs from a moral root? That takes some honest self-examination. John Calvin pointed out that our thought processes, even when we believe we are being objective, are controlled by our desires. Freud added a second to this and went on to describe the process. Evidently we repress our less rational evil desires and confine them to the cellars of our minds so that they may escape scrutiny. In that way our house may seem to be in order and our thinking has the appearance of straightforwardness. We are convinced and try to convince others that our conclusions have been arrived at without determined bias.

Jesus declares, however, that the mind reasons from reasons it does not reason with. Unbelief may not be rational at all. Part of the reason that men and women do not find God, he says, is that they do not want to find him, any more than a thief wants to find a policeman. One basic reason that we do not hear Christ speak is that he may be saying things we do not wish to hear. Or, in our selfishness and sin, we may fashion a concept of God with which we are comfortable; and if we discover that God is not there, we may choose to believe that no God exists at all.

A student listened to the claims of Christ and seemed deeply impressed, but he would not respond to faith. When pressed about his refusal, he shrugged: 'Look, I can give you a bunch of reasons that sound good, but the fact is Jesus would upset my sex life'. While Christ might have wept at his choice, he would have commended the integrity of his answer. We often do not believe because we do not want to believe.

> Lord, help us to be honest in what we think, in what we believe and in what we say we believe.

Further reading: Jn 3:16-21, 8:12.

HWR

March 28

Fit for the Kingdom of God

Jesus said to him, 'No one who puts his hand to the plough and looks back is fit for the kingdom of God'. Luke 9:62

On the road to Jerusalem, three men encounter Jesus; two pledge their desire to follow him; to the third Jesus calls, 'Follow me' (Lk 9:57-62).

To be his follower involves 'following', 'leaving' and 'going and proclaiming the kingdom of God'. This is the only way to be 'fit for the kingdom of God', *not* fit *to enter* the kingdom of God. To be 'fit' is to be useful, suitable for work in the kingdom of God (rather than to qualify to enjoy it).

Often as undergraduates, we may hear the call of Christ to serve him and needy fellow human beings, and we begin with high ideals. But as we progress the 'buts' of custom, convention, duty to home and loved ones and comforts of luxury and security crowd in.

Jesus says that once we commence ploughing, the only way to drive a straight furrow (one that is fit for the kingdom of God) is to keep looking ahead to him and not looking back with self-confidence, excuses, compromises or half-heartedness. There must be an absolute commitment to Jesus — his standards (example and commands), his empowering and his glory.

Michael Wilcock envisages Jesus speaking today; 'Suppose I were to lead you towards work in which income would be lower, or your prospects more uncertain (humanly speaking), and your accustomed standard of living non-existent? Or suppose I were to ask you to do something for me which according to most people of your class and background is simply "not done"? Or suppose I were to summon you to my service with such a peremptory call that your nearest and dearest would have to be left without an explanation? Would you even then come my way?'

The call of Christ must take priority even over the call of medicine! The most difficult choices in life are not between the good and the evil, but between the good and the best.

> Gracious Father, we thank you that your Son, our Saviour, fully complied with every one of the demands which he enjoins upon his followers; help us by your Holy Spirit so to follow him by setting priorities and making our values, attitudes and work fit for your kingdom.

Further reading: Mk 10:32-34. Heb 12:1-2.

LT

March 29

Failure

Simon, Simon, behold, Satan demanded to have you, that he might sift you like wheat, but I have prayed for you that your faith may not fail.
Luke 22:31

Peter had failed his Lord desperately. A broken man, he had gone out into the night and wept bitterly (Lk 22:62). But the security of the believer depends ultimately on his Lord, and he had prayed for Peter that his faith would not fail (Lk 22:31). So the Lord sent Peter a special message after his resurrection (Mk 16:7) and invited him, with the other disciples, to a meeting in Galilee at which he could effect Peter's restoration to a position of love, trust and purpose. The scene in Galilee was carefully prepared; and again before a fire, Peter is questioned three times: 'Lovest though me?' (Jn 21). Twice Peter answered, but how his heart must have been condemning him: 'You say you love your Lord, but just think of what you did, don't you remember the oaths...?' On the third question Peter, as it were, confessed his failure and acknowledged his wretchedness: 'Lord, though knowest all things, thou knowest that I love thee'... despite what I have done, forgive, and help me to do better the next time!

John, who had been with Peter on both occasions (Jn 18:15-16; 21:20), seems to have been deeply moved by Peter's experience. In his first letter, which is all about assurance in Christian things, he seems to have had the experience of Peter in mind. In chapter 3:19-24 he says 'Be assured, we are of the truth: and if our hearts condemn us'... perhaps because something in our lives has not been consistent with the truth... (God is great, he knows and understands) — go on, and seek to be more pleasing to him next time!

And this is exactly what happened with Peter. There was another time when Peter was in the High Priest's house, but this time he was in the hot seat — before the Sanhedrin and not just in front of a slip of a maid (Acts 4:1-23). The outcome this time was utterly different: 'They saw the courage of Peter and John and noted that they had been with Jesus' (v13).

> Lord, your love and understanding are greater than my failures; You know that I love you despite the mess I have made of things; Lord, forgive the past and help me to live in a way more pleasing to you.

Further reading: 1 Jn 3:19-24. Heb 2:16-18, 4:14-16.

PCE

March 30

Empathy

He had to be made like his brethren in every respect, so that he might become a merciful and faithful high priest... Hebrews 2:17

I used to think I was a fairly decent paediatrician — providing sound medical care while helping patients and their families cope with both health and illness. But last week, my ability to understand parents increased by at least a degree of magnitude. My six-month-old son cried out for most of two nights. I tried all the clever tricks I knew, but to no avail. Whispering, talking, singing, bouncing, running, sitting, lying, walking — none of my manipulations of his environment consoled him. My wife and I had frustrating and fitful sleep as we took turns with our son. Before, I had imagined what it must be like for parents to deal with a sick child. Now, I have some personal experience. Already, I've been able to deal with people with a new dimension of empathy.

The book of Hebrews instructs us to 'consider Jesus'. As I consider his omniscience, I realise that he could imagine pretty well what life is like on earth. Yet he didn't settle for a carefully calculated understanding of the human condition. He chose to experience humanness, personally. He lived as we live. He faced limitation and hardship. He accepted emotional and physical fatigue and discomfort. And through it all, he became personally able to sympathise with our weakness and to deal empathetically with us. The second and fourth chapters of Hebrews tell us of some of the consequences of Jesus' incarnation, of the Eternal One's choice to experience human life personally. First (Heb 2:14), he was able to conquer death. By subjecting himself to death and by rising victoriously, he has overcome Satan's deathly reign. Death need not be feared. Physical mortality is not the end. We can live victoriously before, through and after death.

Second (Heb 2:17), by being a human sacrifice, the Lamb of God has paid the penalty for our sin. No longer are we bound to sin and to the limitations of the old nature. We can share in his own deliverance. We can live in the light of the new nature.

But somehow incarnation, resurrection and propitiation all seem somewhat distant when I'm tired and frustrated in the middle of a sleepless night. That's where a third result of Jesus' fleshliness comes in. He has been through it all: he can sympathise with us: he can come to our aid. In the daily (and nightly) details of life, he can help us. He does understand. I need only with confidence to 'draw near to the throne of grace...' (Heb 4:15-16).

Even as God gives me the best that Heaven can offer, I can provide for my patients the best of what medical science can offer. And as Jesus understandingly deals with me, so I can and should deal empathetically with my patients.

> Have this mind among yourselves,
> which is yours in Christ Jesus.

Phil 2:5

Further reading: Heb 2:9-18, 4:14-16. Phil 2:3-8, 4:4-9.

PRF

March 31

The Touch of a Human Hand

Jesus... touched him. Mark 1:41

I once had a leprosy patient for whom there seemed little we could do. His legs were a mass of ulcers, and each really needed amputation. His leprosy (tuberculoid) was burned out, but he felt rejected and had 'turned his face to the wall'. I was reading a book about Paul Brand at the time and was struck by a comment that leprosy patients need to feel the touch of a human hand. So we shook hands with him on ward rounds — all of us. The transformation was almost unbelievable. He began to smile, to enjoy the little daily ritual that cost us so little. He began to trust us — even to the point of allowing us to amputate both his legs and fit him with prostheses. He walked — perhaps for the first time for years. He was always to be seen around the town after that, smiling, and talking to people. The last time I saw him he was back at the hospital — but this time as a sick visitor — visiting one of the nurses who had tended him — now herself ill (though not with leprosy).

It cannot have been coincidence that the thought that inspired our action came from the biography of a Christian who has taken much of the initiative in leprosy work. For the Christian is merely following in his Master's footsteps. The same challenge comes to us in different clinical situations — the elderly patient who gets 'passed by' on the ward round, the difficult depressive or schizophrenic, the smelly incontinent man, the alcoholic, the delinquent boy. All need human contact — our eyes to meet theirs, our hands to touch theirs, and our words to go out to meet them in their need. I have a colleague who, at times when technological medicine has little to offer, shares with the patient a precious word from his store of poetry. What do we share?

> I pray today for my least attractive patients. Help me to see
> them through your eyes, to accept and understand them as

you accept and understand me, and to love them with your love as those with whom you are glad to associate, and for whom you found it worthwhile to give your life.

Further reading: Mk 1:40-45. Mt 9:9-13. Lk 14:16-24.

PCB

Easter Readings

Good Friday

Serpent on a Pole

I, when I am lifted up from the earth, will draw all men to myself. John 12:32

The familiar medical symbol, the serpent entwined around a staff, undoubtedly comes to us in a direct line from the Greek cult of Asklepios (Aesculapius the Romans later called him). It links us with a system of medicine which had some real merit, especially by contrast with much of what passed for medicine in the ancient world. Its temples of healing, always set in attractive surroundings, with their features of rest, simple diet, washing and anointing, combined with powerful positive suggestion, must often have been beneficial.

How the staff and serpent came to be associated with the healing god is a complex and fascinating story, wrapped around with all the elusive features of Greek myth. It almost certainly had to do with life and even resurrection — the life of the tree (staff) springing from the earth, and the serpent, symbol of wisdom to the Greeks, coming out of the earth and regularly shedding its skin in an act of seeming renewal.

Is the rod and staff symbol of the Greeks connected with the brass serpent which Moses set up by God's command in the wilderness (Nu 21:9)? There seems to be no established historical connection, though the two certainly came to be linked, at least by mediaeval times. Our symbol is Greek. But the Old Testament record is medically very much to the point: the deadly plague of serpents, the symbol of healing directly derived from the plague, the requirement of faith and obedience in order to be healed. It is wonderful and, in a way, startling to find the Lord Jesus making it a direct picture of himself (Jn 3:14): the Son of Man lifted up on the cross, being made sin for us, though he knew no sin (2 Cor 5:21).

To be healed from the death-dealing plague of sin, of unbelief, of disobedience and rebellion, we look to the cross in faith and obedience, and in glad surrender. And we say thank you. Our staff and serpent symbol is always there to remind us.

O my Saviour, lifted
   From the earth for me
Draw me, in thy mercy,
   Nearer unto thee.

Lift my earth-bound longings,
   Fix them, Lord, above;
Draw me with the magnet
   Of thy mighty love.

William Walsham How

Further reading: Nu 21:4-9, 2 Cor 5:16-21.

RRW

Easter Saturday

God is Dead

I am the first and the last, and the living one; I died, and behold I am alive for evermore, and I have the keys of Death and Hades. Revelation 1:17-18

'God is dead', say some. Of course, we do not agree with that. Nevertheless, a long time ago Christ did die — and rose again. That resurrection is at the centre of our Christian faith. For he is God.

It must have been a real physical tangible resurrection if it is to be the basis of real physical tangible faith. And for that to be so, Jesus must really have been dead. So, both his death and his resurrection, if they are indeed true, are two of the most important facts in history.

The modern medical world is greatly concerned with the determination of death — the certainty that death has occurred — for a number of essentially contemporary reasons, to do with artificial prolongation of life, use of organs for transplantation and so on. Much careful thought is being given to it. But it has, of course, always been important.

What evidence is there that Jesus was really dead when they took him down from the cross? Some say he had only swooned.

Can doctors believe that? Much historical evidence points to a real death. Who, at the time, believed he was dead?

Hardened Roman soldiers. They knew death when they saw it. And they did not even bother to break his legs (as they did to the two others crucified with him).

A Roman centurion. He was obviously impressed, possibly even puzzled, by Jesus as a man, and by the manner of his death. But he was under orders — and he reported to Pilate.

The Jewish leaders. They asked for a seal on the rolling stone, and a guard to be set over it.

Joseph and Nicodemus. They in a courageous act of sympathy collected the body and found no evidence of life.

The common people. For them 'the show was over'. They dispersed and went home.

The disciples. They mourned. Some gathered in a room, fearful for their own safety. Some walked to Emmaus and got a shock.

The women. They prepared ointment for anointing the body and were most upset when they found the body gone.

That is only a fraction of the evidence of Jesus' real death.

But to believe that he did not die one has to be amazingly credulous or to be aggressively seeking some — any — alternative to the resurrection.

His real death allowed of a real resurrection — and a real faith in his power to change the world.

> Thank you, Lord, for the many evidences of your living reality as the way, the truth and the life. Help me to seek and learn them, that the faith you have given me may for ever be strengthened and that I may faithfully work for and through you for others.

Further reading: Mt 27:56-65, 28:1-8. Mk 15:37-47, 16:1. Lk 23:46-56, 24:1-13. Jn 19:30-42.

SMT

Easter Sunday

Body and Soul

We know that if the earthly tent we live in is destroyed, we have a building from God, a house not made with hands, eternal in the heavens. Here indeed we groan, and long to put on our heavenly dwelling, so that by putting it on we may not be found naked. For while we are still in this tent, we sigh with anxiety; not that we would be unclothed, but that we would be further clothed, so that what is mortal may be swallowed up by life. 2 Corinthians 5:1-4

Paul is writing to Greeks in Corinth. Before they became Christians they had probably believed, as did most Greeks, in the immortality of the soul — that divine and pure spirit as they understood it, imprisoned during earthly life in the corrupt and degrading body from which it escapes at death. In an earlier letter Paul had given (1 Cor 15) a long and impassioned answer to questions about the new teaching — new to

Greeks, that is — about the resurrection of the body. Pagan Greeks had sneered at the Christian hope of bodily resurrection. 'The raising of corpses from the grave' they called it.

But in the light of the resurrection of Jesus, all this had to be re-thought. The risen Jesus had stood there and said: 'handle me and see, for a spirit has not flesh and bones as you see that I have' (Lk 24:39). A doctor recorded that, and also observed that Jesus ate food with his disciples. This Christian certainty that believers will rise from death, as Jesus did, to a new and glorious life with a new, 'given' and glorious body is an infinitely richer inheritance than the 'immortal soul' of the Greeks. It will not be the nakedness (2 Cor 5:3) of the disembodied spirit of Greek immortality, but the rich vesture of a body beside which the one we wear now will seem but the rags of poverty. The dim senses which serve us imperfectly here will then be exquisitely tuned to the perfect colours and sounds of that new world. Imperfect recognition and understanding which are the best we know here will give place to the acute perceptions of bodies made new after the pattern of that which Christ took into the presence of God, 'with all things appertaining to the perfection of man's nature' (Art iv, Articles of Religion, Book of Common Prayer).

Paul concludes his main discourse on the subject with this word of encouragement (1 Cor 15:58):

> 'Therefore my beloved brethren, be steadfast, immovable, always abounding in the work of the Lord, knowing that in the Lord your labour is not in vain.'

Further reading: 1 Cor 15. 2 Cor 5:1-10.

AMB

Easter Monday

The Resurrection and the Life

Jesus said, 'I am the resurrection and the life'. John 11:25

Before Jesus raised Lazarus from the dead, he made it clear to Martha that he was (and is) the resurrection and the life. At the time, the great excitement of the event was that Lazarus came alive. We tremble with mixed emotions as we hear Jesus cry, 'Lazarus, come forth', and see a man, still tightly wrapped in grave clothes, come out of the tomb. But we know perfectly well that Lazarus is dead now. He had to die twice. What thrills us now is that Jesus is alive for ever.

In medicine we fight death off, or we delay it a little. Saving someone from death or the prolongation of a life strikes us as a major triumph. And so it should be, or we would not be worth our salt as doctors. But at times we feel it is a losing battle. Old age or cancer or tragic road accidents take their toll. We look at the pale corpse and the eyes which used to sparkle — then we go from the ward back to our room and wonder what life is all about. The answer to our wondering is Jesus Christ. He is the resurrection and the life. The fact that Christ is alive now and always will be is one of the most powerful and important truths in the world today. It has two implications. Firstly, the living Christ is with us throughout the whole of today. It is a comforting thought — yes — but also a very frightening one. He will watch our performance (whether or not we invite him to), he will cut straight to the root of our thinking, and he will listen quietly with unwavering attention to everything we say. How much of what he sees and hears will cause him pleasure, and how much will cause him grief before nightfall?

Secondly, the living Jesus Christ does not simply wait passively to see what we will do today. Since we belong to him and love him, he waits to act and speak through us. Surely this is an awesome responsibility: if my words are unloving, and my actions selfish and careless, what sort of view of him will my patient have?

Take heart! He who will live through you today will transform and work through the imperfections. If you really love him and walk humbly today, you will know his presence, his encouragement and his strength. Be sure that his love, just like his life, will never stop.

> Thank you, Lord Jesus, that you are alive. Please live in me
> today, and may I live every minute of the day for you.

Further reading: Ps 139. 2 Cor 3:2-3. Col 3:22-24.

JT

April 1

Election — for what?

Elect according to the foreknowledge of God. 1 Peter 1:2 (AV)

Election is one of the oldest grounds of dispute and the subject of much profitless debate. However, there is nothing contentious in this phrase. Peter's two letters face the world as it is. The second letter especially spells out its confusion, perversion, rebellion and ultimate judgment. God's judgment of man is correct as well as inevitable. God is moral and not arbitrary. 'The wrath of God is not vindictive, like the wrath of man; it is purely vindicative. It is simply the vindication of the right, before the eyes of all intelligent and moral creatures' (Douty).

Peter reminds us, however, that God is not willing that any should perish (2 Pet 3:9). A way of escape is provided which is firmly based on the two advents of Christ — the first which led to the crucifixion, and the second which will entail a 'new heaven and a new earth', as well as final judgment. Peter's other great theme is a corollary — in view of all this — wherefore — forasmuch — seeing — likewise — because God has done so much for us, we should be a people with a difference.

Strangely enough this is the election which concerns Peter. It is not one to be a topic of sterile debate and contention between Christians, but the thing which makes Christians different. It is purposive. God is calling people to serve and function in obedience to him; to live in a new way; to walk humbly because of what we are while also walking tall because we are so privileged. It is exactly the same in Romans, chapters 8-11, where Paul enlarges on the extent of God's love in Christ, but follows inevitably and without a break into Chapter 12 — 'therefore give yourselves unreservedly to God'.

General elections take place so that free countries can be governed. God has elected believers to live in the light of his love in work that he has planned for them. Regardless of difficulties that may come our way today, nothing can change our standing and purpose in life. People with a destiny live differently.

Called to be different — how different are you?

Look at Matthew Arnold's uncertainty:

> We but dream we have our wish'd for powers.
> Ends we seek we never shall attain.
> Ah, some power exists there, which is ours?
> Some end is there, we indeed may gain?

Then look at Murray McCheyne's confident resolve:

> Chosen not for good in me,
> Wakened up from wrath to flee,
> Hidden in the Saviour's side,
> By the Spirit sanctified.
> Teach me, Lord, on earth to show
> By my love, how much I owe.

Further reading: 2 Pet 1:2-11. Rom 8:28-30.

DEBP

April 2

Be Shrewd

The people of this world are more shrewd... than are the people of the light. Luke 16:8 (NIV)

At first glance the parable commonly known as the parable of the unjust steward is an unusual one. Why does Jesus apparently commend the shrewd manager who by dishonest means saved himself from disaster? Which of the man's characteristics is Jesus encouraging us to emulate? Jesus commended him to us not because of his dishonesty but because he was shrewd in his use of material possessions.

Improvidence commonly takes one of two forms: firstly, spending all that we have here and now on things of no permanent value — the principle of 'eat, drink and be merry for tomorrow we die', and secondly, squandering our money without ensuring a reasonable and worthwhile return — the failure to use it to 'store up treasures in heaven, where moth and rust do not destroy, and where thieves do not break in and steal'.

For most of us starting house jobs represents a sudden increase in our income, so that we now have more than we require for our immediate physical needs. It is easy to let money slip through our fingers, either to gratify ourselves or with a thoughtless generosity to others that achieves nothing.

Jesus is asking us to think very carefully about the way we spend this new-found wealth. Habits formed now tend to last a lifetime. Now is the time to face with God whether money and material possessions are ours or his, and if his, to consider how he would have us use them. Some of us have responsibilities to family or dependents. Some need to save for known future commitments. Our personal needs and circumstances vary, but they are all known to God. We must consider how much we should, or rather can, give directly to the Lord's work and in what ways this can be most effectively dispensed, remembering that all our material possessions come as a gift from him, and that, as a profession, we are more liberally endowed than many.

But why stop at money and possessions? Do we not owe him all that we are as well as all that we have? Time spent in thinking what really are his gifts to us and how best to use them could not be better spent.

> Lord, thank you for all you have given me. Deliver me from the sin of thinking of money, possessions or talents as being my own. Give me the grace to give back to you all that I have and all that I am.

Further reading: Lk 16:1-9. Dt 8:11-19.

DCM

April 3

The Way (4) — The Maker of the Way

In him we live and move and have our being. Acts 17:28

Each one of us who follows the broad way of medicine, no matter on which of the many tracks it offers, must sometimes ponder on the wonder of life, its creation and its sustaining. Especially wonderful is human life, with which all in the health team have much close contact. We need to remind ourselves constantly that behind it all is God.

When the apostle Paul visited Athens he was greatly disturbed to see how many trivial and inadequate and unworthy gods they had. Then he saw that they had made provision for 'an unknown God' — a quaint way of leaving their options open. He soon made it clear that they were missing out on the only god who mattered — in fact, the only God, who not only created all things but gives life and being to all living creatures.

Some people when they start to think about this are frightened off by the mystery of God's nature, especially the idea of the trinity: Father, Son and Holy Spirit, three Persons in one God. They put it in the 'too hard' basket and forget about it.

That is a big mistake. The fact that it is a mystery is no warrant for rejecting it. Would we really expect the nature of the eternal infinite God to be easy to comprehend? It is worth the most careful and reverent study (C S Lewis deals with it very helpfully in his book *Mere Christianity*).

This God not only made us and the world in which we live, he also made the Way by which we may come to know him. And he put it into effect in the most practical fashion. The Father gave his Son (God gave — for us). The Son took our nature and gave his life (God died — for us). The Spirit came to be with us and in us (God lives — for us). God has made the Way and shines his light in it. It is up to us to take it and follow it.

> Lord of all being, throned afar,
> Thy glory flames from sun and star;
> Centre and Soul of every sphere,
> Yet to each loving heart how near!
> Sun of our life, thy quickening ray
> Sheds on our path the glow of day.

Oliver Wendell Holmes

Further reading: Acts 17:15-34.

RRW

April 4

Hearing and Doing

Do not merely listen to the word, and so deceive yourselves. Do what it says. James 1:22 (NIV)

For the past six months, I have been studying French in Europe as preparation for missionary service in Africa. While at a continuing medical education conference in Lyon, France, this week, I was encouraged by my progress. I understood practically everything the French speakers said. I could have been deluded into thinking I knew French.

French people use the same phrase to say politely both 'please' and 'you're welcome'. In casual conversation with other physicians, I errantly used that expression to say 'thank you'. I am certainly grateful for my progress thus far, but my oral mistakes serve as a frequent reminder that hearing with understanding comes long before successful spontaneous speech.

As far as language acquisition goes, my instructors are 'Baptists'; they believe in 'total immersion'! One must be in a setting to hear the language daily. The student must study newly acquired information. And, most importantly, the language must be spoken; it must be practised and used. 'Speak, speak, speak,' was the advice of one teacher as the year began.

Having been a Christian for many years, I have a tendency to hear God's word apathetically. But God has reminded me that the same guidelines that I've been given to learn French apply to my life spiritually. James knew that the readers of his epistle had heard the word of God. Yet he challenged them to look at the word 'intently'. We, too, must handle the Bible with diligence; we must spend time studying it. James went on to say that as we continually look intently into God's word, we must then be 'doing it'; we must put it into practice. This leaves us vulnerable. God has put us on the battlefield of his kingdom. We each stand at the individual interfaces where God's kingdom meets the world. We must act according to his word.

Each time I open my mouth to speak French, I risk failure. At each moment we live as Christians, we risk failure. Yet God himself promises to uphold us, to strengthen us, to provide for us. We need simply to act on the basis of his word. Then, as James told his readers (Jas 1:25), we shall be blessed in what we do:

> 'He who looks into the perfect law,
> the law of liberty and perseveres,
> being no hearer that forgets but a doer that acts,
> he shall be blessed in his doing'.

Further reading: Jas 1:19-27.

PRF

April 5

Hope (1) — The Other Side of Faith

Hope in God; for I shall again praise him, my help and my God. Psalm 42:5

Hope is a wonderful and life-changing concept. Hope is the confident and favourable expectation of something good. Hope is confident, serene and expectant. Hope creates an inner attitude of openness to God, to other people and to life. Hope is the other side of faith, by which one commits oneself to God or another person.

Hope is the confidence that what I offer to God or to another person will be appreciated and responded to. Hope believes that God values what I offer him and will respond to my prayer. Therefore I am open to receive that response. It takes faith and hope to create love.

Hope does not disappoint because the love of God has been poured out in our hearts by the Holy Spirit (Rom 5:5). Long ago the psalmist could say with confidence: 'Hope in God, for I shall again praise him for the help of his presence'. Because God is a God of hope, every Christian should have a constant attitude of confident expectation.

> Gracious Lord, God of hope, thank you for pouring out
> your love in our hearts by the Holy Spirit. Fill our hearts
> also with hope and grant us faith that in you we shall not be
> disappointed.

Further reading: Ps 42.

KOT

April 6

Hope (2) — Its Therapeutic Value

... let us put on the breastplate of faith and love, and for a helmet the hope of salvation. 1 Thessalonians 5:8

Hope is meant to be a guardian of the mind, the perfect protection against depression, worry, pessimism and all the forms of rejective thinking. Hope has great therapeutic value for disturbed feelings. Because we know that God's choices for us are motivated by infinite love and guided by infinite wisdom, our hope comprising an attitude of openness and expectancy gives us emotional balance.

There are no hopeless situations — only people who have grown hopeless about them. King David knew the great therapeutic value of hope for disturbed emotions. In his own distress (Ps 42) he cried out: 'Why are you downcast, O my soul? Why so disturbed within me?' He soon found the answer: 'Hope in God, for I shall again praise him for the help of his presence' (NIV).

'When we were utterly helpless with no way of escape, Christ came at just the right time and died for us sinners who had no use for him' (Rom 5:6 LB). Every day then is a time for hope — 'For God so loved the world that he gave his only Son, that whoever believes in him should not perish but have eternal life' (Jn 3:16). 'And hope does not disappoint us because God's love has been poured into our hearts through the Holy Spirit which has been given to us' (Rom 5:5).

> Make us mindful always, Lord, of the helmet you have given us, which is the hope of salvation. So keep our minds at all times, knowing that in quietness and confidence in you is our strength.

Further reading: 1 Thes 5:8-11.

KOT

April 7

Hope (3) — In Problems and Trials

... hope does not disappoint us. Romans 5:5

Because of hope, we can rejoice when we run into troubles and trials, for we know that they are good for us. They help us to learn to be patient. And patience develops strength of character in us and helps us trust God more each time we use it until finally our hope and faith are strong and steady.

Then we are able to hold our heads high no matter what happens. We know that all is well for we know how dearly God loves us. We feel this warm love everywhere within us because God has given us the Holy Spirit to fill our hearts with his love (Rom 5:3-5 LB).

We are saved by trusting. And trusting means looking forward to getting something we do not yet have — for a man who already has something doesn't need to hope and trust that he will get it. But if we must keep trusting God for something that hasn't happened yet, it teaches us to wait patiently and confidently (Rom 8:24-25 LB).

> Lord God, giver of hope, fill us with your peace as we believe in you. And help us to overflow with hope in you through the power of the Holy Spirit.

Further reading: Rom 5:1-11.

KOT

April 8

Stress: The Normal Pattern of Life

Do not be surprised at the painful test you are suffering, as though something unusual were happening to you. 1 Peter 4:12 (GNB)

The stresses experienced by a 1st century apostle seem very reminiscent of those encountered by 20th century Christian physicians! In 2 Corinthians 6:1-10 Paul identifies three such areas of stress.

1. Physical extremity (vv4-5). How often, particularly when doing a house-job does life seem more a survival of the fittest doctor than survival of the least fit patient! Paul knew the spiritual problems of fatigue too (v5) and the nervous tension produced by calamities (v4). Did ever a man show such 'great endurance'?

2. Christian integrity (vv6-7). Paul could often have compromised as a preacher. Every day we too have opportunity somewhere to compromise our Christian integrity. 'Purity, forbearance, kindness, genuine love, truthful speech' — these should characterise our behaviour as Christians in medicine. And it is so easy to live like everyone else. But in so doing, it becomes difficult to live with ourselves.

3. Personal antipathy (vv8-10). It is hard to be disliked or despised (v8). It is frustrating to be junior, 'as unknown' (v9). It is wretched to be reproved, 'as punished' (v9). But these familiar areas of stress were all shared by the apostle.

How then did Paul respond to those stresses of life?

(a) He accepted stress as inevitable. For 'all who desire to live a godly life in Christ Jesus will be persecuted' (2 Tim 3:12). Did not Christ himself suffer those very same stresses? 'A disciple is not above his teacher' (Mt 10:24).

(b) He acceded to them as invaluable. It is in these very areas of stress that the Christian can often most vividly commend the source of his inner life to others (v9), most really experience the power of God the Holy Spirit (v7), most sadly learn the paucity of his own natural resources, and yet most certainly find, too, that his own inadequacy can prove God's complete adequacy (vv9-10).

> 'Every trial that we pass through is capable of being the seed of a noble character. Every temptation that we meet in the path of duty is another chance of filling our souls with the power of heaven.'
>
> William Temple

> 'It is not what happens to us that matters, but how we react to what happens.'
>
> Fred Mitchell

BW

April 9

My Shepherd (4)

He restores my soul. Psalm 23:3

The thought of restoration implies the bringing back to a proper state: to reinstate or to revive. We may restore a lost treasure to its owner or be restored by a cup of coffee. To restore a patient to life may be first to resuscitate him and later to send him home in full health and vigour. He is then doubly restored.

For a soul to be restored suggests that it was either lost or lacking lustre. Our Creator made us to have fellowship with him and to be in his image. An illustration of his intention is the rapt and adoring gaze of young infants as they respond to the smiling faces of their parents. That unclouded, radiant love is what he longs to see in us — his love reflected back from our souls to him and through our lives to others. The image is spoilt by anything that intrudes upon this central relationship. Between humans, a preoccupation with one's own affairs dislodges attention from the other person. In spiritual terms, estrangement develops when we become independent of him, bent on having our own way, or so immersed in our daily routine that we stop the habit of looking and listening to him. When, for the first time, a person realises that life has no focus or purpose, to hear then that the Shepherd has laid down his life in seeking to find and to save (Jn 10:11) and that he longs to restore the broken relationship may be what brings about conversion and starts the wonderful process of restoration into his image. Yet this is only the beginning — the resuscitation. From then on, Christians continue to need day-by-day restoration. His image in us will fade at any point of departure from his path or disobedience to his will. As a human shepherd pursues and assists his bleating, wandering sheep, so our heavenly Shepherd does the same for us. As the one disentangles from brambles and attends to minor wounds, so the Other releases and cleanses from all that dims his image. The way to restoration is for us to respond to his searching, sacrificial love and to clear it all up with him in that atmosphere. To shift the gaze from self to him brings repentance and renewal and has us following wholeheartedly once again.

> Perverse and foolish oft I strayed;
>   But yet in love he sought me,
> And on his shoulder gently laid,
>   And home, rejoicing, brought me.

H W Baker

Further reading: Lk 15:3-7, 11-24. Ps 51.

JG

April 10

My Shepherd (4 cont'd)

He restores my soul. Psalm 23:3

It is not only our relationship with the Shepherd that may need restoring, but our attitude towards the other sheep. Sheer fatigue as much as shifted focus can make us cross, crabby or complaining and adversely affect our working relationships. Is the receptionist suddenly a little cooler, or the telephonist unusually abrupt? For full restoration, such damaged relationships may need attention, apology or explanation. The Shepherd will do the necessary prompting if we are willing to hear him. It may be in such simple ways that he is going to reach someone else who was first alerted to look for him because of our humble attempts at reconciliation.

If tension is becoming a recurrent problem, it may be sanity that needs to be restored as much as spirituality. Restoration then may come through recreation as well as repentance. A return visit to the green pastures and still waters, even for half a day, can put us back onto the path with renewed vigour, confident of his continued leading, feeding and restoring. He has promised never to put us to more strain that can be borne (1 Cor 10:13). He is always ready to restore.

Come ye and rest; the journey is too great,
   And ye will faint beside the way and sink;
The bread of life is here for you to eat,
   And here for you the wine of love to drink.

E H Bickersteth

Further reading: 1 Ki 19:4-8. Is 40:28-31.

JG

April 11

A Legitimate Release (1)

When the cares of my heart are many thy consolations cheer my soul.
Psalm 94:19

Is there any way for us as Christians to find a legitimate release from the tensions imposed by having to be in the hospital on a 'one-in-two' rota for a year or perhaps longer?

A friend of mine was discussing this with the pastor of his church, a much-respected Christian leader, who expressed the matter frankly: 'Of course, in many ways it's far easier for your pagan colleagues who only have themselves to think about. Once they come off duty — or maybe even before — they can find release by leaping into bed with any partner who takes their fancy, or they can drink themselves to temporary oblivion, and so on.'

Unfortunately, in the heat of the moment it is not only our 'pagan colleagues' who end up finding their release in this way. Sadly some Christians deliberately get into situations which they later regret deeply, or find themselves trapped by habits — sexual or otherwise — from which they can't break free.

What then are we to do? Of course there are practical measures one should take to try to avoid trouble — the fellow who knowingly arranges to be alone at night with a nurse in the residence has already lost the battle. But, equally important, we should make plans to occupy free evenings in a definite, relaxing, but nonetheless positive way.

However, there are days when no matter how careful we are, we find ourselves feeling spiritually low, and a superb temptation falls right into our lap. (As a matter of fact I have had such a day while writing this!) But even here there is an answer.

The psalmist in Psalm 61:2 (AV) says 'when my heart is overwhelmed I cry to thee'. As God's children we must similarly learn to turn to him immediately the heat is turned on and we find we are in difficulties. To do this is, of course, far from a natural response. And in order to make it we need to condition our spiritual reflexes by spending time consciously with God throughout the day and not only in a fixed period specially set aside for that purpose (essential as that undoubtedly is). This sort of habit is not easy to cultivate, and for most of us it takes a long time. But it is infinitely worthwhile.

> Lord, I confess that one of the reasons why I am so prone to fall into temptation is because we spend so little time together, and my relationship with you is so shallow. It is my sincere desire that I should know you better and I pray that in the midst of a very busy life I may give priority to growing in the knowledge of you.

Further reading: Ps 94:12-23. Pr 18:10.

TGS

April 12

A Legitimate Release (2)

I have hidden your word in my heart, that I might not sin against you. Psalm 119:11 (NIV)

If yesterday's suggestions sound like a lot of 'pie-in-the-sky' to you, may I say humbly but with the benefit of experience, 'try it'. Carry around a pocket New Testament — or even better a whole Bible — in your white coat, and when those times come when you feel the pressure building up, read, memorise and meditate on God's promises to those who have been in your shoes in the past.

In order to do that, you need to be familiar with the relevant passages. As you read through the Bible, you will discover more and more of these for yourself. But in order to help you today, here are some verses which I found of great value during my final clinical year. Why not underline them in your Bible or copy them out now? You never know when you might need them.

A king is not saved by his great army; a warrior is not delivered by his great strength (Ps 33:16).

He will deliver my soul in safety from the battle that I wage (Ps 55:18).

I pour out my complaint before him. I tell my trouble before him. When my spirit is faint thou knowest my way (Ps 142:2-3).

Cast your burden on the Lord and he will sustain you (Ps 55:22).

No temptation has overtaken you that is not common to man. God is faithful and he will not let you be tempted beyond your strength, but with the temptation will also provide the way of escape that you may be able to endure it (1 Cor 10:13).

Though he fall, he shall not be cast headlong, for the Lord is the stay of his hand (Ps 37:24).

He delivered me from my strong enemy (Ps 18:17).

Lead me to the rock that is higher than I; for thou art my refuge, a strong tower against the enemy (Ps 61:2-3).

Thou, O lord, art a shield about me, my glory, and the lifter of my head (Ps 3:3).

I kept my faith, even when I said, 'I am greatly afflicted' (Ps 116:10).

Peace I leave with you; my peace I give to you, not as the world gives do I give to you. Let not your hearts be troubled, neither let them be afraid (Jn 14:27).

Blessed are the men whose strength is in thee, in whose heart are the highways of Zion. As they go through the valley of misery they make it a place of springs (Ps 84:5-6).

> Thank you, Lord, for your strong word. Help me to find in it not only encouragement but challenge.

TGS

April 13

Do-Gooders and Doers of Good

He went about doing good. Acts 10:38

The epitaph of the Lord Jesus, which came from the lips of a close friend and follower, was that 'He went about doing good' (Acts 10:38). Unfortunately, the phrase 'doing good' is debased coinage in current usage. The 'do-gooder' is thought of as a meddler, the amateur of mixed psychological motives who dips into other people's business with little benefit and sometimes the reverse. Such people can of course be tiresome and can do harm. But this does not justify a general attitude of contempt towards the desire to do good.

Doctors, nurses, social workers and all whose business it is to provide medical care, counselling and the like, know that they must be objective in their approach if they are to survive emotionally. But if all such activity is to be coldly clinical without compassion or sense of service, the outlook is bleak. Sentimentality is certainly not wanted. But a human approach and humane motivation cannot be discarded without ultimate loss.

The best of men of every age, and certainly the Christian doctor, will surely agree with Michael Faraday, scientific genius and humble Christian: 'It is not he who has soared above his fellow creatures in power, it is not he who can command most readily the pampering couch or the costly luxury; but it is he who has done most good to his fellows, he who has directed them in the doubtful moment, strengthened them in the weak moment, aided them in the moment of necessity, and enlightened them in their ignorance that leads the ranks of mankind'.

In quoting Faraday's words during a Lister Centenary Address in 1967, Arnold Aldis put the matter plainly — at least as the doctor of Christian persuasion must face it — when he said that 'all men are the objects of God's love and our responsive love for God must issue in love for our fellow-men. Indeed to fail to treat our patients at this deepest level is to add to the dehumanising of man. For it is to treat him as less than human, an object to be treated rather than a person to be helped.' So then as we have opportunity, let us do good to all men (Gal 6:10).

> Lord Jesus, I know that in your earthly ministry you went
> about doing good. Help me to follow in your steps.

Further reading: 1 Jn 4:7-12.

RRW

April 14

Lord, let me Share...

Bear one another's burdens, and so fulfil the law of Christ. Galatians 6:2

Lord God, the more I get to know the patients entrusted to my care, the more I sense the burden on their soul — their unvoiced fears of illness and death: of being 'abandoned' by relatives, and totally dependent on the provision of nursing care; of possible loss of jobs; what a heavy load on their hearts and minds and, added to that, their physical suffering!

How often have I prayed for that deep and loving understanding of yours, dear Lord, such as when you responded to the special need of the Samaritan woman at the well and unmasked her desire for 'life-giving water'. But I recognise that I must first draw my living water from you, daily and humbly, in the total commitment of prayer — or all will be of no avail.

> To be there before you, Lord, that's all,
> To shut the eyes of my body,
> To shut the eyes of my soul,
> And to be still and silent,
> To be exposed to you who are there exposed to me.

Empty of all ideas, of all images,
Here I am, Lord, to meet you without obstacle.

But, Lord, I am not alone
I can no longer be alone,
For men live within me,
I have met them;
They have settled down;
They have worried me;
They have tormented me;
They have devoured me;
And I have allowed them Lord,
So they might be refreshed.

I bring them to you, Lord, as I come before you;
I expose them to you in exposing myself to you.
Here I am and here they are, Lord, before you.

Michel Quoist

Further reading: Mk 6:30-37a. Jn 15:4-17.

L-MN

April 15

Man of Power

Moses was educated in all the wisdom of the Egyptians, and was powerful in speech and action. Acts 7:22 (NIV)

God worked miraculously to allow Moses to survive infancy and to provide him with a superb education. The result was that Moses became a very powerful man. When we were physicians-in-training, we were afforded great opportunities for education and for personal, intellectual growth. Based on our training and on our role as health care providers, we too exercise power through what we say and what we do.

How should we deal with such power? First, like Moses, we must remain humble. We must not think too highly of ourselves. Second, like Moses, we must maintain a proper perspective of life. We must see the real importance of various activities. As we complete each phase of our training, we tend to think that we 'know it all', and that we are invincible. We might compare ourselves with some of our unfortunate patients and come to the conclusion that we are better than they are. It is then easy to believe that we deserve the best of life's comforts. A big house, nice cars and expensive vacations can become the goals of our labours.

Moses faced similar challenges, but he kept a godly perspective on himself. Though the riches of Egypt were within his grasp, he chose to align himself with God's people rather than to enjoy personal, passing pleasures. So, third, we, like Moses, must make a conscious decision to work for God's kingdom. How do we live it out day by day? Again, we can follow Moses' example. We must live by faith. It was not because of priorities of the visible realm that Moses chose to leave Pharaoh's household. Moses, by faith, had extended his vision to the realm of the invisible. By faith, Hebrews 11 tells us, Moses acted 'as seeing him who is invisible'. We, too, must look to God for real power and for guidance as to how properly to implement that power. Some of us will be directed to serve away from the land of our upbringing. Others, with clear vision of the same God and of his priorities, will serve faithfully within our homeland. All of us must, by faith, see God's direction. And each of us must faithfully and obediently live as he leads.

> Trust and obey
> For there's no other way
> To be happy in Jesus
> But to trust and obey.

J H Sammis

Further reading: Acts 7:20-35. Nu 12:3. Rom 12:3. Heb 11:23-29.

PRF

April 16

Togetherness

... let us consider how to stir up one another to love and good works, not neglecting to meet together, as is the habit of some, but encouraging one another. Hebrews 10:24-25

'Togetherness' is something of an 'in' word these days. It gives a good clue to one way in which we can — and should — obey our Lord's 'new commandment' to his disciples, 'that you love one another' (Jn 13:34). It is simply by meeting together.

Some of us, doctors by no means excepted, find reason to excuse ourselves from this, so avoiding involvement in our church's activities. We are too busy or too involved in other things (worthwhile things, of course), the style of church service or music is not in our line, we have too little in common (culturally, intellectually, etc, etc) with other church people, and so on.

Reasons of this kind can be a bit thin, like the excuses in the parable of the great banquet (Lk 14:16-24). But if they really do weigh heavily with us, we need to watch them, particularly the one about other people. Christians come in all shapes and sizes, whether considered physically, intellectually, culturally or what you will, and so they are not always to our personal taste. The cynical sentimentalist can say: 'Of course I love my fellow men, it's people I can't stand'. That attitude is not an option which the Lord Jesus leaves open to his disciples. He does not say we must always like one another and one another's funny little ways. Indeed, I know myself too well to expect everyone to like me and my funny little ways. The commandment is to love one another, as he has loved us.

C S Lewis, university professor, man of intellect and culture, has told how, when he first became a Christian, he thought he could get along quite well without going to church. He considered the pros and cons, and he seems at first to have found the cons beguiling. Among other things, 'I disliked their hymns, which I considered fifth-rate poems set to sixth-rate music', he writes. 'But as I went on I saw the great merit of it. I came up against different people of quite different outlooks and realised that the hymns (which were just sixth-rate music) were, nevertheless, being sung with devotion and benefit by an old saint in elastic-sided boots in the opposite pew and then you realise that you aren't fit to clean those boots. It gets you out of your solitary conceit.'

Is solitary conceit our problem — or part of it? It does not belong to the mind of Christ. Conceit and love are just not compatible.

Teach me, master, to love as you love.

Further reading: Jn 13:31-35. Heb 10:19-25.

RRW

April 17

Cart before Horse

By grace you have been saved, through faith; and this is not of your own doing, it is the gift of God — not because of works, lest any man should boast. For we are his workmanship, created in Christ Jesus for good works, which God prepared beforehand that we should walk in them. Ephesians 2:8-10

Many people in the world today, including professing Christians, are trying to save their own souls by religious observances and by good deeds. It can't be done! However much he tries, man can neither atone for his past nor live up to God's standards in the present or the future. Had this been possible, Christ would not have died on the Cross, for just as a surgeon would not amputate a limb for a condition which would respond to conservative treatment, so God would not have allowed his Son to endure the terrible physical and spiritual agony of Calvary in order to save men who could have saved themselves.

We cannot earn our salvation, but we can accept it as an utterly undeserved free gift. 'What makes a man right with God is not the performance of the works that the laws lay down, but the simple trust of complete yieldedness which takes God at his word, and which believes that God still loves us when we have done nothing to deserve that love' (William Barclay). Only then do we start to have a life which is pleasing to him; only then do our good works become acceptable to him, good works which God had planned to do through us, and for which he makes us into suitable instruments as we hand over our lives to him.

We have the double privilege of showing our gratitude to him by our obedient service and by having a part in his great work of saving those around us.

> I cannot work my soul to save,
>   For that my Lord has done;
> But I will work like any slave
>   For love of God's dear Son.

Further reading: Eph 2:1-10. Heb 13:20-21.

DCT

April 18

Though... yet...

Though the fig tree does not bud and there are no grapes on the vines, though the olive crop fails and the fields produce no food, though there are no sheep in the pen and no cattle in the stalls, yet I will rejoice in the Lord, I will be joyful in God my Saviour. Habakkuk 3:17-18 (NIV)

It is very common among Christians today, with the popularity of the prosperity doctrine, to have our faith so closely tied to our material well-being that we become unable to discern joy and peace in the Lord unless we experience the kind of security the world provides. In a relatively affluent profession like medicine the danger of this is increased.

In his short book, Habakkuk recorded how he learnt that the almighty God is still sovereign and in control over the affairs of this world. Though Israel would be taken into captivity by the Babylonians, and though the latter seemed invincible, there would come a day of reckoning when the Babylonians would be punished. Habakkuk was also told to exercise patience as he waited for an answer from the Lord.

How is it possible for Habakkuk to be joyful in the Lord despite the news of such calamities? We too have similar experiences in our own times when every day we read of nothing but disasters and wars and destruction. Our economic forecasters have nothing but gloom for our future. We shall certainly be very anxious if our ultimate welfare is tied to our material well-being.

Habakkuk's secret was his faith in the Lord. 'The righteous will live by his faith' (Hab 2:4). It was this implicit trust in the Lord that brought peace and joy to Habakkuk despite all the calamities that were to come to the land of Judah. Habakkuk did not put his trust in the material well-being of the land. It did not matter what was going on in his time. He continued to rejoice in the Lord because of his faith in the sovereign God.

We need to re-discover this faith in our lives. It is easy to say with our lips that we trust God when we live in a land of plenty and in relative security. Many of us grew up with an emphasis on the external expression of our faith; but with our formal religion, we must not be immune to the great adventure that faith will lead us into. Despite our abundance and security, we need to see with our spiritual eyes beyond these horizons to the God who has provided us with all good things.

> Whatever may happen to me, Lord, grant me grace to rest
> my faith always in you and in you only.

Further reading: Mt 6:24-34.

S-KT

April 19

Get some Rest

Remember the Sabbath day by keeping it holy. Exodus 20:8 (NIV)
Jesus said to his disciples 'Come with me by yourselves to a quiet place and get some rest'. So they went away by themselves in a boat to a solitary place. Mark 6:31-32 (NIV)

Sunday presents a real problem in hospital. Jesus was no legalist about the sabbath, but, we are told, his custom was to attend the synagogue services. He emphasised the need for the rest and change that the fourth commandment prescribed. Even if our medical duties confine us to hospital for a Sunday, we should plan to set aside part of it for worshipping God. A hospital radio or TV service will often be possible, and an hour set aside in your own room for a devotional cassette tape or prayer and Bible study. The effort may be considerable but will prove tremendously worthwhile. The Bible's teaching on a day of rest is important and often neglected. As a result many busy Christians suffer physical, mental and spiritual problems. Often the 'sabbath' has to be on a weekday. It is a day for re-creation, for regular physical exercise, the mental refreshment of meeting friends (preferably non-medical!), for cultural activities and for Christian fellowship. Best of all we can hear Jesus say, 'Come with me by yourselves to a quiet place'.

Many years ago I heard the Rev Sidlow Baxter say, 'In the twentieth century, with all its pressures on us, I doubt whether it is possible to maintain a Christian life on less than an hour a day spent with God'. 'Impossible in my job!' you say. Perhaps it is not so difficult as we sometimes imagine. I am more convinced than ever that he was right.

> You have made known to me the path of life;
>> You fill me with joy in your presence,
> with eternal pleasures at your right hand.

Ps 16:11 NIV

O Lord, your days were more full than mine will ever be, more people came to you for help and healing, more needs, more agonising cries, more calls on your time. Yet you were often alone in your Father's presence seeking his will, his refreshment and his renewal. Help me to do the same.

Further reading: Ps 84.

CDA

April 20

Eternal Easter

Christ being raised from the dead will never die again. Romans 6:9

Every doctor is familiar with childbirth. The bringing of another baby into the world can be just routine — a job which calls for know-how and appropriate skill and care. It is easy to overlook the wonder of it, the emergence of a new life. But it is indeed wonderful. Wonderful also is the birth of a soul into the kingdom of God. It all looks back to the rising of Jesus from the dead.

During a visit to Leningrad in the early 1920s, Hugh Redwood went into the Cathedral. He describes the scene in his book *God in the shadows*. It was just before Easter. Despite the strong anti-God campaign being waged by the Soviet government, the great church contained many worshippers. One, who was clearly a lady, though her dress was poor, saw him watching her and addressed him in English.

'You are an Englishman, sir,' she said, ' and in England it is Easter now. But here we have no Easter, because Christ has been abolished by law. What wickedness! Christ is not dead, even in Russia. They think that they have taken him away, as they have taken away our Easter, but we shall keep Easter in our hearts, and there he will rise again...'

For many, Easter comes and goes. To some it means nothing. To some it brings a fleeting glimpse of hope, but then is put aside for another year. For the Christian who keeps Easter in his heart, it is present all the year round.

Christmas tells of a baby in a manger and of a supreme miracle. God was made man on a day in history. For the Christian who keeps Easter in his heart, it tells of new God-given life born in every human heart that opens itself to the living Christ.

Good Friday tells of a Man on a Cross, and a superb act of love. God offered himself as a ransom to save us. For the Christian who keeps Easter in his heart, it tells of pardon, peace and the power to live, freely bestowed by the living Christ. And because Christ is alive, it tells of hope — not only hope for us who follow him but hope to take out to others who know no such hope.

> Eternal God, living Lord, you have given us a living hope
> by the resurrection of Jesus Christ from the dead. Grant that
> we, being risen with him, may seek the things that are
> above and may rejoice in eternal life and in certain hope.

Further reading: Rom 6:1-11.

RRW

April 21

God the Healer

Heal the sick. Luke 10:9

The Bible does not say very much about physicians, and much of what it does say is not very complimentary. We find, for example, that Joseph did not call in the physicians to his father Jacob until after he had died, when he wanted his body embalmed (Gen 50:2). The only really effective Healer in the Old Testament is the Lord himself; one of his titles is 'The Lord, your healer' (Ex 15:26).

When the Lord Jesus performed his miracles of healing, he was, as ever, doing the works of his Father (Jn 5:19). When Christian doctors go in his name to do their ministry of healing, they are doing, with different tools and in different ways, what their Master did here on earth. As we go about our work today, let us keep his words in our minds. God himself is the great healer. All we can do with our modern scientific medicine is apply the principles we know to counteract the factors which hinder healing and facilitate those which aid it. And here, so often, we need wisdom to discern just what those factors are.

> Lord, you are the Great Physician. As I move among my
> patients today, grant me in a special way your wisdom to

know what best I can do to promote that healing of body, soul and spirit that you alone can give. Grant that I may be hindered from doing anything which would cause physical, mental or spiritual harm to those I seek to serve. Use me as your instrument of healing today.

Further reading: Mark 5:25-29. Lk 10:1-9.

JWMcM

April 22

The Only Way

Jesus said, 'I am the way...; no one comes to the Father, but by me'. John 14:6

At a mission hospital in Thailand, we found that a lot of the older rural patients were illiterate. For them it was no use having notices telling them where to find the Pathology Laboratory and the X-ray Department. At hospital committee we decided on a system of coloured arrows — red ones for a blood test, yellow ones for a urine test, blue for an X-ray etc. These arrows were painted on the floor, and when in use they led to a rather comic, rather sad spectacle of aged Thai farmers walking, head down, following the arrows and hoping to reach their destination. We don't know how many heads banged together during this procedure!

Our goal is important, but so is the route by which we get there. Jesus tells us that our goal is our Heavenly Father, and that Jesus is himself our Way. His words were spoken to Thomas, who was both confused and irritated, but they remain true for us today. Throughout each day our journey continues, our destination an eternity of joy with God and an unclouded view of him. I'm not suggesting that we'll get there by the end of the day, but we can certainly get several steps nearer. And those steps are taken in Christ — our WAY. We take the steps by faith — ie knowing that he is with us, and keeping our eyes upon him, we follow his footsteps obediently. As we do this, the end and the means become one, so that we need only to concentrate on one thing — staying with Jesus — our WAY. He will take us to the Father — no doubt about that. Our only worry is lest we wander off into our own way instead of his.

So we ask Jesus to keep us close to him today, and to whisper — or shout if necessary (though he should not need to shout) — a simple warning if at any moment we waver, or take a step off the road.

I said to the man who stood at the gate of the year —
'Give me a light that I may tread safely into the unknown'.

And he replied

> 'Go on into the darkness and put your hand into the hand of God,
> That shall be to you better than light and safer than a way'.*

M L Haskins

Further reading: Jn 14:1-11. Heb 10:19-23.

JT

April 23

Why, Master, Why?

Though he slay me, yet will I trust him. Job 13:15 (AV)

He was a very small puppy when he came into my life. Soon he had wriggled his way into my heart. I attended to his needs, saw that he was fed, took him for runs. The bond between us grew. I became his god.

My presence, it seemed, was what mattered to him. When I left in the morning, the protest was loud and vigorous. My arrival home in the evening brought joy unbounded. He shadowed me everywhere in the house, content to lie on the floor all eyes for me when I worked at my desk, up to be with me when I moved, sleeping by my bed.

Then he got distemper — my fault, as I should have had him immunised, and I offer no excuse for that. With the help of a good veterinary friend, I nursed him, getting out of bed by the clock during the night to be sure he received his medication. And he recovered, so it seemed.

When I moved from home to a student hostel, he had to come with me. But he was different. His personality was changing. From being a friendly little dog, he was becoming snappy and aggressive, though not towards me. I had to assume that the distemper had left permanent cerebral damage.

In the new environment it was virtually impossible to control him when I was away during the day. No one else seemed able to manage him. He ran wild. He bit the milkman. Something had to be done.

Again I went to my veterinary friend. We sadly agreed on the little dog's fate even while he was standing up pawing me affectionately. 'It will cause him no pain' I was assured, as I handed the lead to my friend. When he brought it back with the empty collar dangling at the end, I could say nothing. Nor could he, for he too loved little animals. I went away out of sight and wept for a little dog. Though he had trusted me, I had slain him. If he had known what was happening and had been able to comprehend the point of it, would he have said like Job, 'Though he slay me, yet will I trust him'? Or would he have said, 'I gave you all my love, all my trust. Yet you did this to me. Why, master, why?' I loved him. I had done what I believed was best. But I would have found it hard to explain in terms that he could understand. Is that perhaps God's dilemma (Is 55:8-9)?

Since then, when things in life have puzzled me, I have been able to say, 'I don't understand, master, but I trust you'. Job had it right.

> When things in life puzzle us, Lord, help us to understand
> as much as we can. And for what we cannot understand,
> grant us the grace to trust you.

Further reading: Rom 8:28-39. Jb 40:1-9, 42:1-6.

RRW

April 24

Brinkmanship

About the fourth watch of the night he came to them... Mark 6:48

We all have a touch of the 'brinkman' about us, some more than others! Out of bed at the last possible moment — toast munched, as we scurry down the corridor — wet towel and black coffee as we swot in the all-too-short months before an exam — midnight oil burnt for the report due yesterday — the results not obtained, the X-rays not fetched, the investigations not done, that send everybody else, quite unfairly, into a panic-stricken fever of activity! O the misery to ourselves and the nail-biting anxiety of others of the vicious circle of 'never doing today what we can possibly leave till tomorrow!'

Have you ever noticed how often God seems to act right at the last moment? Yet his brinkmanship is of a totally different order. He is never in a hurry, yet, in spite of our impatient apprehension, he is never late. His seeming delays are never because of a lack of care for us. It was because he saw their heavy going against a head wind that he came to them about the fourth watch of the night, walking on the sea (Mk 6:48). (Would we have left it until the morning?) How typical of us that they were surprised and frightened by his coming and nearly let him pass by without inviting him into the ship! It was the very night before Herod's proposed execution of Peter that the angel rescued him from prison. All honour to Peter's faith that he could spend his last night on earth asleep, chained to two soldiers (Acts 12:6).

Why does God seem to leave it so late before he intervenes? Is it that he can only act when we have exhausted our puny resources? Or that he will not share his glory with anyone else, and we and the world have got to see how he alone did it (1 Cor 1:28-29)? Is it to strengthen our faith in his unslumbering care (Ps 121:4)? Or perhaps to bless us more than we had ever thought possible (Jn 11:5-6, 15, 40)?

'In the fullness of time' — his time — 'God sent forth his son...' (Gal 4:4 AV). If he could do that at the right time, can we not trust him with the events of our lives?

> Lord, teach me that sometimes you have to wait until I have
> come to the end of myself before you can bless me, until I
> have finished trying my own plans before you can show me
> yours. Help me to recognise your perfect timing, and to
> know that you will never let me down.

Further reading: Mk 6:45-51. Acts 12:1-11.

MC

April 25

Lessons in Unemployment (1) — Why so hard to be Unemployed?

The apostles returned and met with Jesus, and told him all they had done and taught. There were so many people coming and going that Jesus and his disciples didn't even have time to eat. So he said to them 'Let us go off by ourselves to some place where we will be alone and you can rest for a while'. Mark 6:30-31 (GNB)

Eight o'clock on a sunny August morning, and suddenly I'm no longer on call; in fact I'm no longer employed. The patients I've admitted overnight are now the responsibility of my successor, my bleep is silent, and I'm free. Leaving the hospital, I meet some other members of the firm on their way to breakfast before outpatients, and already I feel an outsider. I've been unemployed for fifteen minutes, and I hate it.

The usual lift of the spirits at the start of a holiday isn't there. Life outside the hospital goes on as before, but it doesn't take long to see that medicine has taken up so much of my energy and enthusiasm that there isn't much life outside the hospital for me. Lesson one: it is hard to be unemployed because it makes me face the poverty of my interests.

Insecurity, a change of pace and the loss of the sense of being needed were all aspects of unemployment I had expected, being warned about them by my patients. What I didn't expect, and find the hardest to hear, is the silence of my mind. I have no list of jobs to do, no problems to unravel, no new skills to challenge me. The stamp of a working, active God seems to be so deep within us that unemployment causes a tension which is continually there, sometimes drowned temporarily, but always returning. Lesson two: it is hard to be unemployed because there is no shape or form to it — and it seems to be purposeless.

> O Lord, who gave us work to do, may I never make my work an end in itself — an idol. If unemployment comes my way, teach me its lessons, help me to understand my own negative reactions, and find grace to help, not only for myself but for others like me.

Further reading: 1 Ki 17:1-6, 18:1.

PIMA

April 26

Lessons in Unemployment (2) — Can I find meaning in Unemployment?

But when God was pleased to reveal his Son to me... I did not confer with flesh and blood,... but I went away into Arabia. Galatians 1:15-17

Do I really mean that God has allowed me to be unemployed with no reason? There is much to be learned from the experience, not least in sharing the feelings of so many in Britain today. But I think there is more — Jesus and his disciples, in the middle of purposeful and constant activity, suddenly withdrew (Mk 6:32). They had been busy travelling and teaching, caught up with their work so much that they could not even snatch a bite. I remember on occasions running straight from theatre to outpatients because the list had over-run. Jesus stepped into this busyness, and took his apostles out of it for a while — to be alone together. Taking stock of my life is easier when I am isolated from my usual employment. Lesson three: unemployment can be a chance to reconsider and redirect my efforts. Indeed its very formlessness is a help as I am not constrained by existing plans.

Before, every day was brimful of details which filled my attention. The short gaps that are evenings and weekends off were filled with domestic and social activity, the ordinary recreation of life. Now, Jesus takes me out of that sort of living: I need to be alone with him, free from responsibility and bustle, to make sense of the whole. Work too easily comes to mean too much. It gives me value in society, it gives me security and meaning in my life. However, these are all being detached from their real source, which is God. If I can have all these from him, I am freed from my dependence on activity for its own sake. I no longer need to work, though I certainly want to. Now, after several months I begin to put employment back into its right place.

'You have six days in which to do your work, but the seventh day is a day of rest dedicated to me. On that day no one is to work — neither you, your children, your slaves, your animals, nor the foreigners who live in your country. In six days I, the Lord made the earth, the sky, the sea, and everything in them, but on the seventh day I rested' (Ex 20:9-11 GNB).

The principle of the day without work — to rest and remember what life is really about — applies to unemployment too.

> O Lord, who created us to be your fellow workers, teach me that employed or unemployed by society I still have work to do with and for you. Grant that I may never be ashamed of enforced unemployment, but may use it to find fulfilment in fellowship with you, and direct me and others like me into new avenues of service that you have planned for us.

Further reading: 1 Ki 19:3-18.

PIMA

April 27

The Extra Mile

If any one forces you to go one mile, go with him two miles. Matthew 5:41

'Going the second mile' is often taken to mean that Christians should always do more than duty demands. But when should they do this, and for what purpose? The context shows that the phrase does not mean that we should always be trying to excel our brightest colleagues in study, in the care of patients and in endless service for others. Such an attitude can clearly lead to over-tiredness, inefficiency and even breakdown.

The context shows that Christ was correcting the Pharisee's view about retaliation and getting our own back! The Old Testament had laid down basic justice. The just penalty did not have to be exacted, and certainly was not to be exceeded. But now, Christ says something more: 'resist not the evil person' — in the sense of not rendering evil for evil. Do not attempt to get even with him, or bear him a grudge, or say 'he began it'. Go beyond that natural reaction and forgive him. It is a chance to show that you follow Christ's way.

Then Christ gave these illustrations: a blow on the cheek — an injury to the body, and perhaps to one's pride; the loss of a coat — an injury to one's possessions; and being compelled to go out of one's own way — an infringement of liberty and a use of our time and effort. The Roman occupying forces could compel a Jew to carry certain burdens a distance of

131

a mile: Christ taught that we should be prepared to suffer such injustice readily to turn an oppressor into a friend.

This then is the lesson of 'going the second mile'. We should forgiv generously any colleague or patient who harms or inconveniences us, t make him our friend. Who is my 'bete noire'?

> This (experience of persecution) will be your chance to witness for me.

Lk 21:13 JBP

Further reading: Mt 5:38-42. Acts 7:54-60.

DMcGJ

April 28

Sheep and Goats

Inasmuch as ye did it not... ye did it not to me. Matthew 25:45 (AV)

Is it a coincidence that this passage comes immediately after the parable o the servants and the talents? Standing on its own, it paints a terrifyin picture of the final judgment and is indeed one of the 'hard sayings' of ou Lord. For which of us has not passed by someone in need at some time o other? Could it be, indeed, that this passage is in part supposed t illustrate the misuse of talents given to us for the benefit of our fellov men? If so, the responsibility laid on us as doctors is grave indeed, for w have had 'talents' heaped upon us in the form of our medical training an experience. There is, of course, another side to the parable, for every tim we use our talents in the relief of suffering, we are, in a very special sense 'doing it unto him' — our Master himself. And it is a thought to comfor as well as challenge that, whether we are tending septic legs in a varicos ulcer clinic, giving comfort for the recently bereaved, seeing patients ir prison, putting up drips, giving morphine, inducing anaesthesia, treatin the aged or the unwilling, or even caring for the unlovely, we can regar that work as being done to our Lord himself. This thought alone can 'keer us going' when we are tired, irritable or perhaps even disgusted by th work that we have to perform. How grateful a patient can be after i manual disimpaction of the rectum! It may not be blasphemy to thinl when we are doing such tasks that we are doing them with the care an attention to detail that would be called for if the tasks were being done t our Lord himself.

But what if we have been guilty of standing by on the other side in th presence of need? Surely this is where the gospel comes in! Of course w have to admit that we have sinned (not always easy), but then we have th reassurance of Jesus' own words in another place: 'The man who hears what I have to say and believes in the one who has sent me has eternal life. He does not have to face judgment; he has already passed from death into life' (Jn 5:24 JBP). What does this mean for us? It means surely that we are freed from worry about the past — Christ has dealt with that through his death on the Cross — but freed to allow ourselves to be moulded into a new pattern of living — a pattern of joyful service of our fellow man 'as though he were Christ'.

> Teach me my God and King
>   In all things thee to see,
> And what I do in anything
>   To do it as for thee.
> All may of thee partake;
>   Nothing can be so mean,
> Which with this tincture, 'For thy sake'
>   Will not grow bright and clean.

George Herbert

Further reading: Mt 25:14-46.

PCB

April 29

Realism in Perspective

What does the worker gain from his toil? Ecclesiastes 3:9 (NIV)

Those who live and work on the medical scene can appreciate the earthy realism of the book Ecclesiastes. Rose-coloured spectacles have no place in medicine's view of life — or in that of the Teacher, who wrote this remarkable book.

He is a cynic, say some. But in fact he faces reality. He sees life as it is and makes no pretence. So must the doctor or the nurse or whoever has the care of sick people in the real world.

Yet the refrain comes again and again: 'All is meaningless. All, all is vanity'. Life set in an empty universe is pointless, a rat race on a cosmic treadmill: a time for this and a time for that, a time to be born and a time to die...and all in vanity. There is nothing before the beginning and nothing after the ending in an empty universe.

An empty universe? Why must it be empty? For the Teacher it was not empty. For him, God was there. For us, God is here. We, like the Teacher, may feel the treadmill of chapter 3 under our feet — a time for this and a time for that in a seemingly endless drone — and we gasp out: 'What does the worker gain from his toil?' The answer comes: 'I have seen the burden

God has laid on men' and then, sweet and clear, 'He has made everything beautiful in its time. He has also set eternity in the hearts of men.'

Much is still not explained — 'they cannot fathom what God has done from beginning to end' — and so it often is in medicine. But the ultimate hope keeps it in perspective, for God has set eternity in our hearts.

> Thank you, Lord, that you have set eternity in my heart. Help me to see life realistically, yet always to live in the perspective of hope.

Further reading: Ec 3. 2 Cor 4:8-18.

RRW

April 30

A Proper Respect

Live as free men, but do not use your freedom as a cover-up for evil; live as servants of God. Show proper respect to everyone: Love the brotherhood of believers, fear God, honour the king. Slaves submit yourselves to your masters with all respect, not only to those who are good and considerate but also to those who are harsh. 1 Peter 2:16-18 (NIV)

It is easy (and scriptural) to respect the worthy. It is another thing to respect all. This does not mean that we are to be so easygoing that we tacitly approve the false or mean. But there is a respect that is due to everyone.

What is our attitude to others? What is their worth to us? Doctors often deal with people who differ from them in many ways — if only because they are sick and vulnerable. But they will certainly have feelings just like our own. This also applies to our colleagues — even those who may give the impression of being so hardbitten as to be insensitive, or to 'chiefs' who are unreasonable and difficult to work with. We are all significant to God, which is why this command is linked with that to 'fear God'. If we show disrespect to another, we are devaluing one to whom God has given life, and for whom Jesus sacrificed his own life.

This thought must be at the heart of all our creed and conduct when facing issues of real life and death — not only on ultimate questions such as euthanasia, but in our daily contacts with the awkward or slow-witted outpatient, the demanding or hostile parent, the terminally ill, and the untreatable but 'interesting case'. When I insert that intravenous drip, is my action consistent with respect for the patient?

The principle holds too in questions of truth. Can I lie to someone respect, be he patient or colleague? Equally my honesty must be tempered with sensitivity and compassion for the suffering and problems of others.

> Forget not thou hast often sinned,
> and sinful yet must be;
> Deal gently with thy brother, then,
> as God has dealt with thee.

J A Fletcher

Further reading: Col 3:12-4:1.

DEBP

May 1

Run to Obtain

Train yourself in godliness, for while bodily training is of some value, godliness is of value in every way, as it holds promise for the present life and also for the life to come. 1 Timothy 4:7-8

As Timothy was continuing his job as pastor and teacher at Ephesus, Paul might have wished and prayed for him for much in the way of gifts and endowments to do the work. But this is not his theme. Again and again in his letters to Timothy he urges him to aim at godliness. In the context of 1 Timothy 4:8 and 2 Timothy 4:7-8 Paul likens the pursuit of godliness to physical training as a prolonged struggle — 'the good fight of faith'. Godliness is not something that magically supervenes after an appropriate length of time as a Christian; it is something that has to be strained after and fought for.

We are all familiar with the sight of thousands of people, clad in singlets and shorts, pounding the streets of our major cities in the 'people's marathons'. These individuals have often given up hours every week to train their muscles to accept the load that, legend has it, killed the sole runner of the first marathon. How much more should we be prepared to train ourselves in godliness, day in day out, at the cost of a struggle.

But training has a negative as well as a positive aspect. Timothy is instructed on the one hand to have nothing to do with — to refuse (AV) — godless and silly myths (v7), and on the other hand to train himself in godliness. In 1 Timothy 6:11 he is told to shun — flee from (AV) — the foolish and hurtful things as well as to aim at — follow after (AV) — godliness.

The spirit of the age in which we live, with its false beliefs, dependence on human wisdom, inverted values and superstitions, can be seen in agnosticism, humanism, the worship of money and possessions, and preoccupation with astrology and the occult. These are the things we need to shun as we pursue the righteousness, faith, love, endurance and gentleness which are godliness (1 Tim 6:11), so that we attain God's promise not only for the present life but also for the life to come.

> Heavenly Father, help me daily to lay aside those sins which cling so closely, and, looking to you, to persevere in pursuit of your high calling. May I so run as to attain the promise of the life to come.

Further reading: 2 Pet 1:1-11. 1 Cor 9:24-25.

TAG

May 2

The Lord's Keeping

I am the vine, you are the branches. He who abides in me, and I in him, he it is that bears much fruit. John 15:5

'Beware! When you become a houseman you will fall away unless you keep links with other Christians.' Advice like this was frequent during my last year or so as a medical student — and it rang true! However, here I was in a classically hectic house-job with no Christian medical colleagues and very little off-duty for seeking fellowship. Would I be too busy to take time and listen to the Lord? Would the fascination of my medical work be too preoccupying to allow me to make the effort to be with his people? Would I slip out of his grasp on my life in the sometimes dubious atmosphere of the medical staff quarters?

Our Lord's words in John 15 were a powerful corrective to these anxious questions and negative attitudes. My calling was to 'abide in him', stay close to him, in the assurance of his presence and keeping. He, the Vine, was the source of life and strength to me — one of his many, unique branches. The Father needed to prune me, to cut me down to size, but, as I took what opportunities I could for worship, fellowship, prayer and Bible study (all aids in 'abiding' in him), I had the continuing conviction of his power, not only to keep, but to help me lead a fruitful life.

> Dear Father, be a Vinedresser in my life. Help me, in today's busyness, to remember I am a unique branch of the Vine and that, although I need cutting down to size, I am secure for ever as I stay close to Jesus, strengthened and kept by the nourishment of your word in the power of the Holy Spirit.

Further reading: Jn 10:27-30, 15:1-11

PFH

May 3

The Way (5) — The Barrier on the Way

Jesus said: Those who are well have no need of a physician, but those who are sick; I have not come to call the righteous, but sinners to repentance. Luke 5:31-32

We constantly lament the failure of people with serious, though curable, disease to seek help early enough, or indeed to seek it at all. So often they brush aside their symptoms, refusing to admit even to themselves that there is anything wrong.

It is the same with the sickness of the soul. And here Jesus puts his finger right on the problem. He is dining with tax collectors and sinners to the holy horror of the Pharisees and scribes. He is bringing help to those who have no illusions about their faults, sinners who can be called to repentance. He is unable to help 'the righteous', who just do not know, or at any rate admit, that they are sick. This is the barrier that blocks their entrance to the Way.

If we ask why so few do in fact enter on the Way, the answer is in one word — sin. Unhappily this word is too often misunderstood. Sin is essentially that rebellious attitude of mind and heart that refuses to accept God's sovereignty, that flouts his laws, that asserts our right to live our own lives.

The Pharisees would, of course, have been shocked at any suggestion that they were guilty of that. But they were. They were guilty as we may be of the basic sin of pride — the sin of setting up ourselves as our own gods, relying on self-righteousness and self-sufficiency.

Pride often masquerades as self-respect, as honest independence. But it is no more than the futile pitting of man's will against God — the God who made us and can alone order our lives and make us really happy, the God who loves our human race so much that in Christ he suffered to the utmost to reconcile us to himself, to establish a living relationship with himself.

We should differentiate sins from sin, just as we differentiate symptoms from an underlying disease or disorder. The ugly vicious sins are the fruit of the corrupt seed of rebellion and pride in people's hearts. But that same pride can be working under the most seemingly virtuous exterior, a symptomless cancer, a latent infection. Its effect is the same. It disables, it destroys, it kills, sooner or later. It makes a barrier to or on the Way. It creates a tragic diversion from the hope of healing for the soul's sickness, a diversion from the Way, which is the way of spiritual life, to the way of spiritual death. It separates us from God. And sadly it not only shuts people off from entering the Way. It can still block progress on the Way for the unwary wayfarer. And it can black out our vision of Christ.

> Sun of my soul, thou Saviour dear,
>   It is not night if thou be near;
> O may no earth-born cloud arise
>   To hide thee from thy servant's eyes.

John Keble

Further reading: Lk 5:27-32.

RRW

May 4

The Eye of the Storm

Peace I leave with you, my peace I give unto you. John 14:27

Peace in the usual sense of the word is hardly descriptive of the life of a junior hospital doctor. Demands for our services come thick and fast and often all at once. The ubiquitous 'bleep' intrudes on meals, conversations, relaxation, sleep and everything else we do. But Jesus promises his peace to reign in our hearts, a peace like no other peace, independent of circumstances and in spite of all that would harass us.

What is it? It is peace with God, the peace of forgiven sin and reconciliation with him: 'justified by faith we have peace with God through our Lord Jesus Christ' (Rom 5:1). Nothing can equal or disturb the peace that springs from his free saving grace.

He tells us, too, that since we are at peace with God, and trusting in him, his resources are available for every need and all eventualities. He wants to garrison our hearts all day and every day from fear and every anxious thought. 'You will keep in perfect peace him whose mind is steadfast because he trusts in you' (Is 26:3 NIV).

But we have a part to play. Our Master not only assures us, he commands us, 'Let not your hearts be troubled, neither let them be afraid' (Jn 14:27). 'Let the peace of Christ rule in your hearts, to which indeed you were called' (Col 3:15).

> Peace, perfect peace, in this dark world of sin?
>   The blood of Jesus whispers peace within.
> Peace, perfect peace, by thronging duties pressed?
>   To do the will of Jesus, this is rest.
> Peace, perfect peace, our future all unknown?
>   Jesus we know, and he is on the throne.

Edward Bickersteth

Further reading: Phil 4:4-9.

JHCM

May 5

Frail Children of Dust

...he knows our frame; he remembers that we are dust. Psalm 103:14

Every doctor knows the frailty of the human body and mind, even while acknowledging that we are fearfully and wonderfully made (Ps 139:14 AV). Perhaps more than most, the casualty surgeon knows how easily the body can be broken, and the psychiatrist knows how the mind can be thrown into chaos. We know it is true of ourselves as well as of patients. This earthly tent that we live in, as Paul calls it (2 Cor 5:1), is very vulnerable and has a limited life. Meantime the doctor's task is to look after it to the best of his or her ability.

What we too often neglect, however, is the spiritual being who lives in this tent, this temporal home. We live and think and work very much in the 'now' of life, forgetting the eternity that not only is to be but already surrounds us. Thank God his vision of things is not so limited. He knows our frame. He remembers that we are dust. 'Our days are like grass', says the Psalmist. 'But the steadfast love of the Lord is from everlasting to everlasting upon those who fear him.'

While being grateful always for God's steadfast love towards us personally, we can also see here a pattern for a right attitude in medical practice. It is not for the doctor to play God, though that accusation is sometimes made as a jibe. But patients do trust their doctor, and he or she can scarcely do less than follow the Lord's example of showing tenderness and faithfulness towards those who trust him.

> Frail children of dust, and feeble as frail,
> In thee do we trust, nor find thee to fail:
> Thy mercies how tender, how firm to the end,
> Our Maker, Defender, Redeemer and Friend.

Robert Grant

Further reading: Ps 103.

RRW

May 6

D G

Whatsoever you do, do all to the glory of God. 1 Corinthians 10:31

I never did like examinations. I always came at the very last moment and rushed away as soon as I could. I thought little of those who claimed that examinations were harder for the examiner than for the students, but I had to become an examiner before I came across the two initials DG at the top of some answer papers.

They puzzled me. After a while it became clear that it was the mark of Catholic students. D G — Deo Gloria — to the glory of God. It challenged me. Here was a group of people who were willing to advertise their answer as being to the glory of God. I often wish that I had had the courage and the knowledge to do this as an undergraduate. In order to be able to put D G on a written paper one has to be confident that all the necessary hard work has been done beforehand and then the answer committed in prayer to the glory of God. Not only at times of testing but in all our lives everything we do should be D G. Whether we take a history in outpatients, examine an old lady in the wards, set up an intravenous drip on a new born baby, counsel a disturbed adult, all should be done in a manner that will glorify God.

I like the term St Paul uses of himself: an ambassador for Christ (2 Cor 5:20). It may be difficult to think of ourselves as ambassadors in the middle of a general practice surgery or at 3am doing an appendicectomy, or at 1.45pm still doing morning outpatients, but that is what we are. St Paul had a most unusual assignment; he was ambassador in chains as a prisoner. What an unlikely situation for an appointed ambassador for the most high God! He must have wanted to be free to preach the Gospel there in Rome and other places. But God had put him there, and the letters that he wrote from the Roman gaol have been to the blessing of many and to the turning of the world upside down. God can use us for his glory wherever we are if we are loyal and obedient. His ambassadors are rarely in high places, but often in the undesirable parts of the world, and working at unsociable hours. No wonder a Christian may wonder if he is in the right place doing the right thing! St Paul must have had the same thought many a time. The greatest writer the world has ever seen did his work in bonds serving in a most inappropriate place in an impossible situation, but Deo Gloria.

> Lord, help me never to fall into the trap of thinking that 'the grass is greener' in the place where you have not put me, or that I could serve you better in someone else's

circumstances, or with the gifts and personality of another.
Grant that this day I may bring glory to your name, by
doing my best for your sake, just as I am, and where I am.

Further reading: Mt 5:13-16. 2 Cor 3:1-6.

OPG

May 7

Don't be Dumb

*Do not be afraid of anyone. But have reverence for Christ in your hearts,
and honour him as Lord. Be ready at all times to answer anyone who asks
you to explain the hope you have in you, but do it with gentleness and
respect. 1 Peter 3:14-16 (GNB)*

Many have had the embarrassment of suffering at the hands of a 'hot-
gospeller' — the type who is not simply ready to speak if necessary, but
ready with inappropriate zeal to pounce whenever there is a chance to
intrude with a pat verse or trite challenge. However, such belong to a dis-
appearing species.

We have, rather, become decorous and dumb. Christians are a minority in
medicine. Christianity has unpopular things to say: the Bible teaches that
all are lost apart from Christ, and the 'all' includes our colleagues and
patients. The Bible emphasises sin as a reality, which explains not only our
lostness but much of our suffering. It points to our hope of salvation which
is Jesus Christ. These truths, though some of them may be unpalatable,
should always be in our minds. Otherwise we cannot 'always be ready'.

The readiness required is not that of being quick to blurt out, but to
answer, and an answer is a reply to a question asked — 'what is the
secret?'...'what makes him tick?' We should be the sort of people who
prompt this type of bewildered query. Martyn Lloyd-Jones points out that
a Christian should be an enigma to the unbeliever (*Studies in the Sermon on
the Mount*). When we do reply to the question, we are to do so with
'gentleness and respect'.

Are we ever asked? and anyway, what is the reason for the hope that is in
us? Have we really thought? Find out some answers from the suggested
further reading.

> Go forth and tell! Men still in darkness lie;
> In wealth or want, in sin they live and die.
> Give us, O Lord, concern of heart and mind,
> A love like thine that cares for all mankind.
> Go forth and tell! The doors are open wide;
> Share God's good gifts with man so long denied.

Live out your life as Christ, your Lord shall choose,
Your ransomed powers for his sole glory use.

J E Seddon

Further reading: 1 Pet 1:3-9. Rom 8:28-30. Col 1:27.

DEBP

May 8

Months of Emptiness

I was allotted months of emptiness, and nights of misery are apportioned to me. Job 7:3

There is not space to relate all the complex circumstances that precipitated it — and they will be different for you in any case. The fact remains that in my final two student years I became increasingly more depressed and unable to cope with life. It was not just a passing phase either; people said it would soon lift but it didn't. And as month followed upon month there seemed no end to the sleeplessness, the aimlessness and the emptiness. The whole of life was breaking up for me.

And where was God in all this? I had been a Christian for some eight years and had always known such joy and fulfilment in life up to this point. Indeed, my Christian commitment was a key factor in my choosing medicine as a career, and now it seemed that my very future in it was in severe jeopardy.

It was during the second year of this depression that the book of Job became so meaningful to me. It was not that I found there any answers to my questions at the time, but I found such help in the fact that here was someone who was feeling just the same agony, someone with whom I could identify. The knowledge that you are not the only one brings untold release and comfort. G K Chesterton puts this so well in *The Man who was Thursday*: 'There are no words to express the abyss between isolation and having an ally. It may be conceded to the mathematicians that four is twice two, but two is not twice one; two is two thousand times one.' And it was this issue of not being alone that eventually proved to be one of the key answers to the question 'Why did you let this happen, Lord?'

Eventually I did get better, and obtained a tremendously satisfying house-job in the oncology unit at the hospital where I trained. During this job I saw that God had over the months of my depression, been equipping me to be better able to help others cope with the psychological trauma and suicidal feelings accompanying severe illness.

Paul tells us in his opening paragraphs of 2 Corinthians that God 'comforts us in all our afflictions, so that we may be able to comfort those

143

who are in any affliction'. What a privilege then for those who are working each day with the sick and injured. If we look to him, the Lord will cause any experience — no matter how devastating at the time — to be used for ultimate good in our lives and for the help and enrichment of our patients too.

> Lord, thank you that you never cause us needless pain, that it is true that all things work together for good for those who love you. Help us to be patient under the trials that we face, knowing that you do have a purpose in them because your love is constant and everlasting.

Further reading: Jb 7:1-10.

TGS

May 9

My Shepherd (5)

He leads me in paths of righteousness for his name's sake. Psalm 23:3

The retrospectoscope is a wonderful instrument for appreciating the fact of the Lord's leading. Those at the start of their careers can be encouraged by the life stories of others — it is true that he leads. Sheep have to learn to know and respond to their shepherd's voice, and the ways in which the Good Shepherd leads are also learnt by experience and will have individual variations. We can be sure that we are not hearing his voice if we set foot on paths of unrighteousness or even of self-righteousness. The paths of his righteousness may at first sound narrow and forbidding to the uninitiated, but assurance of the Shepherd's constant care for his flock must surely assure us right at the start that he has our interests at heart. He leads not merely to satisfy himself, but to bring us into satisfying pastures, not just to indicate his authority, but to reveal to each of us new evidence of his careful, personal, individual planning. Other paths may look more beguiling, and the right track may well require a committed will and self control. We may stumble and stray, but only as we find the paths where he leads shall we continue to hear the calling of his voice, to see the print of his foot and to be assured that we are not setting out into the unknown alone.

Doctors in training change jobs more than most other workers. Do we pray about which of the many doors we should try? When each house-job has scores, if not hundreds, of applicants, can we trust him to lead us to the post of his choice? The experience we glean, the colleagues we have and the contacts we make will all become woven into the pattern of our lives and can have important implications for the future. He alone sees the end from the beginning and is thinking today of our tomorrow. How vital that we ask him to lead the way and then follow. It is very likely for each of us that there will be times of great uncertainty and even of unemployment. Closed doors may be one way by which our paths are being directed. These setbacks need not mean that we are off his path: each of us needs to learn the value of developing patience in waiting upon God.

> O light that followest all my way,
> I yield my flickering torch to thee;
> My heart restores its borrowed ray,
> That in thy sunshine's blaze its day
> May brighter, fairer be.

George Matheson

Further reading: Jn 8:12. Ex 13:21-22. Nu 9:15-23.

JG

May 10

My Shepherd (5 cont'd)

He leads me in paths of righteousness for his name's sake. Psalm 23:3

It requires practice to keep looking to him expectantly, despite delays or dashed hopes. Each experience of his leading will add to the encouragement to trust him in the next crisis. He has a way of suddenly making dead ends open up or finding ways around apparently impenetrable barriers. This comes as an affirmation of his presence and assurance of his leading. So often, too, he speaks to us clearly through his word if we have established the habit of reading it day by day. Words of encouragement or direction will be read which the attentive heart will recognise to be personally directed by his Spirit. At other times, an apparently chance encounter, an unexpected invitation, or a bewildering closure of a planned route can be his way of showing us the next step. We can rely on him to be faithful, and the reason for his faithfulness is his love. For him to behave otherwise would be inconsistent and contrary to his good name. When he leads and I follow, this brings praise and glory to him. It is indeed for his name's sake.

These thoughts were written on a train journey which had been fraught with practical problems from the start. At times, it seemed that I could not hope to reach my destination in time, yet on arrival was expected to entertain others to a special celebration lunch. Timing was vital! To crown all, I was surrounded by hundreds of milling football fans. It took a deliberate act of will and of trust not to fret and fume, but to rely on the Lord's loving involvement and concern. It was a little time before I realised that the fans, too, were heading for my home town, that they, too, had a time limit (kick-off time exactly matching my own deadline) and that every effort was being made to get them there in time and therefore to get me there in time. Later, over lunch, the story made a conversation piece, and someone commented that even before I had learned that my original train was cancelled, a great master plan had already swung into action to come to my rescue and ensure that obligations were fulfilled. The remark was made lightly, but my spirit gave a glad assent — the Shepherd had done it again! So let not your heart be troubled. If he cares about successful lunch parties, he can surely be relied on to clarify career plans as well. He really does lead.

> Ever be thou our guide,
> Our Shepherd and our pride,
>   Our staff and song:
> Jesus, thou Christ of God,
> By thy perennial word
> Lead us where thou hast trod,
>   Make our faith strong.

Clement of Alexandria
(Translated from the Greek by H M Dexter)

Further reading: Jn 10:1-10.

JG

May 11

Beyond the Reasonable Call of Duty

Whosoever of you will be the chiefest, shall be the servant of all. Mark 10:44 (AV)

This passage is worth reading in its full context, for it is preceded by the episode in which two disciples asked for the chief places in the Kingdom, and Jesus countered them by saying that true greatness went with service and ministry. It is followed by the episode of blind Bartimaeus, sitting by the highway begging.

Bartimaeus cried out to Jesus as he passed by, only to be hushed up (by the healthy, one supposes!). He was getting in their way, a nuisance, preventing them from doing what to them was more important. But seeing his fleeting chance of help Bartimaeus refused to be silenced, and Jesus was not one to stand on his dignity — he had come to serve, not to be served. Here was one needing service. Jesus always held himself available for people like Bartimaeus.

One of the problems of being a doctor is that so many people seem to expect us to be available at all times. They may not necessarily be patients — they may be relatives, or nurses needing some question answered.

Often the request for our time comes when we are tired, or are just leaving work for some well deserved relaxation. Often the request seems unjustified and trivial compared with our need for some privacy and leisure. Yet when and if we answer the request, we often find that it is more urgent than we had anticipated, or that it reveals some unspoken anguish or misapprehension at which we had not guessed. This is not always so — sometimes the request really is trivial. But if we are following in our Master's footsteps, we dare not stand on our dignity and behave as if we were 'the great ones' not to be troubled by trivia. 'For even the Son of man came not to be ministered unto, but to minister, and to give his life a ransom for many' (v45) — the key to our reading.

> Lord help me not to be impatient with those who make what seem to be unnecessary demands on my time. Give me the grace to be courteous, and ready to give of myself to those whose requests appear trivial but whose needs may be greater than I realise.

Further reading: Mk 10:35-52.

PCB

May 12

Guidance (1) — Recognising God's Guidance

The Lord will guide you continually. Isaiah 58:11

God's promise of guidance is certain and repeated. He has recreated us and has a prepared plan for our lives (Eph 2:10). Jesus himself promised that his followers would not walk in darkness but have the light of life (Jn 8:12). Yet recognising God's will remains a practical problem, particularly perhaps for junior doctors who have to make frequent job decisions which could determine their whole future. We can be caught between the Scylla of rushing ahead with our own plans, assuming them right, and the Charybdis of being reduced to jittering indecision, lest we are making a mistake.

The following stem from long experience:

1. God is more anxious than we that we should know his will, trying neither to delude us nor to obscure his plans. But his promises are not magic formulae triggered with a magic wand. We are not always ready for the answer for which we ask. God's promises are often conditional on prerequisites in the recipient. 'In all thy ways acknowledge him and he shall direct thy paths' (Pr 3:6 AV). 'Seek ye first the kingdom of God...and all these things shall be added' (Mt 6:33); 'If ye abide in me, and my words abide in you, ye shall ask whatever you will and it shall be done for you' (Jn 15:7).

2. God sometimes withholds guidance, having some better thing for us, 'therefore the Lord waits to be gracious to you' (Is 30:18). His delays are for our greater blessing.

3. Guidance comes in different ways to different people and in different ways to the same person. He is a living God of resource and initiative, seldom working in the same way twice. We sometimes pray for guidance and fail to recognise it when it comes.

4. We may not be acutely aware of God's guidance at the time, but with hindsight can see how unerring it has been. A multiplicity of 'coincidences' of circumstance and timing assure our hearts of his good hand upon us. In his good time we see the picture emerging from the jig-saw pieces.

> Child of my love, fear not the unknown morrow,
>   Fear not the new demand life makes on thee.
> Thy ignorance shall be no cause for sorrow
>   Since what thou knowest not is known to me.

Further reading: Ps 121. Jn 10:1-14.

MC

May 13

Guidance (2) — Keep 'On Course'

I being in the way, the Lord led me. Genesis 24:27 (AV)

God's guidance is a natural consequence of being 'on course'. Anything that disrupts our fellowship with him obscures our vision and blunts our perception. Given a right relationship with God, his guidance may be unobtrusive, almost outside our conscious awareness, many decisions being dictated by common sense, albeit the common sense of a renewed mind. God promises to guide the meek in judgment (Ps 25:9). We are not to be stupid and mulish, to be pushed and pulled, but to be those with understanding minds enlightened and instructed (Ps 32:9), attuned to the mind of Christ. Maybe we can see only one step ahead. Take it and the way will open as do automatic doors on our approach.

Guidance may be by restraint. In Acts 16:6-10 Paul and Silas were forbidden by the Holy Spirit to speak the word in Asia. How (since it seemed so good a thing to do)? By a spoken word? a vision? or just a disquiet of heart, a lack of assurance, an unease, a 'something' that held them back? Then they saw a door marked 'Push'. They tried it. It did not yield (no harm in testing the doors). God has promised to tell us if we take a step in the wrong direction (Is 30:21). But for every door that closes there is one that opens. The invitation came to Macedonia. They weighed it up. They became satisfied ('assuredly gathering' AV, 'concluding' RSV) that this was God's call. Immediately they pushed forward. The way opened up. The wide door for effective work in Greece lay open, and it was a door that none could shut.

But sometimes God not only restrains us, he 'ejects' us from where we are. Paul longed to preach to the Jews (Rom 9:3). For this he was eminently fitted. But God had a different sphere for him, hence his rejection by the Jews; 'make haste and get quickly out...Depart, for I will send you far away...' (Acts 22:18-21). Well qualified for a particular appointment? Trained and prepared for it? In 'the running' — even promised it and then by-passed? Don't bang your head against the brick wall of non-acceptance. Sometimes a misfit in one sphere is eminently suited for a successful and fruitful life in another. (But — be certain that your rejection is not due to unpleasantness or incompetence!)

> One step thou seest, then go forward boldly,
> One step is far enough for faith to see.
> Take that, and thy next duty shall be shown thee,
> For dark and light are both alike to me.

Further reading: Acts 16:6-10. Acts 22:17-22. Acts 13:44-49.

MC

May 14

Guidance (3) — Conductive Deafness

He who has ears to hear let him hear. Matthew 11:15

There is a saying that there are none so deaf as those who won't hear. It is possible to shut our ears purposely (Zc 7:11). In fact problems of the will may be more significant than those of spiritual perception. Words of Jesus, taken completely out of context, yet enshrine a principle, 'If any man's will is to do his will, he shall know' (Jn 7:17). It is true in experience that not until we are truly willing can God make clear to us which of the options before us is right. This may involve a major spiritual battle. We may think we are unbiased when we are not.

God's guidance may come in the language of a look (Ps 32:8 AV) — provided that we are watching for it (Ps 123:2); or by the whisper of the Spirit in the heart, as with Simeon and Philip (Lk 2:27; Acts 8:29). If we do not hear his whisper, he may speak, or even shout to make himself heard. If we are still unresponsive, he may need to 'goad us' to attract our attention, or even to stop us in our tracks (Acts 26:13-14). And all the time we are wondering what is happening to our lives!

The trouble sometimes is that we are seeking his will with minds already made up, and asking him to confirm our plans rather than reveal his own. We can deceive not only ourselves but other people into thinking that we only want God's will, thus effectively stifling any further discussion in the matter.

> O give me Samuel's ear,
> The open ear O Lord,
> Alive and quick to hear
>   Each whisper of thy word.
> Like him to answer at thy call
>   And to obey thee first of all.

James Drummond Burns

Further reading: Acts 26:9-16. Je 42:1-6, 20-22. Heb 4:12-13.

MC

May 15

Guidance (4) — What if things go Wrong?

This man could have been set free if... Acts 26:32

There was no doubt about the rightness of his decision. Directed by the Spirit he had planned to visit Rome (Acts 19:21). His wish to go was certainly of God (Rom 15:22-24), and his call was later explicitly confirmed (Acts 23:11). Paul saw the future mapped out in front of him; he would finish his work in Macedonia and Achaia, deliver the gifts to the church in Jerusalem, then set out for Spain via Rome.

But things went badly wrong. Arrested in Jerusalem because of a total misunderstanding (Acts 21:28-29), he became the object of a smear campaign. The scandal grew. His enemies were quick to cash in on the situation and brought charges against him on accusations that were totally false and which he persistently and vehemently denied. But it was no good. The trip to Spain was 'off', and he found himself instead unjustly jailed for two years in Caesarea (Acts 24:27). And then — what irony — justice at last — but too late! Agrippa's judgment was in his favour, 'this man is doing nothing to deserve death or imprisonment...He could have been set free if he had not appealed to Caesar' (Acts 26:31-32). Had he made a horrible mistake? could he have gone to Rome and Spain a free agent just as he had originally planned?

But Paul's plan would never have materialised. He would have been murdered in Jerusalem before he even started, God's plan was better. He actually used Paul's captors to save his life, to facilitate his work and to ensure the spread of the gospel to the west. Five times the Romans saved him from death (can you find them between Acts 21:31 and 27:44?). They gave him free and safe travel, so different from his missionary journeys. Not least they gave him guaranteed accommodation for four years under military protection, with his friends coming and going at will, with freedom to preach, teach and write unhindered (Acts 24:23; 28:16-24, 30-31).

Worried about injustices in job appointments? about unfairness and favouritism? about the malicious and false things people say? Afraid that God's plan for our lives is being spoilt? Our plans may not materialise, but God's always do.

> The soul that on Jesus has leaned for repose
> He will not, He cannot desert to its foes.
> That soul though all hell should endeavour to shake,
> He'll never, no never, no never forsake.

Richard Keen

Further reading: Passages indicated in the text.

MC

May 16

Guidance (5) — Not thy Will but Mine

God's anger was kindled because he went. Numbers 22:22

A comment was heard recently, 'It's extraordinary how often God seems to have changed his mind in guiding Mr & Mrs X!' Does God change his mind? or is it we who try to change it for him? Balaam asked God a straight question, should he go with the messengers of Balak? He was given an equally straight answer, 'You shall not go with them'. Balaam's immediate reaction was decisive and right, 'The Lord has refused to let me go with you. I could not go beyond the command of the Lord my God to do less or more.'

But gradually his resistance was worn down. To comply with Balak's request would bring great financial gain. Already he was being sought after by 'high-ups' who could influence his future career, and even the King promised to grant his every request. In a position like that, what an influence he could exert for good and for God! And after all perhaps he had a responsibility to his family! It might be worth asking God again. Did he really mean what he said? Did these new considerations make a difference? And God did apparently change his mind, 'Go with them' he said, and delightedly Balaam got up in the morning, saddled his ass and went with the eminent emissaries.

The result?

1. God's anger was kindled because he went.

2. God, who had been his master and guide, became his adversary, standing in his way.

3. God drove him into an impossible situation, no way forward and none to right or left. 'I have come to withstand you, because your way is perverse before me.'

4. And then, as commonly happens, Balaam began to 'take it out' on an innocent victim of his frustration.

5. Of course he was remorseful of what he had done, and was anxious to go back, but he could not retrace his steps.

6. He had to learn the hard way. It was costly and time-consuming, and he lost all the hoped-for advancement.

There are some clear commands in God's word. If he says, 'Don't do it' we are foolish to expect him to contradict himself or make an exception of us. If he has made his will clear in a matter not explicitly dealt with in his word, we cannot expect further or different guidance. If we do, we may have to be content with God's second best, or find, like the Israelites, that 'he gave them their request but sent leanness into their soul' (Ps 106:15 AV).

C S Lewis comments that in the end there are only two kinds of people: 'There are those who say to God "Thy will be done", and those to whom God says "thy will be done".'

Further reading: Nu 22-24.

MC

May 17

Guidance (6) — The Role of Christian Friends

...That we may be mutually encouraged by each other's faith, both yours and mine. Romans 1:12

Christian friendship is one of God's greatest gifts with its mutual encouragement, support, fellowship and advice. We need to consider the role of other Christians in the matter of guidance.

1. *Example* While benefiting from their example and experience, don't try to copy them. Don't assume that God's plan for your life is identical with theirs. Don't force yourself or be forced into their mould. Joseph, a nomadic shepherd boy, became president of Egypt to save God's people; whereas Moses, steeped in the language and culture of Egypt and influential in Pharaoh's court, was banished to Midian to serve the

same purpose. Both men knew what God would do, but neither knew how he would do it (Gn 37:7,9; Acts 7:25).

2. *Advice* The advice of Christian friends may be invaluable. 'The onlooker sees most of the game.' Paul's zeal would have precipitated him into the uproar of the Ephesian amphitheatre, courting unnecessary trouble, had not the disciples and influential friends dissuaded him (Acts 19:30-31). The town clerk dispersed the hostile mob, and Paul disappeared to continue his work elsewhere. Discretion prevailed. Jesus acted similarly when 'his hour had not yet come'. Older Christians in the profession can be of great help to us. They can assess our capabilities better than we, give us advice about likely specialty openings, and tell us how to set about fulfilling what we believe to be God's will.

But the wise counsellor always encourages us to look to the Lord for his leading. Ananias, knowing God's plan for Paul, only told him to turn to the Lord in repentance, faith, and commitment. It was the Lord's prerogative to show him what this would mean, 'for I will show him...' (Acts 9:15-16). The genius of Barnabas was to advise young Christians to 'cleave to the Lord' (Acts 11:23 AV), and for all his friendship, encouragement, teaching and training, Paul never dominated his life, and was content to let him obey his conscience when their opinions differed (Acts 15:36- 41).

3. *Ultimate Accountability* The divide between profiting from the experience and advice of another, and allowing someone else to determine our future for us is a fine one. In Acts 21, we read of people who had been told by the Holy Spirit of the danger awaiting Paul in Jerusalem, confirming what he already knew. In addition, some sought to prevent him from going. Paul, however, was not moved. He knew where his ministry lay, and was confident of God's guidance in the matter. It is noteworthy that when the advisers failed to persuade him they stopped pressing him, saying, 'The will of the Lord be done'. Can God-given insight spill over into human persuasion? May it be better to risk an honest mistake, believing it to be God's will, than to give blind obedience to the dictates of others?

> Lord, I thank you for your promise that your followers shall not walk in darkness. Grant that I may be humble enough to take advice, but discerning enough to distinguish between your will and mere human opinion.

Further reading: Acts 15:36-41, 20:22-25, 21:3-15.

MC

May 18

Only a Youth

Then I said, 'Ah, Lord God! Behold, I do not know how to speak, for I am only a youth'. Jeremiah 1:6

My first week in hospital after graduation found me interviewing new outpatients. The mature-looking woman who had just come in was obviously surprised. 'Are you the doctor?' was less a question than an exclamation, tinged (I felt) with dismay and even scorn. Who could blame her? I was only 22, and I looked much younger. Like Jeremiah, I was acutely conscious of my youth. But I listened, arranged for an interview with an appropriate specialist, and all was well. I felt not quite so young. Then another woman sat facing me. Her lined face and hunted eyes told their own story. Oblivious of my youth, she poured out her misery — illness and pain of body and mind in an atmosphere of domestic hell. The detail was intimate, frank and to me horrifying. Again I listened, referred her for specialist advice, and all was well. But this time I knew I was young with much to learn.

Jeremiah was at most in his early twenties when God called him to an awesome task — to be a 'prophet to the nations'. He shrank back. 'I am only a youth,' he pleaded. Many translations say 'only a child'. He felt very, very young.

But the Lord would have none of it: 'Do not say, "I am only a youth": for to all to whom I send you you shall go, and whatever I command you you shall speak. Be not afraid of them for I am with you to deliver you'. 'Then', writes Jeremiah, 'the Lord put forth his hand and touched my mouth...' And he went out to a life of tough service.

Many a newly fledged doctor, young man or young woman, must feel like Jeremiah. I did, and I still remember it, though it was many years ago. Most of us are not called to Jeremiah's kind of life. But a medical life is one of great responsibility and privilege. It can be tough. If God calls us to it, he will equip us for it. He will undertake for youth or for age and for much else.

> Lord, take me just as I am. Use me to meet the needs of others as you show them to me. And touch my mouth that I may know when and how to speak, and when to keep silent and listen.

Further reading: Je 1:1-10.

RRW

May 19

The Testing of Faith

For a little while you may have to suffer various trials, so that the genuineness of your faith, more precious than gold which though perishable is tested by fire, may redound to praise and glory and honour at the revelation of Jesus Christ. 1 Peter 1:6-7

Peter had stood before a fire and had denied his Lord with oaths and curses (Mk 14:66-72). Why had his Lord not warned him to avoid the High Priest's house that night? After all, if he is God, he must have known... But Christ had simply told Peter: 'You will deny me, but I have prayed for you, that your faith may not fail' (Lk 22:31-32). In the upper room Christ had explained that he was telling his disciples about certain things, so that when they happened they would know that 'I AM' (Jn 13:19). Not just afterwards, when they had time to think things through, but in the very moment of distress they would know that he had known all along, he understood, he cared and he was in control (Lk 22:61).

Peter's attitude had been all wrong. His bravado, the 'big man' attitude (Mt 26:33,35; Lk 22:33), had indicated a complete lack of dependence on his Lord. Peter had not been teachable in the upper room. So he had to be allowed to make an utter mess of things. It was the only way he would learn!

Peter never forgot the lesson, and in his letter he writes of the trial of faith. Gold, he explains, has to be refined; and from a bucketful of ore only a small nugget of the metal survives the fire. But the nugget is infinitely more precious than all the dross. So with our faith — the bravado, the self-esteem and the pride have to be destroyed by the fiery trial. But what emerges, in terms of a greater evaluation of the Lord and a closer dependence on him, is infinitely precious.

> Our Father, which art in heaven, hallowed be thy name,
> thy kingdom come, thy will be done... Lord, make me
> teachable, but when I won't learn, when you have to expose
> me to temptation, be with me and pray that my faith fail
> not, and deliver me from evil... for thine is the power and
> the glory, for ever and ever. Amen.

Further reading: 1 Pet 1:3-9.

PCE

May 20

Christ, the Centre of Life

Whatever you do, whether in word or deed, do it all in the name of the Lord Jesus, giving thanks to God the Father through him. Colossians 3:17 (NIV)

It is essential that Christ should be the centre of every part of our life. Someone said: 'If you don't worship the Lord at home, if you don't worship the Lord at work, in the office, in the school, you will know very little of worship on Sunday morning'.

So often we lose sight of the purpose of Christ's redeeming work, that we may have eternal life, that we may know the Father, the only true God, and Jesus Christ, whom he has sent. That means that Christ is the centre of every facet of our life. Christianity is God-centred, and not self-centred. We should call ourselves doctoring Christians, and not Christian doctors. Our primary function in this world is to be Christians; we happen to be doctors. Our purpose is then to glorify Christ now and forever. This helps to comfort us in times of despair, when we are overworked, when we feel depressed or used, and to bring us down to earth when we feel omniscient and omnipotent.

To achieve it, we must abide in him. 'I am the vine; you are the branches. If a man remains in me and I in him, he will bear much fruit; apart from me you can do nothing' (Jn 15:5). What is the purpose of the fruit? 'This is to my Father's glory, that you bear much fruit, showing yourselves to be my disciples' (v8).

Christ should be our worship whatever our professional eminence, in our church life, at home, at work and socially. He is all and in all that we are, so that people may see us and give glory to God in heaven. He is the aim of our life, the end of our life.

> Yea thro' life, death, thro' sorrow and thro' sinning
> He shall suffice me, for he hath sufficed:
> Christ is the end, for Christ was the beginning,
> Christ the beginning, for the end is Christ.

F W H Meyer, St Paul

Further reading: Col 3:12-17.

GKGL

May 21

Tomorrow

Jesus said, 'Do not worry about tomorrow'. Matthew 6:34 (NIV)

How much of our time do we spend worrying over or imagining what might happen tomorrow? In my early teens one of our family treats was to go to the cinema on the last day of the school holidays. I saw some of the best films on those days, but they were all ruined! In the most exciting part of the film I would suddenly remember that tomorrow I would be at school — and the enjoyment would vanish.

Jesus did not tell us that we shouldn't plan: he did tell us not to worry. Since he always practised what he preached, it is interesting to look at his own life. Each day was packed with activity — travelling, teaching, preaching to crowds, talking to individuals, healing. He concentrated on doing what needed to be done at that particular moment: he depended upon his father for wisdom and strength for each task and did it to the best of his ability — ie he did it perfectly.

What a contrast this is to the way we so often dissipate our mental and emotional energy! We bite our nails and knit our brows at things which may happen. If we have strong imaginations we may even imagine difficult or aggressive conversations with people we fear or dislike. We become nervous wrecks when we should be towers of strength.

The key to the problem is in the preceding verse, 'Seek first his kingdom'. We can do this throughout today — we must, because Jesus has told us to. We begin by offering the day — with every detail in it — to the Lord. We then take his hand and give our best effort and full concentration to each thing to be done and every conversation held. So, at the end of today, having shared in the task of bringing his kingdom upon earth, we shall be ready, without fear, for tomorrow.

> Lord, for tomorrow and its needs I do not pray;
> But keep me, guide me, hold me, Lord,
> Just for today.
>
> J H Burke

Lord Jesus, today belongs to you. Help me to use every minute wisely and to work with you in bringing the kingdom of God a step nearer. Thank you that tomorrow is in your hands — and that's where I gladly leave it.

Further reading: Mt 6:19-34.

JT

May 22

An Impossible Situation

Peter was kept in prison; but earnest prayer for him was made to God by the church. Acts 12:5

Put yourself in Peter's position. Things appeared desperate. James his friend and fellow fisherman had been killed by Herod, and the Jews were pleased. Now Herod had got him. Four squads of soldiers guarded him, and at night he was chained to two of them. Why should he expect a better fate than James? Did he, even for a moment, regret his bold witness in those heady days after Pentecost? This must be the end.

The church was in an impossible situation too. They had lost James, now they were going to lose Peter. There seemed no end to it. Who would be the next? One by one their leaders were being taken away, how could the defenceless infant church survive? Their high hopes were being dashed. They must have felt very low.

But there was one significant thing: 'earnest prayer for him was made to God by the church'. I wonder what they prayed for. If it was for courage and peace of heart for Peter, their prayer was certainly answered — he was so fast asleep on the night before his execution, in spite of his physical discomfort, that the angel had to strike him to wake him up, and even then he was so dazed that subsequent events seemed unreal. (Have you ever felt like that when called for an emergency at night?).

If their prayer was for Peter's release from prison, their faith did not stretch to that, especially as time had all but run out. The reader cannot help smiling at the humour of vv14-15; one can almost hear a church member rebuking Rhoda for interrupting their prayer for Peter with a joke in such bad taste. But God answered that prayer too, although they never expected it.

At times we find ourselves in an impossible position. How important do we find prayer — ours and that of others? And do we really pray for Christian friends facing similar problems? If our prayer is only from habit, God graciously honours it and sometimes with big surprises.

> Lord, thank you for the times when prayer seems easy and natural, but help me to persevere when the heavens feel like brass, I feel like lead, and I can see no way out – even for you.

Further reading: Acts 12:1-17.

WGB

May 23

Christian doctor — or Christian Doctor?

You are a chosen people, a royal priesthood. 1 Peter 2:9 (NIV)

A truth, rediscovered at the Reformation, is that every believer is a priest of God — all have direct access to him through Christ. The logical sequence is that all are in full-time Christian service.

Medicine and Christianity are both full-time professions. Although doctors have 'off-duty' times, in an emergency they must be available and, if resuscitation or advice is needed on holiday, they will not withhold their services. This can happen in most unusual ways. The writer when crossing the Atlantic as a passenger on the Queen Elizabeth answered an emergency call and was second signatory to the death certificate of a rabbi who was to be buried at sea before the sunset which heralded the Jewish sabbath. Many will ask our advice simply because we are medical doctors, and after a number of years of 'living and thinking' medicine we often offer advice when it is not asked for.

How about Christianity? We refer to ministers or missionaries as being in 'full-time' Christian service: but we are all servants of God, no less full-time. Have you ever thought seriously about this? Much publicity was given to the actor James Fox who, after a number of years in so-called full-time Christian service, returned to the theatre to serve Christ in this field. Likewise we can serve him in our medical practice. We are called to offer our bodies as sacrifices holy and pleasing to God (Rom 12:1 NIV), and this includes our minds, our thoughts and indeed our work. We are no less in Christian service during a ward round than when worshipping in church.

St Paul (Rom 12:6-8) reminds us of our individual gifts. As the human body is made up of different parts with different functions, so likewise the body of Christ is made up of his servants in every branch of human activity. We should be Christian doctors with equal emphasis on both aspects of our calling.

Further reading: The whole of Romans 12 as a 'job description'.

JWD

May 24

The Lighting of the Lamps

You are the light of the world. Matthew 5:14

Most of life is routine, even in hospital or in medical practice. Rarely is life exciting; often it is dull. Sometimes, as the light of a day fades, the dusk settles heavily on us, and we know what T S Eliot (in his Preludes) means by 'the burnt-out ends of smoky days'. Weary of doing, we sink under the weight of oncoming night, imprisoned by the ordinary things. Eliot's poem concludes:

> The showers beat
> On broken blinds and chimney-pots,
> And at the corner of the street
> A lonely cab horse steams and stamps.
> And then the lighting of the lamps.

The change is sudden and vivid: 'And then the lighting of the lamps'. The darkness is pushed back. The shadowy shapes take on meaning again. Brains clear, voices brighten, hearts lift. And we go on.

The greatest darkness is that which settles about the soul, weighing down hearts, befogging minds, insisting on the futility of life. But Jesus Christ says: 'I am the light of the world; he who follows me will not walk in darkness, but will have the light of life' (Jn 8:12).

Do you ever think how the evening settles down about your patients' hearts, with pain, loneliness, worry or fear? Is your coming the 'lighting of the lamps' to them? It can be, though it need not be self-consciously so. Certainly it should not be sanctimoniously so. The Saviour's statement, 'You are the light of the world', becomes true in fact as (and only as) his followers look to him with unclouded eyes and hear him say: 'I am the light of the world'.

He alone is the true light. It is the glory of the moon to burst into light, reflecting the sun's splendour, at the very moment of dusk when the sun is slipping from the sight of the world.

> Lord Jesus, true light of the world, shine in our hearts, we pray: so that your light may push back the darkness from our souls and may be reflected into the hearts of others to dispel their darkness.

Further reading: Mt 5:14-16. Jn 1:1-9.

RRW

May 25

Forgiveness

Jesus said 'Neither do I condemn thee; go and sin no more'. John 8:11 (AV)

A doctor friend of mine was working in a refugee camp in North Thailand. I visited him in his room. It was in the upstairs part of a simple wooden building. On his wall he had pinned maps, photographs — even lists of things which he needed to do. But what caught my eye was a scrap of paper, pinned over his desk, on which he had written 'Remember you have been forgiven'.

This message is the heart of the good news which dawns on us every morning. We really do start the day with a clean slate — not because we deserve to, but because God loves us and has wiped the slate clean for us. To go into the day knowing we are forgiven gives an inner strength and confidence and joy that only Christians know. As we examine the next patient or look at the next chart we can feel the same sort of relief as though we had just passed an exam. To know that we are forgiven clears our minds of worries and nagging fears. It helps us to give our full attention to the next thing we should do — and this is how we are meant to live.

But — be careful — don't luxuriate too much in the feeling of forgiveness. Remember that many people you meet today won't have a clue what it means to be forgiven. All their lives will have been spent building up their self-image and suppressing the thoughts and feelings which they know are wrong or dirty or unworthy. They think that they need to be congratulated or encouraged, but certainly not to be forgiven. But today you may find a patient in despair. Through his illness or fear of death, or financial anxieties he may suddenly find that the bottom has dropped out of his life. He will probably be very inarticulate, but go and spend some time with him. It is just at the time when life seems to be falling apart that the message of the love and forgiveness of Christ is the only one which will help. 'This is a faithful saying and worthy of all acceptation, that Christ Jesus came into the world to save sinners.'

> Thank you, Lord Jesus, for the wonder of your forgiveness.
> May someone I meet find that same forgiveness today.

Further reading: 1 Jn 1. Col 2:13-15.

JT

May 26

Pens for God

Luke, the beloved physician, sends you his greetings. Colossians 4:14

One of the most valued colleagues of the apostle Paul was Luke, the physician. We know very little about Dr Luke's medical career; where he studied, and where and when he practised his profession. He is remembered most of all as a writer, one of many medical men who have laid aside scalpel and stethoscope for pen or typewriter. Luke's contribution to the New Testament is substantial. There is a two volume work: Luke's Gospel and the Acts of the Apostles.

The first tells us what Jesus began to do and teach: the second what the risen Lord continued to do through his apostles by the Holy Spirit. Both books are marked by careful research. The second includes excerpts from Dr Luke's diary: we can pick them out when the pronoun quietly changes from 'they' to 'we'. All of the powers of observation which a physician still needs — and needed so much more in a world without special investigations — are used by God to produce some of the most valued parts of the New Testament.

Today God still needs physicians who can use their pens for him. This can be done in all kinds of ways: in private correspondence, in letters to magazines and newspapers, in magazine articles, in books, and even in contributing to a devotional booklet like this.

> Lord, I give myself to you once again. You know your plans for me today. Lead me step by step in the pathway of your perfect will. May I, like St Luke, be willing to be used as your instrument to do your will, for the blessing of others.

Further reading: Lk 1:1-4. Acts 15:22-31.

JWMcM

May 27

Einbahnstrasse

The unspiritual man does not receive the gifts of the Spirit of God, for they are folly to him, and he is not able to understand them, because they are spiritually discerned. 1 Corinthians 2:14

While recently driving with my family in Germany, I struggled to orientate myself to a German road map and to German street signs. After a half hour of unsuccessfully trying to find our hotel, I realised I had seen several directional signs labelled 'Einbahnstrasse'. Figuring 'Einbahnstrasse' must be a site of some significance, I followed the signs with the expectation of stopping at 'Einbahnstrasse' to orientate myself to the map. A series of right and left turns led us nowhere, and my father correctly concluded that 'Einbahnstrasse' meant 'One Way Street'.

It was as if a light of understanding went on in my head. With one word of German vocabulary, I could avoid further futile searches. I thought of the new-born Christian who senses new insight and freedom as the Spirit begins to reveal spiritual truth to him.

Over the next few days of our German visit, however, I still felt lost in a foreign world. One word of German vocabulary is a nice starting foundation, but it doesn't go very far.

I am thankful, as I look back over my beginning years in medical school, for the factual foundation I received. Sadly though, much of what I learned has been forgotten. The material I reviewed, studied and applied, however, is the material I can still recall to use in patient care.

Spiritually, we have a sure foundation in Jesus Christ. Each of us must, Paul warned, be careful how we build on this foundation. Just as continuing medical education is vital to our ongoing good medical practice, so continuing spiritual education is vital to our Christian growth. Peter urged us to grow in knowledge, and we can do so as we study God's word and as we get regular biblical teaching. We also grow in grace as we commune with God and as we apply his truth in our daily lives.

As Christians, we need not forever chase 'One Way Street' signs. Equally though, we must not settle for a limited spiritual vocabulary. Following God's direction, we can grow to enjoy him more.

> I count everything loss because of the surpassing worth of knowing Christ Jesus my Lord.

Phil 3:8a

Further reading: 1 Cor 2:6-3:18, 2 Pet 3:17-18.

PRF

May 28

Slow to Anger

Everyone should be quick to listen, slow to speak and slow to become angry. James 1:19 (NIV)

One day I was running later than usual. I greeted the next patient in the waiting room — but she did not return my smile, and I could sense that her handshake was unwilling. She looked grim! We had hardly sat down in my consulting room when she burst out with 'You kept me waiting nearly forty minutes and I had to rush from work to get here on time. You care more for your other patients than for me — you should keep them to their time. I don't go over my time!'

The patient had been in intensive psychotherapy with me for some months. For a moment I felt hurt and angry, for I had invested much thought and emotional energy in her therapy, and her accusation seemed unfair. Moreover, I had had a lot of phone calls that day and had steadily slipped behind in my appointment schedule. I hadn't asked for those phone calls!

Fortunately, I quickly remembered an important principle of counselling and psychotherapy — it is usually better to explore anger than to return it.

That way, the potential quarrel can be turned to good therapeutic use. And the gift of the Holy Spirit for which I prayed that morning, was with me. So I replied: 'I'm so sorry — and I'm glad you can tell me how you feel...' She interrupted: 'I know, I know. My adult tells me you couldn't help being late and I shouldn't be angry — but I am — my little girl feels shut out and angry, as if you don't really care about me...'

I listened as she went on, and she recalled that her father often derided her and closed the door on her — and she used to lie awake terrified as a child when her parents were late home after evening outings. Her anger subsided, and the usual warm rapport and trust returned.

What would have happened if in my own anger I had forgotten my therapeutic and Christian principles? I think it likely that if I had been quick to become angry and had given her a stern lecture about what a hard day I had endured, etc, etc, she would have retreated into crushed silence as she used to with her father, and the opportunity for self-expression, insight and growth would have been lost.

> Lord, help me to love my patients with your kind of love
> and to be sensitive to the pain that so often lies behind their
> anger.

Further reading: Tit 1:7-9.

BP

May 29

Terminal illness

In those days Hezekiah became sick and was at the point of death. Isaiah 38:1

It is never easy to care for a terminally ill patient. Hezekiah seems to have had a carbuncle of some kind. There were no antibiotics in those days. No one knew anything about bacteriology. Hezekiah must have developed septicaemia, and it was obvious to those caring for him that his condition was rapidly getting worse, and that there was nothing that any man could do about it.

Their fears were confirmed when the king was visited by the prophet Isaiah, who brought him the stern message: 'Thus says the Lord; "Set your house in order; for you shall die, you shall not recover"'.

The king turned his face to the wall, and prayed, and wept with a great weeping. The Lord heard his prayer, and while Isaiah was still in the middle court of the palace sent him back with a new message to the king. It was this: 'Thus says the Lord: "I have heard your prayer, I have seen your tears; behold, I will add fifteen years to your life"'.

Hezekiah did recover, and the psalm or poem which he composed after his recovery is one of the most poignant writings in all literature. Read it for yourself in Isaiah 38:9-20.

> Lord, give me special grace today as I have contact with any who are terminally ill. May I bring them, by my words and action, some comfort from yourself, the God of all comfort. Give to your children who may be dying this day the knowledge that you hear their prayers and see their tears, and that you are planning in love for them, whatever happens.

Further reading: Jn 14:1-7, 27. Is 38:9-20.

JWMcM

May 30

Healing with Jesus

Then again Jesus laid his hands upon his eyes; and he looked intently and was restored, and saw everything clearly. Mark 8:25

The chronological context of this healing recorded in Mark 8:22-26 is significant. Prior to it, Jesus admonished his disciples: 'Having eyes do you not see, and having ears do you not hear?...Do you not yet understand' (vv18,21)? The healing is followed by the confession of Peter 'You are the Christ' (v29), Christ's first prediction of his suffering (vv31ff), and the transfiguration on the mount (9:1-8).

In our calling, we are often tempted to draw distinctions between medical or scientific therapy, psychological recovery, and spiritual healing. In this narrative, one of the two miracles recounted only by Mark, we see a gradual healing where every aspect of the human person is involved — body, mind, emotions and spirit.

Friends had brought this blind man to Jesus — as we need to bring our patients to God, the Great Physician, in prayer, 'begging him to touch' them. His friends wanted for him the gift of God's healing; Jesus gave himself, the Giver! Jesus led the blind man out of the village, spat on his eyes and laid his hands upon him.

Jesus, possibly conscious of some lack of faith in the recipient, asked 'Do you not see anything?' (v23). When we ask God for signs, we ask him to do something for us and, indeed, he does do much for us. But he loves better to do things WITH us — he seeks our co-operation. If we were more ready to respond and do things WITH him, he would be able to do much more FOR us.

This man had to make his own effort and contribution. After Jesus had AGAIN laid his hands upon his eyes, he looked intently (ie opened his eyes wide), and saw everything clearly.

Unlike the Pharisees who refused to see (Jn 9:39-41), the disciples of Jesus, of whom Peter was chief, went on from the first stage of recovery (confused knowledge of Christ) to clear sight — of his transfiguration, death, resurrection, ascension and the sending of his Spirit.

Jesus doesn't do his work by halves — in his thoroughness, he will only be satisfied with perfection!

> Heavenly Father, help me to see and understand by your word and your Holy Spirit what you want to do in me and with me, that I may this day and always co-operate more readily with your purpose and power in healing men and making them whole persons in Christ.

Further reading: Jn 9:24-41. Mk 7:31-37.

LT

May 31

Strength in Weakness

For the sake of Christ, then, I am content with weaknesses...for when I am weak, then I am strong. 2 Corinthians 12:10

The university where I received postgraduate medical training placed a copy of its emblem, a huge letter U, on a hillside near the medical centre. The U was surrounded by lights which were illuminated during sports events. At the conclusion of each contest, the U announced the outcome to the surrounding community — the strong lights flashed with each victory. The president of the university explained the symbolism of the lights saying that the university flashed with enthusiastic celebration in victory, yet remained consistent and sure even in defeat. It is true that our real character may be revealed in the manner in which we deal with adversity.

The Apostle Paul knew much of adversity. From shipwreck to stonings and from conflict to confinement, he frequently faced difficult times. And he learned that God does not always choose to relieve personal discomfort. Nonetheless, Paul saw God's strength as the means of overcoming periods of distress.

We, like Paul, will face difficult times. We might be over-burdened by the demands of our profession. We might find difficulty dealing with the results of personal failings. Or we might face overt persecution as we stand firm for God's ways. Paul's example can serve to instruct and encourage us as we face undesired situations.

Paul realised that he was not omnipotent. He even suggested that some of his discomfort, his 'thorn in the flesh', was intended to remind him not to exalt himself. We too must face up to our own limitations.

Paul knew that God is almighty. He realised that God's power was also personally applicable. He could, he told believers in Philippi, do all things through Christ. It was in facing up to his own weakness that Paul was able to appropriate God's strength. Thus Paul found his utmost strength in his own weakness. Perhaps we can avoid some of our own difficulties by recognising our own weakness and calling on our strong God before we get ourselves into trouble.

With God's strength, Paul knew how to live through adversity; he persevered. He could be down but not out. He could be perplexed but not despairing. He kept living with the attitude of a servant despite the adversity in which he found himself.

Like Paul, we shall face adversity. We, too, must learn to recognise our own weakness, to appropriate God's strength, and to keep pressing on. Thus, we can shine brightly even in seeming defeat.

> We have this treasure in earthen vessels, to show that the transcendent power belongs to God and not to us.
>
> 2 Cor 4:7

Further reading: 2 Cor 4:5-10, 6:1-10, 12:7-10. Phil 4:11-13.

PRF

June 1

Doctor, Be Still: The Voice of Stillness

... and after the fire a still small voice. 1 Kings 19:12

Does life ever overwhelm you? So many things can happen — good things, bad things, all kinds of things — that they knock you flat. Do you wonder when they will stop — when the tumult will cease? Can medicine never be the quiet life?

Elijah was one of the great men of God, but things got him down sometimes. When Jezebel put him on her death list he packed up completely. Rather paradoxically he asked God to let him die. God treated him gently and strengthened him. He wandered off, but was obviously still unhappy. He came to Horeb, the mount of God, took refuge in a cave and had another attack of the miseries, pouring out his heart to the Lord in a stream of self-pity.

This time God was not so gentle. Elijah really got the treatment: 'And behold the Lord passed by, and a great and strong wind rent the mountains, and broke in pieces the rocks before the Lord, but the Lord was not in the wind; and after the wind an earthquake; but the Lord was not in the earthquake and, after the earthquake a fire, but the Lord was not in the fire...'

God was showing his power. Elijah apparently needed to be made aware of it. The demonstration must have been terrifying, but Elijah had to learn the hard way. The demonstration had, however, been made, and the message was getting through. Elijah was ready for something different, and something different came: 'after the fire a still small voice'. Another translation says: 'a voice of stillness'. And in the stillness he was again able to tell his troubles.

Somehow the atmosphere is now different. Perhaps in the stillness Elijah is now listening, really listening. God shows him the way ahead. Communication is restored. Confidence is restored.

The story is worth pondering. Sometimes we think we have had enough, whether it is sheer physical exhaustion, deadness of heart, discouragement, even a sense of spiritual abandonment. God may then treat us gently, and we at least pretend to take the healing with gratitude. But we may not be really listening. Self-pity can cause severe deafness. And God may have to give us the treatment, as he did to Elijah.

The experience can be rough and tough and tumultuous.

'Where is the god of love?' we then ask, unheeding of the fact that Love is shouting at us. When we are ready to listen, then — only then — comes the still small voice, the voice of stillness. And in the stillness God reaches us.

> God, who was not in the earth when it was shaken,
>> Could not be found in fury of the flame,
> Then to his seer, the faithful and forsaken,
>> Softly was manifest and spake by name.

F W H Meyer, St Paul

Further reading: 1 Ki 19:1-21.

RRW

June 2

Fatalism or Faith

Come, now, you who say, 'Today or tomorrow we will go into such and such a town, and spend a year there...; whereas you do not know about tomorrow... Instead you ought to say, 'If the Lord wills, we shall live and we shall do this or that'. James 4:13-15

I am writing these words in hospital — in bed, as a patient. I've just had a biopsy, and am awaiting the result. Is it inflammatory or malignant? I shall know in a few days. Whatever the result, God is in charge, and I know that he does all things well. This is not a kind of whistling to keep one's spirits up, or 'putting a brave face on it'; it is a sincere affirmation of complete faith in God and in his will. We make our plans — and so we ought — but always with the proviso 'if the Lord wills'.

Twenty-five years ago, I faced a similar situation. The lump was benign, but statistically it should have been malignant.

Forty-five years ago I was in another situation which might have spelt the end. I was facing an angry horde of armed savages in Central Africa advancing on me and my two African companions. I was scared. Then I remembered the promise, 'Thou shalt not be afraid for the terror by night, nor for the arrow that flieth by day' (Ps 91:5). God was there. Later that night we sang together:

> 'Ye that are men, now serve Him
> Against unnumbered foes;'

and there were the foes lurking threateningly behind the forest trees. We encouraged each other with the words 'I will trust and not be afraid' (Is 12:2).

This note of confidence, of utter trust in God sounds strongly throughout scripture. Whatever the appearances, God is in charge. However black the night, however delayed and uncertain the dawn, God is still in charge; he always has been, 'out of them all the Lord delivered me' (2 Tim 3:11 AV); he is now, 'He delivered us...and he will yet deliver us' (2 Cor 1:10 AV); he always will be, 'Though I pass through the valley of the shadow of death, I will fear no evil: for thou art with me' (Ps 23:4).

Nothing — no, nothing — can separate us from the love of God. Rest in that assurance. 'Man's chief end is to glorify God, and to enjoy him for evermore' (Scottish Catechism).

> God's will for us is to be enjoyed, not endured.

Further reading: 2 Cor 12:7-10. Rom 8:35-39.

SGB

June 3

The Way (6) — The Open Gate

Jesus said: I have come that you might have life — life in all its fullness.
John 10:10 (GNB)

When the diagnosis of a serious disease or disability has been made, and effective treatment is available, it would seem crazy to refuse or ignore that treatment. Yet some people do just that, for reasons that may be clear or unclear. Others accept the treatment at first and then give it up, gradually or suddenly. This is sad when it happens in the physical or mental sphere. It is even sadder when it happens in the spiritual realm.

The Way to true spiritual life, to life in all its fullness, to eternal life, is wide open to those who will enter it. It remains wide open to those who will continue in it. The mission of Jesus was to open the gate and to hold it wide open in gracious welcome to all who are willing to enter. This is the offer of salvation — his offer. To pass it by or to opt out is surely crazy — and ungrateful.

The gate to the Way was flung wide open when the Lord Jesus by his death on the cross broke down the barrier of sin between God and man. This had begun in the eternal councils of God as a living plan to meet the desperate soul-sickness of mankind. 'God so loved the world that he gave his only Son, that whoever believes in him should not perish but have eternal life' (Jn 3:16).

So the Son of God came among us, shared not only our life but our very humanity (Jn 1:14) and in due time gave his life as 'a ransom for many' (Mk 10:45). 'He himself bore our sins in his body on the tree', writes the apostle Peter (1 Pet 2:24). There he took the load of our death-dealing sins, as our Representative and our Substitute. Only because he was man could he represent mankind. Only because he was God could his death atone for the sins of the whole world.

On the cross not only was the power of sin and death and the devil broken, but the love of God was supremely revealed. 'God was in Christ reconciling the world unto himself' (2 Cor 5:19 AV). Paul sums up a great deal in a few words: 'God our Saviour...wants all men to be saved and to come to a knowledge of the truth. For there is one God and one mediator between God and men, the man Christ Jesus, who gave himself as a ransom for all men' (1 Tim 2:3-5 NIV). We cannot add to that. But the least we can do is to say 'Thank you' as we enter the open gate and to go on saying 'Thank you' in practical terms every step of the Way.

> Love so amazing, so divine,
> Demands my soul, my life, my all.

Isaac Watts

Further reading: Jn 10:7-18. 2 Cor 5:16-21. Heb 2:14-18.

RRW

June 4

Communication

The Word became flesh and dwelt among us... full of grace and truth. John 1:14

We communicate in many ways, but basically by the spoken and written word. Yet in the most effective contacts we also communicate by our attitude. It is not simply what is said that matters, but the way it is said, and the actions that accompany and follow.

God communicated with man over many centuries, by the spoken, and by the written word. But finally, he communicated in the most effective way possible by coming among men — the Living Communication: the Word. The infinite and absolute qualities of Deity have now become knowable in human terms! Just try to describe 'infinite power' — or simply ponder a miracle of Christ. Define 'infinite knowledge' — or just speak of the way our Lord knew what was in the hearts of men. Expound 'absolute love' — or just point to his concern for a blind man, a fallen woman, or a dying thief. After all, he came to reveal the Father: 'Father, I have shown your Name (your Nature) unto the men you have given me' (Jn 17:6).*

Moses craved a deeper relationship with God: 'Show me now thy ways, that I may know thee' (Ex 33:13). We have the inestimable privilege that the Way has become man — God has become knowable in human terms. Philip asked: 'Show us God'. 'See Me — see God', Jesus replied (Jn 14:6-9).*

And what about men to whom the Word means nothing? We are a letter to them, says Paul. 'You are a letter from Christ'... 'written not with ink, but with the Spirit of the living God' (2 Cor 3:3 AV). He made the invisible God visible, he made absolute Holiness infinitely attractive...do we?

> Let the beauty of Jesus be seen in me,
>   All his wondrous compassion and purity.
> O thou Spirit Divine, all my nature refine,
>   Till the beauty of Jesus be seen in me.

Tom Jones

Further reading: 1 Jn 1:1-4. Jn 14:1-11.

PCE

* The actual text has been paraphrased.

June 5

The Thorn

I besought the Lord about this, that it should leave me... 2 Corinthians 12:8-9a

As soon as I saw this particular patient lying on his bed I knew that the agony of the thorn was going to start all over again.

The young man had presented with pyrexia of unknown origin, and I was sent to see him. At eighteen, good-looking, well built and intelligent, he fitted well into what may be described as the 'Greek God' category. And as I carefully examined him — felt the smooth enlarged glands in his neck, palpated his abdomen methodically for any liver or splenic enlargement and looked into his bright steel-blue eyes — I wondered if he had any idea at all of the way I felt about him.

Did he know the waves of emotion he was firing in me? Was he conscious of the quickening of my pulse and the slight tremor of my hands? I doubt it. This was not the first time I had had to cope with such an internal crisis, and God, over the years, has given me more than adequate grace to come through these trials without anyone being aware of the struggle within.

I have been conscious of a homosexual trait since I was at secondary school. Though it has waxed and waned throughout my life, and many times I have pleaded with the Lord to take it away from me — and perhaps one day he will — so far it remains as the most persistent and painful 'thorn' I have ever known.

My reason for writing this is not to elicit pity, however. It is because I believe that every Christian who means business with God encounters some kind of thorn in his life, which usually comes, as in Paul's case (2 Cor

12:7), to counteract the even more serious problem of spiritual conceit.

God has given me a keen mind — and scholarships, prizes and (so far at least) a fulfilling and successful series of good jobs have come to me with relative ease. If it were not for this hardship in another area of life, I often wonder if my ambition would have caused me to abandon the road of discipleship long ago.

The blind George Matheson once wrote 'My God, I have never thanked thee for my thorns... I have been looking to a world where I shall get compensation for my cross; but I have never thought of my cross as itself a present glory. Teach me the glory of my cross: teach me the value of my thorn.'

I thank God that I have come to that place of thankfulness and contentment in spite of pain, and I rest at peace in the fact that God keeps us weak that the power of Christ may be seen in us, and may not be obscured by our own self-sufficiency.

Further reading: 2 Cor 12:1-10. 1 Cor 1:21-31. 2 Cor 4:1-5:10.

Anonymous

June 6

Sin's Sad Entail

God gave them up... Romans 1:26

The second half of the first chapter of Paul's letter to the Romans is one of the saddest portions in the whole of Scripture. Paul is about to expound the grand doctrine of justification by faith. But before he does so, he paints in black colours the devastating effects of sin and disobedience go God. If you are unfamiliar with the passage, please read Romans 1:18-32 before you read on.

As I write the first cases of AIDS have been reported in Australia. Much still needs to be known about this disease, but it seems evident that infection with HIV, with its horrific spread and devastating effects, is associated with the misuse of our sexuality by both men and women, as described in Romans 1:24-27. Further, promiscuity (both hetero- and homosexual) accounts for the involvement of both innocent and guilty. Together with the debasing of parenthood and the breakdown of family life so prevalent in our permissive society, it fills hospital beds and saps national resources. The God who made us — including our sexuality — is the God who inspired the Scriptures, and it should be no surprise to find that disobedience to his commands in this area leads to sad and terrible effects in our bodies and in society. As we think of these matters, there are two great biblical principles which we need to keep firmly in mind. The first is that stated by the apostle Paul in Galatians 6:7 (NEB): 'God is not to be fooled: a man reaps what he sows'. This principle is as true in human life as it is in agriculture. We need to be careful in all that we do, as we shall surely reap what we sow.

The second is the wonderful truth stated by the apostle John in 1 John 1:8 — 'The blood of Jesus, his son, cleanses us from all sin'. 'All sin' includes the sins that Paul wrote about in Romans 1. When he wrote to the church in Corinth, Paul again listed some of those sins, which were so characteristic of the great pagan temple cities of the Middle East and Greece. Then he went on to say: 'And such were some of you: but you were washed, you were sanctified, you were justified in the name of our Lord Jesus Christ and by the Spirit of our God' (1 Cor 6:11). There is salvation for every sinner who turns to God through faith in our Lord Jesus.

> Lord, as I treat people with diseases which have been acquired through actions which are contrary to your word, whether done by the patients themselves or by others, let me always remember that while you hate sin, you love the sinner and help me to follow your example.

Further reading: Rom 1:18-32.

JWMcM

June 7

Not my Own

You are not your own; you were bought with a price. So glorify God in your body. 1 Corinthians 6:19-20

Bleep, bleep! There it goes again! I'm wanted somewhere in the hospital. If only they would leave me alone to finish what I am doing! There's not a minute's peace!

It reminds me of our life as Christians; we have no rights, we have been bought with a price, we are not our own. We have deliberately chosen, and must continue to choose moment by moment to belong to God. We are 'on call' for Jesus.

My bleep is long range; God can call me wherever I am. It works one way; it is for me to listen to it and answer the call. It can call me at any time; I must always be ready to hear it. Every day it needs recharging as does my life in God. I must spend time seeking his resources as I read the Bible carefully and prayerfully, and as I bring myself to him to be moulded into his pattern, and as I pray for the needs of others whom I shall meet today. For all who are led by the Spirit of God are sons of God (Rom 8:14).

> The entrance fee to the kingdom of God is nothing,
> the annual subscription is everything.

Henry Drummond

Now read the story of a man who heard God's call wherever he was, whatever he was doing, whenever it came, and did at once whatever he was asked to do. Acts 8:5-12, 26-40.

FMJ & RMJ

June 8

Burden and Liberation

Blessed is he whose transgression is forgiven, whose sin is covered... Be glad in the Lord, and rejoice, O righteous, and shout for joy, all you upright in heart! Psalm 32:1,11

Carl Gustave Jung mentioned once that people today go to see a psychiatrist, whereas formerly they went to the minister. By this statement he wanted to indicate the need to learn to deal with guilt and guilt-feelings, in order to maintain mental health. Psalm 32 is a wonderful guideline and help in this direction.

The experience of forgiveness of guilt produces a sense of freedom (vv1-2). Sometimes psychotherapy deals with the (psychic) background of guilt feelings; but the burden will come back after a short time of counselling. Where guilt-feelings are a symptom of neurosis, depression or psychic reaction to inner or outer conflicts, we have to be aware of two abnormal aspects: either we suppress the guilt (feelings), accentuating the inner conflict, or we exaggerate them, using them as a hanger (pretext) for other hidden conflicts. There are depressive people who exaggerate their guilt-conscience, accusing themselves even of the sin against the Holy Spirit. Instead of discussing with the patient whether his guilt-feelings are 'real' or just an expression of depression, it is better to follow an empirical way: offer him forgiveness. If he accepts it and feels free then it was a matter of authentic guilt. If the guilt-feelings come back then it is a psychological matter, and treatment is medical or psychological.

Even if people in olden days liked to exaggerate, the expression 'When I declared not my sin, my body wasted away' (v3a) is most illustrative. The whole person suffers and is confused. The expression 'through my groaning all day long' reveals a depressive mood.

It seems that verses 3-4 express a spiritual condition rather than a depression in the medical sense, for verse 5 relates the experience of God's grace in the forgiveness of sin. Verses 1 and 6-7 show the real result of confession of sin: they express mental comfort, and demonstrate the healing power of prayer. The 'godly' person is the person who admits his powerlessness, and is ready to accept God's help.

Verses 8-10 teach us the divine aspect of faith. Most people think of faith as human trust in God's help. But faith means also that God himself believes in us, and trusts us as a father his child. Thus faith is a bi-polar action: man trusts God and God offers man his grace and trust. Therefore faith represents a personal relationship. This is the experience of witnesses in both Old and New Testaments. We are invited to a similar experience, and the life, death and resurrection of Jesus Christ are the guarantee of its realisation.

Verse 11 mentions joy as a result of the experience of forgiveness of sin. The 'righteous' man is a person who has had such an experience. Is there a better sign of mental health than to live with such a joy? The words of Psalm 66:20 are then a very real prayer of thanksgiving:

> Blessed be God, because he has not rejected my prayer
> or removed his steadfast love from me.

Further reading: Ps 32.

BH

June 9

My Shepherd (6)

Even thou I walk through the valley of the shadow of death, I fear no evil; for thou art with me. Psalm 23:4

We can rejoice in the Shepherd's clear leading and share enthusiastically with others that he never fails — until he suddenly seems to lead us into a blind alley. Does the trust then evaporate and the rejoicing stop? Whatever the initial impact may be and however we arrived there, this is a chance to discover that our Lord does not lead into blind alleys, yet he sometimes allows us to enter dark valleys. At times, it may seem that the long, dark, uncharted way will last forever, and that I may even die there (if only I could...). Yet it seems that David is not here referring to death itself, as verse 5 speaks of enemies so cannot refer to heaven; yet even the shadow of death conveys a picture of loss, of grief and of gloom. The dark night of the soul may be precipitated through the loss of a loved one, or of a patient, by personal illness, or the slow death of hopes (even of hope itself) taking us into an experience of desolation and deprivation hitherto unknown.

Yet, as the shadow of a wolf is not a wolf (however fearful), so the shadow of death is not death. We do not need to fear the shadows, however real they may seem, when the substance has been conquered by our resurrected Lord. The presence of a shadow across our path often indicates that there is sunshine not far away — indeed, shadows may fall precisely because we have our backs to the light. Even when completely in the dark we can trust that the Light of the world will finally break through. Bewildered and frightened sheep are not left by their shepherd to panic alone in the valley, and neither are we. There is no possible evil that our Good Shepherd cannot either keep at bay, or slay. He is a match for them all.

> Christ, who knows all his sheep,
>   will all in safety keep.
> He will not lose one soul,
>   nor ever fail us;
> Nor we the promised goal,
>   though hell assail us.

Richard Baxter

Further reading: Jn 8:12. Jn 14:1-6.

JG

June 10

My Shepherd (6 cont'd)

Even though I walk through the valley of the shadow of death, I fear no evil, for thou art with me. Psalm 23:4

It is possible for us, as for sheep, to have got into our valley imperceptibly, by wandering on without listening for orders, or more precipitately by running heedlessly after other (or another) wayward sheep. It is also possible for a completely unforeseeable valley experience to have me taken aback or even resentful and embittered. This sort of reaction can indicate that it was about time that my complacency, and perhaps my self-righteousness, were brought up short. The sides of a dark valley are so steep and awesome that a lost sheep must feel woefully small and intimidated there. I, too, can only cry out in a new and painful awareness of my own inadequacies, at last shown up in the face of such difficulty, danger and darkness. My answers are no longer slick, my confidence no longer in myself. I recall the Lord's 'why?' in his valley with deeper insight and a warmer response (Mt 27:46). I now see the answer to his question in the light of the resurrection: he sees now the answer to mine. As then, so now, he loves me. His presence will never fail. His power will open up the way and bring me out into the clear again. I cannot fly out of this valley, nor run away from it, but I will walk through it, step by step, with his help. In this dark, strange, confined and fearful place I shall get to know the

Shepherd more personally than I have ever known him before. 'He' becomes 'Thou'. 'He leads' — but in the valley 'Thou art with me'.

Some years ago, an African nurse invited me to her home in a tall apartment building. She met me at the entrance to the liftshaft, carrying her little boy, just a few months old, and as we got into the lift apologised that the light bulb had failed. It was a noisy lift, and conversation stopped as we went up in total darkness, surrounded by ominous clangs and clashes. No sound came from the baby, but as we reached the top and the door opened, there he was, eyes wide with apprehension but now turning eagerly to the light, his arms still wrapped tightly around his mother's neck. She saw my glance and said in a voice full of loving satisfaction, 'Ah, he fears the dark, so he holds on to me'. He was too little to know Psalm 23, but he had just experienced the message of its fourth verse!

In time, I shall be able to thank my Shepherd for all that he came to mean to me in the valley, but until then the moment by moment task is to reach out for his presence and trust to his love.

> When through the deep waters He calls thee to go,
> The rivers of grief shall not thee overflow;
> For He will be with thee in trouble to bless,
> And sanctify to thee thy deepest distress.

Rippon's Collection

Further reading: 2 Cor 4:8-18. Rom 8:25-39.

JG

June 11

What is Man?

What is man that thou makest much of him and turnest thy thoughts towards him, only to punish him morning by morning or to test him every hour of the day? Job 7:17-18 (NEB)

From 1942 to 1946 I was a medical student in Tokyo, and learned much about what the war really was. In March 1945 downtown Tokyo was heavily bombed and largely destroyed by fire, leaving thousands of half-charred bodies scattered over the burnt earth and scorched debris. Hundreds of soaked and swollen corpses were floating in the Sumida river together with the packages of clothes and utensils which people were carrying on their shoulders when they fled from the fire. It was a scene which nobody could bear to look at.

In August 1945 atomic bombs exploded above the cities of Hiroshima and Nagasaki, leaving thousands of burnt bones and scorched bodies with eroded skins, depilated heads and bleeding limbs. The pictures and paintings of the time tell us how abhorrent it was.

What then impressed me most was that man is so feeble and subject to sorrow. 'Dust you are, to dust you shall return.' After becoming a Christian, I could realise that God makes much of us and turns his thought towards us.

> Take pity on us, Lord, as we are feeble and subject to sorrow.
> Make us strong in faith to follow you, serving our neighbours who need our love to them.

Further reading: Mt 6:25-33.

S-IY

June 12

Who needs a Physician?

Those who are well have no need of a physician, but those who are sick.
Matthew 9:12

It would hardly seem necessary to remind doctors of this one of our Lord's sayings. Two sides of it are familiar in medical experience. First, there are those who take up the physician's time unnecessarily — the hypochondriacs and the over-anxious, who have no need of a physician or would seem to have no such need. But that last qualification is important. The absence of apparent physical or mental illness does not necessarily mean absence of need. The wise physician will be looking for the hidden need to see if it can be met in some way.

So the other side of the picture is of those who do need a physician but either do not know it or will not admit it. The serious condition that is diagnosed too late is all too tragically familiar. Ignorance, fear, denial or something of that sort has inhibited action.

Jesus was, of course, talking about spiritual sickness. The Pharisees were raising their self-righteous eyebrows at the fact that he was eating with tax collectors and sinners. It was they whom he had come to help, for they (or many of them) were aware of their need. The 'righteous' Pharisees were unaware of their need. There was real irony in the Lord's comment. And it is still relevant today.

C S Lewis, who accepted many invitations to present the Christian faith to service men and women during World War II, has recorded some of the difficulties in these assignments. One great difficulty was linguistic, because of the different educational backgrounds of speaker and audience. The speaker had to learn and use the language the audience understood. Apart from this, he writes, 'the greatest barrier I have met is the almost total absence from the minds of my audience of any sense of sin... The early Christian preachers could assume in their hearers... a sense of guilt... Thus the Christian message was in those days unmistakably the Evangelion, the Good News. It promised healing to those who knew they were sick. We have to convince our hearers of the unwelcome diagnosis before we can expect them to welcome the news of the remedy.'

> Help us, Lord, in communicating with people, whether patients or others. Make us aware that in both medical and spiritual matters there are barriers of both language and understanding. Grant us both wisdom and patience in seeking to overcome those barriers.

Further reading: Mt 9:9-13.

RRW

June 13

The Simple Life.

Teach me thy way, O Lord, and lead me in a plain path. I had fainted, unless I had believed to see the goodness of the Lord in the land of the living. Wait on the Lord: be of good courage and he shall strengthen thine heart: wait, I say, on the Lord. Psalm 27:11, 13-14 (AV)

A medical training carries the danger of glamourising the complex. The student is notoriously liable to remember the small print stuff, or to identify the sparrow as a canary. But even in medicine the great advances have often been simple. Cholera eradication is Britain owed more to sewage control than to advances in bacteriology. Nowadays, economic factors prompt us to take decisions on priorities. The question changes from 'can we?' to 'should we?'

There is a general awareness of the forbiddingly complex nature of our society, and its vulnerability when one link in the chain is disrupted. Hence we see the rise of ecology parties, the development of cottage industries and disillusion with high technology.

The Christian also, for greater reasons, should aim to simplify life. He, more than any, should take the 'long, cool view'. Why 'be with it'? Why complicate domestic or professional life? When we recall the 'ordinariness' of Jesus' life, it is little wonder that those who have done most for him have been those whose lives have been noted for their simplicity. Such a life will, to some degree, entail a deliberate withdrawal from the general trend — a retreat. The psalmist, before asking for a plain path, has already confessed his one desire to 'dwell in the house of the Lord'. We choose where we live, and in order to live in one place we have to withdraw from any other.

> 'A man must keep a little back shop where he can be
> himself without reserve. In solitude alone can he
> know true freedom.'
>
> Montaigne

> Lord, that I may learn of thee,
> Give me true simplicity;
> Wean my soul, and keep it low,
> Willing thee alone to know.
>
> Charles Wesley

Further reading: Pr 3:1-10. Phil 4:10-13.

DEBP

June 14

Beatitudes (1) — Thoughts on the Beatitudes

Seeing the crowds, Jesus went up on the mountain, and when he sat down his disciples came to him. And he opened his mouth and taught them...
Matthew 5:1-2

Professor William Barclay has noted that 'the Sermon on the Mount is the summary and the essence and the core of all that Jesus continuously and habitually taught...It is the opening of Jesus' whole mind to his disciples'. It contains the essential truths he wanted them to live by and give to the world. Thus nothing more significant than these three chapters of St Matthew's 'Good News' has perhaps ever been written. The Beatitudes encapsulate some of these thoughts in the forms of teaching aphorisms.

The word *makarios* (Gr) or *beatus* (L) is translated 'blessed'. Makarios means supremely joyous — 'at the root of my being' joyous because I am in the favour of God. But why and how can this be so? Jesus explains it in these sayings, which are guidelines for the joyous or favoured life. I see these as the distinctive qualities of a new order of human beings, the living constituents of the new society, the Body of Christ.

> Lord, teach me your way, and grant me grace to follow it,
> that I may know your joy.

Further reading: Mt 5:1-2.

DA

June 15

Beatitudes (2) — The Poor in Spirit

Blessed are the poor in spirit, for theirs is the kingdom of heaven.
Matthew 5:3

'Blessed are the spiritually destitute' is another and perhaps better way of translating the opening words here.

For the heavy responsibilities I have, I am totally inadequate spiritually and in my fundamental personal characteristics. Without rich resources coming from God I am inadequate in so many ways — as a doctor or as a patient, as a parent or as a child, or whatever. I can't even begin to conquer personal temptation or the evil flooding about me in society.

And the promise — 'for theirs is the kingdom of heaven'. This immense concept is a central theme in Jesus' teaching; the essence of his ideology. Every doctor everywhere would do well to ponder Jesus' meaning. It is the highest good which can be conceived. It is present: it is future. It is personal: it is universal. It is the 'place' where God's will is sought and done, where what he says is done. It is the new society; the new mutant in human life, the new man and woman. In this beatitude Jesus is saying that anyone who knows his or her need can turn to God to find his way and be given the grace and power to follow it. His disciples living this way are the new society, the 'kingdom of heaven'. I have found that a sure way to become aware of my need is to ask God to make me aware of it. It never fails to work!

> Keep me mindful Lord, of my own inadequacy and of your boundless resources; so that I might be used to effect your eternal purposes.

Further reading: Jn 15:1-11.

DA

June 16

Beatitudes (3) — The Mourners

Blessed are they that mourn, for they shall be comforted. Matthew 5:4

There is a profound truth here that many interpreters have failed to appreciate. But doctors, nurses and clergy who meet dying people and bereaved families know that mourning in bereavement leads to comfort and eventual healing. It is those who do not mourn we should worry about. Such people are not blessed. Instead they are at grave risk spiritually and emotionally, for the symptoms resulting from suppressed grief may blight their lives and affect their families for decades ahead. An evangelical Christian woman of 23 was pregnant when her sailor husband drowned when his ship was torpedoed. She bore it bravely without emotion, as she had been taught Christians should. Forty years later the symptoms of spiritual pain still dominated her life as she herself was dying, and caused unhappiness and near despair in her daughter's family and those who missed her.

I wonder whether Jesus was thinking of a particular person or small group of bereaved people when he said this? That would be so like him!

> Divine Comforter, thank you that we can look to you when
> we mourn, knowing that you can in your time and in your
> way turn our sorrow into joy.

Further reading: Is 61:1-3. Lk 4:16-21.

DA

June 17

Beatitudes (4) — The Meek

Blessed are the meek, for they shall inherit the earth. Matthew 5:5

Jesus quotes from Psalm 37:11. I wonder if he was talking to his nationalist, guerrilla friends, furious and out for Roman blood? For Jesus, like ourselves, was teaching his ideology within a political context full of hatred and rebellion against a foreign repressive power, flaunting its domination. As doctors we cannot ignore the political strife around us, and some of us may be called to bring 'healing to the nations' in a political sense.

So what is meant by meekness? As used in the Old Testament it is a quality of royal leadership. Moses had it, and so did David. Supremely so did Jesus. It is an inner attitude of disciplined committal of oneself to God's sovereignty. It is inner obedience, responsiveness to orders, the ability to 'take it' in adversity or under personal attack. Am I ready to accept and carry out God's will, not my own? It was this quality of meekness that a Roman officer recognised and responded to in Jesus when he said 'I also am a man under authority'. In Gethsemane the night before his crucifixion Jesus said the words which most perfectly express meekness: 'Father, if it be possible, let this cup pass from me; nevertheless not as I will but as thou wilt'. That made the Cross, the resurrection, the forgiveness and rebirth of the human family possible.

> Lord, teach me to be truly meek as you were meek, and to
> know the strength that lies in that meekness.

Further reading: Mt 11:25-30.

DA

June 18

Beatitudes (5) — The Longing for Righteousness.

Blessed are those who hunger and thirst for righteousness, for they shall be filled. Matthew 5:6

William Barclay points out that in these quotes Jesus' choice of words is as strong as possible. He didn't say...'those who are not averse to a bit of righteousness'! He meant those who long for it like a famished man lost in the desert longs for food and water. That strong!

In the business and professional world of western medicine, where big money can be gained in the cities, there are those who sneer at the idea of 'righteousness'. They hope for a square business deal for themselves, but they would be embarrassed to be labelled square themselves. Some respect integrity in others, but in practice go for the dishonest option. Jesus says that you and I need to long with all our being for the quality of righteousness.

We confuse righteousness with self-righteousness. The first is a quality of God best seen in the words and acts of Jesus. The other is the quality of the smug prig. Jesus personified total integrity, purity of motive and compassion. (Think of his stories of the good Samaritan or the prodigal son and how he dealt with the adulterous woman, or the dead girl, and with the heart-broken Peter after his betrayal.) That is righteousness. Do I long for that in my dealings with my family, patients, staff, colleagues? The corresponding promise is: 'they shall be filled'. So we long for the quality, pray for it, work at it, and the promise will be granted. For more on this point about righteousness as seen by Jesus check out Matthew 6.

> Lord, give me a hunger and thirst for righteousness so that,
> being filled, I may be completely yours to do your work.

Further reading: Mt 6.

DA

June 19

Beatitudes (6) — The Merciful.

Blessed are the merciful, for they shall obtain mercy. Matthew 5:7

Ruthlessness and mercy are opposites.

Because we deal with people when they are at their weakest, we doctors can be either ruthless or merciful in our attitudes or management plans. Often we don't recognise the motives hidden within ourselves or built into our 'system of health care delivery', driving us along paths which are ruthless rather than merciful. Our patients are too weak, too dependent to protest at the useless investigations or the doubtful therapy.

The Hebrew *chesedh* translated merciful means 'the ability to get right inside the other person's skin until we can see things with his eyes, think things with his mind, and feel things with his feelings' (Barclay). It is far more potent than our usual interpretation of the word 'mercy'. *Chesedh* is a virtue indispensable to the best doctoring. The promise is that those who develop this virtue will receive it in return. If *chesedh* means an attitude rather than an isolated act, experience vindicates this promise. It is an attitude that can be spread by example: it catches on.

> Lord, grant me the love and wisdom that will make me merciful in all that I do and say.

Further reading: Lk 6:32-38.

DA

June 20

Beatitudes (7) — The Pure in Heart.

Blessed are the pure in heart, for they shall see God. Matthew 5:8

We think of purity in relation to sex, mainly because the sexual drive is so powerful a factor in human affairs. As doctors we understand that people's sexuality is a biological variable, and the sexual temptation may affect anyone past puberty.

Katharos (Gr) means pure or clean, the opposite of dirty. Dirt obscures and diminishes the picture or porcelain or surgical instrument or microscope lens; remove the dirt and purity of colour, form or function becomes a sheer delight. Purity is a positive and creative virtue. In the Bible, wilful decisions are made in 'the heart', while emotion springs from 'the bowels'. It is the single-minded with no ulterior motives who 'shall see God'.

Experiences of many known and unknown saints of God testify to the truth of this promise. If the vision of God in Jesus Christ has been lost and your life has become dark, you might find it profitable to review the moral standards by which you are living.

> Lord, grant me purity of heart and true holiness without which no one will see you.

Further reading: Phil 4:8-9. Heb 12:12-14.

DA

June 21

Beatitudes (8) — The Peacemakers

Blessed are the peacemakers, for they shall be called the children of God.
Matthew 5:9 (AV)

Peacemaking is different from protesting at war and the nuclear arms race. Creating peace between people who hate each other demands commitment and often personal sacrifice, for the peacemaker may get in the line of fire from both sides of a conflict. Turning enemies into friends is a healing of society as surely as a surgical operation or a correctly prescribed medicament is a cure for disharmony within the body, and so Christian doctors have a part to play as peacemakers.

It is worth pondering differences in meaning of the word 'peace'. What is 'peace' to a Christian is not 'peace' to a Marxist. So we need to be wary! We need 'the peace of God which passes understanding...' Nevertheless, there is a link between societal peace and social justice. Peace is constructive, never static. It is a pathway, a way of travelling, and stems from change in entrenched attitudes. None of this denies that both personal and societal peace is a fruit of the Spirit. But God uses human hands to bring peace to fruition. Jesus said peacemakers are blessed, not peaceful people. There is a distinction — and it is the former who 'shall be called the children of God'.

> Lord, make me an instrument of thy peace;
> Where there is hatred, let me show love;
> Where there is injury, pardon;
> Where there is discord, union.
> Where there is doubt, faith;
> Where there is despair, hope.
> Where there is darkness, light;
> And where there is sadness, joy.

Attributed to St Francis

Further reading: Is 58:6-12.

DA

June 22

Beatitudes (9) — For the Sake of Righteousness

Blessed are those who are persecuted for righteousness' sake, for theirs is the kingdom of heaven. Matthew 5:10

'Righteousness' is not a good word. Indeed it is often used as a pejorative about a person's character. Absolute integrity, purity, a selfless disregard for oneself and a love which seeks nothing in return are the components of righteousness. A character displaying such moral qualities may attract some people and repel others. Those who are repelled usually react by intolerance, opposition, persecution. Jesus was a realist and experienced both reactions in full measure. It is worth considering why Jesus linked personal morality ('righteousness') with something with social/political overtones (the 'kingdom of heaven'). An individual's personal morality is often connected with national security in biblical stories, especially in the Old Testament. Here Jesus promises that these moral qualities actually are the moral constituents of a new society — the kingdom of heaven. So the family, the hospital, the community where Christ's moral standards are the norm of human relationships really is the kingdom of heaven. Our practical aim in life is nothing less than to be part of such an amazing new society.

> Help us, Lord, to understand and to practise what makes for true righteousness, and to be prepared to suffer for its sake.

Further reading: 1 Pet 3:13-18.

DA

June 23

Beatitudes (10) — Persecution for Christ's Sake

Blessed are you when people insult you, persecute you and falsely say all kinds of evil against you because of me. Rejoice and be glad, because great is your reward in heaven, for in the same way they persecuted the prophets who were before you. Matthew 5:11-12 (NIV)

Few attacks on evil will go unchallenged. If we align ourselves with Jesus in our behaviour we shall get insults, persecutions and lies thrown at us. So what do you do? Cringe? Actually you rejoice and give out positive vibes! People who live the moral and spiritual behaviour patterns set by the Master inevitably challenge evil — in society and in people around them.

As doctors who walk this path is there some unique response we are asked to make to evil? Surely, is it not to heal the disease of pride etc, and help change the person behind the evil? If so — and it is the path Jesus took — it is a dangerous route. At times political action or force may be justified, but the unique challenge of the gospel — the essence of the good news — is that human nature can be changed, not by force but by the forgiveness, healing and education of the Holy Spirit. And the reward? Just be glad and rejoice for you are in a good historical tradition. 'Your reward is in heaven.'

Thank you, Lord Jesus, that you are willing to suffer for my sake. Help me to be willing to suffer for your sake.

Further reading: Jn 15:18-21, 16:1-4.

DA

June 24

Two Sides of Life (1) — The Trivial Round

And he (Jesus) went down with them (Joseph and Mary) and came to Nazareth and was obedient to them... And Jesus increased in wisdom and in stature, and in favour with God and man. Luke 2:51-52

Every life has its share of the trivial round. A medical life, no matter what form of special aspects it embraces, has its dull side and its routine. The exciting and romantic things in the television medical series don't happen all the time. Pity help us if they did! No mortal frame could stand it. Busyness and pressures come — and often don't go, even when we feel we have had more than enough. But the boring side can come too — and can seem just as interminable and unacceptable. Both must be coped with.

Putting aside the problem of frenetic activity for the moment, let's look at the trivial round in the light of our Master's experience. Do we realise that before the few years of his actual ministry, about eighteen years of his life (between the age of twelve and thirty) were spent in Nazareth growing up as the carpenter's son? For most of that time, we may fairly assume, he worked in Joseph's carpenter's shop.

What a trivial beginning for the most important life ever lived in mankind's history! He must have been aware (as Mary was) of his own destiny, and we can only remotely and quite inadequately guess at what went on in his mind as he did the routine jobs. One thing we can feel sure about is that the jobs would have been done well.

Does it seem too much of a platitude to emphasise that for us it is still and always important to do the trivial things well? No matter how boring they seem to us, they matter to those who are seeking help, and they are worth doing. It is all part of our reasonable service (Rom 12:1 AV) and our spiritual worship (RSV).

> The trivial round, the common task,
> Will furnish all we ought to ask;
> Room to deny ourselves; a road
> To bring us daily nearer God.

John Keble

Further reading: Lk 2:39-52.

RRW

June 25

Two Sides of Life (2) — The Tyranny of Busyness

... so many people were coming and going that they did not even have a chance to eat. Mark 6:31 (NIV)

Does that sound familiar to you? It happens often enough — too often — in hospital life and in many a medical practice. It happened again and again to Jesus and his personal band of followers during his ministry. Great crowds followed him everywhere (Matthew's Gospel has at least 15 separate references to such crowds). Their motives were sometimes mixed, as he was not slow to tell them (Jn 6:26). But he taught them and healed their sick. At the same time, we read again and again that he dismissed the crowds or avoided them and got away to a quiet place. Repeatedly he took his disciples away so that they could rest. The one motive that overruled his need for rest was compassion.

At times in a medical life there just seems to be too much to do. It can be genuinely inevitable, and then one must cope. Nevertheless it is well to examine one's motives if life seems constantly too busy. In looking at the tyranny of busyness, we need to look honestly for the real tyrant. Is the tyrant perhaps ourselves? Is there always genuine pressing need? Is there sometimes a wish to impress others? Is there sometimes a wish to impress ourselves — to feel important, to feel 'needed', to satisfy an excessive perfectionism, to enjoy a little self-pity, even to be 'very Christian'? Most of us have a remarkable capacity to deceive ourselves when it comes to motive. It is worth some frank thought.

A young Christian once said to me: 'I've been told that Christians should not take holidays. What do you think?' I said: 'As a doctor, I think that is nonsense'. It is not a sin to have a holiday when we do absolutely nothing useful or to take an afternoon off for golf or to go fishing.

Of course we must do our work well and willingly, and with compassion, but we shall not do it efficiently if we are physically and/or mentally exhausted. Of course we must play our reasonable part in the work of the Kingdom, but we do not need to be on 57 committees. We do not need to flatter ourselves that nobody else can do anything properly (which means like we would do it!). Certainly there is no warrant to think that busyness is next to godliness. The Master says to us as he said to his disciples long ago, after they had been on a busy and demanding assignment (Mk 6:31 NIV): 'Come with me by yourselves to a quiet place and get some rest'.

> Lord, take from our souls the strain and stress
> And let our ordered lives confess
> The beauty of thy peace.

J G Whittier

Further reading: Mk 6:1-12, 30-44.

RRW

June 26

Jesus Weeps Today?

Greater love has no man that this, that... (he)... lay down his life for his friends. John 15:13

Visitors to the Holy Land are often upset by the commercialism, the lack of respect for historical sites and the competition between various Christian traditions. Yet often a place, a word or an event may speak to us in an unforgettable way. On the slopes of the Mount of Olives is a small Franciscan Church, Dominus Flevit, built in the shape of a tear by the French architect Barluzzi. This is reputed to be on the site where Jesus wept over Jerusalem (Lk 19:4). Earlier he had expressed his concern for the city. 'O Jerusalem, Jerusalem...how often would I have gathered your children together as a hen gathers her brood under her wings, and you would not' (Lk 13:34).

In our medical practice we shall be involved with patients who have, seemingly without thought, brought disaster or ill health on themselves. In many instances innocent people may suffer as a result of their folly. The drunken driver comes to mind, or the avoidable head injury because a seat belt was not worn. The distress of the relatives and remorse of the patient dying from cancer of the lung or oesophageal varices and the recently reported case of fetal alcoholism syndrome are other examples. It may be difficult for us to treat these patients with the care they need, particularly if the innocent victim is in the same ward as the one responsible for his plight. Those who have treated terrorists and their victims in adjacent beds know this only too well. Irrespective of the authenticity of the site of the Dominus Flevit Church, its message speaks to us in these difficult situations. Through its single large window we see the ancient city with its domes, its minarets and its churches. On the inside of the window is a single empty cross signifying the lengths to which Jesus went in caring not only for Jerusalem, but for the whole world. This is the supreme example of caring. No one else can ever go to this extent, but we often have opportunities for applying the same principles in our practice.

A plaque on the wall opposite the entrance to the Chapel, freely translated, reads: 'The love of God is mourning, O unfathomable grief!

God mourns that man, whom he created, has strayed so far from him. Today in love he is calling — your Saviour Jesus Christ. God is calling, calling, calling. Turn round and come back home today.'

> My Saviour weeps: his heart is rent.
> I hear his loving sad lament
> Upon the Mount of Olives.
> Come home, my children, come to me,
> I want and yearn so fervently:
> For you my heart is open.

Basilea Schlink
The Holy Land Today

Further reading: Is 53:4-6. Jn 12:20-33.

JWD

June 27

The Least of These — My Brethren.

Suffer little children, and forbid them not. Matthew 19:14 (AV)

Children can be pests at times, demanding and unreasonable: egocentric — 'me first'; negativist — 'no! no!'; questioning — 'why? why?'; non-compliant — 'I won't!' and at the end of a tiring day they can be so much the more exasperating. But after all they are tired too. They choose unreasonable times to be ill — holidays or the middle of the night — but they can't help it. When they go to sleep, head on pillows, sheets pulled down, they look for all the world like little angels. Perhaps they are. Sometimes when they are ill they can be far more appealing and certainly much less demanding. They are dependent upon us for good, warmth, nursing and medical care, yet often unable or unwilling to thank us. They can't command attention as can adults. They can't report us to the health authority. They are at the mercy almost entirely of our commitment, care and concern. We are measured in eternity by our responsiveness and our responses, as well as by our total commitment to their need. 'Forbid them not', said the Saviour at a time when the needs of other people seemed far more important than those of mere children. Our Lord could see their need and gave them his full attention. He would still have done so had it been in the middle of the night. He went on to say, 'for of such is the kingdom of heaven'.

Whenever we care for a child, we are caring for one of God's creatures known and loved by him. We have an awful responsibility and yet a tremendous opportunity — and 'inasmuch as you do it unto one of these, you do it unto me'. The devotion of your mind and person, your care and concern for the child's body, mind and soul, your love for the loveless, your smile, your gentleness and patience are all in his name. Our whole approach to a child (or adult), in outpatients or on the ward, is altered if we realise that he is precious in God's sight, worthy of our prayers and our blessings. It takes two, possibly three seconds to look at a child — or indeed anyone — and silently, at the start of a physical examination, to seek God's blessing on him. You will never know the effect upon the child. Perhaps if they ever knew about it, your worldly friends would think you superstitious or worse. One thing is sure, you are a different person when you approach a child whom you have just silently blessed and whom you see as one for whom Christ died.

> Lord, teach us to regard all others as better than ourselves.
> Give us your grace as we minister to your creatures. Give us
> the strength to love the unlovely, to help the rebel and to
> give our all when nobody else can know it — but you. Make
> our lives be unto your glory.

Further reading: Mk 10:13-16. Mt 25:31-46.

OPG

June 28

Listening to People

Then the woman, scared and shaking all over because she knew that she was the one to whom this thing had happened, came and flung herself before him and told him the whole story. Mark 5:33 (JBP)

This woman, with her severe and worsening menorrhagia, had come to Jesus in despair, had secretly touched his cloak and had experienced healing. Jesus insisted on making personal contact with her. And he listened while she told him the whole story.

Listening to people is always important, both for the doctor and for the patient. Doctors don't listen, patients say. Why don't we listen? No time, we say. That's a pity. Perhaps we could make a little more time if we tried. Some doctors do. But is shortage of time always the reason? Is the exercise tedious to us? Do we think that patient has nothing to tell us? Do we just not want to hear about the pains and aches and coughs and limps, or — more tedious, but often more important — the frustrations and burdens and miseries that make us feel helpless? Are we impatient to get on with ordering the X-ray examinations and the pathology tests, or to reach for the prescription pad to order the placebo or the panacea? It is not always easy to listen, whatever people say. But listening always matters, listening both to what the patient says and to what he (often more loudly) does not say. It is important diagnostically. It can be vital therapeutically. It can bring great healing to the spirit. Jesus listened — not only to the woman with her debilitating menorrhagia, but to Nicodemus, to the woman of Samaria, to the Centurion at Capernaum, to the Syrophoenician woman, to tempestuous Peter, to blind Bartimaeus, to lepers and sinners and outcasts. He was good at listening and clearly saw the value of it. Perhaps that was because he was always listening to his Father.

> Lord, strengthen me, that, while I stand
>   Firm on the rock, and strong in thee,
> I may stretch out a loving hand
>   To wrestlers with the troubled sea.

Frances Ridley Havergal

Further reading: Mk 5:24-34.

RRW

June 29

A Word in Season

Let your speech always be gracious, seasoned with salt. Colossians 4:6

It seems that wherever there is plenty of stress there will also be plenty of swearing. The bigger the crisis, the more blatant the cursing becomes. Certainly my experience of hospital staff is that no one blasphemes quite so much as those working in the intensive care unit or the labour suite.

When I first became an SHO in obstetrics, the bad language of the midwifery staff upset me greatly. One particular afternoon, when we had been very busy on the labour ward, Sister said 'Jesus Christ' once too often, and I felt such an anger rising up inside that I wanted to take her to task over it. I was about to do so when the Lord seemed to say in my heart, 'no, it's not the best moment', and of course he was right. Sister would have felt very threatened in the presence of junior nursing staff, and , with a mother critically ill from a massive post-partum haemorrhage in the next room it was hardly the right time to give an explanation of the meaning of Jesus' name!

So I waited and prayed that Jesus himself would give me a suitable opportunity to mention the matter. About a fortnight later, when we had no patients in labour, Sister and I were alone on the ward when 'Jesus' passed her lips yet again. To my surprise I found myself gently saying: 'You know, Sister, I think you must be one of the few midwives I've met who talks about the Lord Jesus more than I do!' Immediately the message got across without raising her hostility, and although after that the words would occasionally slip out she really made a determined effort not to swear. Perhaps more important our esteem for one another increased enormously — so much so that when I eventually left the hospital, that particular Sister had organised a collection for the biggest farewell gift I have ever had, and on the accompanying card she had simply written the words 'keep the faith'.

Hastily spoken words do nothing to further the cause of Christ and Scripture clearly tells us that we are always to be gracious in our speech, never rude. Yet this does not mean our words have to be continually weak and ineffectual. They are to have a real 'bite' to them that gets the point across without being destructive. Let us pray that God will teach us to be truly incisive without being offensive.

Further reading: Jas 3:6-12. Eph 4:29.

TGS

June 30

Be Not Dismayed

Be not dismayed. Joshua 1:9

The exuberant on-top-of-the-world life is not for all of us. True, we may experience this feeling at special times, immediately after our conversion, or when we pass 'finals'. But the mountain top experience does not last, and we often have our setbacks. Things go wrong despite all our efforts. The word said in kindness is misunderstood. Lack of sleep last night and the night before takes its toll, so that it is all too easy to wonder whether all our efforts are worth it, and whether it is any good to go on striving for excellence. Would it not be better to alter our standards and, indeed our job? Why ever did we do medicine at all? Dismay can seep into the soul and affect our way of living and our reason for it. One of the first things to suffer is our life in Christ, our prayer time, our Bible reading and our everyday witness. That is why Joshua was told that he needed courage and strength to go on studying and obeying God's word (Jos 1:7-8). The murmurings of the discontented people of Israel did not leave Moses and Joshua unscathed. Some of the rebellious talk sank into their souls (Nu 11:10-15). That is why God had to say 'Be not dismayed'. It required an act of obedience by them — and it does by us too. This is a command for us to obey. Not to be dismayed is one of the hardest things to do. It requires much prayer and trust and can be one of the biggest trials of our faith.

The houseman years can be very difficult. After the friendship of the Christian Union, the joy of graduation, there follows the time of testing. The long hours, the responsibility which at times is awful, the calls which demand a knowledge and skill well beyond any preparation that the medical school gave us, these sap both our physical and spiritual strength. The n'th job applied for and denied, another intravenous drip into the tissues, the third dry lumbar puncture in succession, the families who break up before our very eyes, these all tax our courage, tenacity and Christian faith. And, just when we need it most, time for God is at a premium. The man of the world tackles the possible, the Christian the impossible. To do so the Christian requires not only courage but 'stickability', tenacity, the ability not to be deflected by dismay and the sure knowledge that he is commissioned in his everyday work by the King of Kings, who gives the strength for each new demand and who does not measure a man's life by worldly achievements but by his acts of obedience.

> When we have exhausted our store of endurance,
> When our strength has failed ere the day is half done,
> When we reach the end of our hoarded resources,
> Our Father's full giving has only begun.
>
> His love has no limit, His grace has no measure,
> His power no boundary known unto man,
> For out of his infinite riches in Jesus
> He giveth and giveth and giveth again.

Annie Johnson Flint

Further reading: Jos 1:1-9. Ex 14:13-22.

OPG

July 1

Abundant Life for a Sheep

I am come that they might have life, and that they might have it more abundantly. John 10:10 (AV)

This well known verse, set in the context of a shepherd and his sheep, is usually interpreted in an emotional sense. Abundant life is 'joie de vivre' or 'life to the full' (NIV) or 'life in its fullness' (NEB).

But can we not go a little deeper by looking at the context? The first half of the verse provides a contrast. The thief comes to steal and to kill and to destroy. The shepherd comes to bring life. The difference is stark. The thief steals for his own purpose, perhaps to fatten and put on his own family table. He kills — and the word used means to make a sacrifice presumably for ritual purposes. He destroys, and for what other reason than malice?

The shepherd came to the fold to bring life. But he did not want the sheep just to be able to exist. He wanted them to have the fullest possible life of which a sheep is capable. But can we define what this means to a sheep? What is a sheep's abundant life? We are told in the preceding verse. It means to 'go in and out, and find pasture'.

To 'go in' means security. The fold, guarded by a shepherd, offers safety for the sheep when wolves prowl and thieves are more likely to be active. Just so, we Christians are secure in Christ. No man shall ever be able to pluck us out of his hand.

To 'go out' spells liberty. We are free to wander where we like, always provided we keep within range of the Shepherd's voice and follow his lead. And if we happen to stray, he will be watching and will give us a call or come after us.

To 'find pasture' speaks of sustenance, of food and water enough for every day. Even in mountains or desert the Shepherd knows our need and provides for it.

If this is the kind of abundant life the Shepherd offers, there is only one thing to do, and that is to stick close by him.

> Good Shepherd, may I sing your praise
> Within your house for ever.

Further reading: Jn 10:10-15. Ps 23.

CGS

July 2

Success

Uzziah... was marvellously helped, till he was strong. 2 Chronicles 26:15

Unquestionably there is a potential danger in success. Many men, like Uzziah, have found success harder to cope with than adversity. Paul wrote 'I know how to be abased, and I know how to abound' (Phil 4:12). The latter may be the harder test, for self-confidence can be disastrous. On the other hand ambition and success are not intrinsically wrong. It was God's plan that Esther should hold an influential position in the court of the king, and it was equally true of Joseph and Daniel.

The vital thing is to remember constantly that all we have and are is due entirely to the goodness of God. When we see the consequences of sin in the lives of others we should acknowledge that, 'There but for the grace of God go I'. It is equally important, when we are granted advancement or success, to remember, 'Here am I purely by the grace of God'. In the injunction 'Do you seek great things for yourself? Seek them not' (Je 45:5), the crucial words are 'for yourself'. After all, what is success? If it be but professional advancement, financial gain, or popular acclaim, it is an empty bubble. Let us remember that God sees the motive rather than the achievement, and rates faithfulness above success. It is through being faithful that we truly achieve (1 Cor 15:58).

> 'I dedicate myself — my time — my capabilities —
> my ambition — everything to Him. Blessed Lord,
> sanctify me to Thy uses. Give me no worldly
> success which may not lead me nearer my Saviour!'

From the diary of Kelly
co-founder of John Hopkins Hospital
on the day of his graduation

Further reading: 1 Cor 4:1-7. Dt 8:11-19.

DPB

July 3

The Way (7) — The Call to the Way

Jesus said: Come to me, all who labour and are heavy laden, and I will give you rest. Matthew 11:28

These precious words of the Lord Jesus lie at the heart of Christian hope and experience. They lie at the heart of the Call to the Way.

Two things, perhaps more than all others, play a part in this Call. One is our need. The other is God's love. Behind it all is God's sovereign will.

A sense of need is, of course, familiar to us as the driving force that brings people to seek medical advice and care. They have a need of body or mind which it is the doctor's role to try to meet. But the help that God gives to those who come to him in repentance and faith is infinitely deeper and more significant and more effective than anything that even the best human physician can give to a patient. He gives forgiveness for sin, peace to the guilt-ridden soul, rest for the weary and restless, hope for now and eternity. He opens up the Way to the bewildered and the lost.

God's love, love to the uttermost, is revealed in Christ. It was seen supremely and poignantly on the Cross. That amazing act of love has broken the rebellious hearts of multitudes, turning fear into adoration, mistrust into love, and disobedience into allegiance. And we know his love continuingly and constantly in his daily presence and care for those who trust him.

Christ calls us to the Way by our need and by his love. We still hear his words: 'All that the Father gives me will come to me; and him who comes to me I will not cast out' (Jn 6:37). We enter on the Way when we acknowledge him with mind and heart and will as personal Saviour, Lord and God. Our need and his love keep us in the Way. Ultimately his love is the one supreme and abiding factor.

John has written: 'Beloved, if God so loved us, we also ought to love one another ... We love, because he first loved us' (1 Jn 4:11,19). It might be a salutary exercise for us to consider what is in the minds of those who come to us for help. Their need is real. How far can they count on being met with love?

> O Saviour, I have nought to plead,
>   In earth beneath or heaven above,
> But just my own exceeding need,
>   And thy exceeding love.
> The need will soon be past and gone,
>   Exceeding great but quickly o'er;
> The love unbought is all thine own,
>   And lasts for evermore.

Jane Crewdson

Further reading: Mt 11:25-30. Jn 6:35-40. 1 Jn 4:7-21.

RRW

(*Faith Under Test* was written by a 52 year-old Australian surgeon shortly before his death in 1984. We are grateful for permission to republish it from the magazine of his parish church, Holy Trinity, Adelaide, South Australia, in which it first appeared)

July 4

Faith Under Test

Your Father who is in heaven will give good things to those who ask Him.
Matthew 7:11

Most of you will know that some weeks ago I was hospitalised at very short notice. Lethal tumours had been found, so major surgery was the only answer, even though that surgery carried significant risks, and I was not at all looking forward to it, especially the post-operative recovery period.

During the crisis, prayers tended to be fairly brief and simple (although I guess it is part of my nature to try to avoid 'heaping up empty phrases') asking for strengthening of faith to keep trusting God whatever he had in store in the days ahead, and if possible removal of the offending tumours, not too much pain and torture post-operatively, together with comfort for my family. Interspersed with this were a hundred other thoughts running around in my head, like 'Will someone remember to water the side garden? Or look at Mr Blogg's X-rays?' And even, 'Does anyone knows where my Will is?' etc, etc.

God had been trustworthy in the past, and I felt quite sure that I could trust him through this escapade also, but I was sensible and practical in my requests for the post-operative period, as I knew that this would be a bit of a trial by the very nature of the surgery.

However, as day followed day, I found to my surprise that he had almost completely abolished the pain and torments I had expected. The medical and nursing care was excellent, and this was an important help, but I realised with fresh clarity (and great thankfulness) the truth of Paul's words: 'he is able to do far more abundantly than all that we ask or think, to him be the glory in the church and in Jesus Christ'.

In the Psalms, David sometimes sings of his desire to praise God in the congregation as a response to deliverance, and I am praising him on this page (as it were in the congregation) for my deliverance; and also for the faithful support of you all in prayer and fellowship.

The future is uncertain. There may still be further trials on the road ahead. Despite the uncertainty of life, we know even more certainly than ever, that God remains faithful. Even when we come to that last valley we need fear no evil.

> Grant me the grace, Lord, when I come
> to that last valley, to fear no evil.

Further reading: Eph 3:14-21.

KFC

July 5

The Night Before...

Have I not commanded you? Fear not. Joshua 1:9 (NIV)

There are some who appear positively to enjoy a lecture to a big audience, or presenting a case for the seminar or grand round. It is a challenge, and they delight in it. But for most of us these occasions are associated with a fearful apprehension that gives us an uneasy night's sleep beforehand, and a quickening of the pulse and paling of the face at the time. Yet these things have to be faced. The words given to Joshua can be a great support to us: 'Fear not, have I not commanded you?' The Christian goes as God's ambassador about his daily duties, and this includes public appearances. As an ambassador he does his very best, prepares well beforehand, rehearses, thinks about the important points and seeks the help of others. But having done all this, when the occasion comes, he goes as a servant of the living God, even though speaking on secular matters. He relies on the strength and courage that God gives in response to his prayers and knows that God will be with him. The words he uses, the standard he sets, the grace and consideration he shows towards the patient whose case he demonstrates, these all come from his maker. And so the burden becomes lighter, the accomplishment greater, and God's name is honoured.

Joshua did all that was humanly possible to prepare for the taking of Jericho, and he was right to do so. But, military genius though he was, he only found victorious power when, on the eve of the battle, he met the Captain of the host of the Lord, drawn sword in hand, and fell down and worshipped him (Jos 5:13-15).

It was for Joshua to do his best in total reliance on the Lord. It was for the Lord to magnify him in the eyes of other people as he saw fit (Jos 4:14).

> Teach us good Lord to serve thee as thou deservest,
> to give and not to count the cost,
> to fight and not to heed the wounds,
> to toil and not to seek for rest,
> to labour and not to ask for any reward
> save that of knowing that we do thy will.

Ignatius Loyola

Further reading: 2 Cor 11:24-30. 2 Cor 5:14-15.

OPG

July 6

The Rabbi (1) — A Visitor

I was humming 'Amazing Grace' — one of my favourite hymns. I was precisely at the highest point in the song — 'that saved a wretch like me' when the door opened and a voice was heard asking 'Are you The Friends of Israel's doctors?' Perhaps it was my habit of seeing people through the eyes of a practising physician that caused me to see first a plastered arm in a sling, but immediately thereafter I realised that the arm, plaster and sling all belonged to a rabbi. 'Of course we are, and for many reasons, rabbi,' I said, cordially inviting him to come in.

'I do hope one of your reasons will allow you to help me with this,' he said, as he held out his arm and crossed the threshold of our clinic here in Buenos Aires.

Once he was in, I noticed the perfect plaster cast he had on his arm and wondered what could be the ultimate reason he came to us. As if he were reading my thoughts, he said, 'In these days of anti-Semitism, our enemies come to us freely. I think now is a good time for us Jews to get closer to our friends.' No doubt he was a brave rabbi, a man accustomed to facing all sorts of situations.

It was difficult to guess his age because of his long beard. His accent, from somewhere in Europe, led me to ask 'Have you met many friends of Israel in the world?' 'Not as many as I would have wished — and not so few as I would have expected' he answered. 'Among them, have you met any Christians?' I asked. He replied, 'Haven't you, doctor? Everybody does.' 'Did it make any vital change in your life, rabbi? I ask you this because something I once learned from a fellow- Christian was the turning point of my life,' I told him.

'I wonder what it could have been,' he murmured, not having the slightest idea that I was about to relate to him my testimony and how I had recognised my Messiah. After listening to my account of personal salvation through faith in the Lord Jesus Christ, he looked at me like an entomologist would look at a rare insect for the first time. Then he asked, 'Who do you think you are talking to about religious affairs? Are you crazy?' 'And who do you think you are talking to about psychiatric disorders?' I asked. 'After all, I am supposed to give the diagnosis.' He murmured something I couldn't quite hear, and then said acquiescently, 'How can an intelligent man like you believe in such a fantastic tale?' Sincere in his beliefs, he was concerned for what he thought were my misguided persuasions.

Further reading: Jn 9:24-38.

A and AE

July 7

The Rabbi (2) — A Challenge

Soon I had arranged my tools on the table. I plugged in a small electric saw and... buzzzzz! It sounded awful I admit. 'Hold it! Hold it! Are you planning to use that on me?' he shouted. 'Yes, of course,' I replied, trying to reassure him by the tone of my voice. 'But what do you really want to do to me? Are you going to remove the plaster from my arm — or split my whole body in two?'

'Don't worry, rabbi,' I said. 'This may look like any other saw, but it is entirely different. It has been engineered to cut plaster and only plaster. Would you like to have a practical demonstration?' 'As long as you use your own flesh for the test,' he quickly responded.

I then moved the blade of the saw to the palm of my hand. As soon as it touched the skin, it stopped. I knew it would. There was no risk involved. The continuous buzzing of the electric saw accompanied my words as I proceeded to cut through the cast. 'You see, rabbi, it cuts the plaster perfectly, but causes no harm to soft surfaces. It looks frightening, but it is real.'

I then steered the conversation to a spiritual course again. 'I was humming a song when you entered my office a little while ago, rabbi. That song says that I was a wretch, but God's amazing grace saved me. It probably sounded frightening to you, but it was real! You are a rabbi, and here you are listening to the testimony of a Christian doctor. Twenty minutes ago you would have said, 'It is impossible' but here you are. It's real! How can you deny that Jesus fulfilled all the Old Testament prophesies concerning the Messiah by saying it's impossible and not give yourself the opportunity to see it's reality?'

The eyes of the rabbi were fixed on me. What sort of thoughts were dashing through his mind, I do not know.

Further reading: Jn 3:1-17.

A and AE

July 8

The Rabbi (3) — Messiah is Coming

Soon the job was done, and he was free from the plaster. Sliding the fingers of his other hand over the cast, he said, 'I'm going to miss this. It was very useful to write telephone numbers and dates on. You know, doctor, I haven't missed an appointment since I broke my arm — but it sure feels good to be free. Yes, it is so nice to be free.'

I turned off the electric saw, and a heavy silence came upon us. He glanced at the table where the saw lay dead. Striding to the exit door and shaking his head, he said, 'A doctor who talks like a rabbi — a saw that is mighty and cuts plaster, but stops when it touches flesh — and, wonder of wonders, a rabbi who keeps silent when he should be telling you so many things. It must be the end times for things like this to be happening. Surely, the Messiah is coming soon!' And having said that, he left, repeating, 'Messiah is coming soon!'

He was right. Time is short. The Messiah is coming again. Somewhere in this city of Buenos Aires there is a man whom God loves, a man with a long beard and a prayer shawl whom God sees. In the agenda of this man's life, he has been missing the most important appointment of all. He may now be considering for the first time in his life the fact that the Messiah has already come! Men like him once asked before, '... Rabbi, when camest thou here?' (Jn 6:25). Let us pray that it will not be long before he confesses to Jesus, '... Rabbi... thou art the King of Israel!' (Jn 1:49).

Further reading: Mt 16:13-17.

A and AE

(*The Rabbi* sections used by permission. The Friends of Israel Gospel Ministries Inc)

July 9

My Shepherd (7)

Thy rod and thy staff, they comfort me. Psalm 23:4

Commentators vary slightly over the function of rods and staffs in shepherding, but one who has been a shepherd himself (Phillip Keller: *A Shepherd looks at Psalm 23*) suggests that the rod (a kind of club) acts as an extension of the shepherd's right arm. Symbol of authority and power, it could be both weapon and warning. Thrown directly at an enemy, it becomes a deadly missile, while pitched into a wandering sheep's track it would act as deterrent. Ezekiel speaks, too, of sheep being counted as they pass 'under the rod' (Ez 20:37) as a check that all are present and correct. A sheep found to be sick or in need of special treatment would then be drawn out for personal attention by the shepherd before rejoining the flock. A rod scarcely sounds comforting, yet as a symbol of God's authority against evil it may be so. If it sometimes seems that he is holding back his hand, this is in mercy, not in impotence.

A scene in the Bayeux tapestry is described as King Harold 'comforting' his troops, yet portrays the monarch prodding them on with his spear. The old word comfort included the idea of urging on. So those who claim to be the sheep of his pasture must be willing to submit to God's authority and be assured (rather than alarmed) that his loving, searching glance will see all our defects and apply correction. Even so, his rod does not fall on us in anger, but we read the amazing fact that 'He was bruised for our iniquities' (Is 53:5). Punishment has been borne on our behalf by the Shepherd himself: the rod is not to slay us but to restrain us when straying and to convict us when sinning — to separate us, to sort us out and to send us on again. Keller likens the rod to the word of God, authoritative and challenging, and the staff to the Spirit of God, comforting and strengthening.

> O Saviour Christ, our woes dispel;
> For some are sick and some are sad,
> And some have never loved Thee well,
> And some have lost the love they had.
> Thy kind but searching glance can scan
> The very wounds that shame would hide.

Henry Twells

Further reading: Ho 4:16, 14:4-7.

JG

July 10

My Shepherd (7 cont'd)

Thy rod and thy staff, they comfort me. Psalm 23:4

Keller likens the rod to the Word of God, authoritative and challenging, and the staff to the Spirit of God, comforting and strengthening. With this image in mind, we find the function of a shepherd's staff to be versatile and gentle. Because of its integral crook, it may be used to lift newborn lambs nearer to their mothers, to extricate sheep from entanglements or difficulty (whether or not of their own making) or simply as a means of maintaining contact. Thus, a shepherd may be seen walking alongside a tired or nervous sheep, his staff keeping it close to him, so offering evidence of his reassuring presence and protective care. The crook is unique to shepherds; swineherds and cowherds do not use one. Its whole design and purpose are directed towards the needs of sheep. Unlike the rod, the staff is never for long range use and to know its comfort, sheep must be within the shepherd's reach. So the Holy Spirit is described as the Comforter — one brought alongside to help (Jn 14:16 AV).

David mentions the rod and staff in the context of the valley, and it is in their valleys that some of our patients (or colleagues) may first call upon God, be it in anger or panic. For some, the rod is clearly of their own making, as with those suffering from drug overdoses, including nicotine and alcohol. Even so, they may question his control of his compassion, either denying his existence altogether or the possibility of his care. There is a further risk that they will be treated as second class citizens by their official caregivers because their ills are self-induced. Yet the crisis may indeed be his rod, selecting them out and giving to an undershepherd the chance to draw them close to himself. Stern warning may be needful, but a loving word or deed accompanying professional advice may make all the difference to their lives. Sometimes we ourselves are impelled to cry out in despair or rage as to why God has permitted some tragedy, such as death in childbirth. The rod and staff remind us again that he is Lord and Shepherd. Even though we cannot always understand his ways, authority blended with concern are inseparable aspects of his character. If we care, he cares far more and can even bring great good from great tragedy.

Isaiah, in adjacent verses says 'His arm shall rule ... He shall gather the lambs with his arm and carry them in his bosom' (Is 40:10-11 AV). The same arm that hurls the club at the wolf may stop any of us in our tracks. It also lifts up and cradles the weaklings. His rod exposes but his staff transposes. They both assure us that the Comforter is close.

> Thy rod and staff my comfort still,
> Thy cross before to guide me.

H W Baker

Further reading: Jn 14:16-20, 26-27. Jn 6:37.

JG

July 11

Doing What We Can

She has done what she could. Mark 14:8

Very seldom, if ever, should a doctor say to a patient: 'I can do nothing for you'. We may have to say: 'You need special treatment which I am not trained to give you, so I shall send you to a specialist'. At times we may have to say: 'We cannot give you anything which will cure your condition, but we can give you something to relieve the pain and make you more comfortable'. It is unkind, and usually unnecessary, to say: 'There is nothing we can do for you'. We should, like Mary of Bethany, do what we can.

Mary knew that the Lord Jesus was on a 'collision course' with the Jewish authorities ever since he raised her brother Lazarus from the dead. She had sat at Jesus' feet, listening to his words, and had more spiritual insight than most people. She knew that there might be no opportunity to anoint his body after he died, so she did it beforehand. The fragrance of the nard perfume — grown in the Himalayas, and carried by slow camel or other animal transport all the way to the land of Israel — would have clung to his feet for days, and was probably still there when he was nailed to the cross.

We cannot cure all of those who seek our attention, but let us be sure that we do all that we can to help them physically, mentally, and spiritually, either personally or in co-operation with others.

> Lord, as people seek my help today, give me the strength to do all that I reasonably can do to help them. If there is no way that they can be healed, show me how best I can help them in every way. Above all, help me to point people's attention to you, the Great Physician.

Further reading: Mk 14:3-9.

JWMcM

July 12

Integrity

May the God of peace make you holy through and through. May you be kept in soul and mind and body in spotless integrity until the coming of our Lord Jesus Christ. He who calls you is utterly faithful and he will finish what he has set out to do. 1 Thessalonians 5:23-24 (JBP)

If there is one quality above all else expected of a doctor it is integrity. The word is not an easy one to explain, but we all know what it means and what it implies.

The patient of necessity trusts the doctor. Innermost thoughts are confided. Potent drugs are swallowed on the doctor's say-so. Consciousness is surrendered under the surgeon's knife. Life and welfare are put into the doctor's hands. It is awesome.

In all this the patient assumes the doctor's integrity, the quality of being trustworthy, of being rock-solid reliable. The Greek word which Paul uses, and which J B Phillips translates by the phrase 'in spotless integrity', appears in other translations as 'blameless', 'sound', 'complete' and 'without break or blame'. There is in it the idea of soundness and wholeness, which is well conveyed by the word 'integrity'.

In a purely medical and social context, the idea of integrity underlies several aspects of the Hippocratic standard. It is even more relevant by the

Christian standard. And here, as Paul makes clear, it goes far beyond a matter of right behaviour and reliability before people. It relates to how we stand before God, before the Lord Jesus at his coming. By God's grace it is made a reality in us if we trust him. His integrity is beyond question.

> Lord, keep me in soul and mind and body in spotless integrity until the coming of our Lord Jesus Christ.

Further reading: 1 Thes 5:12-24.

RRW

July 13

Melchizedek

Then Melchizedek king of Salem brought out bread and wine. He was priest of God Most High, and he blessed Abram, saying, 'Blessed be Abram by God Most High, Creator of heaven and earth'. Genesis 14:18-19 (NIV)

The writer to the Hebrews tells us that this mysterious figure was 'made like unto the Son of God' (Heb 7:3 AV), and that Christ 'is a Priest for ever after the order of Melchizedek' (Heb 5:6 AV). He implies that the way Melchizedek helped Abraham is a model of how our Great High Priest would operate with us.

In the incident involving Melchizedek, in Genesis 14, we read that Abraham, having rescued Lot and others, and having recovered all their goods, was about to meet the king of Sodom, a crass, evil and perverted materialist. This is to be a crucial event — a confrontation between a pilgrim, seeking the government of God is his life, and a 'prince of this world'. Suddenly, 'out of the blue' Melchizedek interposes himself, and prepares Abraham. How? ... By giving him a set of do's and don'ts relevant to his meeting with Sodom? No! By teaching him about God, 'The most High ... Possessor of heaven and earth'. Abraham could well have protested and demanded advice as to how to cope with his immediate problem — a crowd of hungry refugees! But Abraham learnt well, and the next day, in answer to Sodom's offer of a 'dirty deal', he repeats what Melchizedek has taught him, and goes on to apply it to his immediate situation (vv 22, 23): 'God is The Most High, and it is to him and not to you, king of Sodom, that I am accountable. Moreover, he is the Possessor of all these things, and therefore I will accept no deal with you: I will put myself under no obligation to you.'

So the Lord would teach us. Answers to our problems seldom come straight from Scripture. Rather a principle is there which has to be worked out in practice under the leading of his Spirit. Let us study and absorb these principles of Scripture, however dry and irrelevant they may seem at the time — tomorrow they may suddenly become crucially relevant. 'Study' said Darby, 'till your very blood be Bibline!'

Ultimately however, the Truth is a Person, 'I am the Truth' (Jn 14:6). It is not just 'I am truthful and dependable', nor even simply 'I bring you truth you would otherwise not know', but rather 'Learn of Me, My Person, My Nature, My Character — and then work out the implications day by day, situation by situation'.

Put on the Lord Jesus Christ... the truth is in Jesus.

Rom 13:14, Eph 4:21

Further reading: Gn 14:16-23.

PCE

July 14

Confidence

For the spirit that God gave us is no craven spirit, but one to inspire strength, love, and self-discipline. 2 Timothy 1:7 (NEB)

Christians have no need to be afraid. Knowledge of our sin need not sap our confidence: we are to be confident not in ourselves but in God. The Christian way is not negative; it is positive with positive virtues.

At the beginning of another day, let us ask God that we may be bold in his service. It needs courage to witness to Christ in a secular environment. It needs faith to trust God for our capacity to cope with the problems which will arise.

God's Spirit gives us strength. This strength is not for ourselves but that we may serve others. Our patients often feel bereft of strength, physical, mental or spiritual. Let us seek to strengthen others through the strength which God gives us.

God's Spirit inspires love. Our patients need all the knowledge, skill and experience we can give. The aim of a Christian must be to practise first-class medicine in a spirit of love — genuinely seeking the welfare of our patients, regarding them all as people who matter, going out of our way to help them in every way possible.

God's Spirit inspires self-discipline. Life tends to be very busy, demands are made upon us from every side. We need self-discipline to organise our lives, so that we use our time effectively. We need self-discipline to overcome bad habits which so easily enslave us.

Let us pray for that gift of God, the Spirit who can empower us, fill us with love and give us control over ourselves.

> Gracious Spirit, dwell with me!
>   I myself would gracious be,
> And with words that help and heal
>   Would thy life in mind reveal,
> And with actions bold and meek
>   Would for Christ my Saviour speak.

T T Lynch

Further reading: Gal 5:22-24. 2 Pet 1:2-8.

JEL-J

July 15

What is Enough?

There is great gain in godliness with contentment. 1 Timothy 6:6

God promises that the needs of his children will be met. But wants have a habit of becoming needs, and luxuries necessities. It may well be right to have a life-style commensurate with our professional status. It is right and responsible to make provision for our dependents (1 Tim 5:8), but hoarding 'to be on the safe side' can insidiously grow out of all proportion; as Dr John White observes, we say that we only want enough, yet with the years enough is constantly redefined.

'Money is not evil but dangerous.' 'The rich fool was not a fool for harvesting abundant crops. He was a fool for letting his crops fill his horizon and determine his life-style' (*The Golden Cow*, John White). The preacher of Ecclesiastes certainly knew about its dangers. The problems of plenty are as great as those of want (Ec 5:10-16). Money accumulating in the bank is no good to anyone (v11), and hoarding only damages the hoarder (v13). The more we have the more we want (v10). Priding ourselves on our pious disregard of 'terms and conditions', we are only too glad if others negotiate them favourably for us. The more we have the more we find to spend it on (v11) — a sort of 'Parkinson's law' — and wealth, far from easing our worries often robs us of our peace (v12).

What a tragedy if, in seeking financial security for ourselves and our families, we rob our children of the chance to prove the faithfulness of God on whom we profess to be dependent.

Should we then despise money? Should we get rid of it all as evil? As a relatively well paid profession we cannot opt out of our stewardship. God has infinite resources, but he usually dispenses them via the Christian pocket. Perhaps some in missionary service can hardly be said to have enough! It is a salutary exercise to keep account for one week of money spent for ourselves and that spent for God.

> Lord, who has given us richly all things to enjoy, touch and control our pockets as well as our hearts, so that our commitment to you may involve all that we have as well as all that we are.

Further reading: 1 Tim 6:17-21.

MC

July 16

Luke (1) — Physician

Luke the beloved physician and Demas greet you. Colossians 4:14

So wrote the apostle Paul from his Roman prison, of one of his closest friends and, so it would seem, his personal physician. It was a strange and wonderful adventure that the Greek doctor, Luke, had got caught up in — travelling the then-known world with one of history's most dynamic men 'to testify to the gospel of the grace of God' (Acts 20:24).

It would have been no easy assignment. Paul would have been no easy patient. What Paul's physical ailments were is a matter only of speculation. Many people have opted for some serious eye trouble. Some sceptics have suggested that he was epileptic because of what happened on the Damascus Road. Others suggest that he had malaria, and so on.

However that may be, Paul undoubtedly drove himself hard. Luke may well have had the doubly difficult task of keeping up with Paul and, at the same time, of trying to get him to put the brakes on. What we do know, however, is that to Paul Luke was 'the beloved physician'.

How good a physician might Luke have been? By his day much of the glory had faded from the Greek medicine identified with Hippocrates and his school — beyond question the finest medicine of all the ancient world. It may be that some of its quality lingered on to touch the knowledge and standards of this Greek doctor. Was this one of God's provisions to sustain Paul in his enormous task? How well could one of us have done the job? Would we have earned, like Luke, the title 'the beloved physician'?

> Lord, wherever you put me in life, help me to use my knowledge and skill well, to maintain standards that please you and try to be, like Luke, a beloved physician.

Further reading: Acts 20:17-27.

RRW

July 17

Luke (2) — Worker for God

Epaphras, my fellow prisoner in Christ Jesus, sends greetings to you, and so do Mark, Aristarchus, Demas and Luke, my fellow workers. Philemon 24

The apostle Paul never minced words. When he listed Luke among his fellow workers, it had to mean a great deal. Paul scoured land and sea in a far harsher world than most of us know today to do the work of Christ, whom he had just as relentlessly persecuted in the days of his blindness. Luke was with Paul (sometimes his only companion) on many of his travels and shared in many of his hardships.

The 'we' passages in Luke's book *The Acts of the Apostles* record his accompanying Paul on that important visit to Macedonia. A case can be made for identifying Luke with the 'man of Macedonia' in Paul's vision (Acts 16:9). The 'we' passage ceases when Paul and Silas leave Philippi (was that Luke's home town?) and resumes when Paul returns to Philippi (Acts 20:6). Then Luke remains with Paul in his journeying, through the fracas in Jerusalem, the appeal to Caesar and the voyage to Rome, including the shipwreck at Malta.

The whole tone of Luke's account, as well as specific phrases (such as Acts 16:10), make it clear that Luke was not just a medical camp follower or even only a faithful friend, but was part of the gospel team. He does not tell us, but we can well imagine, that the care of the beloved physician not only kept Paul going, but helped to open hearts to the message of the Great Physician, in which Luke was counted a fellow worker.

> Lord, grant that medical work, including my own, may be the means of opening hearts to the knowledge and acceptance of the love of God in Christ.

Further reading: Acts 16:6-15.

RRW

July 18

Luke (3) — Reliable Friend

Luke alone is with me. 2 Timothy 4:11

All three of Paul's references to Luke are in letters written from prison in Rome. But this is the most poignant of them. In the other letters Luke was mentioned as part of a group with the apostle. Now it is only Luke. For

211

good or poor reasons, the others have all gone. Clearly Luke was not one to run out on his patients.

G B Caird, in his Pelican commentary on Luke's Gospel, has well said of Luke: 'He was more interested in people than in ideas. He had a lively social conscience and an inexhaustible sympathy for other people's troubles.' What a fine and challenging description of a doctor! Luke was like his Master, Jesus. And like his Master, he did not leave his patients at a time when he was most needed, even though things were awkward.

Do we know such times? When a patient is being particularly trying, but is really crying out silently but desperately for help? When there seems to be 'nothing more to be done' from a curative point of view for the dying patient — who still needs help to cope, whether medical, psychological, spiritual or just personal? When a patient's relatives are sorely needing the support and understanding that may not seem to be 'part of our job'? What would Luke have done?

> Lord, help us to be reliable and faithful to our patients and
> to others who need us. Help us to be willing to give our love
> as well as medicine, to give ourselves as well as our skills.

Further reading: Acts 28:11-31.

RRW

July 19

Luke (4) — Evangelist

... it seemed good to me... having followed all things closely for some time past, to write an orderly account... Luke 1:3

It is an eye-opener for us, having noted what the apostle Paul had to say about Luke, to look back at his Gospel. There are no 'we' passages here, as in the Acts, but Luke unconsciously tells us much about himself as he writes faithfully about his Lord — and indeed, many times he does call Jesus, 'Lord'.

The opening words addressed to Theophilus surely show Hippocratic influence. Extant writings of the Hippocratic school contain case histories which indicate that the recording physician had 'followed all things closely' and had set himself 'to write an orderly account' — a characteristic approach of the Hippocratic school unmatched in the ancient world.

The medical flavour in Luke's writing continues to come through as the narrative develops. To whom but an understanding physician would Mary have confided the details (recorded nowhere else) of Jesus' conception and birth and childhood? Our Lord's acts of healing are closely followed, often with special attention to detail and a real feeling for the compassion which was so essentially a part of the Lord Jesus' ministry. Is it strange that Luke was the one to record the parables of the Good Samaritan and the Prodigal Son? Or that women and children have a sympathetic place in his story? To Luke, Jesus was clearly both Lord and Saviour, and his mind and heart were his Lord's.

> Thank you, Lord, for the example of doctors like Luke, who confessed you as Lord, trusted you as Saviour and loved you as Master and Friend — and who for your sake truly loved their neighbours. Help me to follow in their train.

Further reading: Lk 1:1-4.

RRW

July 20

Whose Wisdom?

The foolishness of God is wiser than men. 1 Corinthians 1:25

There exists in many doctors' lives a very real, but often undetected, dichotomy between their faith and their medical practice. It is not that the two are totally unrelated; indeed most Christian doctors would acknowledge that it is for their Saviour's sake that they endeavour to treat their patients as people and not just as cases. This is of course much to be encouraged, but how many of us allow the Lord to play an even more integral part in our working lives? After six or more years of painstaking scientific training in recognising clinical signs and logically working through differential diagnosis it is far from easy to allow God access where we have been taught to 'walk by sight'.

This is well illustrated by a consultation I had recently with a middle-aged woman who was complaining of a variety of abdominal symptoms. As I was mentally running through a list of what my training had taught me it could be, I felt the Lord say in the still small voice with which he speaks to us, that this patient's symptoms were stemming from her central problem of loneliness. A few careful questions confirmed this to be the case, and the consultation which might otherwise have ended in a request for a barium meal led instead to appropriate counsel.

This kind of thing does not happen very often, and I am certainly not suggesting that Christians should not bother to acquire the highest possible standards of knowledge and skill in their particular discipline — an incompetent doctor brings no honour to Christ's name. However, if our human ability and knowledge exclude the Lord from intervening in our routine work in this direct way, then we and our patients will be the losers. We should not only share our human ability but also speak the wisdom that is taught by the Spirit.

'Whatever you get, get insight.'

Pr 4:7

Further reading: 1 Cor 1:26-31. Pr 2:1-9.

TGS

July 21

Forgiving Others

And forgive us... as we also have forgiven... Matthew 6:12

The readiness to forgive those who have wronged us is a fundamental part of Jesus' teaching about our own forgiveness, as we see from those words in the Lord's Prayer. It is brought out vividly in the parable about the servant who owed the king 'millions of pounds' which he could not pay (Mt 18:21-35 GNB). When the king ordered him to be sold into slavery, he begged for time to pay.

'The king felt sorry for him so he forgave him the debt and let him go. The man went out and met one of his fellow-servants who owed him a few pounds. He grabbed him and started choking him. "Pay back what you owe me!"... he had him thrown into jail until he should pay the debt... So the king called the servant in. "You worthless slave!" he said. "I forgave you the whole amount you owed me, just because you asked me to. You should have had mercy on your fellow-servant, just as I had mercy on you."'

This parable is couched in harsh terms, merely to emphasise the importance of this aspect of our Christian work. Our forgiveness cost the Lord Jesus everything: compared with that any forgiveness we may offer is cheap, yet by withholding it we dishonour our Saviour before our fellows.

The principle can arise quite subtly in the most everyday happenings, so we need to be on our guard. Simple examples in hospital life readily come to mind. Duty rotas inevitably result in 'our' patients being treated by other doctors. How easily we resent their mistakes or omissions, perhaps forgetting the problems associated with unfamiliar patients, to which we are equally vulnerable — and forgetting our own wish to be forgiven in comparable circumstances. Rotas also have a tendency to be 'unfair'. Should we always expect our exact ration of off-duty — and want to blame someone if we do not get it? We can all think of more examples of 'forgive as forgiven'.

Lord, as I have been forgiven by so great a sacrifice, grant me a forgiving spirit, not grudging, but willing to make sacrifices.

Further reading: Mt 6:12-15, 18:21-35. Col 3:12-13.

PDC

July 22

Housedog or Hound of the Lord

As it is, there are many parts, yet one body. The eye cannot say to the hand, 'I have no need of you', nor again the head to the feet, 'I have no need of you'...But God has so composed the body, giving the greater honour to the inferior part, that there may be no discord in the body, but that the members may have the same care for one another. 1 Corinthians 12:20-21, 24-25

'For a long time he lived in the toy cupboard or on the nursery floor, and no one thought very much about him. He was naturally shy, and being only made of velveteen, some of the more expensive toys quite snubbed him. The mechanical toys were very superior, and looked down upon everyone else; they were full of modern ideas, and pretended they were real. The model boat, who had lived through two seasons and lost most of his paint, caught the tone from them and never missed an opportunity of referring to his rigging in technical terms. The Rabbit could not claim to be a model of anything, for he didn't know that real rabbits existed; he thought they were all stuffed with sawdust, like himself, and he understood that sawdust was quite out-of-date and should never be mentioned in modern circles.' (*The Velveteen Rabbit* by Margery Williams).*

Two Senior House Officers were overheard discussing the rota for January. 'Has your houseman had his holidays yet?' asked one. 'No, he's taking the last two weeks, but it doesn't make any difference if he's there or not', was the reply. Medicine is full of people competing with each other. The sad thing is that there are very few who are outstandingly better than the rest. As jobs become scarce, the competition hots up, and the struggle to be noticed intensifies. How easy it is then to try to boost a dented ego by little remarks which diminish our colleagues. How shoddy! The Rabbit was no worse — and no better — than the other toys. His contribution in the nursery was important, and could no more be fulfilled by the others than he could fulfil theirs. But while we can laugh at the toys, it is somehow harder to see that we are subject to the same emotions.

Perhaps it is really about acceptance. If I know that I am important to someone, that I am loved, then I do not need to seek respect from others. But I have to believe that I am lovable. I need to be reminded that, for the

Christian, real acceptance comes in remembering that knowing me, God loves me. Nothing hidden, nothing earned. I don't need modern ideas, or complicated rigging to impress God. Knowing the right words or having the right connections doesn't matter.

To think about: 'What impresses me?'

Further reading: Zp 3:16-18. Lk 7:36-50.

PIMA

July 23

The Mastery of Time — but who is Master?

For everything there is a season, and a time for every matter under heaven.
Ecclesiastes 3:1

The writer of Ecclesiastes speaks powerfully and sometimes uncomfortably to our generation, but was he ever a houseman? There just isn't time to examine all the patients, no time to see relatives; I never get my half-day and ... there goes the bleep again! We soon lose the excitement of qualifying as we battle with tiredness and the disillusionment of finding how much of medicine is routine. I wonder if all the housemen feel themselves to be a combination of clerk and phlebotomist! And what about time for Christian witness as we find there are — three 'chest pains' in casualty and no beds, the consultant's round going on and the drip we've just put up leaking into the tissue? How can we be expected to obey Paul's injunction to 'let your speech be always gracious' (Col 4:6)?

The philosopher is right though, there is a time for everything, including the trivia of house jobs. Never again does the opportunity come to be so involved in the day-to-day care of patients. The satisfaction of mastering new techniques and seeing patients respond to treatment is not so fresh and thrilling as we become more senior. Perhaps it is never again quite so easy to share with patients, relatives and nurses the Christian hope that is ours.

None of this disguises the fact that the pre-registration year is a testing time; yet here is the chance to lay down the pattern for our own future medical practice, to learn to discriminate between important and unimportant, to get priorities right, to find that speed sometimes matters more than perfection, and that it is possible to do what is right at the wrong time.

Above all we must take time for fellowship with God and with other Christians, in hospital and church, and to stimulate our spiritual growth by Christian reading. Impossible? Not if we look to him who assures us there is time for everything — that is, everything that he wants us to do.

> Lord, help me today to discern what to do and garrison my
> heart with your peace as I do it.

Further reading: Ec 3:1-10. Col 3:22-24.

PMC

July 24

Battle for the Mind

Do not be conformed to this world but be transformed by the renewal of your mind, that you may prove what is the will of God, what is good and acceptable and perfect. Romans 12:2

The pattern of this world has an insidious influence, and we are here told to stand out from it. The secret of being different is clearly stated. It does not lie in our feverish activity of self reform, but it starts with the renewing of our mind. Our thoughts are not God's thoughts, and our whole outlook needs changing. Everything else will follow. Attitudes determine action, and beliefs behaviour. This renewing of the mind is something that God alone can do, but we are instructed not only to allow him to do it but to co-operate with him by the 'direction' of our thinking — the 'set' of our minds (Rom 8:5-6).

Think over today and meditate on what a renewed mind — the mind of Christ (1 Cor 2:16) should have been thinking about; whatever is true, honourable, just, pure, lovely, gracious, excellent and worthy of praise (Phil 4:8). Has my thinking today slipped into any of the following categories?

> The selfishness that puts my career above God's demands.
> The laziness which means that I did not do my utmost for
>   the patient today.
> The mental dirt I allowed to accumulate.
> The way I have allowed the world to condition what I think
>   of others.
> The materialism implicit in my life-style.
> The needless anxiety I have felt about my daily needs
>   when God has said he will care for them.
> My unavailability to those who need me.
> The set of my mind on earthly things.

> > May the mind of Christ my Saviour
> > Live in me from day to day,

By his love and power controlling
All I do and say.

Katie Barclay Wilkinson

O Lord, my thoughts are so difficult to control, and it is easy to be discouraged when I realise how often my thinking reflects the world's viewpoint instead of yours. Cleanse the thoughts of my heart and mind today, and help me to bring into captivity every thought to the obedience of Christ.

Further reading: Col 3:1-3. Eph 4:17-32.

TAG

July 25

Wanting to Pray

... one of his disciples said to him 'Lord, teach us to pray... Luke 11:1

Here was a straight request from a disciple, who was by inference ('teach us') speaking for others. They wanted to pray. So they turned for guidance to their Master. They knew he prayed. They also wanted to pray.

How often do we really want to pray? In an emergency, yes. But what about it at other times? Is it just a duty, even a chore? Do we then pray perfunctorily, our minds half on something else? Do we just 'say our prayers'? Sometimes (too often) it is like that with me. But last night I was praying about many things when I suddenly found I just wanted to say — and did say: 'Thank you, Lord, for letting me pray. It is so good just to pray. To talk to you.'

Why don't I always feel like that? Many reasons why, I suppose: laziness, pre-occupation with other things (not least with myself), not in real touch with God...and ultimately being too stupid to know what is good for me and to get it into my head and heart that Almighty God wants me to call him 'Father' and to talk things over with him.

There is really so much to talk about with our heavenly Father, different things in each of our own lives and in the lives of others: personal needs of people (patients are people, family and friends are people, critics and enemies [if we have any] are people), problems, hopes, things enjoyed, disappointments, achievements, failures. And, yes, sins to be confessed. And gratitude to be expressed. Many many things. Make up your own list. And above all God's presence with us and his love shown to us in Christ, with all that it means and should draw out from us in adoration. The little gem of a prayer that he taught his disciples says so much of this in beautiful miniature.

Lord, teach us to pray... and help us to want to pray.

Further reading: Lk 11:1-4. Mt 6:9-13.

RRW

July 26

Pause for Thought

Whatever you do, work at it with all your heart, as working for the Lord, not for men. Colossians 3:23 (NIV)

This is no new principle to a follower of the Lord Jesus. Tiredness can, however, weaken the strongest will. My experience of being jolted awake by the jarring sound of a bleep, after perhaps just having fallen asleep, is by no means unique. Maybe my reaction, on finding that I had to go down to casualty to attend to what I may have regarded as an unnecessary or irritating call, is also echoed in your experience. However 'hard done by' I felt, I did also realise as I thought about the matter that these were the most testing times for me as a Christian.

My tiredness inclined me to feel angry and resentful. But there was a part of me, a small but strident voice against the inner screams of indignation, that asserted and desired deeply the Spirit-given qualities of kindness, patience and self-control.

It does make a difference to reflect on whom you serve, so that you may 'work at it with all your heart'. It wasn't infrequently that I had reason to be thankful that it took me five minutes to walk from my room to casualty.

Father, forgive me that I often forget whom I serve, and that my behaviour doesn't always match up to what I profess. Write these words of yours on my heart that I may remember them in times of tiredness, and characterise my life by the fruit of your Spirit.

Further reading: Col 3:22-24. Eph 6:5-8. Gal 5:22-25. Jas 3:17-18.

JSdeC

July 27

Inasmuch...

Is not this the fast that I choose? Is it not to share your bread with the hungry and bring the homeless poor into your house ...? Isaiah 58:6-7

The King will answer them, 'As you did it to one of the least of these my brethren you did it to me'. Matthew 25:40

Astrid was the eighteen-year-old twin sister of my patient Edna. Orphans, they were homeless, jobless and sick, Astrid with an undiagnosed kidney disease, and Edna a psychiatric outpatient with a personality problem. Her illness and the emotional trauma of separation from her mother made Astrid remote and withdrawn, with an acute reactive depression exacerbated by her sister's rudeness and neglect, and fear of hospitalisation.

I asked Edna to bring her. She 'dumped' Astrid on me, rolling in pain, but refusing investigation and admission. She made my office her home, and I changed my routine to sleep with her, seeing patients elsewhere. Gradually she began to regard me as a friend, and through a therapeutic and prayerful relationship, her depression lifted and she agreed to an intravenous pyelogram as an outpatient. Finally a Christian family took her into their home, in return for help in the house.

After two days she failed to return after an outpatient visit. We could not find her. Three days later Edna's friends saw her lying unkempt and dirty in Luneta Park. She did not recognise them, and Edna, to my annoyance, would not fetch her.

That evening I became worried. Astrid was oliguric, haematuric, and dysuric with left loin pain. Was she developing metabolic encephalopathy? I prayed, and God spoke to me through Matthew 25:40. How much did I really care? and for whom? I decided to look for her myself together with a Christian third year medical student. We asked everyone we met, called at police stations and searched fruitlessly for hours in the park. We had to 'call it a day' and committed Astrid to God.

Next day Astrid was at the hospital gate untidy and withdrawn but refusing admission. Patiently and firmly, unhelped by Edna, I persuaded her to come in and again my office became her home. There she attended Bible studies I and my co-residents held. She finally agreed to proper investigation and treatment.

> Lord God, help me to know and to trust the fact that you honour and answer persistent, prevailing prayer.

Further reading: Lk 11:5-13, 18:1-8a.

ME

July 28

Still Waters Run Deep

Be still and know that I am God; I will be exalted among the nations.
Psalm 46:10 (NIV)

Medicine can easily consume all our waking hours, and probably nowhere more so than during housejobs. The new responsibility, the volume of work, perhaps not being able to get away from hospital during off duty hours because the residency is in the hospital — all these things contribute to make it difficult to take time off, mentally and physically.

Life becomes busy, full and tiring. It's a very stark contrast to be asked to 'be still'. For one thing, it can be surprisingly difficult to be still after being busy. I'm often reminded of Elijah in this context, in his severe depression after being God's champion on Mount Carmel.

He needed spiritual and physical refreshment, both of which God provided. But God really touched the heart of Elijah's need, not in the obvious power and noise of earthquake or fire, but in a still, small voice — just, I think, what he did not expect after God's mighty demonstration of power on Carmel.

It's hard to be still amid a busy schedule, and we shall always have the temptation of other things to occupy us. God wants to and does speak to us when we are still — give him time to; he alone, by allowing us to experience and know him, can give our lives the perspective they need.

> Father, don't let me be so swamped with a busy schedule that emptiness and depression characterise my inner life. Refresh me and assure me of your strength, as you let me know you in stillness. Let me hear your still, small voice daily.

Further reading: 1 Ki 19:1-13. Is 40:28-31.

JSdeC

July 29

Changes in Sexual Points of View

... for in Christ Jesus you are all sons of God through faith. There is neither Jew nor Greek, there is neither slave nor free, there is neither male nor female; for you are all one in Christ Jesus. Galatians 3:26, 28

'When we were young, if a boy caused a girl to be pregnant, it was a disaster for him. There was just no way out of the situation.' So remarked a colleague who studied medicine at the same time as myself, 25 years ago. He blames the contraceptive pill for a vast social change. As he went on to explain; nowadays, if a girl becomes pregnant, it is regarded by most people as being her own fault, because she was not taking 'the pill'. So the male partner very often feels no responsibility towards her.

My doctor friend also remarked that he had observed that many young women were very aggressive in their pursuit of boy friends today. This is in sharp contrast to the situation which prevailed when we were young. In those days the girl would wait to be asked out by the young man. My friend blames the pill for this change also. He pointed out that, while taking the pill, girls felt safe from the main consequence of casual sex (omitting VD) and so were out to gratify their desires and sense of conquest.

The above is not the only reason for change in this area. Thanks to the feminist movement, many young people are confused about sexual roles, and many women wish to act like men. However, the Bible does not teach that women are inferior to men — rather that they are equal, yet different. Different they are, too — physically, functionally, physiologically and even spiritually at times, and yet 'before the cross the ground is level'.

Another reason for change in sexual patterns of young people is the propaganda and pressure of the 'permissive society'. The prevailing climate of opinion on a subject has a tremendous impact for good or ill on individuals. Only a spiritual revival can help to change it in our day and in our nation. Let it begin with you and me.

> Grant to us, Lord, a right view of the value of people and a right perspective on human relationships. And help us to share this with others, especially our patients, with sympathy and understanding.

Further reading: 1 Cor 6:9-20. Col 3:5-10.

DAB

July 30

Perspective on People

And he said to her, 'Daughter...' Mark 5:34

Jesus was on his way to the house of Jairus, the supervisor of the synagogue, whose 12-year-old daughter was dying.

A woman with gynaecological bleeding for those same 12 years — an outcast economically, socially and religiously because of her disease — saw hope in Jesus passing by and tried to grasp only the hem of the garment he wore... and was healed.

The woman was alone, unnamed, outcast, unwanted, suffering, poor and (of all medical specialties) gynaecological. She should not have been there. Jesus healed her, but not without cost. He realised that power had left him. Our greatest work is that which costs us most. This gives a greater sense of achievement.

Jesus brought her onto the centre stage. So often we tend to keep such people out of the centre — reserving that for the prominent, the financially rewarding, the attractive or the politically appropriate.

She was unnamed, but Jesus went past naming her. In the family we sometimes use terms of endearment that are even more expressive than a name. Jesus used such a word here — the same word Jairus used (v23) for his only child. Jesus took her from being an outcast to the point of belonging, not only in the crowd, but in the inner family.

We are concerned with numbers of people in medicine, with attempts at solving overall problems. In so doing we lose sight of the individual, especially those of no account, when to work with such people would cost us something. Jesus made her the focus of his attention and his care. The rich, religious, politically aware, suffering Jairus just had to wait — for an outcast.

> Teach us, Lord, that people of no account are really of great account in your order of things. Help us to have your perspective in all our contact with people.

Further reading: Mk 5:21-35.

LS

July 31

Chosen... For What?

You are a chosen people, a royal priesthood, a holy nation, a people belonging to God, that you may declare the praises of him who called you out of darkness into his wonderful light. 1 Peter 2:9 (NIV)

One of the most frustrating things about being a houseman is that you so often feel like a small, impersonal cog in an immense impersonal machine, just a 'pair of hands' to fill up forms, and do repetitive procedures. This can be frustrating and threatening to your sense of identity, both as a doctor and as a child of God.

Peter reminds us that as Christians we have been individually chosen by God (1 Pet 2:9) and Paul adds that this choice 'was made in Christ before the creation of the world' (Eph 1:4). We are each therefore of importance to our Creator himself. He is personally concerned with our welfare and

...estiny. What a privilege is ours! To realise it is to find the cure for feeling insignificant and of little consequence in the vast hospital complex.

But we need to notice, too, God's purpose in choosing us. It is 'that you may declare ('show forth' AV) the praise of him who called you out of darkness into his wonderful light'. We declare his praises not only by what we say about him, but by the people that we are, the things that we do and the way we do them. 'Live such good lives among the pagans that they may see your good deeds and glorify God' (1 Pet 2:12).

As we draw on his resources through the lifeline of prayer and reading his word, he will show forth his character in us even in the most unpromising situations, and we shall be 'to the praise of his glorious grace' (Eph 1:6).

> To him that chose us first
> Before the world began;
> To him that bore the curse
> To save rebellious man;
> To him that formed our hearts anew
> Is endless praise and glory due.

Isaac Watts

Further reading: Eph 1:1-14.

JHCM

August 1

Guidance

I am the true vine and my Father is the vinedresser. John 15:1

Just a few years ago, a small peach tree was planted at the home of my in-laws. My uncle, with a futuristic twinkle in his eyes, explained to me how each of the branches would grow. The following year, I watched as the tree was pruned. The branches, some barely more than twigs, were considered and selected. Some branches were left; others were removed. Now, after careful feeding and watering, the tree is large and productive. The sun is setting on a summer evening as I write this on an outdoor patio. The tree sits to my left with its lush green leaves shading branches heavy with ripening peaches. God has designed for us to be fruitful and productive as vines under his care. Even as the tree or the vine has its growth guided by the manipulation of the caretaker, so God wants to direct us. How can we discern his leading?

Solomon was a wise man, and he sought to share his wisdom with generations to follow. In the third chapter of his Proverbs, he passed on principles to instruct us in how to avail ourselves of God's guidance. He tells us, in verse 5, to trust in God fully. Certainly, our initial relationship with God was entered by faith, and it is by faith that we continue with him. We must believe that God does indeed know what is best for us and that he will, as he promised, reveal directions to us. Trust in God must be complete; it rules out the possibility of leaning on our own human understanding.

While trusting him as we're seeking guidance, we must also talk to God. 'Acknowledge him,' instructed Solomon. We should openly admit that it is God who is giving the directions. We should acknowledge God's presence in our daily lives. Whether we're making major career decisions or trivial choices, God is with us. He has promised that he will be with us always, and that we may abide in him. We should remain cognizant of his daily involvement in our lives.

Trusting in him and talking with him, we can then take from him. He will give us straight paths. We should accept them and walk in them. He will provide for us; we have the privilege of taking from him. As we delight in him, he will do his will.

Thus, Solomon has advised us — trusting in him, talking with him, and taking from him, we can enjoy clear direction and guidance from God. Like a healthy peach tree, we can grow and be productive in him.

He is like a tree planted by streams of water,
that yields its fruit in its season,
and its leaf does not wither;
and in all that he does, he prospers.

Ps 1:3

Further reading: Jn 15:1-14. Pr 3:5-6. Ps 137:4-5.

PRF

August 2

Possessions

When the young man heard this he went away sorrowful: for he had great possessions. Matthew 19:22

The evening service had greatly impressed me. It was about 'possessions'. All through the sermon I was suffering qualms of conscience because some of my possessions seemed very dear to me. I thought of some of my precious books about my favourite sport rugby, the piano which helps me to be creative, our comfortable home with all the necessities of life and more. I wondered if perhaps I could be partially excused because I share most of my possessions. Then the picture of my wardrobe flashed before my eyes. Those clothes were not really being shared: two summer suits, two winter suits, several pairs of casual trousers, about 15 pairs of shorts, 20 pairs of socks, and so on.

As I shook hands with the minister on my way out, I said: 'You touched me on a raw spot tonight'. He replied: 'After my mother's death father lived alone. He was a fine old Christian who lived as near to Christ's teaching as he possibly could. When God called him home, the family went to his house to dispose of his worldly possessions. There was only one suit, his Sunday suit, hanging in the wardrobe.'

It makes one think of the story of Jesus and the rich young ruler. Whether this is the pattern for every Christian's life is a matter of conscience before God, but it warrants a lot of honest thinking. And although the context of the hymn 'Rock of Ages' is different, two lines in it may well bear on keeping our perspective right in life and death:

Nothing in my hand I bring,
Simply to thy cross I cling.

Further reading: Mt 19:16-22.

ASW

August 3

The Way (8) — The Comradeship of the Way

Jesus said: A new commandment I give you: love one another. As I have loved you, so you must love one another. All men will know that you are my disciples, if you love one another. John 13:34-35 (NIV)

Here the Master set the pattern of love for those who follow the Way. Just before his death he prayed that those who believed in him might be one (Jn 17:11, 21). A deep comradeship with a special quality was the mark of his disciples. Do we have that mark?

Many others follow the Way. They know its joys, its difficulties, its challenges, its hopes, as we do. They trust in the same Saviour, acknowledge the same master, bear the same Name, are children of the same Father. They need our fellowship, as we need theirs. With individual differences, at the core we are one. Many practical implications emerge from Paul's development of the theme of the body of Christ. His delightful anatomical and physiological metaphors should appeal to us and are well worth pondering (see Further reading).

In a busy medical life we cannot always do things just as we wish. We certainly should belong to a church and join regularly in worshipping God in company with others. But we may need to get across (gently and tactfully, but still firmly) that for us involvement in too many church activities is just not on. Indeed, doing too many things, and perhaps not doing any of them well, does no honour to our Lord and is little help to others.

Christian fellowship between not only doctors but all involved in medical and health fields can be exciting, as those who have met colleagues from and in other parts of the world will know. They may see the pressures under which some live and work and the loneliness that they suffer. They may experience, as I have, the kindness and caring love they can show to a visitor. But whether or not we have any direct contact with them, we can pray for them and look for other ways of fostering the oneness in love that our Master wants us all to encourage and enjoy.

Recently a radio programme told of Australian soldiers working and dying on the infamous Burma-Thailand railway during World War II. Despite the surrounding horror more than one man died, the narrator said, 'with his head in a mate's lap and another mate holding his hand — dying in an atmosphere of love'. How far does our Christian fellowship measure up to that level of mateship?

Grant us grace, Lord, to love one another as you have loved us.

Further reading: Jn 13:12-17, 31-35, 15:12-17. Rom 12:3-5. 1 Cor 12:12-27. Eph 4:15-16.

RRW

August 4

The Discipline of Hardship

Endure hardship — like a good soldier of Jesus Christ. 2 Timothy 2:3 (NIV)

Few would deny that the pre-registration year involves hardship. Physical exhaustion, mental fatigue and emotional stress are all part and parcel of a houseman's lot. God's word encourages us to see this experience as valuable discipline under his almighty hand. If our faith has not been tested before it will be now. If we have never had problems organising our day (and which of us has not?), we will have now. If we have never been exposed to temptations to immorality, we will be when we are housemen. The rigours of hospital life can make all these things seem hardships for us as God's people, but we must see them rather as part of his sovereign purpose in our lives, and go to him for sustaining grace, not only to bear them but to profit by them. Let us notice that whatever the source of the pressures, it is his hand alone that mediates and uses them (Rom 8:28-29).

Soldiers who have never been exposed to stress in training will not survive real battle conditions. Similarly, we shall never be mature reliable Christians unless we have been through the training of God's discipline. The pre-registration year is an opportunity to grow under his hand. Certainly, as we read in Hebrews 12:11, it may seem unpleasant at the time, perhaps even painful. Later on, however, it produces a harvest of righteousness and peace to those who have been trained by it. We must play our part, in responding rightly to the opportunity, as God's adopted children, to benefit and grow from his discipline.

> When through fiery trials thy pathway shall lie,
> His grace all-sufficient shall be thy supply.
> The flame shall not hurt thee, his only design
> Thy dross to consume and thy gold to refine.

Rippon's Selection

Further reading: Rom 5:1-5. Heb 12:7-11.

JHCM

August 5

A Testimony or a Front? (1)

But understand this, that in the last days will come times of stress. 2 Timothy 3:1

We were in the anaesthetic room, and the consultant anaesthetist was explaining in his affable friendly way some of the special points about anaesthesia for cataract extraction — affable, that is, until he came to induce the patient, when in his haste, he pricked his finger quite badly on a 'butterfly' needle. Instantly his plastic smile vanished, and his face flushed angrily as he poured out a stream of cursing and four-letter words.

It was only a minor incident to be sure. But I remember it so well because it was the first of many later occasions when I saw the thin veneer behind which many doctors hide break down completely, and the anger and frustration of their true selves break through, often at the very slightest provocation. Their friendliness and apparent calm and control were in reality just a front.

How do we as Christians stand up to the test of stress? Do we have a real and vital day-to-day experience of the Holy Spirit making us more like Christ, or do we simply have a Christian facade? a form of godliness but denying the power thereof (2 Tim 3:5 AV)?

During the last week of my second housejob, one of the ward-clerks bidding me farewell said 'It's been so good working with you because you are always the same. You've never got to ask the nurses, "Is X in a good mood today?" You know you're always approachable.'

That deeply moved me, as I had no idea that she had been watching my life so closely. I gave thanks to God that to one person at least I had shown consistent testimony, and that this woman could see that Jesus really did make a difference in my life, and it wasn't just an act. It is my prayer that you too — albeit unconsciously — may show something of the constancy and love of the living Lord as you go about your work today.

> Lord, please deliver me from pretending to be what I am not. In the areas where you show me I am wrong, help me to turn to you for the strength to change, and not to be content with just glossing over them.

Further reading: Mt 12:35-37.

TGS

August 6

A Testimony or a Front? (2)

You shall receive power when the Holy Spirit has come upon you and you shall be my witnesses. Acts 1:8

I managed to stifle back the tears while on the ward. But as soon as I walked into the corridor, the dam broke, and I went quickly to my office to work it out of my system. I had grown to know Mr 'B' quite well over the months he was with us, and now suddenly he had died. Moreover, his was the ninth death on my ward that week. Though, when working on a cancer unit, one becomes accustomed to sudden death, this particular week had exacted a very heavy emotional toll. I could not suppress my feelings any longer, and I wept unashamedly. Was I wrong in that? There are many today who tell us that as Christians we should be above such things; that we should be perpetually-praising, constantly-clapping, unceasingly-smiling, 'Allelujah-all the way' ambassadors of the Gospel, with never a wrinkle on our brow. I am sure this attitude is a very distorted one, and Scripture teaches us that witness is more than skin-deep.

Jesus tells us that witness is not a technique to master or an act to perform, 'You shall be witnesses unto me', he told his disciples. We do not primarily bear witness to what a blessed state it is to be a Christian (though indeed it is!), but to Christ himself, and to what he means to us not only in our triumphs and joys, but in our pains and fears as well. As Prof John White writes in *The Fight*, 'You have nothing to hide. The truth itself is infinitely more powerful than the filtered version of the truth that your vanity might prefer.'

I know a young woman doctor, now a senior house officer in pathology, who as a medical student became a Christian through the power of such an unfiltered witness. A friend of hers (not a medic incidentally!) who had spoken many times about Christ, hit a very rough patch — her parents' marriage was on the rocks, and she herself had recently broken up with her boyfriend. As the parents' inevitable divorce eventually went through, the hurt was obvious and very deep. Yet as my friend expressed it, 'she held together. Her faith was unshaken and I could see that Jesus Christ was real in her whole being.' It wasn't just words.

Paul reminds us in 1 Corinthians 4:20 that the kingdom of God is not just a matter of talk but of power. May we know (as did those early disciples in Acts 1) the power of the Holy Spirit upon us in every aspect of our lives as we bear witness today to him.

> Since we have this treasure in earthen vessels to show that the transcendent power belongs to God and not to us (2 Cor 4:7), Lord, please may your power be present in me, your vessel today.

Further reading: Acts 1:6-11. 1 Cor 1:26-31. 2 Cor 12:9-10.

TGS

August 7

Biblical Case Histories (2) — Elijah's Depression Problem

'I have had enough, Lord' he said, 'Take my life'. 1 Kings 19:4 (NIV)

Elijah met his depression problems towards the end of his life. In his zeal for God, he had incurred the hatred of King Ahab's wicked queen, Jezebel. She swore to have him killed — and sent a messenger to tell him so. Jezebel did nothing by half measure.

The case record goes on:

Elijah was afraid and ran for his life. When he came to Beersheba in Judah, he left his servant there, while he himself went a day's journey into the desert. He came to a broom tree, and sat down under it and prayed that he might die. 'I have had enough, Lord', he said, 'Take my life; I am no better than my ancestors'. Then he lay down under the tree and fell asleep.

This was just the culminating event in a life for God that had been physically, mentally and spiritually demanding almost to the limit of human endurance. Elijah had had enough, as he said, and God treated him gently. There were some tasks still to be done, but God's resources were at hand. Food and water strengthened Elijah's body. A vision of the Lord himself renewed his spirit. He learnt that Elisha was to take over his work as prophet. So he was encouraged and enabled to do the rest of what God had for him to do. And he was taken up to heaven in a blaze of glory.

The experience of this great man of God was not unique. It would scarcely be said that his depression was any more than a natural reaction to a prolonged stressful experience. But it did get him down. And God gave him the help that he needed — just as our Lord found strength from his Father after the temptation in the wilderness and when he agonised in Gethsemane. The same Lord is with us to understand and help when things get us down, when we have had enough.

> Drop thy still dews of quietness,
>   Till all our strivings cease;
> Take from our souls the strain and stress,
>   And let our ordered lives confess
> The beauty of thy peace.

J G Whittier

Further reading: 1 Ki 19:1-9.

RRW

August 8

The Handless Christ

Behold my hands... Luke 24:39 (AV)

The story goes that during World War II a statue of Christ in a European village was knocked over. At the end of the war, when the villagers went to restore the statue, they discovered it fairly well intact, except for the hands. These were missing and could not be found. Rather than manufacture new hands, the people left the statue as it was.

Now a story like that just calls out to be used as a sermon illustration. In fact, that's where I heard it. The speaker said that Christ without hands was exactly as he is today. He went on to say that we are his hands, and that we must be responsible for doing his work in the world. To quote the old poem —

> He has no other hands than our hands
> He has no other feet than our feet...

Appealing, isn't it? Appealing — but wrong to the point of blasphemy. It appeals, I guess because it satisfied human pride to have it thought that we are somehow absolutely vital to God's purposes. We like the idea that he needs us. It appeals, too, because it cuts Christ down to size so to speak. It makes him more like us, and gives us a chance to use him. It is little wonder that God forbade the construction of images. They divert our attention from his inspired word and give us false ideas of ourselves.

The truth is, of course, that (to quote the Bible) 'all power on heaven and earth' has been given to Jesus Christ. By his word and by his Spirit he can and does accomplish whatever he pleases, with or without us. We are meant to worship him, not to compete with him. But, when we are perfectly clear about that point, we may also notice this stupendous truth. In his grace and mercy, Christ does use us to do his will. He does employ our puny efforts, in prayer, in service, in speaking, in doing, to accomplish his ends. But we are the servants, he is the Master.

> A handless Christ? God forbid!
> 'Jesus Christ is Lord' — that is the Christian Gospel.
> Grant me, Lord, the grace and the faith never to forget it.

Further reading: Mt 28:16-20, 8:5-13.

PJ

August 9

My Shepherd (8)

Thou preparest a table before me in the presence of mine enemies. Psalm 23:5

After the rigours of winter, livestock are taken up from the valleys to graze on lush tablelands. So, an Eastern shepherd will lead his flock from the valley onto higher ground, relieved to have survived, but needing time to relax and be refreshed. A good shepherd prepares the ground before taking his flock there. Selecting good pasture, he weeds out poisonous plants, clears waterholes and looks out for vipers or other predators. Harm can befall his sheep unless he remains watchful. Clearly, those who stay closest will be safest, for as they concentrate on grazing he will protect them from danger of which they are unaware. So lush is the pasture that for a time there will be no need for them to scatter as they graze in contented companionship, gladdening the shepherd's heart.

'Setting the table' or 'preparing a meal' bring to the word 'table' a sense of conviviality and sociability. After the hardships of the valley may come the literal pleasure of the table in a celebration dinner; others may prefer to feed the mind with music or an undisturbed good read. Either way, it is vital to retain closeness to the Shepherd if we are not to risk attack by more subtle hazards than those we meet in the valley. There we were forced to seek his aid, here we may feel able to cope on our own or allow the bliss of unwinding to take priority over our personal times with him.

Some Christians may give a wide berth to the mess party or the hospital show, as being 'worldly'. Others may feel that they provide opportunity to relax with, befriend and witness to colleagues. Whatever form of respite we enjoy take care that to be off duty is not also to be off guard. The Enemy is ever present and, particularly in the aftermath of battle, will try to beguile us away from the Shepherd into a place definitely not prepared for us. Yet equally he can come upon us suddenly and unexpectedly, even in the midst of a very 'holy huddle'. Destructive criticism, wrong appetites, professional jealousy, or loss of restraint — all these may poison us even in pastures or pastimes of apparent innocence. We shall in time each learn to know the secret weapon that he best likes to use for our personal defeat, but be it of the world or the flesh, it is all of the Devil. To beware of occupations or occasions which we have learned will invariably invite his attack is only common sense, but takes experience and vigilance. If we fail, how vital to return to the Shepherd in repentance, seeking his forgiveness quickly and renewing the closeness which we had learned so much about in the valley.

To meet with others around a table can be enjoyable. To meet at the Lord's own table is a reminder of his love and sacrifice for us, and an inspiration to remain in fellowship with him and with each other. By together maintaining a closer walk with our Shepherd, we shall all learn to be careful in checking where he has put clear warnings to 'keep off the grass' and come to avoid areas that he has not prepared and tables not set by him.

> Prone to wander — Lord, I feel it –
> Prone to leave the God I love;
> Here's my heart, O take and seal it,
> Seal it from thy courts above.

Robert Robinson

Further reading: 1 Ki 11:1-6. Ps 51:1-4, 10-12. 1 Jn 1:3-9.

JG

August 10

A Disciple, but Secretly

Joseph of Arimathea, who was a disciple of Jesus, but secretly, for fear of the Jews, asked Pilate that he might take away the body of Jesus... Nicodemus also, who had at first come to him by night, came... John 19:38-39

I have been interested and sometimes surprised to notice the number and kind of patients who, on admission, openly put a Bible on the bedside locker (incidentally a valuable point of contact). There must be many disciples of Jesus, but secretly, for fear. But what fear?

Is it the niggling, perhaps long suppressed unease about our standing before God — an uncertainty that springs not about the faithfulness of God but about the reality or otherwise of our belief in him, and whether our plea to know him as Saviour and Lord was made with an invitation sincere enough or a commitment complete enough; a fear enhanced by the paucity of the exuberance and assurance experienced by others; a fear that makes us say 'I hope I am a Christian, I try to be' rather than 'I am one!'? God bids us base our assurance on his finished work on the Cross, rather than on the adequacy or otherwise of our faith, and to lay hold with both hands, and unreserved dependence upon the gift of life already obtained for us (1 Tim 6:12. Heb 9:12).

Or is it the fear of what people might say or do that keeps us on the touchline? Nicodemus was set to lose the respect and good opinion of his colleagues, particularly the religious ones, who might well regard him as an odd fanatic. Joseph faced the loss of his honourable position, influence and respectability, maybe even his wealth and way of life.

Or is it the fear of what total involvement might cost in terms of what God himself might demand of us? Where might he ask us to go? What might he ask us to do? What might it mean in terms of future prospects for us and our families?

But Jesus never pressed them to confess him openly. He graciously welcomed Nicodemus at night and leisurely revealed the truth that he had never understood. There is no record of his meeting with Joseph. That is left to our imagination. But faith deepened and courage grew, until Nicodemus surprised himself when he demanded of the council a fair hearing for Jesus (Jn 7:48-52), while the councillor Joseph raised a lone dissident voice against the motion to crucify him (Lk 23:50-51).

But faith finally blossomed, Joseph threw all discretion to the winds and, risking the jeers of Jewry and the sneers of Rome, begged Pilate for the body of Jesus. His courage, as so often happens, brought Nicodemus out into the open, and together and with loving care they laid him in the tomb. What were their thoughts now? Were they conscious of the hostile crowd? or only aware that they had done all they could, but too late, to demonstrate their love? One thing is certain; it was the Cross that overcame their fear and made them see things in their real light.

And how did they feel on Easter morning?

Further reading: Jn 7:45-52, 19:38-42. Mt 10:32-33.

MC

August 11

Stones of Encouragement

These stones will remind the people of what the Lord has done. Joshua 4:6 (GNB)

For the first time for years I am facing the future. At school, it was relatively easy to decide to become a doctor. And once the decision was taken, I felt I had some influence over achieving it; if I worked hard enough, I should be successful. Since then I have been occupied with the mechanics of qualifying. Suddenly at the end of my pre-registration year, I am faced with deciding how best to use my skills, and I am surrounded by those whose priorities are influenced by their conviction that this life is all there is.

It is fine to look back — remembering the occasions before when I didn't know where to turn, or when my own well-laid plans went disastrously awry. At each crisis, God stepped in, teaching me to look to him for direction and to wait for his answer, reminding me that I am his servant now. Frequently he showed me that his thoughts are not our thoughts, neither are his ways our ways. And, in directing me to something quite beyond my own expectations, he showed me that my God was too small. These stones of remembrance endure; they not only encourage at the time, but also are intended for reminders to us and others in the future. The psalmist too knew the value of remembering God's past dealings with his people:

> Give thanks to the Lord, proclaim his greatness;
> Tell the nations what he has done.
> Sing praise to the Lord;
> Tell of the wonderful things he has done.
> Be glad that we belong to him;
> Let all who worship him rejoice,
> Go to the Lord for help, and worship him continually.
> You descendants of Abraham, his servant,
> You descendants of Jacob, the man he chose,
> Remember the miracles that God performed
> And the judgments that he gave.

Ps 105:1-6 (GNB)

Further reading: Jos 4:19-24.

PIMA

August 12

Where to Find Jesus

Were not our hearts burning within us while he talked with us on the road, and opened the Scriptures to us? Luke 24:32 (NIV)

The walk to Emmaus is a masterpiece of story-telling by Luke the physician. But if we look too closely at the human comments and reactions, we shall miss the whole point.

As they slowly walked home, two deeply disconsolate disciples were discussing the events surrounding the shameful and brutal death by crucifixion of Jesus of Nazareth. Why did he have to come to this awful end? Then, suddenly, the subject of their conversation quietly came up from behind and joined them — 'but they were kept from recognising him' (v16).

How easily in an instant, he could have shown himself, raised from the dead, gloriously alive. What a scoop if would have been for them! But no. He wanted to give them something far more valuable. He wanted to give them a secure foundation for a personal faith in him for all time.

He embarked on a Bible-study. He opened their eyes to truth which is hidden in the Scriptures. Beginning with Moses — the first five books —

he went right through to the end. All Scripture speaks of him and of God's purpose to call out a people for himself. He is there in the prophets and their challenge to right living. He is in the priestly offices which give us a picture of making atonement for sin. He is there in the kingly characters and the examples they gave.

Today, we have more. We have the very words of Jesus himself (as well as the apostles' interpretation of the meaning for us of his death and resurrection and ascension). His words are much better to us than any picture or photograph of him can ever be, better than any tokens or emblems of his presence, better than any system of government on any magical gifts which he might have bequeathed to us. His words tell us what is in his heart and mind.

If we want to find Jesus, he is there in the Bible when we come humbly, eagerly to it to read and meditate over it — and to listen.

Further reading: Lk 24:25-32, 44-48. Eph 1:15-23.

CGS

August 13

Alone or Lonely?

They were on the road, going up to Jerusalem, and Jesus was walking ahead of them; and they were amazed, and those who followed were afraid. Mark 10:32

Some of us are gregarious, some of us are loners. Given the choice, I should prefer a day bird-watching or hill-walking to being at an exuberant party or watching a football match! Whether we are sociable beings or not, working in a hospital can be a lonely pursuit. Although we may be on a crowded ward or part of an operating team, we can feel lonely if we lack colleagues or friends that we can share with.

However, loneliness and aloneness are not the same thing! Jesus could be alone with the Father as he prayed on a hillside and yet not feel lonely. On the road to Jerusalem his disciples shrank back from him in fear and puzzlement at this man who walked with steadfast face towards certain death; he was not alone, and yet it is likely that he felt a measure of loneliness. He said in another place, 'A time is coming and has come, when you will be scattered, each to his own home. You will leave me all alone'... humanly speaking very lonely, 'yet I am not alone, for my Father is with me' (Jn 16:32 NIV). But he endured supreme loneliness on the cross when he cried, 'My God, my God, why have you forsaken me?' Jesus knows about loneliness, as well as aloneness.

So whether you are a loner by nature or fond of company, whether you lack close companions or are surrounded by real friends, you can find strength for times of loneliness by recalling our Lord's promise, 'Surely I will be with you always, to the very end of the age' (Mt 28:20 NIV). You may, as a Christian, feel lonely from time to time, but you are never alone!

> Lord, thank you for enduring misunderstanding, betrayal, desertion and denial for me. Thank you for experiencing the horror of loneliness on the Cross. Help me when I feel lonely to know that I am never alone. Help me, in turn, to be a caring companion to others.

Further reading: Mk 10:32-34. Jn 16:25-33.

RFH

August 14

God and the Man Born Blind (1) — Why?

As Jesus passed by, he saw a man blind from his birth. And his disciples asked him, 'Rabbi, who sinned, this man or his parents, that he was born blind?' Jesus answered, 'It was not that this man sinned, or his parents, but that the works of God might be made manifest in him'. John 9:1-3

This is the opening of a thought-provoking story. Jesus restores both the physical and the spiritual sight of a man blind from birth and starts a raging controversy. The story itself raises more questions than it answers. But, as often happens, the absence of answers — or the giving of an answer that seems irrelevant — may be because the right question was not asked.

The disciples asked Jesus the wrong question based on a wrong premise. His answer was designed to put them back on the right track.

However, these words of Jesus have raised further questions in other people's minds ever since. A very good friend of mine, a medical colleague and a sincere Christian, has expressed puzzlement at them. He put it very bluntly: 'Is it fair that a man should have been born blind and remained blind to mature years just so that God could go on an ego trip?' This is blasphemous, some would say, or at best irreverent. But my friend is no blasphemer. He holds his faith the more dearly, I am sure, because (like Job) he thinks about it honestly.

The trouble, as I see it, is that he asks the wrong question. It is based on a wrong premise. By the nature of things, God just cannot 'go on an ego trip'. To use another piece of modern jargon, God cannot 'expand his ego'. His 'ego' is already infinite, eternal and absolute. 'In the beginning God...' says Genesis 1:1. The creation of the cosmos follows. When Moses asked

238

God what he should say if the people asked his name, the answer came (Ex 3:14) 'I AM WHO I AM... Say this to the people of Israel: "I AM has sent me to you"'. God is the Eternal First Person living in the Eternal Present Tense.

If one of us is called 'a great I am', it means that he is a poseur and a bore. It is not so with God. The Revelation to John sums it up:

> 'I am the Alpha and Omega,' says the Lord God,
> 'who is and who was and who is to come, the Almighty'.

Rev 1:8

This is no boast. This is the nature of things. We can do no less than join those who cast their crowns before the throne in heaven, singing:

> Worthy art thou, our Lord and God,
> to receive glory and honour and power,
> for thou didst create all things,
> and by thy will they existed and were created.

Rev 4:11

Further reading: Jn 9:1-41.

RRW

August 15

God and the Man Born Blind (2) — Is it fair?

Then the Lord answered Job out of the whirlwind: '... Will you even put me in the wrong? Will you condemn me that you may be justified?' Job 40:6, 8

What about the 'Is it fair?' part of my friend's question? It was the sort of question that Job asked God. And the conclusion of that story makes it clear that God respected Job's honesty and sincerity, while at the same time completely demolishing his arguments.

The response to my friend's question (or part of the response) is that again the question can be said to be irrelevant. God is sovereign, and that is that. And if our belief were only in a transcendent Almighty One, aloof and unheeding, we should have to stop there. Yet to many sincere people this just seems not to be enough.

Well, there is something more to say, a very big something, a breath-taking paradox. The God whose ego cannot be expanded can — and did — act in the opposite direction. God the Son put aside his glory and made himself of no reputation. He took the form of a servant and was made in human likeness. He humbled himself and became obedient to death — death on a cross (Phil 2:5-8). All this was to rescue lost mankind. God was in Christ reconciling the world to himself (2 Cor 5:19).

We may still not understand everything. But do we really need or want to ask any more questions? Job said (in effect): 'I give up. I haven't a leg to stand on'. And then came the positive bit, the transforming bit, which meant that Job was never the same again: 'I had heard of thee by the hearing of the ear, but now my eye sees thee' (Jb 42:5). Amy Carmichael, who served God for many years in India and was a long-time sufferer from physical pain and disability, has put it in another way: 'Thy Calvary stills all our questions'.

> Gracious God, help us to see you clearly and to know that you are not only a God of infinite power and might, but a God of infinite wisdom and love.

Further reading: 1 Jn 4:7-21.

RRW

August 16

True Humility

Humble yourselves before the Lord and he will exalt you. James 4:10

The Revelation to John, chapter 5, paints a vivid picture of the magnificence, greatness and worthiness of Jesus Christ. There he is exalted, seated at the right hand of God the Father, where he still bears the unhealed wounds of his crucifixion. 'Worthy is the Lamb that was slain to receive power, and riches, and wisdom, and strength, and honour, and glory, and blessing' (Rev 5:12 AV). Yet it was this same Jesus who completely humbled himself, and made himself of no reputation in the eyes of the world, becoming a slave to men, and dying a criminal's death (Phil 2:7-8).

As members of the medical profession we are given by society many privileges. We have benefited from educational opportunities and have financial security. People turn to us in their need and entrust us with the most intimate details of their lives. We are given the ability to heal and allay suffering. All this affords us considerable status in the world and enhances our feeling of self-worth. Yet God expects us to have Christ's humility. In our work self-righteousness, ambition and pride are tremendous stumbling blocks, and our hearts can easily be hardened by them. It is a dangerous path we walk. Satan offers us worldly success, reputation and comfort, and he often acts in a very subtle way to destroy our relationship with God. If we accept what he offers us, we are denying Christ and his perfect example. It is important to remember that righteousness comes from God alone on the basis of faith (Phil 3:9), and that only through faith in the living God will he exalt us.

> Lord Jesus, thank you for your life and sacrifice. Work in me, Lord, exposing any false pride or self-righteousness

that I may be clinging onto, and creating in me the same
humility that you displayed.

Further reading: Mt 23:2-12.

August 17

Whose Faithfulness?

He who calls you is faithful, and he will do it. 1 Thessalonians 5:24

The whole basis of our Christian life is faith. It is by the grace of God that we are saved through faith. It is the way the Christian should be walking from day to day, by faith not by sight. Christ himself, the ultimate goal, is both the Author and Finisher of our faith.

In the verse above we are reminded that it is because God is faithful that we can fully place our faith in him. We can completely trust ourselves to him when he calls us because he is trustworthy. Faithfulness is a constant divine characteristic upon which we can build our lives. He remains faithful even if we are faithless, for he cannot deny himself (2 Tim 2:13). He is the sovereign Lord who never changes. He is the same yesterday, today and forever (Heb 13:8). What a tremendous encouragement this is to us whose faith is so unstable!

In medical practice we are constantly subject to the pressures and strains of our work, we inevitably suffer overtiredness and mental as well as physical fatigue. Alongside our patients in the crises of life and death, we cannot divorce ourselves from their problems, their depression, anxiety or hopelessness, and like them we are subject to illness and changes of mood. Thank God that his faithfulness endures in spite of our feelings, and the rock on which we are building our lives is secure.

> Great is thy faithfulness, O God my Father,
> There is no shadow of turning with Thee;
> Thou changest not, Thy compassions they fail not;
> As Thou has been Thou for ever wilt be...
> Great is Thy faithfulness, Lord, unto me!

T O Chisholm

Lord, I believe, help thou my unbelief.

Further reading: Gal 3:1-9. Eph 2:4-10.

DPC

August 18

Being Cruel to be Kind

For the moment all discipline seems painful rather than pleasant; later it yields the peaceful fruit of righteousness to those who have been trained by it. Hebrews 12:11

No medical person needs to be told that sometimes we must be cruel to be kind. The days of surgery without anaesthesia and of nauseous drugs (remember castor oil?) are mercifully over. But most necessary surgery is still painful at some stage. The side effects of potent modern drugs must be weighed against their therapeutic value. A rigorous diet-exercise regime can be a sore trial to an over-weight patient. And so on. One must sometimes be cruel to be kind. It is a medical cliche.

In everyday life it is still a cliche. But like most cliches it is true enough — with some qualifications. It is never an excuse for deliberate and unwarranted cruelty, for the malicious gossip or the wielder of the poison-pen who, 'speaking as a friend', creates a havoc of suspicion or despair; for the sadistic parent who takes it out on his family 'for their own good'; for the lazy doctor who neglects his patients 'because it is not good to pander to their whims'.

The Bible has many examples of the sort of thing the writer of the letter to the Hebrews is talking about: merciful rebukes, salutary disciplines, inescapable judgments. God is loving and patient, long-suffering and of great goodness. But he is not an indulgent grandfather. His love is deeper and more constructive than that. So he allows and uses many circumstances and happenings as discipline. It is important to understand that discipline is not necessarily punishment. We do not have to feel guilty every time something goes wrong. But it is time to take stock. What has happened may be the result of our own foolishness, neglect or ignorance, but we should be listening for the warning bell. Often we can hear the voice of God speaking through the circumstances. And it may not be a voice of soft comfort. It will still be the voice of love.

> Thank you, Lord, that you care enough about me to discipline me. Help me to understand and co-operate.

Further reading: Heb 12:1-11. Rev 3:14-22.

RRW

August 19

Thirst

Jesus stood up and proclaimed, 'If any one thirst, let him come to me and drink'. John 7:37

The trouble with us, working in a temperate climate in a developed country, is that we rarely experience severe thirst. I recently travelled in the sparsely populated vast Chaco region of Paraguay with two companions. Even though one of them was a capable Indian guide, we lost our way, spent a night in the open, and for twenty- four hours had no water to drink. I understood thirst in a new way. The longing for a drink grew and grew until it dominated my mind. I didn't dare to think of water anymore as we travelled slowly on through the arid thorn scrub land. When at last we reached human habitation where we were given water, we eagerly drank cupful after cupful until the sensation of thirst began to ease off.

Jesus, as always, used a simple illustration of his own nature and of our need to come to him. 'When you are thirsty, come to me', he cried. Our problem is two-fold: usually we aren't thirsty, and, even if we are, we often go to the wrong water supply (Je 2:13). May I suggest that now, or at least some time today, we stop and switch out of the busy routine of the day long enough to think of Christ and of what life would be like without him. Let's remember that without him we should be totally lost and in chaos. Then let's beg him to fill us today and satisfy that thirst which only he can quench.

I'd like to suggest too that today you take a fresh look at the effects of shock or clinical dehydration on patients. Possibly today you will have the opportunity to watch the urgent rehydration of a patient. While he is still dehydrated, look at his dry tongue, his sunken eyes and his inelastic skin. Watch the way he breathes, and the restless anxious look on his face. Then, when he is rehydrated, check him again — what a difference! 'But', we might say, 'that difference is only because there is more water in him'. Precisely — but remember that he is meant to be well over 70% water!

So with us — Jesus has come into our lives, and unless he daily fills us and satisfies us we are spiritually dehydrated and in acute need. How tragic that our spiritual dehydration often escapes our notice! One thing is certain: if we thirst for Jesus and cry out to him with longing — even with desperation — he will satisfy us.

Lord Jesus, please make me thirsty for you, and then satisfy that thirst.

Further reading: Ps 63. Jn 4:1-14.

JT

August 20

Facts or Feelings

If any man will come after me, let him deny himself, and take up his cross daily, and follow me. Luke 9:23 (AV)

We all know how our moods fluctuate in the course of a day with the ups and downs our work inevitably brings. We know, too, just how frequently we give in to our fickle feelings, and, as the day ends, dissatisfied and full of self-pity, we realise our innate weakness and our love of self.

The Christian, however, is called to forsake self and to resist rather than indulge in his changeable feelings since they do not reflect the unchangeable character of God. It is not that we can avoid the angry or resentful emotions that boil up within us. Nor can we escape the temptation to gossip, or to give vent to the cynical judgments we pass on everyone but ourselves. We do not ask for or expect immunity from temptation, but rather the ability to resist the self-gratifying emotions. Some may think that it doesn't matter what we feel inside, but how can we ever expect to be trusted in greater things if we fail to be faithful to our Master in little things? God promises that if we resist the devil he will flee from us (Jas 4:7).

Christ remains our prime example; weakened and exhausted by hunger, he met the full force of the devil's temptation in the wilderness, yet fought and won by the power of the word of God. The only one who yielded nothing to the enemy was also the only one to know the full extent of Satan's power. And he to whom angels ministered has sent us his Comforter to strengthen and sustain us (Jn 14:16). He who daily denies himself will daily find God's unchangeable and inexhaustible resources.

> Give up yourself and you will find your real self.
> Lose life and you will save it.
> Submit to death of your ambitions and favourite wishes
> every day and death of your whole body in the end.
> Submit every fibre of your being and you will find eternal life.

C S Lewis

Further reading: Mt 4:1-11. Jn 12:24-26.

L-MN

August 21

Cleanliness is next...

... he shall wash his clothes, and bathe himself in water... Leviticus 15:8

In the month of April in the year 1857, at the time when Vienna was enjoying the waltzes of Strauss, Ignaz Semmelweis, a young Hungarian obstetrician, saw 57 women die in his midwifery wards in a Vienna hospital. They died from haemolytic streptococcal infection (childbirth fever, puerperal sepsis). Semmelweis noted that the women who died were those who had been examined by medical students who had just come from the post-mortem room. So he ordered that before a doctor or student examined a woman he must wash his hands in water containing chloride of lime. In the month of June following this edict only one woman died. Semmelweis had lighted on the fact that childbirth fever was a bacterial disease, and the bacteria were carried from the post-mortem room to the patient by the doctor or student.

This was a world-shattering discovery, but Semmelweis made one fatal mistake — he blamed the doctors. The result was that prejudiced obstetricians, jealous superiors and lazy medical students belittled him. He was turned out of the hospital. The strain of continued criticism and the death cries of infected women — women he knew he could have saved — so haunted his sensitive mind that it finally broke. He died in a mental institution without ever having received the recognition he deserved.

Over 3,000 years before Semmelweis rediscovered these facts, God gave Moses detailed instructions on cleansing the hands and body and clothes after handling the dead or the infected living. In Leviticus 15 the phrase 'bathe in water' occurs 15 times, and it occurs in other places also. Semmelweis added chloride of lime to the water (and that is not unimportant), and since then there have been many refinements. But the principle of cleansing by washing is basic. God made this clear to Moses, who recorded it. The pity is that for so many centuries it was ignored.

> Help us, Lord, to listen to what you teach us, to acknowledge it as your wisdom and to act on it.

Further reading: Lv 15.

GJH

August 22

The Marks of Peace (1) — Love for the Word of God

If you, even you, had only known on this day what would bring you peace... Luke 19:42 (NIV)

Every day of our working life we are rubbing shoulders with patients who are looking for peace, and to help them in their quest we must be sure that we ourselves are living in peace. This is not easy in our pressured age, but just recently I did a rapid survey of the factors associated in the Bible with peace and discovered at least fourteen to start with. Three of these are particularly important, as the peace they bring is qualified by the description 'great' or 'perfect'. We look at these over the next three days.

The first is love for the word of God (Ps 119:165). God's word can bring peace because it is powerful. Today's reading (Ps 29) is full of the mighty effects of God's voice, which strips the forest bare. This is why he can bless his people with peace (v11). The Lord Jesus could calm a raging storm with just the power of his word (Mk 4:39), and he told his disciples '... I have spoken to you that in me you might have peace' (Jn 16:33). What God speaks gives us peace because of its strength.

If this is really so, how is it then that we can fail to benefit from it? James surely gives us the answer when he tells us to 'receive with meekness the implanted word, which is able to save...' (Jas 1:21). To produce its effect, the word has to be received and implanted in the soil of our heart.

Jesus himself gave us a solemn warning in the all-too-familiar parable of the sower (Mt 13:18-23) of the danger of a defective incorporation of his word. A hard heart, a shallow heart, a heart cluttered up with other things — these are the soils in which his word cannot fulfil its true potential, and these, too, describe the Christians who never fully experience the peace of God which passes understanding. How very different was the attitude of the Thessalonian Christians. To them Paul wrote that he thanks God constantly that 'when you received the word of God, which you heard from us, you accepted it not as the word of men, but as it actually is, the word of God, which is at work in you' (1 Thes 2:13). Was it any wonder that such believers should know the Lord as the God of peace (1 Thes 5:23, 2 Thes 3:16)? May God help us to know him like this too.

> Lord, teach me to love your word, and so to obey it that I
> may know your reign of peace in my heart today.

Further reading: Ps 29.

TGS

August 23

The Marks of Peace (2) — Meekness

The meek will inherit the land and enjoy great peace. Psalm 37:11 (NIV)

We continue our examination of the factors associated with peace in the Scriptures by looking at meekness. This is a word very closely linked with humility and, indeed, the two words are often used interchangeably in different translations. Perhaps meekness could be defined as the outward manifestation of an inner humility. If so, then it surely brings peace because it does not have an image to maintain.

In today's reading we see that Jesus, even though he was God himself, 'made himself of no reputation, and took the form of a servant' (v7 AV). When he entered Jerusalem as king he came 'gentle and riding on a donkey' (Mt 21:5), and because he is meek and lowly he can give us rest and peace (Mt 11:29).

By contrast how much peace we lose in our struggle to keep up our reputation as doctors. And the more experienced in the profession we get, the fiercer the struggle becomes. I have lost count of the number of post-graduate meetings and clinical presentations I have attended where different consultants have bitterly insulted each other — not because vital matters of patient care are at stake, but because reputations have to be defended. In dealing with opposition we need to hear Paul's advice to Timothy that 'the Lord's servant must not be quarrelsome but kindly to every one... correcting his opponents with gentleness (or meekness)' (2 Tim 2:24-25). Does this not apply in clinical meetings as much as in defending the faith?

Another area in which meekness is essential to peace in the doctor's life is in the realm of counselling patients. If we think that we must have all the answers, we feel very threatened when confronted with a problem we cannot immediately solve. In pastoral ministry Paul teaches that those who are spiritual should restore others in a 'spirit of gentleness' (Gal 6:1). Likewise in our ministry of restoring sick bodies and minds it is well to have a humble approach. We are not infallible, and those who try to 'play God' often pay a high price in loss of peace.

> Lord, grant me the peace that comes from humble dependence on you, so that the serenity of my life may bring peace to those with whom I come in contact.

Further reading: Phil 2:5-11

TGS

247

August 24

The Marks of Peace (3) — Steadfastness

You will keep in perfect peace him whose mind is steadfast... Isaiah 26:3 (NIV)

We conclude our study of the biblical factors associated with peace by considering steadfastness. This brings peace because it is sure and will never change its mind.

As in meekness, so in steadfastness Jesus is our supreme example. For him, the temptation to turn back from the way of the cross did not begin in Gethsemane. Long before that, he had been rejected because people saw that he had 'set his face to go to Jerusalem' (Lk 9:51). Jesus must have been familiar with our reading, which prophetically told of the suffering he would face and how he would set his face like a flint in regard to it. When a man has his heart fixed like this, nothing can shake his peace.

Medicine, in common with many other callings, is not an easy one in which to follow Christ. There are many pitfalls, and sadly some who lay their hands to the plough do look back and become unfit for the Kingdom (Lk 9:62). I well remember as a student attending a Christian Medical Fellowship breakfast in London where the speaker looked round the hundred or so medics there and said it was a hard fact of experience that in five years time not all of us would still be active followers of Christ. I prayed there and then that I would remain steadfast, and by God's grace to date it has been so.

Our world is one in which depth of commitment is often measured purely in terms of depth of emotion, but this need not be an accurate gauge. Both Ruth and Orpah expressed great emotion to Naomi (and rightly so), but it was only Ruth who clung to her (Ru 1:14). Can we cry with the Psalmist, 'My heart is fixed, O God, my heart is fixed' (Ps 57:7 AV)?

Has this vital issue been settled for you? Have you really determined that come what may, you will take your stand with Christ? If you have, it will be costly, but your life will be characterised by a peace that will be an enigma to patients and colleagues alike. And should some of them ask you about its Source, I'm sure you'll be very happy to let them in on the secret.

Lord, keep me steadfast in your love, just for today.

Further reading: Is 50:4-9.

TGS

August 25

The Body and the Flesh

I know that nothing good dwells within me, that is, in my flesh. I can will what is right, but I cannot do it. Romans 7:18

I appeal to you therefore, brethren, by the mercies of God, to present your bodies as a living sacrifice, holy and acceptable to God, which is your spiritual worship. Romans 12:1

Paul makes many references to 'the body' and 'the flesh' especially in his letter to the Romans. It is easy to confuse them and to misunderstand completely the important message he brings. The medical mind automatically thinks of the body as flesh and so equates the two terms. That doubles the confusion.

Some time ago I copied into a notebook a very helpful succinct statement that I had read somewhere on this subject. Foolishly I did not note where I had copied it from. If I knew the source, I should gladly write and ask for permission to quote it. Since I cannot do that, I hope the author will forgive me for passing it on without formal permission. I am grateful to be able to share it. This is what it says:

> What Paul says about the 'flesh' in the sense of unregenerate human nature must not be taken as applying to the physical body. Of the 'flesh' in this sense he has nothing good to say; but the believer's body, while once used by the master-power of sin as an instrument of unrighteousness (Rom 6:13), can be presented to God as 'a living sacrifice' for the doing of his will (Rom 12:1), is indwelt by his Spirit (Rom 8:11; cf 1 Cor 6:19f), and will one day be redeemed from mortality and invested with glory (Rom 8:23; cf Phil 3:21). Paul does not share the Greek philosophers' contempt for the body as the fetter or prison-house of the soul.

> Help me, Lord, to put away the works of the flesh and to present my body to you as a living sacrifice for your service.

Further reading: Look up the references.

RRW

August 26

Crisis

No one who puts his hand to the plough and looks back is fit for the Kingdom of God. Luke 9:62

The Greek physician Hippocrates set great store by the healing power of nature — the power by which Nature tended to restore harmony to the disordered body. In Hippocratic terms, the turning point at which bodily harmony might be resolved was the 'crisis', the parting of the ways. From there the patient either went on to recovery or began the inexorable descent towards death. Fundamentally those ideas still contain a modicum of truth, though we have long since discarded the ancient humoral theory on which they were based. Today we know more about the forces that battle in our bodies and about ways to aid the powers of recovery. But we still know the parting of the ways, the triumph of success, the weariness of defeat.

And we know the close parallel in our spiritual warfare — either winning or losing, moving either towards victory and life or towards failure and death — in New Testament terms 'being saved' or 'perishing' (1 Cor 1:18). Some people don't like those words, and certainly they have been misused, but the ideas that lie behind them are woven into the whole fabric of Christian thought. The sense of spiritual direction implied in them is just as real as the divergence of the stream of physical life towards recovery or death.

The critical point, the watershed, is at the cross of Christ. Our course is determined by our response to that superb act of love in which the Son of God died to make us free. From there we move out in faith and obedience to follow his way to eternal life. Or we go on our own way and carry our burden to defeat. The choice is ours. But if we have set our feet on the way of life, don't let us, like Lot's wife, look back.

> Lord Jesus, help me to run the face that is set before me,
> looking always to you, the Author and Finisher of my faith.

Further reading: Lk 9:57-62.

RRW

August 27

Buying up Time

Turn my eyes away from worthless things; renew my life according to your word. Psalm 119:37 (NIV)

The pre-registration year can mean many long hours in a hospital bedroom or common room waiting for the next call. Slack on-call weekends can drift imperceptibly by in a haze of wasted time, with nothing achieved. Of course there is a right and necessary place for total relaxation, but this must be by design and not by drift. It is important not just to allow the 'worthless things', the trivial television programmes or trashy newspaper articles, to take over the quiet unoccupied on-call hours, filling our minds and leaving no room for spiritual life and growth. How often on other days do we deplore our lack of time; yet how slow we are to buy up the opportunities that do arise to pray and read God's word, or to talk to colleagues or patients.

The trouble is that we find we have neither the inclination nor the ability within ourselves to stir ourselves to do anything about it. Failure to feed spiritually leads quickly to a diminishing appetite and finally to anorexia. We need to pray the psalmist's prayer: 'Turn my eyes away from worthless things; renew my life according to your word'. We need God's renewing grace each day to break in on our spiritual lethargy, to give us the desire to read and to pray. As we obey, his word will speak to us, mould us and become our delight. As we feed, our appetite will grow again.

Let us give the unoccupied on-call hours to him to our eternal blessing and that of others.

> Oh to grace how great a debtor daily I'm constrained to be!
> Let that grace, Lord, like a fetter bind my wandering heart to thee.
> Prone to wander, Lord, I feel it, prone to leave the God I love;
> Take my heart, O take and seal it, seal it from thy courts above.

Robert Robinson

Further reading: Col 3:1-10.

JHCM

August 28

Death and Dying

I know that my Redeemer liveth, and that he shall stand at the latter day upon the earth; and though after my skin worms destroy this body, yet in my flesh shall I see God; whom I shall see for myself, and mine eyes shall behold, and not as a stranger. Job 19:25-27 (AV)

The Bible is realistic! Nowhere does it say that we should not face dying. Dying can be a distressing and painful process. It would be irresponsible for us to say we could lightly leave those who are dependent on us. Our Lord wept at a tomb, and he offered prayers and supplications 'with loud cries and tears' before his own death (Heb 5:7). Perhaps, however, the way will not be as fearful or as lonely as we might think, because he who went through it in utter loneliness has promised to come again and receive us unto himself (Jn 14:3).

However, Christ certainly does save us from the fear of death — that is, the fear of being dead (Heb 2:14-18). After the pain, after the parting, we shall be with Christ, which is far better (Phil 1:23). Job, in his suffering, looked forward to the time when 'I shall see him, and not as a stranger' (Job 19:27).

> If life be long I will be glad, that I may long obey;
> If short, why should I be sad to welcome endless day.
>
> Richard Baxter

One of the most poignant contrasts I have seen is that between a dying Christian, and the end of a man who has rejected Christ. For the one, horizons open up, one whom he has come to know waits to greet him 'and not as a stranger'; for the other, horizons close in, the 'great unknown' approaches, and the time that remains is filled with petty distractions.

Our Lord told Peter that in his dying he would 'glorify God' (Jn 21:19). And what an encouragement Peter's confidence and joy, as he approached his 'exodus' (2 Pet 13:15), must have been to the early church. We shall have that same opportunity one day, to 'Glorify God' in the way we face death. But now, by our attitude to death, and by the way we speak to patients close to death, let us seek to glorify God. And let us, day by day, situation by situation, seek to get to know him; so that when we go to be with him, we shall see him... but not as a stranger!

> In the valley of the shadow of death you will be with me,
> Lord. But sensitise me now to your presence, so that you
> will be no stranger to me when we meet.

Further reading: Heb 2:14-18. Rom 8:35-39.

PCE

August 29

On Stigma

There came a leper to Jesus and he touched him. Mark 1:40-41 (AV)

Can you picture the scene? Can you imagine the shudder of horror that must have passed through the crowd of respectable and orthodox people when our Lord actually put out his hand to touch somebody suffering from a condition considered by all and sundry as ritualistically defiling? Our Lord cut through the prejudice and the false assumptions of everybody who saw what he was about to do. He refused to admit the possibility of contamination, or of being contaminated. And he showed by that very act that God cared for needy individuals, especially those who suffered from discrimination of any kind — disease, or nationality (remember the Samaritan?) or sex, or social standing.

The word 'leper' in our Lord's day was not a medical diagnosis, but a prejudiced categorisation, a lumping together — discourteous and hurtful — of the ceremonially unclean. It is the same today in many languages, many cultures. What do you make of the difference between say, 'A person who happens to have a transient infection with Mycobacterium leprae and a leper'? People who have caught leprosy are branded, and the stigma all too often gives rise to cruel ostracism and moral condemnation. It also provides a ready excuse for not thinking and not knowing and not doing anything.

How easily do we doctors fall into the trap of labelling people! We do it, instinctively I suppose, when they come into our consulting room or 'outpatients'. After all, it's what we've been trained to do — to observe. Some obvious feature about them strikes us at once, but in noticing this we may miss other even more important things.

When it comes to diagnosis, we may be so blinded by first impressions that significant points in the history or physical examinations fail to register. We stick a label on, we brand them, and then what we have done colours all our relations with them. It may be the degree of pigmentation of the skin, some tic or habit, or some social distinction or other, or that their symptoms could be psychosomatic and not organic.

Let us be on the watch today and every day that we don't jump to false and stigmatising conclusions.

> Please help me, Lord, to treat everybody I shall meet today with courtesy and consideration — patients, staff, colleagues. Save me from snap and superficial judgments.

Further reading: Mk 1:32-42.

SGB

August 30

Failure is not Final

Jesus said: 'Simon, Simon, behold, Satan demanded to have you, that he might sift you like wheat, but I have prayed for you that your faith may not fail; and when you have turned again, strengthen your brethren'. Luke 22:31-32

A sense of failure can be devastating. Probably all of us experience it sometimes — in personal relationships with people, in service to Christ and not least in the demanding round of medical life. Does it tend to get you down when it happens? Then remember what happened to Simon Peter, and take heart. Be still and listen. Failure is not final.

Peter did fail, wildly and miserably. He openly denied his Master, contrary to all his boasting. And he repented bitterly. What agony of soul he went through as he saw Jesus crucified and laid in the tomb we cannot know. But despite everything, we can scarcely doubt that deep down (as Jesus had prayed) his faith had not failed. Then he saw the empty tomb, and later the Lord appeared to him (Lk 24:34). Though we know nothing about that meeting, hope must then have come — hope to bring a glow to the embers of faith. With Jesus' call to love, made three times corresponding to Peter's three denials (Jn 21:15-17), faith burst into flame.

Many kinds of failure come into our lives. A medical failure, a tragic mistake, misunderstood advice, misjudged surgery, a lapse through inexperience, weariness or stress (each of us can fill in our own detail) — can knock a doctor very hard. As Christians we may see it as dishonouring our Lord (and so failing him just as much, though in a different way, as Peter did) and betraying the trust of people. We cannot, indeed must not, push it aside. It must be faced. Anything must be done that can be done to pick up the pieces. Then we must go on — humbly certainly, but wiser, more tolerant of the failures of others and better equipped to help them when they need it. We should have learnt by then that, as Jesus so gently taught Peter, failure is not final.

> Nay but thou knowest us, Lord Christ, thou knowest,
>   Well thou rememberest our feeble frame,
> Thou canst conceive our highest and our lowest,
>   Pulses of nobleness and aches of shame.

F W H Meyer, St Paul

Further reading: Lk 22:31-34, 54-62. Jn 21:15-19.

RRW

August 31

Following

If any man would come after me, let him deny himself and follow me.
Luke 9:23

Jesus Christ tells us that we are to follow him. It is a very simple but demanding command. What does it involve?

Firstly it involves staying close to him. We cannot follow if Jesus is already out of sight and earshot. When I am driving a car my sense of direction is poor. Sometimes, in cities which are strange to me, a friend will say: 'Follow my car until we are on the outskirts of the town — then I will stop and explain the rest of the way to you'. So I follow behind him. I stick close to him, eagerly, hurrying through amber lights, resenting any car which comes between his and mine. I dread losing sight of him. If I do, I shall, quite literally be lost. But am I as keen to stay close to Jesus Christ? Do I relate all that I do and think to him? Have I spoken to him today, or asked him what he wants to say to me through his word? Have I allowed other things to come between me and him?

Secondly, it involves obedience. Right from childhood we find that obedience is hard work. It goes against the grain. Yet Jesus said: 'You are my friends if you obey me' (Jn 15:14 LB). How determined are we to obey him? When I was working (for the second time!) to take the Primary FRCS examination, a friend said to me: 'Working for Primary is total war!' He was right. It demanded everything I had. Let's ask ourselves today: 'Am I prepared to be as wholehearted and singleminded in knowing and obeying Christ as in my work for higher degrees or in my effort to get the job I want?'

Perhaps the key is in the self-denial commanded in Luke 9:23. Often today our natural inclination will go directly against what we know is the right thing to do. We may recall something in a clinical examination which we forgot to do. We should like to finish our book, our television programme or our thesis, but soon the patient will settle down for the night. We should go now to see him.

And as we hurry down the draughty corridor to the ward, we are suddenly wonderfully aware that the Lord Jesus is with us and that to follow him is better than anything else.

> Lord Jesus Christ, I intend to follow you today.
> Please give me strength to do so.

Further reading: Lk 14:26-33. Mk 14:53-54, 66-72. Jn 14:15-24.

JT

September 1

Doctor, be still: God's Large Place

He brought me forth also into a large place. Psalm 18:19 (AV)

In my student days long ago, the Rector of our parish church used regularly to read his eleven-minute sermons. He wrote them in little books, so that over a period of time we heard them more than once, exactly as before and always read with a quiet serenity. We used to smile when the repeats came up. We knew them all and so perhaps failed to appreciate how thoughtful they were. We even timed them.

Looking back now I realise that those sermons had that quality of detailed care, even a certain perfection, which one expects of miniatures, whether painted or written. Evidence of their value lies in the fact that time has still left some of them in my memory.

In particular, I recall a sermon on Psalm 18:19 (AV, of course, in those days) 'He brought me forth also into a large place'. The detail I forget, but my memory of the man sums up what he would have said. He was a quiet serene man, kindly and understanding. I can never recall seeing him flustered. This, I feel sure, was not just because of a phlegmatic disposition. He knew for himself the secret of God's large place.

It is a place worth knowing about and getting to know. We should be grateful to David for sharing his knowledge of it with us. It must have meant much to him, hard-pressed as he so often was. The 'note to the choirmaster' which prefaces the psalm, says that 'David ... addressed the words to the Lord on the day when the Lord delivered him from the hand of all his enemies, and from the hand of Saul'.

The pressures on us will rarely be of the same kind as the pressures on David. But we can equally well know the value of God's large place. When there seems just too much to do, when an urgent diagnosis baffles us, when skills and judgment are tested at a critical point in a surgical operation, when things are going all wrong — it is possible then to go for just a moment into God's large place and regain calm and perspective. This is not to be something overt, something apparent to those about us. If that happens, they may well think we are having an attack of petit mal! It is essentially a matter of being still in our hearts, as we lift them to God in a special moment of what I imagine Paul meant when he urged the Thessalonians to 'pray without ceasing' (1 Thes 5:17).

> Help us, Lord, to be calm when the pressure is on, and if the pressure seems to be closing in on us, lead us forth into a large place.

Further reading: Ps 18.

RRW

September 2

A Dangerous Belief

Indeed he was ill, near to death... Philippians 2:27

Some of the greatest disasters I have ever seen in the lives of Christians have stemmed from mistaken beliefs. And not uncommonly these beliefs are concerned with healing — or rather with its failure to occur.

Tim was a Christian who must have been born running. His zeal was incredible. During his leadership of our hall Christian Union, some dozen residents gave their lives to Christ in as many months, and many Christians whose lives were tangled up got straightened out again.

They were tremendously exciting days. Yet through it all I was very concerned for Tim himself, since his zeal and enthusiasm so often seemed to deviate from Scriptural teaching, a prime example being his fervent belief that no Christian should ever be sick, or even have any symptoms of disease. All sneezes, snuffles and sore throats had their source directly from Satan and could — and should — be instantly rebuked and removed in prayer.

It is true that we do read of many miraculous healings in the Bible (significantly though, I think, always of serious disease). But equally we read of those who were not healed in such a way, so far as we can tell. Probably the best known example is that of Timothy, who was advised by Paul to take some medication for his stomach complaint (1 Tim 5:23). But it seems that Epaphroditus also had an illness (from which he nearly died), and although we read that God had mercy on him and he survived, there is no indication that any instantaneous healing occurred.

Tim discovered the great danger of his unbalanced belief in no uncertain terms when he attended a wedding one weekend, and quite spontaneously his intestine perforated during the reception and he was admitted for emergency surgery. I went to visit him in hospital, and I remember the saddest thing about it all was not the sight of the drips and drainage tubes running in and out of every orifice, but the fact that his faith had suffered a severe blow from which it never recovered. Instead of listening to what the Lord was saying to him through this crisis, he didn't want to know any more. I wept for him.

I firmly believe that God can and does heal today by a wide variety of means, including the miraculous. But we must always remember that he is the Lord, and we have no right to demand or presume upon his healing power. Let us beware of the danger of an unbalanced view of healing that ultimately brings only hurt and misery in its wake.

Further reading: Phil 2:25-30. 2 Cor 12:7-10.

TGS

September 3

The Way (9) — Communications on the Way

Draw near to God and he will draw near to you. James 4:8

Travellers on the Way have a two-way communication system with base. We can speak to God through prayer. God speaks to us through his word and in our hearts. All this is marvellously monitored by the Holy Spirit.

Prayer is simply talking to God and is the Christian's greatest privilege. 'Pray constantly' writes Paul (1 Thes 5:17). This means not that we must always be engaged in conscious conversation with God, but that our hearts are in that state that they are immediately lifted to God as need or opportunity comes. Prayer in this respect is rather like breathing — continuous but not consciously done unless we need a deep breath or find the going hard.

Regular deep breathing sessions are important. They may include worship of God, confession of sin, praise to God, thanks for all he has done, and petition and intercession, when we ask frankly for the needs of others as well as our own. It must all be scrupulously honest and sincere, and what we ask for in the name of Christ must be worthy of that name.

Prayer can be a great joy. But sometimes it is not easy. We need then to remember that the Holy Spirit is ready to help us in our weakness (Rom 8:26), monitoring our outward calls.

The Holy Spirit also monitors our inward calls. He has inspired Scripture, which he helps us to understand. And he speaks to our hearts, guiding, reasoning and, where necessary, rebuking. We should be humbly dependent on him as we read the Bible, which should be our constant companion. It is not a magic talisman, but it can be trusted in all matters of faith and conduct. Read aright it will not lead anyone astray, and it will bring us close to the mind of God. Reading it aright means not only dependence on the Holy Spirit that he will interpret the words in our hearts, but also full use of the intellect that God has given us, and an honest willingness to live by what he teaches. We should remember what Paul wrote to Timothy: 'All Scripture is inspired by God and profitable for teaching, for reproof, for correction, and for training in righteousness, that the man of God may be complete, equipped for every good work' (2 Tim 3:16-17).

It is vital to keep our communication system in sound working order under regular use. That use may have to be adjusted to the time table of a busy life that is not always ours to regulate. But we neglect it at our peril. Communication is vital — both ways.

Our hearts, if God we seek to know,
  Shall know him and rejoice;
His coming like the morn shall be,
  Like morning songs his voice.

John Morison

Further reading: Lk 11:1-13. Jn 14:12-17, 16:13-15. 2 Pet 1:19-21.

RRW

September 4

Nothing Held Back

And Peter said, 'Lo, we have left our homes and followed you'. Luke 18:28

As an anatomist I have had good reason to be grateful for the public-spirited individuals who offer their bodies for the advancement of science. Many different shapes and sizes of cadavers have passed through my hands in the past quarter-century, but one stands out as the most remarkable. It was the body of a female, so tiny as to occupy only about two-thirds of the length of the seven-foot dissecting table. She was positively diminutive in every respect — dwarf-like in all dimensions. I felt compelled to trace back her record. There had to be an interesting story!

It transpired that she had been a nun in a very exclusive French-Canadian order resembling the Sisters of Silence. She had spent her entire life with this most servile group, doing the unpleasant menial chores of house-keeping for all the other sisters of the Order — scrubbing, laundering, cleaning and sweeping — never speaking or communicating with another living soul. She had devoted her entire life, every minute of it, to her God and to working lovingly for her fellow Christians. And now here she was. She had given freely her last meagre earthly possession for the good of her fellows.

The thought of her utter selflessness still sends shivers down my spine, although the encounter happened almost 15 years ago. It makes me contemplate a verse from the famous old Church of Scotland communion hymn, *When I survey the wondrous cross* (I can even hear the music — the tune Rockingham). The verse reads:

Were the whole realm of nature mine,
  That were an offering far too small;
Love so amazing, so divine,
  Demands my soul, my life, my all.

Isaac Watts

Further reading: Mt 19:23-30.

ASW

September 5

Where do we belong?

Our commonwealth is in heaven, and from it we await a Saviour, the Lord Jesus Christ. Philippians 3:20

Paul tells the Philippians to 'Rejoice in the Lord' (Phil 3:1) but almost immediately warns them of the pitfalls they face. How can this be, since we so often learn of our security in Christ (Jn 10:28-29)?

Philippians 3:18-19 gives three warning signs of falling away:

> *Materialism* 'their God is their belly'. What is my primary concern for the day ahead? Is it that Christ should be glorified in my work and that I should bring something of his care and compassion to my patients? Sadly, I am too often pre-occupied with the car that won't start, the job I should apply for next, terms and conditions, tax relief, superannuation or the intricacies of overtime pay (and it doesn't get easier higher up the ladder!).

> *The world's ways* 'they glory in their shame'. We live in a corrupt society, nowhere more evident than in the doctors' mess. How easy it is to join in gossip, or remain silent when the whole tenor of conversation is contrary to our Christian profession, to keep a low Christian profile, hiding our light under a bushel. Soon we are tempted to do as others do. We need to pray for wisdom and strength to resist the moral laxity round us.

> *Earthly mindedness* 'their minds are set on earthly things'. There are many concerns that rightly occupy our thinking, the ward round, the clinic, relatives to see, patients to encourage and comfort. Yet I suspect I am not alone in being distracted also by the social whirl, spending every evening in pursuits harmless in themselves that gradually undermine the relationship I used to enjoy with my Saviour.

Paul's antidote is not perhaps what we should expect. More Bible study? prayer? church attendance? No, important as they are. It is to look up to our 'commonwealth' in heaven, and the return of our Saviour. True, we belong in this world, but we belong to another, our goal to meet him who will change us to be like him. What a prospect for each new day!

> What kind of people ought you to be... as you look
> forward to the day of God?

2 Pet 3:11-12 (NIV)

Further reading: Heb 11:13-16.

PMC

September 6

Is the Burden too Heavy?

I cannot carry all these people by myself; the burden is too heavy for me!
Numbers 11:14 (NIV)

Do you find that these words of Moses are sometimes your own words? It is good to stop and look at ourselves again and see our position with the Almighty God. Sometimes we are so busy in our work helping people and patching people up, depending on our specialty, or even doing the Lord's work in our local church fellowship. The routine work then gets too heavy, and we find that we cannot cope. Do we say these words of Moses?

From what the Lord had done through him from the time they were in Egypt, Moses knew that it was the Lord who was in control. He did everything, even though he did it through Moses. Many miracles he did through Moses. Moses knew that without the Lord he couldn't achieve anything at all. Yet when the routine got heavy and the going tough (the people had made a golden calf idol, and now they were complaining to Moses again), he spoke as though God had done nothing. He could only look at himself again, his human capability and strength — and of course he could not cope.

Let us reflect on our position in this world again. It is by grace that we have been saved. It is by grace that we are now living the Christian life. It is by grace that we are being sanctified (Eph 2:8-10). The burden may be heavy at times, but it is the Lord who carried it for us (1 Pet 5:7).

> Lord, make these faithless hearts of ours
>   Such lessons learn from birds and flowers:
> Make them from self to cease,
>   Leave all things to a Father's will,
> And taste, before him lying still,
>   E'en in affliction, peace.

J Anstice

Further reading: Nu 11:1-17. Ps 55:22. Gal 3:1-6.

GKGL

September 7

Happy?

Do not rejoice in this... but rejoice that your names are written in heaven.
Luke 10:20

Think what makes you happy: a successful trouble-free ward round? A night off at last? A fascinating case of 'obscuritis unusualans'? A day when things go right, ie when no-one shouts at you? A good meal?

The seventy-two followers of Jesus described in Luke 10:17-20 had something to shout about, something to be happy about; they returned with joy, marvelling at the power Jesus had given them. We can picture them returning from their travels sharing with one another what they had been able to do. We can understand how they felt. By comparison the things that make us happy seem trivial. But look at Jesus' reply: 'Do not rejoice that the spirits are subject to you, but rejoice that your names are written in heaven'.

Jesus puts things into a different perspective. A successful day at work is good; power to control evil spirits may seem better, but how much more wonderful is the salvation that is ours through Christ Jesus! That really is something to shout about. It is something we can rejoice in even when the ward round is not trouble- free, when we have no night off, when we are clerking our twenty-fourth hernia of the day, and yes, even when the food is awful!

> Thank you, Lord, that my name can be written in heaven
> because of what you have done for me. Forgive me that so
> often I see things from the world's perspective. Help me to
> know more of the joy of your salvation.

Further reading: Ps 51:10-17. Tit 3:4-8a.

DCM

September 8

Why Play for Time?

You have been born anew, not of perishable seed but of imperishable, through the living and abiding word of God; for all flesh is like grass and all its glory like the flower of grass. The grass withers, and the flower falls, but the word of the Lord abides for ever. That word is the good news which was preached to you. 1 Peter 1:23-25

Individuals are of unique value — God's son died for them. But we tend to attach more importance to some than to others, especially in medicine, with its traditional hierarchy. The Bible, in fact, while commending a proper respect for seniority and authority, also reminds us repeatedly that 'all men are like grass'.

We are fortunate if our teachers command respect and affection. It may be proper to emulate ability, but it is another to covet success. This is a question of priorities, and whether we are prepared to take the long view. The decline of the famous is sad. The success of some may outlast that of others — but not by much. Sudden or slow, the end is the same — 'They fly forgotten, as a dream ...' The terminal poverty of the person who has lived for his work is as great as the one whose epitaph is 'Born a man. Died a grocer.'

The biblical reminder of the brevity of our lives is always coupled with the reminder of God's permanence. His word is constant, and has been embodied in Jesus Christ who is 'the same, yesterday, today and forever'. 'Listen everyone, everyone! High and low, rich and poor, all around the world.... There is no need to fear when times of trouble come, even though surrounded by enemies! They trust in their wealth and boast about how rich they are, yet not one of them, though rich as kings, can ransom his own brother from the penalty of sin! For a soul is far too precious to be ransomed by mere earthly wealth.... Though a man calls himself happy all through his life — and the world loudly applauds success — yet in the end he dies like everyone else... For man with all his pomp must die like any animal. But as for me, God will redeem my soul from the power of death, for he will receive me' (Ps 49 LB).

Further reading: Ps 103:8-19. 1 Pet 1:18-21.

DEBP

September 9

My Shepherd (9)

Thou anointest my head with oil. Psalm 23:5

Oil in Scripture was multipurpose: for consecration of people and things, for cooking, for fuel or to signify joy. It is hard to see how most of this relates to sheep!

We get nearer to David's meaning by recalling our Lord's reproachful words to Simon the Pharisee, 'You did not anoint my head with oil' (Lk 7:46). A thoughtful host would have offered this service to refresh his guests on arrival. The Good Samaritan knew the soothing property of oil. Both as refreshment and ointment, oil can spell relief.

Oily liniment is used by shepherds to relieve the infection and infestation of a sheep by parasitic flies, buzzing round or burrowing into face and head. Some veterinary ung. emulsificans helps to heal superficial scratches or sores. Oil soothes and heals. How often I, too, need these ministrations of the Shepherd. As sheep can be driven nearly mad by the constant pestering of flies, so can I be irritated by little things. Perhaps the telephone or my 'bleep' act as flies to me, or the unfortunate nurse or relative who innocently says, 'Can I just ask you ...?' and is astonished to be swiped at rather than assisted. My feelings, too, may be hurt or emotions lacerated by the day's happenings. Sheep may catch each other's disorders by rubbing their heads together. Under pressure I may pick up bad practices, language or ideas and need the Shepherd to alert me as to what is happening. I may clash with others and need grace to apologise or to pour oil on troubled waters.

Sheep are not noted for great thoughts; for them the shepherd's oil is for external application only. But the Good Shepherd applies his oil to both mind and heart (Phil 4:7). He does it by the outpouring of his Spirit in our lives, affecting emotions, mind and will: 'He anointed us, set his seal of ownership on us, and put his Spirit in our hearts' (2 Cor 1:21-22 NIV).

We need his daily anointing and recommissioning, to soothe, heal, bear fruit and endow with gifts.

As doctors we have knowledge, but one of our greatest needs is for wisdom in applying it. In making diagnoses, selecting and carrying out treatment, deciding what to tell to our patients and their families, and how to tell it, we all need wisdom, particularly as technology poses new ethical dilemmas. The same Spirit helps here, too: 'You have been anointed by the Holy One .... his anointing teaches you about everything' (1 Jn 2:20,27), for 'we have the mind of Christ' (1 Cor 2:16). The offer is there. We can only say to him 'You did not anoint my head with oil', if we have avoided or rejected the Shepherd's prescription.

> Sun shall not pain them, no burning will torture,
> Jesus the Lamb is their Shepherd and Guide.

C M Idle

Further reading: Eph 3:14-21. 1 Cor 1:26-31.

JG

September 10

St George or the Dragon

The truth is that, although of course we lead normal human lives, the battle we are fighting is on the spiritual level. The very weapons we use are not those of human warfare but powerful in God's warfare for the destruction of the enemy's strongholds. 2 Corinthians 10:3-4 (JBP)

St George seems to have suffered something of an eclipse in recent times. Apparently he is no longer recognised in the gallery of saints. But he certainly remains as a symbol of good triumphing over evil: a mythical picture on the earthly level of the archangel Michael successfully waging war in heaven over the great dragon 'that ancient serpent, who is called the Devil and Satan, the deceiver of the whole world' (Rev 12:9). The great defeat of Satan was, of course, on the cross, where the Son of God and Son of Man gave his life 'that through death he might destroy him who has the power of death, that is, the devil' (Heb 2:14).

It seems, however, that Satan never admits defeat and still prowls around like a roaring lion, seeking someone to devour (1 Pet 5:8). Lion, serpent, dragon or angel of light, he remains the great deceiver, the father of lies. If we do not believe in him, that suits him. And likewise if we under-estimate him. We are less likely to recognise the little dragons he spawns and plants in our way. They are of many kinds, and there is no shortage of them along the medical road, as the enemy seeks to deny the sovereignty of God over human life, the integrity of human personality, the common decencies of everyday living, the paramount values of service and true compassion. Not least are the dragons that assail our personal and professional lives — Mammon, jealousy, ambition and the rest. They must be slain, as they can be through the victory of Christ. It must be St George or the dragon.

> Lord, help me not only to love what is good, but to hate what is evil, and to seek by your grace to cast it out. And help me to slay the dragons in my life.

Further reading: Rev 12:7-11.

RRW

September 11

Dragons (1) — Mammon

You cannot serve God and Mammon. Matthew 6:24

Mammon is a transliteration of an Aramaic word which means simply wealth or profit, but here the Lord Jesus is giving it a more sinister twist. Money in itself is neither good nor evil. What matters is our attitude to it, how we get it and what we do with it. Jesus sees in mammon 'an egocentric covetousness which claims man's heart and thereby estranges him from God: when a man "owns" anything, in reality it owns him' (New Bible Dictionary). Paul does not mince words: 'But those who desire to be rich fall into temptation, into a snare, into many senseless and hurtful desires that plunge men into ruin and destruction. For the love of money is the root of all evils; it is through this craving that some have wandered away from the faith and pierced their hearts with many pangs' (1 Tim 6:9-10).

We can do a great deal of good with money, honestly and fairly gained and wisely used. But the love of it is a very nasty dragon. Rightly or wrongly, doctors are seen as easy — and not always reluctant — preys to it. In most countries they are in the better paid segment of the community — and, to be fair, usually work hard in return. But some are never satisfied. Severely afflicted with the Oliver Twist syndrome, they are always seeking for more. This understandably stirs criticism and accusations of greed, sometimes from high places. The resultant slur on the whole profession grieves honest doctors. It should be unthinkable that Christian doctors would offend in this way. The Scriptures are full of warnings about it, like those already quoted. And anything shady is condemned out of hand: 'Bread gained by deceit is sweet to a man, but afterward his mouth will be full of gravel' (Prov 20:17). Beware of the dragon Mammon! 'To get wisdom is better than gold; to get understanding is to be chosen rather than silver' (Pr 16:16).

> Grant me, Lord, not to mind earthly things, but to love things heavenly; and even now, while I am placed among things that are passing away, to cleave to those that will abide.

Further reading: Mt 6:24-34.

RRW

September 12

Dragons (2) — The Green-Eyed Monster

Love is patient and kind; love is not jealous or boastful. 1 Corinthians 13:4

Jealousy is one of the most destructive of all attitudes. The jealous mind, burning to destroy the object of its jealousy, all too often destroys itself. Iago, with lying motives, yet spoke the truth to Othello:

> O beware, my Lord, of jealousy;
> It is the green-eyed monster which doth mock
> The meat it feeds on.*

He was in fact implanting jealousy in Othello's mind towards Desdemona, and in time both Desdemona and Othello were destroyed. The story is a terrible warning, especially as it shows the trivialities on which jealousy can be based. Iago knew this only too well and put it into words with an ironic twist:

> Trifles light as air
> Are to the jealous confirmation strong
> As proofs of holy writ.*

No one is immune from the attacks of this monster. Our Lord's own disciples quarrelled over which of them was to be regarded as the greatest (Lk 22:24) and resented others doing what they considered their preserve (Mk 9:38). The basis of all such attitudes is jealousy. And there is no shortage of it in medicine, with rivalry over clinical preferment, secretiveness in research, and resentment over someone else's success.

There is, of course, another older meaning of the word jealousy — zeal and solicitude. And the scriptures speak often of the jealousy of God. This is something different and very proper. It is not the 'green-eyed jealousy' of which we all need to beware.

> From bitterness preserve me, Lord
>> From jealous thoughts protect my day,
> Against the stroke of envy's sword
>> Help me to hold my way.
> And grant my soul sufficient grace
>> To gladden at another's prize
> And look upon his eager face
>> With sympathetic eyes.

Further reading: Lk 22:24-27.

RRW

* 'Othello' by William Shakespeare. Act 3, Scene 3.

September 13

Dragons (3) — Ambition

... where you have envy and selfish ambition, there you find disorder and every evil practice. James 3:16 (NIV)

Ambition is both widely cultivated, not least in medicine, and widely condemned. Warnings abound of its dire consequences. Shakespeare's *Macbeth* is the classical example, with his 'vaulting ambition, which o'erleaps itself, and falls on the other'. And we know what a sticky end he came to. The Talmud says, 'Ambition destroys its possessor'. A modern poet has written, rather bleakly:

> Ambition has but one reward for all:
> A little power, a little transient fame,
> A grave to rest in, and a fading name!
>
> William Winter

This is all sadly true of one kind of ambition, the sort that aims at self-aggrandisement or is motivated by greed or love of power.

It is interesting that James in his letter talks about 'selfish ambition'. The adjective is important, for the word 'ambition' is neutral. It can mean simply a goal or aim, something aspired to. In medicine we can — indeed, should — aim at excellence, for medicine is a trust which rightly requires the best. This may well bring success, fame, fortune. But it can be — indeed, for the Christian should be — combined with humility and the desire to bring honour to the Christ whose name we bear. It is then a fine ambition.

But we need to keep on our guard and not fall for the twisted thinking (a favourite ploy of the father of lies) which persuades us that our selfish ambition is aimed at the glory of God. This is tricky and needs watching.

At the other end of the scale from selfish ambition is the great ambition, the striving for a goal which was dear to Paul's heart: 'one thing I do, forgetting what lies behind and straining forward to what lies ahead, I press on toward the goal for the prize of the upward call of God in Christ Jesus' (Phil 3:13-14).

> From prayer that asks that I may be
> Sheltered from winds that beat on Thee,
> From fearing when I should aspire,
> From faltering when I should climb higher,
> From silken self, O Captain, free
> Thy soldier who would follow Thee.
>
> Amy Carmichael

Further reading: Phil 3:8-16.

RRW

268

September 14

Dragons (4) — Moods

Why are you cast down, O my soul, and why are you disquieted within me? Psalm 42:5,11

In one of the loveliest of the Psalms these words come twice as a melancholy refrain. They must often and often have been echoed by hearts bowed down in a black mood of questioning. Why, O my soul, why?

Moods are, in themselves, not necessarily rational. Doctors should not need to be reminded of that. We know that various bodily states — metabolic, digestive or what you will — can determine our moods. But we still can forget this. We can feel depressed, mildly or seriously, for no apparent reason, and yet feel guilty or inhibited or restrained as a result. Moods can swing up and down at different times of day. I tend to have a mild downswing first thing in the morning and so have learnt to be wary of my feelings at that time. For others it can come during the busy part of the day, at twilight or in the night.

If we know that our moods can be unrelated to real circumstances, we need to learn to cope with them. That wise Christian realist, C S Lewis, has said, when talking about faith (*Mere Christianity*, p111), that it 'is the art of holding on to things your reason has once accepted in spite of your changing moods. For moods will change, whatever view your reason takes ... unless you teach your moods "where they get off", you can never be either a sound Christian or even a sound atheist, but just a creature dithering to and fro, with its beliefs dependent on the weather or the state of its digestion.' Moods are dragons to be fought.

Of course, if we feel depression that is persistent or deep, or if we are trying to help a patient in that plight, unless we are skilled in psychiatric matters we may well need to bring a more informed colleague into the picture. Nowadays, as we know, there are different ways of dealing with endogenous depression. Only foolish people think that 'Snap out of it' is good advice. It just is not as easy as that. And Lewis's advice is certainly not meant to be so facile. We may be sure, however, that his advice lines up with the Psalmist's further words: 'Hope in God; for I shall again praise him, my help and my God'.

The next psalm gives us the prayer of hope:

> Oh send out thy light and thy truth;
>   let them lead me,
> Let them bring me to thy holy hill
>   and to thy dwelling!

Then I will go to the altar of God,
    to God my exceeding joy;
And I will praise thee with the lyre,
    O God, my God.

Ps 43:3-4

Further reading: Ps 42 and 43.

RRW

September 15

Dragons (5) — Wormwood

Get rid of all bitterness... Ephesians 4:31 (NIV)

In John's apocalyptic vision (Rev 8:10), he saw a great star fall from heaven, blazing like a torch, 'and it fell on a third of the rivers and on the fountains of water. The name of the star is Wormwood. A third of the waters became wormwood and many men died of the water, because it was made bitter.'

Wormwood is an aromatic herb, notable for its bitterness. C S Lewis, looking for a name for the nasty little junior tempter in *The Screwtape Letters*, aptly called him Wormwood. Wormwood is bitterness. It is a dragon to be fought.

It has been pointed out that the plant wormwood is not actually poisonous, though it spoils all that it contaminates. But bitterness certainly poisons the soul. It is one of those deadly emotional attitudes which does harm to body and soul in a psychosomatic action. The antidote to wormwood is a forgiving spirit.

Bishop Festo Kivengere was asked how he dealt with the bitterness, anger and perhaps hate he must have felt toward Idi Amin, who had done much harm in Uganda and who had Festo on his death list. He replied:

> 'My wife, Mera, and I fled from Amin in 1977. And yes, there was bitterness within me. I was being strangled by hatred of Idi Amin. I saw what he was doing to destroy my people, and I protested. But I was losing my protest. You see, once I began to hate Amin, I was no longer protesting his actions. I was joining him. I had to learn what St Paul said: "Do not be overcome by evil, but overcome evil with good".
>
> On Good Friday 1977, sitting in a London church, I heard the pastor read, "Father, forgive them, they don't

understand what they are doing." Like a flash, the words went right into my heart, showing me Amin. I began to say, "God forgive me. I simply don't have that quality of love. Mine dries so quickly". The Holy Spirit responded, "Don't worry, there is a bank in heaven for people who are bankrupt in love. You put in your application, will you?" And I did. The chains of hatred were broken. I entered a new liberating experience.'

Lord Jesus, help me to get rid of all bitterness, resentment and hatred in my heart. Help me to love others just because you first love me. Help me to forgive as you forgive me.

Further reading: Eph 4:31-32, 5:1-2.

RRW

September 16

Dragons (6) — Magic

When Simon saw that the Spirit was given through the laying on of the apostles' hands, he offered them money, saying, 'Give me also this power...' Acts 8:18-19

Magic can be described as the misuse of power (and, indeed, not only of supernatural power). It is the sort of dragon that Christians think they can spot easily if he appears along the Way. We tend to think of Simon, the former magician and now believer, who tried to buy the Holy Spirit's power with money. He was rebuked by Peter (Acts 8:18-24) and found a permanent dishonourable place in the word 'simonry' in our English dictionary. Or we think of Elymas, the practising magician in Cyprus, who tried to divert the Roman proconsul from the Christian faith, and who was soundly ticked off by Paul as well as being blinded (Acts 13:6-12). We explain the desire of the disciples to call down fire from heaven on those who would not receive Jesus in Samaria (Lk 9:54) as a naive attitude that we should not even think of. We quickly dismiss the trivial pointless miracles attributed to the Boy Jesus in the apocryphal gospels as fanciful tales, which no doubt they are. Yes, we can spot the silly old dragon, magic. Or so we think.

But perhaps it is not so simple. This is the sphere of the prince of darkness, who can appear as an angel of light (2 Cor 11:14). Are we up to his tricks? While we may shy away from the superstitions and the weird things that so many people get themselves sadly tangled up in, do we hanker after spiritual thrills for their own sake? Do we ever feel that we should like to see a spectacular miracle, a real piece of magic? Divine magic, of course. Oh, yes. But it would be nice to be personally involved in it — and so to have something special to talk about, our own personal spiritual thrill. The dragon Magic beckons. His shiny scales have lovely colours. He has a crocodile's grin ('welcoming little fishes in', to quote Lewis Carroll in *Alice in Wonderland*), but his eyes are hypnotic. Magic is fascinating, and this is no time to be self-confident about such matters.

God still does miracles today. We need not doubt that. But it is as he wills, not as we will. Even in the ministry of our Lord Jesus, the important thing about the miraculous events was that they were his 'signs' (Jn 2:11). He was no magician, even when he could have helped himself in a desperate situation (Matt 26:53-54). We must not underestimate the dragon, Magic.

> Grant us, Almighty Lord, a quiet confidence in your over-ruling power in our lives and grace to trust your wisdom and love in all things. For yours is the kingdom, yours is the power and yours is the glory.

Further reading: Acts 8:9-24.

RRW

September 17

Dragons (7) — Ego

He must increase, but I must decrease. John 3:30

So spoke John the Baptist, putting his Ego into place. It seems fair to say that Ego is really only a part-time dragon. We all have an Ego (a self), which can be well behaved and, by the grace of God, a normal part of your life and my life — and not least of a medical professional life. But it can get out of hand, and then: beware! It certainly wrecked everything for Adam. This is a matter of perspective and of maintaining God's order and values. He made us as individuals, and it is clear that his will is to perfect us as individuals. The Christian hope is not one of becoming lost in some vast cosmic non-identity. It is one of growing up in Christ to full spiritual maturity — to the measure of the stature of the fullness of Christ (Eph 4:13) — of putting off the old nature with its practices and putting on 'the new nature, which is being renewed in knowledge after the image of its creator' (Col 3:9-10).

Our Lord's teaching about self is clear: 'Unless a grain of wheat falls into the earth and dies, it remains alone; but if it dies, it bears much fruit' (Jn 12:24). 'Whoever would save his life will lose it, and whoever loses his life for my sake will find it' (Mt 16:25). This is not negative. It is the way to life, the way to the new self that God wants us to be.

John the Baptist's self-abnegation was fervent and sincere. It found expression in action. But no one could say he ceased to be an individual. His Ego under God found a normal place.

On the other hand, Simon Peter's Ego broke through as an untamed dragon again and again. His Master obviously had a constant eye on it — and prayed for him. That dragon was completely tamed long before Peter's martyr death.

Thank God Ego is a very personal dragon, who can be completely transformed. We know about obedience schools for dogs. In God's obedience school Ego can be made a new creature (2 Cor 5:17).

> We thank you, Lord, that you have made us for yourself.
> Help us day by day to become more and more what you
> want us to be.

Further reading: Read the references in their context.

RRW

September 18

Dragons (8) — Hubris

... I bid every one among you not to think of himself more highly than he ought to think. Romans 12:3

A dragon which likes to lurk beside the medical way goes by the name of Hubris. This is a Greek word signifying arrogant pride, something that even the Greeks took a dim view of — in contrast to their attitude that pride was a virtue and humility was to be despised. Hubris (or hybris), it seems, was going too far. According to some versions of the myths surrounding the cult of Asklepios, the Greek god of healing, he started off as a physician in the Thessalian town of Tricca, who became so good at his job that he got tickets on himself and started raising the dead. This upset the gods, and Zeus with the aid of a well-aimed thunderbolt brought a sudden end to the young upstart's promising medical career. By way of compensation Zeus then placed him among the stars, and he came to be venerated as the god of healing. The Romans took him over under the name of Aesculapius.

This is just myth, of course, but like all myth it holds a kernel of truth — a truth which Paul's words state plainly and simply. In particular, the offence of Asklepios warns us of the dragon Hubris setting up ambush along the medical way. It is tragically easy for the doctor's skill and power to go to his head. The old jibe about 'playing God' is often untrue and unfair, but it can be valid. It is worth thinking about — honestly. No matter what the Greeks thought, for the Christian pride in any degree (and hubris is in high degree) is just not on. Pride has been described as the ultimate sin, which lies at the heart of all mankind's rebellion and disorder since our first parents wanted to be 'as gods'. It is not to be confused with a proper delight in doing one's work well. The Lord Jesus delighted in his work of doing the Father's will. But in medicine to cross over the line into self-congratulation is to court disaster. The Christian virtue is not the pride that the Greeks esteemed, but humility, that sublimely paradoxical attribute of God himself. So beware the lurking Hubris! And beware the well-aimed thunderbolt! There is no guaranteed compensatory place among the stars.

> Let holy charity mine outward vesture be,
> and lowliness become mine inner clothing;
> True lowliness of heart,
> Which takes the humbler part,
> And o'er its own shortcomings weeps with loathing.

Bianco da Siena
(Translated by R F Littledale)

Further reading: Rom 12. Phil 2:1-11.

RRW

September 19

Available — For What?

They made me keeper of the vineyards; but, my own vineyard I have not kept! Song of Solomon 1:6

Of all the qualities of a good doctor, easy availability in times of need or crisis is one most appreciated by staff and patients alike. To be at the right place at the right time seems to be the particular gift of some, while the doctor who leaves word of his probable whereabouts inside or outside the hospital is much respected by ward staff and telephone operators.

But while it is true that there is no record that Jesus ever turned down a genuine call for help, yet he did purposefully seek seclusion and solitude for prayer (Lk 5:16), even trying to ensure at times that his whereabouts were not known (Mk 7:24). Availability for our own work or, in emergency, for the work of others is one thing, but availability to be at the beck and call of those who have no claim on our services is another.

In many church situations it is customary to put doctors into positions of leadership just because they are doctors, forgetting the fact that medical status does not confer spiritual ability. Christian doctors are sometimes put 'on a pedestal' because of their professional influence, and suffer in consequence the loneliness of being regarded as 'above need', while all the time they are experiencing the barrenness of a busy life and are in no less need (perhaps in greater need than most) of spiritual help and sustenance. This is particularly true of the junior hospital doctor who moves on too frequently to put down roots, and who is already under pressure from overwork and isolation. The time will come later for involvement in the work of the local Christian community, when the doctor's contribution to the cross-cultural and cross-generational life of the church may be considerable.

In the meantime it may be wise to make the hospital the chief sphere of service, to choose a church which is a spiritual feeding ground, and to spend leisure time in homes where fellowship and refreshment may be found. Thus output and intake will be balanced, and the Christian doctor become a continuing channel rather than an ever diminishing reservoir of God's grace. God asks us to be before we do, to come before we go and to receive before we give.

> Lord, give me wisdom to decide when to respond to the call
> of others for help, and when to refuse that I may be able to
> cultivate 'my own vineyard'.

Further reading: Is 5:1-7. Eph 1:1-14, 2:4-10.

MC

September 20

Priorities

Make me first... 1 Kings 17:13 (AV)

The choice we often face is not between the good and the bad, but between things that matter and things that matter most. None would question the legitimacy of the activity of the widow of Zarephath in assuming her family responsibility, but her wisdom was shown in acknowledging a prior claim. The request of Elijah was the claim of God upon the little she had.

It finds its reflection in the words of Jesus set against the background of a busy life and an affluent society. 'Seek first the kingdom and his righteousness' (Matt 6:33). This is the one safeguard against the thorns and thistles which choke the life of the seed.

Many of us are so taken up with important matters that we have forgotten the highest priorities. We have a habit of putting other pressing duties forward, before we attend to the highest claims of Christ. It is the thin end of a big wedge, an attitude fraught with danger, because there will be no end to such duties if we once admit the principle. Neither shall we or others lose by our putting first things first: the widow of Zarephath found her supply sufficed throughout the days of famine; the promise of Jesus is 'and all these things shall be yours as well'. The Lord is no man's debtor. It takes discipline and determination to do that which is most important first. But if we do so, the urgent things will certainly be done, and perhaps better done as a result.

> Seek ye first, not earthly pleasure,
> Fading joy and failing treasure,
> But the love that knows no measure
> Seek ye first, seek ye first.

Further reading: 1 Ki 17:8-16. Lk 10:38-42.

VW

September 21

What Do I do Now?

A third time Jesus said, 'Simon son of John do you love me?' Peter was sad because Jesus asked him the third time, 'Do you love me?' So he said to him, 'Lord, you know everything; you know that I love you!' John 21:17 (GNB)

I have done it again! The same situation, the same mistake. I am not only sorry for what I have done, I am ashamed that I did not learn the first time. Occasionally we are asked to review our progress in the faith; I cannot hide the weakness from myself, even if I try to disguise it from others.

I like Simon Peter. He has some of the same problems that I have, though his are for all to see. The disciples at his suggestion have gone fishing. They work all night but catch nothing until Jesus gives them directions — a reminder, perhaps, that he should be part of all our activities.

After breakfast, Jesus asks Simon the same question three times. Simon is sad that his Master keeps asking him 'Do you love me?' Can he have already forgotten that only a few nights ago he denied knowing Jesus, three times? After he realised what he had done, Simon was deeply ashamed; now Jesus is giving him another chance to try again, with the past put behind him. I think I most like Simon Peter because he lets me see how God goes on loving him, and gives him another chance, even when he doesn't learn the first time.

Almighty God, our heavenly Father, we have sinned against you and against our fellow men, in thought, word and deed. We are truly sorry and repent of all our sins. For the sake of your son, Jesus Christ, who died for us, forgive us all that is past, and grant that we may serve you in newness of life, to the glory of your name.

Further reading: Ps 40:1-3. Jon 1:1-3, 2:1-3:4.

PIMA

September 22

Sickness of Heart

Hope deferred makes the heart sick, but a desire fulfilled is a tree of life.
Proverbs 13:12

The central part of the book of Proverbs (10:1 to 22:16) is a collection of 'two-limbed' sentences, each consisting of a gem of wisdom. (The scholars call such sentences 'gnomes'.) They contain Solomon's observations of human nature, and as that does not change from age to age, most of them are as relevant to life today as when they were written nearly 3,000 years ago.

A number of psychosomatic illnesses are related to expectations being delayed or never realised. Fulfilment is vital for total well-being. As doctors, we must avoid giving our patients unrealistic hopes, and of entertaining them ourselves. Convalescence after major illness and major surgery can often be a long process, and we need to warn patients not to expect to be active too soon. If we give them unrealistic hopes, and these hopes are not realised, a reactive depression can be added to all the other ills they are suffering from. Our prognosis needs to be as accurate and realistic as possible.

Unfounded expectations regarding the Christian life can also cause depressive illness. Unbalanced teaching about holiness, and especially the unbiblical idea that indwelling sin can be completely eradicated from a Christian's life, can do untold harm to people who realise from experience, as the apostle Paul did, that sin is still dwelling in them. Practical holiness is experienced only as we live in a moment by moment attitude of trusting obedience to our Lord Jesus Christ.

> Lord, you are our hope. Keep us from entertaining false hopes of any kind about ourselves, but hoping only in yourself and your word. We know that those who trust in you will never be disappointed.

Further reading: Rom 8:23-25.

JWMcM

September 23

The Doctor as Servant

Truly, truly, I say to you, a servant is not greater than his master. John 13:16

My fellow house-surgeon and I had been delayed in the theatre for several hours assisting the boss with a very difficult case, and I was exhausted as I just popped into the ward to make sure everything was all right before going to supper.

'Ah', said Sister. 'There are loads of intravenous injections to be given.' I was astonished, as they should have been given hours ago, and our registrar was supposed to have been covering the wards while the housemen were in the theatre. I asked her why Dr X hadn't given them. 'Well, I did ask him, but he merely said that he was a registrar, and it wasn't a registrar's job to give "intra-venouses" and I should wait for the houseman.'

This kind of 'caste-system' thinking seemed to affect many doctors in the teaching hospital where I worked. It was far more important to stress one's rank in the pecking-order than actually to do something to help the patient.

How different from the Lord Jesus, who, although he had absolute power and authority, humbled himself and took the lowest place, that of servant. 'The Son of man came not to be served but to serve' (Mk 10:45). And he has left us an example to follow in his footsteps. If we do so, it will certainly make a difference.

A hideous metamorphosis occurs in medical students when they shed their pupal covering and gain their adult (white) coat. Simultaneously a 'little god' complex becomes implanted in their souls, and humility has seemingly vanished forever.

'I'm sick and tired of being a houseman', a colleague complained to me over coffee one day towards the end of our contract. 'I'm constantly at everyone's beck and call, day and night. I shall be glad when I become a senior house officer. Don't you get fed up with it?'

I explained to him that I could not afford to get fed up with it, since as a Christian I was called to a lifetime of service — not just one brief year. I went on to explain that, of course, I found it hard when my service was abused, as often it was by our seniors, but that didn't change the fact that my whole aim in life as a follower of Christ was to serve him and help others.

May God help you too to follow humbly after him today.

> Serving others is not something that comes easily to us, Lord Jesus, and the pride of life is so hard to combat. Help us to follow your example of humility and service in our work and through all our activities.

Further reading: Jn 13:1-17. Phil 2:3-11.

TGS

September 24

Enough is Enough

He gives power to the faint, and to him who has no might he increases strength. Isaiah 40:29

I was very, very tired. It had been an exceptionally busy night in that particular paediatrics job. A tiny baby, with congenital heart disease, had lapsed into heart failure, and the whole night was spent trying every reasonable medical manoeuvre to save her life. In medical terms we failed! On reaching the haven of my bedroom at about 5.30am, the intrusive 'phone rang once more. Would I return to the ward immediately as a boy of three years or so had been admitted with suspected meningitis? There was no option!

I battled with heavy eyelids while I explained to anxious parents that I needed to do a lumbar puncture on their son. Awake enough to pray for the Lord's strength to see this delicate procedure through, I continued into the demands of another full and hectic day.

Many house officers have had busier episodes than this, stretching over two or three consecutive nights. We all know, the busy and the not-so-busy, that fatigue can be the enemy of good medical and surgical practice. It is irresponsible to court tiredness unnecessarily but I believe, as I found throughout the experience I have described, that the Lord does 'give power to the faint' when we are faced, in the midst of our fatigue, with the pressing need of others.

> Lord, you know about fatigue. You spent whole nights in prayer. You had nowhere to lay your head. You sat at the well in your tiredness to ask for a drink. You slept soundly in the boat during the storm. Help me to take what rest I should, but also increase my strength when patients need my help and my body cries out for sleep.

Further reading: Rom 8:31-39. Is 40:27-31.

RFH

September 25

Do not weary with well doing

Love is patient and kind; love is not jealous or boastful; it is not arrogant or rude. Love does not insist on its own way; it is not irritable or resentful; it does not rejoice at wrong, but rejoices in the right. Love bears all things, believes all things, hopes all things, endures all things. Love never ends. 1 Corinthians 13:4-8

After the Russian invasion of Czechoslovakia, a Czech was asked whether the Russians were their brothers or their friends. 'I think they must be our brothers', he replied. 'You see, we can choose our friends.'

How do I cope with my brothers when I honestly don't like them? Of course, Christianity isn't primarily about being nice; it is about a just God who, because of the love he has for us, is prepared to go to extraordinary lengths to save us from ourselves, and to give us the kind of life we were created to enjoy. He loves us so much that he would die for us — the unlovely who are not even his brothers. But the unlovely are not the problem families, the unemployed youth with spiky hair, dressed in black; they are you and me, saying we believe one thing and then conspicuously failing to live up to it.

Of course, I'm nice to patients, I make the coffee after the ward round, I try to avoid the mess gossip sessions. So do many of my colleagues, whatever their beliefs. Indeed, some of them are far nicer people than I am, despite my faith. There will always be some people I don't like, and some of them will be Christians. I would not choose them for my friends, but I still have a commitment especially to them in sharing love. My responsibility is two-fold: to guard against inconsistency in my own affairs, and knowing my own weakness, to accept theirs.

> 'What is Real?' asked the Rabbit one day, when they were lying side by side near the nursery fender, 'Does it mean having things that buzz inside you and a stick-out handle?' 'Real isn't how you are made' said the Skin Horse. 'It's a thing that happens to you. When a child loves you for a long, long time, not just to play with, but REALLY loves you, then you become Real...'

> 'It doesn't happen all at once. 'You become. It takes a long time. That's why it doesn't often happen to people who break easily, or have sharp edges, or who have to be carefully kept. Generally, by the time you are Real, most of your hair has been loved off, and your eyes drop out and you get loose in the joints and very shabby. But these things

don't matter at all because once you are Real, you can't be ugly, except to people who don't understand.'

The Velveteen Rabbit
Margery Williams*

Further reading: Jn 13:34-35.

PIMA

September 26

Take Time to Pray

For God alone my soul waits in silence, for my hope is in him. Psalm 62:5

> I got up early one morning,
> And rushed right into the day!
> I had so much to accomplish
> That I didn't have time to pray.
>
> Problems just tumbled about me,
> And heavier came each task.
> 'Why doesn't God help me?' I wondered.
> He answered, 'You didn't ask!'
>
> I tried to come into God's presence.
> I used all my keys at the lock.
> God gently and lovingly chided.
> 'Why, child, you didn't knock!'
>
> I wanted to see joy and beauty.
> But the day toiled on, grey and bleak.
> I wondered why God didn't show me.
> He said, 'But you didn't seek!'

This is so often typical of a doctor's life, even a Christian doctor. When was the last time that we actually got up early to spend time with the Lord because we had a lot to do on that day? When Jesus had a hectic day, he went away to pray. Let us focus more on the source of our strength and our life, Jesus Christ, for he said, 'I am the vine... apart from me you can do nothing'. I am sure that not only can we accomplish more, but we shall be a more effective witness in our surgery, and we can be of even greater help to our patients.

Let us see it this way:

> I woke up early this morning
> And paused before entering the day.
> I had so much to accomplish
> That I HAD to take time to pray.

What the writer of Psalm 62 says is worthy of much thought:

> 'For God alone my soul waits in silence, for my hope is from him.'

Further reading: Ps 62:5-8. Mt 7:7-11. Jn 15:1-5.

GKGL

September 27

Unconscious Influence

Let your bearing towards one another arise out of your life in Christ Jesus.
Philippians 2:5 (NEB)

None of us can go through life without unconsciously influencing others for good or for bad. People laid their sick friends where Peter's shadow might fall on them (Acts 5:15). Such an act smacks of superstition, but teaches a lesson. Peter had no idea where his shadow fell; nor do we. But we are casting a shadow all the time, one that helps or hinders, encourages or depresses, transmits comfort or coldness. It has been said that one's unconscious influence greatly outweighs any conscious influence one might have.

Our influence depends on what we are rather than on what we do. A cable can transmit electrical power only if attached to the mains, and a pipe carries water only if it is connected to the tank. So what we transmit depends on the source from which our behaviour and manner of speech derive.

The NEB translation of Philippians 2:5 provides a clue: 'Let your bearing to one another arise out of your life in Christ Jesus'.

Our relationship to God through Christ will determine our behaviour to others. Fulfilling Christ's second commandment, my duty to my neighbour, is dependent on complying with the first. We can only in some small measure reflect Christ if we spend time with him. Do our attitudes or our speech reflect a relationship with our master? The way we talk to or ignore the menial staff, the smile which is or is not present when we talk to patients, colleagues or residents? And remember that a smile has been described as a curve that makes many things straight!

They said to Peter, 'Thy speech betrayeth thee' (Mt 26:73).

> Oh that it might be said of me,
>   Surely thy speech betrayeth thee.
> Thou hast been with Jesus of Galilee,
>   With Jesus of Galilee.

Let it be seen that with thee I have been,
Jesus, my Lord and my Saviour.
Let it be known I am always thine own,
By all my speech and behaviour.

E H G Sargent

Further reading: Mt 26:69-75. Acts 4:13-22.

DPB

September 28

Edge of Eternity

'This night your soul is required of you'. Luke 12:20

'The morning after my admission to the Coronary Care Unit, I lay there absolutely shattered', said 55-year-old Cedric, referring to the day after his admission to hospital for his first, and (one hopes) his last, coronary attack, which had occurred the night before. 'I just didn't think it could happen to me.'

Cedric had lived an active life, was always 'on the go', and yet none of his pursuits included any thought about God.

For many non-Christian men, especially self-made people who have had great drive in the pursuit of material goals or in their climb to power, a heart attack is a huge blow to the ego. It reminds them how vulnerable they are, for we are all only a few heart beats away from eternity. Some will refuse to face this consciously, but even the unconscious knowledge is a severe blow and frequently leads to depression.

Many people who have left God out of their ambitions and goals, are never likely to be as receptive again to the Christian gospel as in the period just after a coronary attack. Another 'soft' time is the puerperium, while a nursing mother is still in hospital with her baby. The people who are ministering to these patients, whether they are doctors, nurses or visiting friends, should remember this fact, and be prepared to spend time listening to them. There will often be a natural opportunity to present the Christian gospel.

There is every reason for coronary patients to feel vulnerable. Any Christian attending such patients should be aware that this may be the last period in which the claims of Christ may be presented to them for consideration.

Help me, Lord, always to be able and ready to present the claims of Christ when you open the way — and especially when the patient is on the edge of eternity.

Further reading: Lk 12:13-21.

DAB

September 29

Cause for Bitterness

See to it... that no root of bitterness springs up. Hebrews 12:15

I particularly wanted to do this man's hydrocoele. He had been cancelled from our list and put onto that of another 'firm'. I arranged my work, asked the senior registrar to put the case late on the list, and the nurses to bleep me when the patient left the ward. Later in the afternoon, surprised at not yet being called, I went to the ward to find the patient just returning from the theatre. Twenty minutes later my opposite number met me, gleefully telling me they had deliberately not called me.

Three months before the start of the course my application was accepted. On the day I had planned to ask my consultant to sign my study leave form I heard that my place had been given to another doctor who had only just applied — four weeks after the closing date. No one supported my objection, and he did the course.

How easy to be bitter about two such deliberate meannesses, to dwell on them, to imagine stinging replies to portray my hurt at their underhandedness. But the remarks are never made, and the anger and frustration are turned inwards — to destroy myself. How can I deal with these situations? Turn the other cheek? repeatedly? Make excuses for them, telling myself I am trying to understand why they did it? Fly off the handle and speak my mind — and a bit more? In the short term my own response has largely been due to the part of me that reacts rapidly and usually thoughtlessly. Confessed and forgiven, those moments still take some living down. I can only trust that God is dealing with this part of me too, and that one day, maybe only in heaven, I shall have real control.

Sometimes the good which God brings out of these experiences is not at first apparent. It was thirteen years before God's plan for Joseph became clear. Moreover, we learn from his story that God's plan for our individual lives is much better than anything we had hoped for or can imagine.

> O Lord, help me to bring the hurts, disappointments and frustrations of everyday life as my living sacrifice to you that I may never be embittered by them but through them prove your good and acceptable and perfect plan for my life, a plan that can never be frustrated by other people.

Further reading: Phil 3:7-14.

PIMA

September 30

A Debtor to Grace

For the grace of God that brings salvation has appeared to all men. It teaches us to say 'No' to ungodliness and worldly passions, and to live self-controlled, upright and godly lives in this present age. Titus 2:11-12 (NIV)

A hospital these days can be a pretty difficult place in which to live a self-controlled, upright and godly life. Often the atmosphere in the mess is one of self-indulgence, drunkenness and immorality, especially on party nights. The pressure of clinical work can make this an attractive way of relaxation and tension-relief, and a number of our colleagues will see nothing wrong in making the most of the opportunities.

It is good to be called back to what should motivate our way of life, the 'grace of God that brings salvation'. What is grace? It is the boundless favour and mercy of God shown to undeserving sinners. It was grace that brought the Lord Jesus Christ, the King of heaven, to earth, to be born in an animal-house, to live as a humble carpenter and to die, 'the righteous for the unrighteous' (1 Pet 3:18) on a cruel wooden cross. But God demonstrates his own love for us in this: 'While we were still sinners, Christ died for us' (Rom 5:8). Was there anything desirable, attractive or good about us that should motivate God to send his Son to die for us? No! We were lost sinners bound for a hell we deserved. It was nothing but pure, full, eternal and 'amazing' grace.

If we involve ourselves in 'ungodliness and worldly passions', we pour scorn on the grace of God, trampling it in the dust of our own selfish desires. If evil inclinations creep into our hearts, we have forgotten the glorious nature of the grace that saved our souls, and have grown cold towards our Saviour. So when the pressures of the world bring temptation, let us remember the grace of God revealed in Christ our Saviour, tortured, bleeding and dying for us. Let us say with Thomas, as we see his pierced hands and side, 'My Lord and my God' (Jn 20:28).

> When I survey the wondrous cross
> Where the young Prince of glory died,
> My richest gain I count but loss,
> And pour contempt on all my pride.
>
> Were the whole realm of nature mine,
> That were a present far too small,
> Love so amazing, so divine,
> Demands my soul, my life, my all.

Isaac Watts

Further reading: Rom 6:1-14.

JHCM

October 1

Where is your heart?

No man can serve two masters: for either he will hate the one and love the other; or he will be devoted to the one and despise the other. You cannot serve God and mammon. Matthew 6:24

The contrast here is profound, a black and white situation. The relationship between servant (or slave) and master used to be very close. The servant literally belonged to his master, made it his aim in life to understand his mind and obeyed him implicitly. As with all close human bonds, love could transform it; but if it went wrong, hate might well replace love. Or if another master came into the picture, the servant's allegiance might be switched. What is humanly impossible is to be loyal and obedient to the needs and wishes of two masters at the same time.

The two masters contrasted here are God and worldy goods. Mammon does not mean being rich, but is a worldly attitude to wealth, desiring it for its own sake, accumulating it, allowing it to mould our attitude to others and to promote our own standing and reputation.

But the particular application which the Lord makes here is surprising. Don't let worldly goods, he says, become a distraction to you. Don't have a divided mind about where your necessary food and drink are coming from or how you are going to get clothes to wear. Look at the birds as they fly. Your Heavenly Father each day gives them all that they need. You cannot even add so little as a few feet to the length of your life's journey by being anxious about these things. Think about the lilies of the field. They are frail and ephemeral, but God has given them a beauty far greater than the richest man can provide for himself.

God has given to all creation the means and resources by which to obtain nourishment and physical identity. Man has his own special gifts allowing him to plan ahead, to sow, to reap, to store and construct with his hands, but, equally, these gifts are from God. Trust him absolutely. Ask for sufficient resources for each day, and he will surely provide.

You are worrying about your next job? You are anxious about keeping your mortgage payments going? You don't know if you can ever hold on in the promotion race? Don't be distracted in this way. It's wrong. Follow the Lord with all your heart and use all the gifts, resources and intelligence he has given you. He will not fail to provide for you.

> Grant to me, Lord, the blessing of singleness of heart, that I may love and serve you before and beyond all else.

Further reading: Mt 6:24-33.

CGS

October 2

You Follow Me

Jesus said to him, '... What is that to you? Follow me'. John 21:22

In the final scene of John's gospel, Jesus and Peter talked intimately. They clarify Peter's love, and Jesus challenges Peter to help believers. Jesus then predicts Peter's death. Peter, distracted by John's presence, changes the subject to ask Jesus about John's fate. Lovingly yet firmly, Jesus redirects Peter to personal commitment. Mention of John is irrelevant to concern for Peter's dedication. Directing Peter to individual responsibility, Jesus says, 'You follow me'. Amidst the many distractions of twentieth century living, Jesus still calls us, individually, to personal commitment.

In the course of medical training, we are repeatedly subjected to evaluation by comparison with our peers. Board exams and other qualifying tests are passed not by achieving a particular level of knowledge but by doing better than a certain percentage of other test-takers. Legal systems, in America for instance, determine the appropriateness of medical care by comparison with the most commonly practised standards. Truly, comparative evaluation is a widespread means of judging human activity.

But is comparison enough? When Peter tried to compare himself with John, Jesus redirected Peter to look only at himself. God does not call us merely to perform as well as our peers. He asks us to perform as well as he did. 'Be perfect' Jesus told his followers, 'as your heavenly Father is perfect'. Not only does being 'good' by comparative standards fall short of God's true calling for us, it also robs us of eternal reward. We should be doing good as God directs, looking to God for strength, and accepting God's 'well done'. We should do our 'work heartily as serving the Lord and not men'.

Along the route of our spiritual pilgrimage, however, human comparison does serve one useful purpose. We can use godly individuals as role models and examples. Thus, as Paul followed Christ, he could encourage others to follow him. Human examples can spur us on in our quest for Christ-likeness.

Amidst a society full of comparisons and relativism, God calls us to perfection. Tempted to build our egos by comparing ourselves with others, he asks us to focus only on him. And when we feel tired as we follow him, he encourages us with his strength and abiding presence. As the writer of Hebrews challenges us, 'Let us also lay aside every weight, and let us run with perseverance the race that is set before us, fixing our eyes on Jesus'.

Help us Lord, to be mindful of your words:
'Enter by the narrow gate; for the gate is wide,
and the way is easy, that leads to destruction,
and those who enter by it are many. For the gate is
narrow, and the way is hard that leads to life,
and those who find it are few.'

Mt 7:13-14

Further reading: Jn 21:15-22. Mt 5:44-6:8. 1 Cor 10:32-11:2.

PRF

October 3

The Way (10) — Those not in the Way

The first thing Andrew did was to find his brother Simon and tell him, 'We have found the Messiah' (that is, the Christ). Then he brought Simon to Jesus. John 1:41- 42 (NIV)

Andrew and Simon seem to have been very different — Andrew quiet and thoughtful, Simon big, bluff and impetuous. But they were brothers and no doubt shared many things. When Andrew met Jesus, he knew he had found someone special. So the first thing he did was to find his brother and tell him about it. And he brought him to Jesus. Jesus did the rest.

The next day Jesus called Philip to follow him. Philip, like Andrew, knew he had found someone special. So he told Nathanael about it. Nathanael was cautious, but Philip said, 'Come and see'. Jesus did the rest.

So began the gathering of the band of disciples, who in their turn were to go out and be fishers of men. We can scarcely doubt that many of these disciples came to Jesus because people like Andrew and Philip brought them to him. Jesus did the rest.

We who know the splendid friendship of the Master of the Way have an obligation to share this with those who are not in the Way. We cannot by argument or by persuasion bring anybody else to true faith. That is the work of the Spirit of God. Our first responsibility is, like Andrew and Philip, to bring people to Jesus. He can do the rest. As F B Meyer has put it, 'Jesus Christ is God's magnet put down amongst men to attract them to himself'.

Why is this an obligation? Indeed, what right have we to intrude into someone else's personal life and beliefs? Is there no such thing as spiritual privacy? Yes, there is such a thing, and we should respect it. But the last thing Jesus said to his disciples was: 'you will be my witnesses' (Acts 1:8). Later, Peter wrote: 'Always be prepared to give an answer to everyone who asks you to give the reason for the hope that you have. But do this with gentleness and respect, keeping a clear conscience...' (1 Pet 3:15-16).

Good news is to be shared. What should we think of a medical adviser who withheld from a patient a curative drug or a rehabilitating procedure that was readily available? Or who refused to refer a patient to a consultant who had the answer to the patient's need? Here, too, in this medical situation there are ways and means of going about it, involving 'gentleness and respect, keeping a clear conscience'. But it is good news and so is to be shared. Infinitely greater is the love of God in Christ.

> Lord, take my lips and speak through them; take my mind
> and think through it; take my heart and set it on fire with
> love for you and for the people you have made.

Further reading: Jn 1:35-47. Acts 1:6-9. Col 4:2-6.

RRW

October 4

Work Out: God is at Work

... work out your own salvation with fear and trembling; for God is at work in you, both to will and to work for his good pleasure. Philippians 2:12-13

We know that nothing we do or do not do can earn us salvation — it is a free gift from God. Sometimes we almost get the feeling when we hear Christians speak that our spiritual growth is also a gift from God for which we can do nothing.

In these verses Paul shows us that the Christian life is, in fact, a partnership between God and ourselves. We do something — 'work out' says Paul; and God does something — 'God is at work'. This should not be too difficult for us to understand for there are parallels in everyday life. You help your patients by providing them with a cure, but they on their part must co-operate actively. To borrow from Paul, they have to 'work out' their healing even as you are 'at work' in (surgeons literally!) them.

As William Barclay puts it so wisely: 'There can be no salvation without God, but what God offers, man must take. It is never God who withholds salvation; it is always man who deprives himself of it.'

Finally, what about 'fear and trembling'? Again, Barclay says: 'It is not the fear and trembling which drives us to hide from God, but rather the fear and trembling which drives us to seek God in the certainty that without his help we cannot effectively face life.'

O Lord, never suffer us to think that we can stand by ourselves, and not need thee.

A prayer attributed to John Donne

Further reading: Phil 2:1-18. 2 Pet 1:1-11.

WGB

October 5

The Wrong Mountain

Happy are those who trust the Lord, who do not turn to idols or join those who worship false gods. Psalm 40:4 (GNB)

As I sat on a log at the top of the pass, I looked up to the white stony mountain and its newly green trees. An hour more and I could be at the top.

I had met such challenges in the past, but this time it was different. My knee was hurting from the chipped cartilage from a previous injury. I knew that climbing this mountain might mean that I would not be able to walk at some point soon in my life. I wondered whether giving in to my desire to climb the mountain was worth that price. It certainly would benefit no one else. I was helping no one but myself, and I was not sure I was even doing that.

So I bade farewell to the mountain, turned back, and resolved to stay healthy in order to serve God.

> Dear Lord, please help us to keep the mountains of our lives from becoming false gods. Give us a clear vision of your will for us, as Jesus had when he prayed, 'Our Father, which art in heaven, hallowed be thy name. Thy kingdom come. Thy will be done in earth, as it is in heaven. Give us this day our daily bread. And forgive us our debts, as we forgive our debtors. And lead us not into temptation, but deliver us from evil. For thine is the kingdom, and the power, and the glory, forever. Amen.'

Thought for the Day:

> With God's help, we can distinguish between worthy challenges and empty challenges.

Further reading: Ps 40:1-5

DJB

Reprinted from *The Upper Room*. Copyright (Sep 5, 1981) by The Upper Room, 1908 Grand Avenue, Nashville, Tennessee. Used by permission.

October 6

Nothing Impossible

Nothing is impossible with God. Luke 1:37 (NIV)

There are many things we cannot alter, much as we should like to. We say: 'If only I could, I would'. What could be better, then, than a faith that makes all things possible for us? But we have already made a subtle but serious shift from a biblical principle. The Christian's God is indeed one with whom 'nothing is impossible', but this is quite different from saying that God will do anything: 'If I cannot, God will'. This is convenient but not scriptural.

This formula, used as a type of incantation, is bound to fail. Experience and commonsense demonstrate it to be false. This is not surprising because Scripture tells us that there are some things that even God cannot do. He cannot belie his nature. The context of the verse is important. In the instance quoted it is the promise of the virgin birth of Jesus, the very incarnation of God himself. With God the utterly impossible actually happened. On another occasion Jesus made the same statement regarding the possibility of a rich man entering God's kingdom (Mt 19:23-26). In yet another Paul is asserting that when God promises something he is able to perform it (Rom 4:21). We see therefore that to impose the necessary strict conditions on the application of this promise in no way limits its stupendous and miraculous possibilities.

All that is consonant with God's nature is possible, all that is true, holy and righteous. More than that, all that is in line with his will no one and nothing can ultimately frustrate. This has been the challenge and the comfort of God's children throughout history. God's dependability is guaranteed to those who depend on him. 'They who trust him wholly find him wholly true' (F R Havergal).

This is the great principle proved in practice by those whose belief and trust is real. Such usually have more than their share of troubles, for God saves us in rather than from our circumstances, while faith remains undimmed and trust in him grows, 'Depend upon it, God's work, done in God's way, will never lack God's supplies' (Hudson Taylor).

For every promise of God is sure to be fulfilled.

Lk 1:37 (JBP)

Further reading: Ps 37:1-5, Heb 11:8-19. Rom 4:16-25

DEBP

October 7

God and the Physician

In the thirty-ninth year of his reign Asa was diseased in his feet, and his disease became severe; yet even in his disease he did not seek the Lord but sought help from the physicians. 2 Chronicles 16:12

King Asa was one of the good kings of the southern kingdom of Judah. He began his reign by doing what was good and right in the sight of the Lord. He listened to Azariah, the Spirit-filled prophet, as he gave God's message to him, and in reliance on the Lord won a great victory. But, as he grew older, his faith grew less. When his enemies threatened him, he sought the military help of the king of Syria against them. Once again the Lord sent a prophet to him, Hanani the seer, and he rebuked the king for his foolishness. Asa was very angry and had the Lord's messenger thrown into prison.

Three years later disease began in his feet, and within two years he died. He did not seek the Lord's help, but rather turned to the physicians. These physicians were men of a different type from the modern physician. Their knowledge was a strange mixture of observation and superstition. They had none of the modern diagnostic aids at their disposal. They could not say whether the ageing king was suffering from diabetes, peripheral arterial disease, gout or some severe form of osteo-arthritis, and they had no scientific basis for their treatment. But the modern Christian physician should remember that, with all his or her scientific knowledge, there is still the need to seek the Lord for his wisdom and grace day by day. Have YOU done so today?

> Lord, I thank you for all the diagnostic tools at my disposal: for X-rays, microscopes and all the other aids I have. Help me never to forget that, day by day and hour by hour, I still need your wisdom and your grace in my dealings with people. May I never, as Asa did, stop relying on you.

Further reading: 2 Ch 16.

JWMcM

October 8

Man: a Breath, a Shadow

Man is like a breath, his days are like a passing shadow. Psalm 144:4

One of the strange paradoxes of life is that the longer it goes on, the shorter it seems. When I was a child and a teenager, I felt that I had been alive for aeons. When I married and graduated at the age of 25, life seemed to stretch ahead unendingly. Now, at 47, when I am at least halfway through my clinical life, I realise a difference has crept up on me. For instance, recently I met a colleague who is near retirement. His wife looked an old lady. Nevertheless, I can remember her as an attractive young woman with two toddlers.

It is not important to consider the transience of life when we are young and it seems unending. Modern physicists tell us that time, space and matter are all inter-related and were created together at, by definition, the beginning of time as we know it. This makes it easier for me to see our temporal existence as something transcended by a different unchanging form of existence called eternity.

Of course, we have not the mental equipment to grasp these concepts any more than an intelligent dog can grasp the concepts of higher mathematics. But we can and should learn to pray with the Psalmist:

Lord, let me know my end, and what is the measure of my days;
let me know how fleeting my life is!
Behold, thou hast made my days a few handbreaths,
and my lifetime is as nothing in thy sight.
Surely every man stands as a mere breath.

Ps 39:4-5

Further reading: Ps 39.

DAB

October 9

My Shepherd (10)

My cup runneth over. Psalm 23:5

In this context, this verse speaks of overflowing contentment. We can almost see the lambs leaping about, wagging their tails with glee and the old sheep looking out benignly over the idyllic scene. All wants supplied, all dangers at bay, all wounds cared for, no limit to supplies. There is more than enough provided for every conceivable need, with the shepherd standing by to keep it that way. The cup of life is indeed full.

For a cup to run over it is either being filled so fast that it overflows or it was full to the brim and has been jolted. Years ago, Paul Brand spoke on this theme. He illustrated the risk of spillage if a full glass were carried across a crowded room. He likened the glass to a Christian and reminded us that what comes out when we are jostled will depend on how our 'glass' has been charged. If we are filled with self- importance or self-pity, irritability or grievance will spill out. If on the other hand the Holy Spirit of God is daily anointing us, cleansing, renewing and refilling us, this will be what overflows when we are jostled, and there will be an unstoppable effect on those around us. Other lives will be touched or made thirsty for the same sparkle. As the Lord Jesus foretold, 'Whoever believes in me, streams of living water will flow from within him', and we shall sometimes be able to share with others his invitation, 'Come to me and drink' (Jn 7:37,38 NIV). More often than not, we shall be quite unconscious of the effect, but the cup will need to be constantly replenished if we are to continue to act as irrigation channels to the dry and barren world about us.

The importance of regular quiet times with the Shepherd cannot be over-emphasised, although there will be times, particularly at the junior hospital stage, when there may be literally little time to sit down in peace. On those days, even one verse to mull over, perhaps while waiting on the telephone, may act as a spiritual 'sprinkler', but the ideal is to find a daily time for prayer and Bible reading. Normally this means to be alone, but to share fellowship occasionally with even one other Christian is of mutual encouragement and stimulus.

> Make me a channel of your peace.
> Where there is hatred let me bring your love;
> Where there is injury, your pardon Lord;
> And where there's doubt, true faith in you.
> Where there's despair in life let me bring hope;
> Where there is darkness, only light;
> And where there's sadness, ever joy.

Sebastian Temple
from a prayer of St Francis

Further reading: Lk 6:43-45. Mk 7:18-23

JG

October 10

My Shepherd (10 cont'd)

My cup runneth over. Psalm 23:5

Are there practical as well as spiritual ways in which a Christian doctor's cup can run over? Whether we like to admit it or not, we are wealthier than many in our own society and rich compared with our third world colleagues. We must each decide before the Lord what sort of lifestyle will honour him most. Remembering how he lowered his standard of living for our sakes may encourage us to pour out more from our own cup to help others. For some, this could involve changing countries so that the contents may flow more readily into areas of greater need. (Why do so few apply for missionary service now? Could it be to do with wanting to preserve a full cup for our own use?) Those whose work is based, here or elsewhere, in a throwaway society, will find drugs or obsolescent equipment to be wasted by the ton. Many items, which could well be boiled up and used again elsewhere, are discarded after one use. One little diabetic girl, by rinsing through and saving her once used plastic syringes and needles, has sent several boxes of them 'to the children in Africa' via her Christian doctor's contact. (That same doctor had been astounded, in an African teaching hospital, to find a record number of injection abscesses and then to see that the two needles being used for 100 patients were as blunt as nails.) Our trash may be useful, but our cash could do more — not merely as handouts, but in supporting medical teachers and others, if we cannot go ourselves. Even so, material gifts are no substitute for prayer: the two go best together.

What, though, if the flow dries up and I seem uninspired either to give or to pray? I must turn again toward the Shepherd, recalling how it is he who has given all things richly to enjoy (and to share). It is he who freely gives, yet the scars on his hands, brow and heart testify to the price that was paid for all that costs me nothing. His cup was bitter, yet he took and drank it all down so that mine could be filled up. If such recollections do not fill my heart to overflowing gratitude, I must make or take time to come closer to him (and others of his), thinking and thanking, until once more my cup runs over.

> O breath of love come breathe within us,
>   Renewing thought and will and heart
> Come, love of Christ, afresh to win us,
>   Revive your Church in every part.

J Wade

Further reading: Rom 12:1-2. Heb 13:15-16

JG

October 11

Take off the Rose-Coloured Spectacles

I the Preacher have been king over Israel in Jerusalem. And I applied my mind to see and to search out by wisdom all that is done under heaven; it is an unhappy business that God has given to the sons of men to be busy with. Ecclesiastes 1:12-13

Doctors, whether young or old, should read the book of Ecclesiastes, the words of the Preacher, provided they read it perceptively. It is a book about life as it is. Some see it as being essentially cynical, but that misses the point. Many parts of it do sound cynical if taken on their own. They are still not to be denied. And again and again the Preacher's mind comes back to God. For all the vanity of life, which he sees with stark realism, his mind is never far from knowing that God is still there — the God who is wisdom and love and power, who knows what he is about, and who knows what life is about when we do not.

Medicine all too often sees the raw side of life, whether in the patient's personal experience or in the world in which people live and with which they have to cope. It may be very real in the doctor's own personal experience (though his patients might be surprised if they knew). It does not help at all to pretend that life is not like that, though of course it can be just the opposite. Indeed, if Solomon really wrote both Ecclesiastes and the Song of Songs, he knew something of both sides of life.

However, come what may, we, like the Preacher, know that God is still there. And we can, like the Preacher, safely take off our rose-coloured spectacles. Moreover, we in our day know something that the Preacher did not know. We know the magnificent reality of a God who has shared our human life, who has drunk its bitterness to the dregs and who has triumphed over it. We know a God who really understands and who fully warrants our trust.

> Christ leads me through no darker rooms
>   Than he went through before;
> He that unto God's kingdom comes
>   Must enter by that door.

Richard Baxter

Further reading: Ec 1:12-18. Heb 2:14-18, 4:14-16.

RRW

October 12

Sight by Faith

We walk by faith, not by sight. 2 Corinthians 5:7

Biblical teaching is clear that we, as Christians, are to live by faith rather than to base our lives only on the realm that is physically seen. Instead of demanding a 'blind faith', however, God gives us the opportunity to see a world that is, humanly, unseen.

It is easy for us as physicians to sense that some things transcend the physical realm as we know it. The ideas of will, conscience and emotion all surpass our anatomical models and descriptions. Though unseen, these aspects of the human mind are very real. So it is with the spiritual realm. God and the heavenly hosts are alive and actively involved in our lives, yet they are not visible to our eyes.

Elisha's servant in 2 Kings 6, was treated to a sight usually seen by faith alone as he saw protective chariots of fire. The chariots had been as real to Elisha, with his sight by faith, as if they had been viewed on visible wavelengths of light. Moses, by faith, was able to live through adversity because he could see 'him who is unseen'. We too, based on guidelines presented in the Bible, can share this view of the heavenly realm.

First, we must believe in the reality of the physically unseen spiritual world. He who comes to God, we read in Hebrews, must believe that he exists, for without faith it is impossible to please him.

Second, we must look at the unseen world; we must set our minds, Paul told Christians in Colosse, on things above. With sight by faith, 'let us fix our eyes on Jesus, the author and perfecter of our faith' (Heb 12:2 NIV).

Believing in the unseen world and looking to its Ruler, we must then take action. Just as a growing infant's vision becomes perception through interaction with his environment, so we too must get involved with our world, based on what we see by faith. 'The righteous,' wrote both Habakkuk and Paul, 'shall live by his faith'. Our sight by faith not only gives us great encouragement; it also gives us illumination by which to live.

> Turn your eyes upon Jesus,
>   Look full in his wonderful face;
>   And the things of earth will grow strangely dim
>   In the light of his glory and grace

Helen H Lemmel*

Further reading: Heb 11:1-12:3. Col 3:1-4. Hab 2:4. Rom 1:17

PRF

* Reproduced by permission of National Christian Education Council

October 13

Roots

Cursed is the man... whose heart turns away from the Lord. He is like a shrub in the desert, and shall not see any good come. He shall dwell in the parched places of the wilderness... Blessed is the man who trusts in the Lord, whose trust is the Lord. He is like a tree planted by water, that sends out its roots by the stream, and does not fear when heat comes, for its leaves remain green, and is not anxious in the year of drought, for it does not cease to bear fruit. Jeremiah 17:5-8

The contrast here is between the shrub with shallow roots and the sturdy tree with roots running deep to derive the hidden moisture seeping through the soil from the river. The former is utterly dependent on circumstances, the prevailing environment of the moment, flourishing in times of rain and withering in seasons of drought. The tree on the other hand is independent of external environment, its nurture being provided by hidden sources reached by its deep and spreading roots. It is fruitful and always green, demonstrating best its environmental independence when the drought withers the surrounding vegetation. The hidden difference is the reliance on roots. The tree 'sends out its roots by the stream'.

A Christian should be one whose 'heart is fixed, trusting in the Lord' (Ps 112:7) and whose 'roots are sent out by the stream'. Security and sources of nourishment should render him or her demonstrably less dependent on environment than are others.

The roots are crucial. When the fig tree failed to bear fruit, it was not the branches or the trunk that were attended to. The ground was dug around the roots and fertilizer applied (Lk 13:7-8). Medical practice of every kind abounds with opportunities to demonstrate dependence on or some degree of independence of environment. Have we, like our Lord, 'meat to eat that they know not of' (Jn 4:32)?

Make your daily (and preferably morning) quiet time a top priority. This has been the mainstay of the writer's life for half a century. Our Lord instructed us to pray for daily bread, and this refers to nourishment for the spirit as well as for the body. If you only collect your bread weekly on Sundays, be honest and drop the word daily. But it is far better to underline it and act accordingly.

Father, give me this day my daily bread.

Further reading: Ps 1.

DPB

October 14

Better off Dead. A Matter of Viewpoint (1)

Cursed be the day on which I was born! Jeremiah 20:14

It is sad but not altogether unusual to hear someone say that he or she would be better off dead.

Jeremiah felt that God had called him to so daunting and impossible a task, that life seemed unbearable. Yet he found that the God who had called him also enabled and protected him (Je 20:9).

For Elijah it was physical exhaustion tinged, perhaps, with self-pity that made him plead for death (1 Ki 19:4,10,14). Rest, food, renewal and recommissioning returned him to effective service.

In our medical practice it is not unheard of for men and women in moments of extreme crisis, or in times of prolonged mental depression or apparently meaningless physical suffering, to feel that life is no longer worth living. But almost always there are means of relief, and often this is a passing phase. Normally life is sweet even for those who are handicapped or are suffering the disabilities of old age or disease.

But there is a new turn in today's society, and doctors are being asked to decide for others whether life is likely to be worthwhile. Some attempts have been made to sue doctors for 'wrongful life' in the first place. Mercifully the law has declined to define what constitutes value in life. As Gareth Jones points out in *Brave New People* decisions regarding potential for real life are being based solely on biological criteria, value choices on the worth of life have been reduced to 'a rating on a scale of excellence'; 'but', he adds, 'life is more than simply a healthy body. It reflects our likeness to God, our creation in his image and our dignity based on his love and concern for us no matter how beautiful or ugly, how successful or fragmented we may appear to those around us.'

The fact that 'life defined as intolerable by physicians might come to be defined differently by parents' was the experience of two shocked by the discovery of Down's syndrome in their firstborn. It took time for the hurt and the fear 'to give place to total acceptance. He enjoys every minute of his young life. God has used him in ways we will never know...There are many people who love and serve our Lord today because we had a little handicapped son. We have three beautiful and very precious children but our firstborn is 'special'. We have heard Down's children described as abnormal or imperfect and other such words, but to us he is none of these — he is just Simon.'

My grace is sufficient for you, for my power is made perfect in weakness (2 Cor 12:9).

Lord, grant us humility, compassion, sensitivity and discernment in our value judgments and choices. Help us to remember how precious in your sight and how close to your heart are some whom the world would regard as worthless.

Further reading: Ps 8. 1 Cor 1:26-29.

MC

October 15

Better off Dead. A Matter of Viewpoint (2)

It would have been better for that man if he had not been born. Matthew 26:24

God's criteria for judging the value of a man's life are in stark contrast to man's. They refer not to biological excellence, but to spiritual relationships.

Man's relationship to him

Referring specifically to Judas, Jesus highlighted the all-importance of the issue of acceptance or rejection of himself. Better not born than knowingly, calculatedly, determinedly and finally to reject the Lord of glory in exchange for transient and worthless things. 'How often would I... and you would not' (Mt 23:37).

Man's relationship to others

Better a millstone... and death by drowning than that we should cause a child who believes in him to stumble or sin (Mt 18:6). As Christians we are perhaps in greater danger here than in the matter of total rejection of the Lord. The world's values rub off, it is easy to conform to and walk in the world's ways and to lose the Christian difference. Paul tells the Christians at Philippi, 'Imitate me!' (Phil 3:17). What will happen to others today if they do just that with me? If they copy my behaviour at the mess party? My degree of integrity in filling up claim forms or job applications? The conscientiousness or otherwise of my routine work? My minor distortions of the truth in covering up my mistakes or blaming others? My casual conversations and slanted gossip? We tend to have a higher standard for others than for ourselves, and to excuse in ourselves what we do not tolerate in others. If everyone I meet today copies me, will the hospital be a better or a worse place in which to live? Or, in those close personal relationships, perhaps hidden from other Christians, is my aim self-gratification or the standing of my friends before God? What a tragedy if friendship with me leads to forgotten ideals, forsaken standards, a diminishing awareness of God's holiness, or a broken relationship between him and one of his followers (or potential followers)!

Man's relationship to himself

There is a sense in which every Christian is 'better off dead', not only because to be out of the world and 'with Christ is far better' (Phil 1:23), but in a spiritual sense here and now because Jesus said 'He who loses his life for my sake will find it' (Mt 10:39). He was not just referring to physical death, though some are called to face that, but rather a death to self to which we are all daily called, and which is the prerequisite of experiencing the risen life of Jesus within us. We should do well to echo Paul's prayer: 'That I may know him and the power of his resurrection, and may share his suffering, becoming like him in his death' (Phil 3:10).

> O Cross that liftest up my head,
> I dare not ask to fly from thee.
> I lay in dust life's glory dead,
> And from the ground there blossoms red
> Life that shall endless be.

George Matheson

Further readings: Jn 3:16-19. Rom. 12:1-2. Jn 12:24-25. Rom 8:10-14.

MC

October 16

Loneliness

Turn thou to me, and be gracious to me; for I am lonely and afflicted. Relieve the troubles of my heart, and bring me out of my distresses. Psalm 25:16-17

If I had to pick out the most common difficulty that faces junior doctors, I would say that it is loneliness. If you are working in an unfamiliar hospital, the barriers to forming good meaningful friendships are considerable. You may be working every other night and weekend, and be so shattered on the intervening evenings that solitude and sleep are much to be preferred to society. In addition, you always have the knowledge that in six months or less you will be moving on — perhaps half-way across the country, and any links you do manage to establish will be geographically severed. In such a situation it is easy to sit on the pity-pot and not make any effort even to start developing relationships.

This, however, can be very harmful. Daphne Du Maurier in her classic study of distrust and suspicion, *My Cousin Rachel*, writes: 'the lonely man is an unnatural man and soon comes to perplexity, from perplexity to fantasy, from fantasy to madness' or as the Scripture expresses it more concisely, 'It is not good for man to be alone' (Gn 2:18). So, even with the limited time at our disposal we should strive to make friends if we possibly can.

Nevertheless we also have to learn to cope with loneliness, as there will be times when human companionship is not possible for us. It is then that the Christian has a tremendous advantage. As John Donne pointed out two centuries ago, 'loneliness is God's great opportunity to draw near to the soul', and more recently John White writes in a similar vein: 'would you despise intimacy with the Almighty in insisting on human intimacy?' (*Eros Defiled*).

One of the deep regrets of my time as a houseman is that I did not make more use of my time of enforced isolation 'on call' for developing relationships with God even when there were often plenty of hours in which to do so. I spent a lot of them idly moping instead. There are things we can only learn when alone with God, and these can greatly strengthen our spiritual lives. One of the criteria of assessment of a man's true character is the answer to the question: 'What does he do when he's on his own?' Let's make sure then that in our periods of loneliness we use the time constructively to build our faith and deepen our relationship with the living Lord.

> I will withdraw me and be quiet,
> Why meddle in life's riot?
> Shut be my door to pain;
> Desire, thou dost befool me, thou shalt cease.
> Vain, vain the word; vain, vain,
> Not in aloofness lieth peace.

Amy Carmichael

Lord, you made me for interaction with others. Help me in the development of firm friendships, but help me to cope with loneliness, knowing that you are always with me.

Further reading: Ps 25:12-22. Jn 16:29-33.

TGS

October 17

Good Intentions

... the noble man makes noble plans, and by noble deeds he stands. Isaiah 32:8 (NIV)

Good intentions by themselves, whether in medicine or in any other department of life, are never enough. Yet many of us indulge in them without finally delivering the goods. Often there are good reasons for this. Too often there are not. In serious medical situations, the results of this kind of failure can be regrettable, disastrous and even tragic. According to an old saying, the road to Hell is paved with good intentions.

Isaiah is certainly not talking about the road to Hell. His subject is the kingdom of righteousness — the Lord's rule — where things are given their right values. 'No longer will the fool be called noble', he writes, 'nor the scoundrel be highly respected'. The fool's failure to do good things tends to be negative; they just don't get done. The scoundrel's failure to do good things is more likely to be positive; they are deliberately rejected. Neither fool nor scoundrel is noble. Nobility by God's standards consists in making noble plans and carrying them out as noble deeds. That is the standard of noble people.

In the language of today's thinking, the word 'noble' does not sit easily on one's lips. It is a bit too grand, a bit too 'good', even a bit pretentious. And certainly it is not a word to be used lightly. Just the same, it is a fine word, which denotes a fine concept. We should not discard it, but should keep it for its right use. Isaiah's sentence gives it very proper use and tells us in the highest terms much more about the very practical matter of good intentions. He makes it very clear that good intentions by themselves are not enough for now or for eternity.

> Help me, Lord, to be both good and thoughtful in my intentions and also responsible and faithful in carrying them out.

Further reading: Is 32:1-8. Pr 20:6.

RRW

October 18

To Have what it Takes

It is by grace you have been saved through faith — and this not of yourselves, it is the gift of God. Ephesians 2:8 (NIV)

It is 3am and your 'bleep' has gone off for the second time in half an hour. You could weep with fatigue, frustration and misery. The human frame is just not designed to cope with the circumstances of a junior hospital doctor. As you mechanically carry out the required task, longing for your bed and sleep, you wonder how you are supposed to survive — as a person, as a member of a family, and as a Christian.

At times like this, we need to let the living and active word of God speak to our hearts, as it is given to do. This verse can help us. Our salvation does not depend one fraction of 1% on ourselves. It is totally, 100%, the work of God. Planned in eternity by the Father, accomplished completely on the Cross by the Son, who as our representative and substitute died bearing the just punishment for our sins, it is applied to our hearts by the Holy Spirit. Even the faith we exercise is the gift of God; we cannot produce it for ourselves.

So when our spiritual survival seems at stake because we are too tired to pray, too busy to study the scriptures, and too tied to the hospital to attend church meetings and worship, it is good to be reminded that we are saved by grace. Temporary interruptions in our co-operation in God's sanctifying work make no difference to our justification. That is his work alone, and Christ has done it all for us. A man as well as God, he understands our fatigue and frustration, and says, 'My grace is sufficient for you' (2 Cor 12:9). So in the midst of physical and mental exhaustion, let us rest in him and his never failing promises.

> My hope is built on nothing less
> Than Jesus' blood and righteousness;...
> When darkness seems to veil his face,
> I rest on his unchanging grace...
> When all around my soul gives way
> He then is all my strength and stay
> On Christ the solid Rock I stand,
> All other ground is sinking sand.

Edward Mote

Further reading: Eph 2:1-10. Rom 3:21-31

JHCM

October 19

An Odd Lot

You have spent enough time in the past doing what pagans choose to do. They think it strange that you do not plunge with them into the same flood of dissipation, and they heap abuse on you. 1 Peter 4:3-4 (NIV)

What impression does the Christian make on others who do not share his belief? Perhaps we all too often make no impression. The wish to conform is strong in most people, especially once they get over the rebelliousness of teens and possibly student years. Thereafter, particularly in a profession such as medicine, the majority wish to be like their peers. Any differences that may be coveted are of another order — those of post, kudos or merit (especially if accompanied by the appropriate award!).

Peter depicts two periods in the lives of his readers. First, a past which carries the label 'no longer'. There were things which once we enjoyed, but now they hold no attraction. What used to be taught as 'separation' is readily held up to ridicule in a permissive culture, but in John Stott's words 'there can be no following without a previous forsaking'. The life of the present is different: Peter is describing a life that has been simplified, that is calm and prayerful. We are called to 'be clearminded and self-controlled' (1 Pet 4:7).

The Christian who is sensitive to God's will for every part of his or her life will know something of the inevitable tension of playing a proper part in the world without being part of it. Perhaps we need to recognise which is the greater danger in our individual case — whether that of compromise or an ugly insularity. This can be, under God, a matter of nice judgment, especially when we recognise the all-pervading nature of the secularism and humanism of today's society. C S Lewis in *Reflection on the Psalms* writes:

> 'I am inclined to think a Christian would be wise to avoid, when he decently can, any meeting with people who are bullies, lascivious, cruel, spiteful and so forth. Not because we are "too good" for them. In a sense we are not good enough. We are not good enough to cope with all the temptation, nor clever enough to cope with all the problems, which an evening spent in such society produces. The temptation is to condone, to connive at, and by our words, looks and laughter, to "consent".'

> Lord, as one who was a friend of publicans and sinners but who never condoned sin, help me to live in the world without being of it, to retain not only my true humanity but also my Christian 'difference', and to love those for whom you died, while hating all that made that sacrifice necessary. I thank you that you prayed not that I should be taken out of the world but that I should be kept from its sins. Keep me just for today, and grant that today I may be 'salt' and 'light' wherever I may be.

Further reading: 1 Pet 2:9-12. Mt 5:13-16.

DEBP

October 20

Understanding People

Jesus knew men so well, all of them, that he needed no evidence from others about a man, for he himself could tell what was in a man. John 2:25 (NEB). He understood human nature. (JBP)

The Lord Jesus did not need to reply on gossip or on the social worker's report or any other roundabout way of assessing a man's character. He himself could tell... he understood. If we have anything at all of his mind, we too should be demonstrating something of his understanding. This may demand conscious effort on our part. It is easier to blame someone for being hard to understand than it is to try to understand him.

Why did our Lord understand human nature so well? Because he had deliberately taken upon himself the likeness of men. He was interested in us and became involved with us. His interest expressed itself as self-effacing love. His involvement went as far as identification and sacrifice.

Does this tell me why I find it hard to understand people? I do not care enough about them, and I avoid getting myself too involved. Therefore I have to rely on the care and involvement of others to explain to me my patient's problems.

This is an era of unprecedented scientific advance. In our enthusiasm for the new knowledge we may be tempted to forget the old wisdom. There is need to remember the person within the patient, to give imaginative as well as intensive care. God is unveiling to us more of his secrets, more of his mind. Although there is no searching of his understanding, yet he wants to share with us more of the understanding that he as Creator has of human structure and of human nature. Interest in our patients must not be confined to elucidating the clinical problems: we must also become involved in reaching a deeper understanding of their personal needs. Indeed, the second may often help toward the first.

> O master, grant that I may never seek
> So much to be consoled as to console;
> To be understood as to understand;
> To be loved as to love with all my soul.

Sebastian Temple

Further reading: 1 Ki 3:7-13.

JG

October 21

Sleep (1) — Restorer and Healer

He gives to his beloved sleep. Psalm 127:2

Sleep is one of God's most wonderful gifts. Much has been written about it that may encourage both doctor and patient. Here are some thoughts:

> Sleep, that knits up the ravell'd sleeve of care.
> The death of each day life, sore labour's bath,
> Balm of hurt minds, great nature's second course.
> Chief nourisher in life's feast.

Shakespeare, *Macbeth*

> O sleep, O gentle sleep
> Nature's soft nurse

Shakespeare, *Henry IV, Part II*

Now blessing light on him that first invented this same sleep; it covers a man all over, thoughts and all like a cloak; it is meat for the hungry, drink for the thirsty, heat for the cold, and cold for the hot. It is the current coin that purchases all the pleasures of the world cheap; and it is the balance that sets the king and the shepherd, the fool and the wise man.

Cervantes

... in so many cases the best way of leading a tired and nervous person back to health is by teaching him to sleep again.

Walter C Alvarez. Mayo Clinic Physician

The sleep of the labouring man is sweet, whether he eat little or much; but the abundance of the rich will not suffer him to sleep

Ec 5:12

Something attempted, something done,
Has earned a night's repose.

Longfellow, The Village Blacksmith

Support us all the day long, till the shades lengthen,
and the evening comes, and the busy world is hushed,
and the fever of life is over, and our work is done.
Then in thy mercy grant us a
safe lodging, a holy rest, and peace at the last,
through Jesus Christ our Lord.

John Henry Newman

Further reading: Pr 3:21-24

RRW

October 22

Sleep (2) — Other Sleep

So then let us not sleep as others do, but let us keep awake and be sober. 1 Thessalonians 5:6

Natural sleep is good and to be treasured. But the Scriptures speak of sleep in at least two other ways that we need to think about. There is a sleep that is not worthy, the sleep of indolence, and unpreparedness. Speaking of being ready for the Lord's return, Paul writes: 'For you yourselves know well that the day of the Lord will come like a thief in the night... you are not in darkness, brethren, for that day to surprise you like a thief... So then let us not sleep as others do, but let us keep awake and be sober... For God has not destined us for wrath, but to obtain salvation through our Lord Jesus Christ, who died for us so that whether we wake or sleep we might live with him' (1 Thes 5:2-10).

And there is that other sleep that is called death. 'We would not have you ignorant, brethren', Paul writes, 'concerning those who are asleep, that you may not grieve as others do who have no hope. For since we believe that Jesus died and rose again, even so, through Jesus, God will bring with him those who have fallen asleep' (1 Thes 4:13-14). 'Christ has been raised from the dead, the first fruits of those who have fallen asleep' (1 Cor 15:20).

Knowing these things we can pray in words attributed to St Augustine:

> Thine is the day, O Lord, and thine the night:
> grant that the sun of righteousness may abide in our hearts,
> to drive away the darkness of evil thoughts.

Further reading: 1 Thes 5:1-11, 4:13-18.

RRW

October 23

Sleep (3) — Good Night

In peace I will both lie down and sleep; for thou alone, O Lord, makest me dwell in safety. Psalm 4:8

For the weary doctor and for the worried patient there should be some balm in the psalmist's words and in what follows:

> O soft embalmer of the still midnight,
> Shutting with careful fingers and benign
> Our gloom-pleased eyes...
> Turn the key deftly in the oiled wards,
> And seal the hush'd casket of my soul.

Keats, *To Sleep*

> The condition which it is most essential to secure is peace of mind. Almost all insomnia is mental in origin, due to some worry, remorse, ambition, or other system of emotional ideas which obsess the mind. In this connection, it is possible only to repeat the proverbial advice about not letting the sun go down upon one's wrath... If, despite our best efforts, sleep is slow in coming, the wise person does not worry. To miss a little sleep does no one any harm, provided he remains calm.

C R McRae, *Concerning You and Me*

Sleep quietly in this quiet room,
O thou — whoe'er thou art —
And let no mournful yesterdays
Disturb thy peaceful heart:
Nor let tomorrow mar thy rest
With dreams of coming ill.
Thy Maker is thy Changeless Friend:
His love surrounds thee still.
Forget thyself and all the world,
Put out each garish light.
The stars are shining overhead —
Sleep sweetly, then. Good night!

Watch thou, dear Lord, with those who wake, or watch or weep tonight, and give thine angels charge over those who sleep. Tend thy sick ones, O Lord Christ. Rest thy weary ones. Bless thy dying ones. Soothe thy suffering ones. Pity thine afflicted ones. Shield thy joyous ones. And all for thy love's sake.

St Augustine

Be present O merciful God, and protect us through the silent hours of this night; so that we who are wearied by the changes and chances of this fleeting world, may repose upon your eternal changelessness.

Compline

Further reading: Ps 121.

RRW

October 24

Be Blessed

God made us alive together with Christ and raised us up with him in the heavenly places that in the coming ages he might show the immeasurable riches of his grace in kindness towards us. Ephesians 2:5-7

As Christians, we are the recipients of God's tremendous blessing. When we were dead in our sin, Paul told the church at Ephesus, God made us alive, raised us up and placed us with him in a heavenly position. Why? Why should God be so generous with us? God has done this, Ephesians 2 tells us, 'in order that in the coming ages he might show the immeasurable riches of his grace toward us'. God is blessing us now so he can bless us more later: God is in the business of blessing. He wants to bless us.

God has arranged the universe to make his blessing available to us. Having saved us, he has 'given us everything we need for life and godliness'. He has also prepared for us good works to be done, for it is in doing good that we experience his blessing. Finally, he has set before us, as Moses explained to Israel, life and prosperity. The abundance of God's kindness is available and is accessible to us.

How, then, shall we make God's blessing ours? Moses and Joshua were each instructed to live according to God's word. It is in obedience to God that we reap his blessing. Yet it is not in our own strength that we obey, for having been crucified with Christ, it is now Christ who lives in us. Obedient to his word, we can do all things through Christ who strengthens us.

Interestingly, however, God's blessings often come to us in disguise. Even the 'trials of many kinds' and the 'painful trial' or 'fiery ordeal' referred to by New Testament writers will lead to deepened faith and a revelation of God's glory. God's blessing will far surpass the difficulties of the present age. Amid the sleep deprivation, pressured circumstances and stressful situations incumbent upon those in the medical profession, God offers a remedy. To the weary, he offers a light yoke. To the workers, he offers the promise of a harvest. We need not succumb to 'burnout'. We can take on his yoke and look beyond burnout to blessing.

It is overwhelming to meditate on the vastness of God's kindness to us. He is blessing us now so he can bless us more in the future. Accepting his provision, even through difficult times, we can obediently choose to live his life with his prosperity.

> Thank you, Lord, for the graciousness of these words of assurance:
> 'I know the plans I have for you,' declares the Lord,
> 'plans for welfare and not for evil,
> to give you a future and a hope'
>
> Je 29:11

Further reading: Eph 2:1-10. 2 Pet 1:3. Dt 30:15-20. Gal 6:9. Mt 11:28-30.

PRF

October 25

An Eye for an Eye

If someone strikes you on the right cheek, turn to him the other also.
Matthew 5:39 (NIV)

So often we get angry — and sin. Our impulse is to retaliate when someone, perhaps a patient, or a friend, hurts or insults us, making us angry. The Jews gave this impulse the seal of approval and codified it as the law of retaliation, the *lex talionis* 'eye for eye, and tooth for tooth' (Mt 5:38).

But Jesus tells us not to retaliate or resist (Mt 5:39). Paul, quoting Psalm 4:4, urges us, 'In your anger, do not sin' (Eph 4:26). My understanding of this is that it is normal to feel hurt and angry when we are attacked or rejected in some way, but it is wrong to allow the anger to flow into retaliation, revenge, hate or destructiveness. We should not hurt back. We should turn the other cheek.

O how hard it is not to hit back! All too often I find myself letting the Lord down on this one. I need the loving power of his Holy Spirit — and a strategy. I think Jesus is teaching us a strategy: turn the other cheek. What does he mean? I do not think he is saying: 'Be nice. Just soak it up and be a doormat'. This is what I assumed I was being taught in my Christian upbringing, and I find that many Christians still have the same assumption. But Christ's teaching about turning the other cheek occurs in a chapter dealing, *inter alia*, with reconciliation and loving even our enemies. I am to love the person who has struck me and try to be reconciled with him. And how else can I turn the other cheek unless I stay with that person rather than walk away? Walking away means to ignore the incident, to sweep it under the carpet. On the other hand, if I use the energy of my anger to stay with my attacker, turning the other cheek (which takes courage), I neither retaliate nor walk away — I face him, I remain vulnerable, I open up the opportunity for dialogue. My attitude is one of love, of seeking reconciliation.

My attacker is surprised, wondering why I did not defend myself or retaliate. I maintain my personal integrity (far from being a doormat). I ask 'Why did you hit me?' and I may discover that he had good reason! Many a friendship started this way. If I had retaliated or just walked away, I would have lost yet another opportunity.

> Dear Lord, what do you really mean when you tell me to turn the other cheek? It is such a hard thing to do. Help me to understand, deeply.

Further reading: Pr 15:1. Mt 5:38-48.

BP

October 26

If I Have Not Love

If I speak in the tongues of men and of angels, but have not love, I am a noisy gong or a clanging cymbal. 1 Corinthians 13:1

The following paraphrase of 1 Corinthians 13 by a Mexican doctor gives thoughtful insight into the place of love in the medical life.

- Though I become a famous scientist or practising physician, and I display in my office many diplomas and degrees, and I am considered as an excellent teacher or convincing speaker; but have no **love**, I am just a sounding brass or tinkling cymbal.

- And though I have the gift of being an unusual clinician making the most difficult diagnoses; and understand all the mysteries of the human body; and feel sure I can treat any kind of disease, even cancer; but have no **love**, I am nobody.

- And though I invest all my money to build the best facilities, buy the best equipment, have the most prominent physicians for the sake of my patients; and I devote all my time for their care, even to the point of neglecting my own family or myself; but have not **love**, it profiteth me nothing.

> Help me, Lord, to appreciate a right perspective, the perspective of love, in all aspects of my medical life. And help me to put it into effect in a way that pleases you.

Further reading: 1 Cor 13:1-3 (in another version).

EC

October 27

Love is an Excellent Medicine

Love is patient and kind; love is not jealous or boastful; it is not arrogant or rude. 1 Corinthians 13:4

The Mexican doctor's paraphrase goes on to describe the qualities of love as a medicine.

- *Love* is an excellent medicine, it is non-toxic; it does not depress the body's defence, but enhances it.

- It can be combined with all kinds of remedies, acting as a wonderful positive catalyst.

- It relieves pain and maintains quality of life at its best level.

- It is tolerated by anyone; never causing allergies or intolerance.

- Common medicines come and go. What was considered good yesterday, is useless now. What is considered good now, will be worthless tomorrow. But *love* has passed all tests and will be effective always.

Help me, Lord, to appreciate the therapeutic value of love
and to incorporate it in all my care for my patients.

Further reading: 1 Cor 13:4-8 (in another version).

EC

October 28

Love is Never out of Date

*So faith, hope, love abide, these three; but the greatest of these is love. 1
Cor 13:13*

The paraphrase concludes by setting out the enduring value of love in
medicine:

- We now know things only partially, and most therapies are only experi-
mental.

- But when all things are understood we shall recognise the value of love.

- It is the only agent capable of creating good rapport between patients,
relative and doctors, so everybody will act not as children but as mature
people.

- Today many truths appear as blurred images to us as physicians and we
can't understand how the things of the Spirit work to maintain life; but
one day we shall see all things very clearly.

- And now remain three basic medications: Faith, Hope and Love; but the
greatest of these is love!

Help me every day, Lord, as I am face to face with people, to
appreciate the enduring values of love. And help me to look
forward with joyful anticipation to the day when I shall be
face to face with you and shall fully understand.

Further reading: 1 Cor 13:8-13 (in another version).

EC

October 29

A Gleam of Light

The Lord said to Paul one night in a vision, 'Do not be afraid, but speak and do not be silent; for I am with you, and no man shall attack you to harm you; for I have many people in this city'. Acts 18:9-10

Paul was facing opposition yet again in his mission to spread the gospel in the heathen, worldly city of Corinth. Despite the presence of Silas and Timothy, Priscilla and Aquila, he must have felt lonely and threatened and, finding the Jews unreceptive and hostile must have wondered if it is was all worthwhile.

Moving from job to job every six months, it is easy for us to get a martyr complex and keep a low Christian profile because we feel lonely, threatened and disheartened. It has certainly been my experience that every time I have timidly put my head above the barricade and witnessed for my Lord, as well as getting 'sniped at', as Paul regularly was in Corinth, I have also made the acquaintance of other Christians. We are all so busy that we rarely chat about anything except our work and the most trivial superficialities. So we may not get to know other Christians until we are about to move on. Perhaps God means to form a fellowship of witnessing Christians in the place where we work. Paul was encouraged to go on, not only with his secular work (v3), but with his missionary ministry, taking every opportunity of witness that God gave him rather than shrinking into anonymity.

Let us then be bold for God, remembering that Jesus promised, 'everyone who acknowledges me before men, I also will acknowledge before my Father who is in heaven' (Mt 10:32), following this with a blunt warning that the converse is also true (v33). As we nail our colours to the mast, unknown fellow Christians at work may be encouraged to declare themselves, and non-Christians be attracted to Christ.

> I'm not ashamed to own my Lord
>   Or to defend his cause;
> Maintain the honour of his word,
>   The glory of his cross.
>
> Jesus, my Lord, I know his name;
>   His name is all my trust;
> Nor will he put my soul to shame,
>   Nor let my hope be lost.

Isaac Watts

Further reading: Phil 1:12-21. 1 Cor 15:58.

TAG

October 30

Making Peace (1)

Blessed are the peacemakers, for they shall be called Sons of God. Matthew 5:9.

So we are ambassadors for Christ, God making his appeal through us. We beseech you on behalf of Christ, be reconciled to God. 2 Corinthians 5:20

Our world is full of divisions and conflicts, big wars and little wars, declared and undeclared. Some are between nations and between all sorts of groups. Some are between individuals. Some are within individuals' own selves. We cannot be indifferent to any of them and must do what we can to foster peace. But those in the last group, those with conflicts within themselves, are the ones of whom doctors are most aware, for they are the patients who come to them for help. In all cases the need is to make peace, to bring about reconciliation. It is something that we know is in the heart of God. For man's greatest and first need is to be reconciled to God, from whom he is separated by his own rebellion. And God has acted to bring about reconciliation: 'in Christ God was reconciling the world to himself, not counting their trespasses against them, and entrusting to us the message of reconciliation' (2 Cor 5:19).

As Christians we are involved in this. And as doctors we are involved not only in this, but in the need for reconciliation, for peace, within people. How often the Christian doctor will find the opportunity, and how far he will feel he has the right to venture into a patient's need for reconciliation to God will no doubt vary. It should never be far from his mind, but it seems that some have a gift for this which others lack. Be that as it may, it always requires much wisdom and grace. It may well be that, just because of what he is going though, a patient is more aware of his spiritual need than he would be at other times. And this will become apparent. But it should never be forgotten that there is such a thing as spiritual privacy. A doctor may not intrude into a patient's private life unless he is invited.

> God of peace and love, take my lips and speak through them; take my mind and think through it; take my heart and set it on fire with love for you and for the people you have made.

Further reading: 2 Cor 5:11-21.

RRW

October 31

What if...?

When he noticed the strong wind he was afraid and started to sink. Matthew 14:30 (GNB)

Some doubts are healthy. They show that we recognise our own fallibility and inexperience. As housejobs progress the doubts do not alter in frequency, merely in nature. I no longer worry about how to arrange a special investigation, or whether I shall sleep through my bleep! The doubts which assail me now when I am tired, perhaps after a weekend on call, are far from healthy; rather they disturb my peace of mind and wear down my defences against self-pity. If I succumb to these doubts, they only breed more.

There are the 'what ifs...?' that are always related to my career or capabilities: what if I don't get that rotation? what it I fail this exam? what if I have to go on moving every six months or so? what if I never get married?

Since I have no way of knowing or influencing what the future holds, such worries and doubts are fruitless. At the very least I could adopt a fatalistic point of view. But the Christian serves a Master who is deeply interested in his people, and who has the power to guide and control the lives of men.

Peter did not falter when his thoughts were taken up with Jesus and with the task in hand. But when he noticed the strong wind, his trust in Jesus' ability to sustain what he had begun wavered, and Peter began to sink. Useless worries, the 'what ifs' of life, have this characteristic, they assail me when I stop concentrating on the job in hand, my current post for which I have been called and equipped, and start to look around.

Recognising a 'what if?' is halfway to dealing with it, and saves expending energy on it. I am learning when to expect them and so am beginning to dismiss them. Anyway, I can seldom remember in the morning what I spent wakeful hours worrying about the previous night. Stanley Browne's words are a help: 'Never forget, you are not alone in deciding your future' (*Mr Leprosy*, P Thompson).

> May the peace of God my Father
> Rule my life in everything,
> That I may be calm to comfort
> Sick and sorrowing.

Kate B Wilkinson

Further reading: Mt 14:22-33.

PIMA

November 1

On God's Guidance

Trust in the Lord, and do good; so shalt thou dwell in the land, and verily thou shalt be fed. Delight thyself also in the Lord; and he shall give thee the desires of thine heart. Psalm 37:3-4 (AV)

One of the most perplexing problems that Christians have to face is to know which way to go, which door to enter, which choice to make out of several possibilities.

It may concern the big decisions in life, personal or professional, such as marriage, or the next job, or the next exam, or it may be one of the more ordinary and humdrum routine matters. We want to do the right thing, and choose the right course... but how to find it? — that's the question.

Start with God. Commit your way honestly to him, and you can be absolutely certain that he will bring 'it' to pass, whatever your 'it' may be.

Then, *consider all the circumstances* in the light of what you know about God — his character, his supreme knowledge, his love and concern for you personally. Bring the possible choices to this touchstone. Our own desires and personal preferences may be helpful, or they can be positively misleading. Be open and honest.

Then, *try to discover if there is any text in scripture,* and passage or incident that throws light on the pathway.

Listen to experienced Christian friends, who can proffer helpful advice, if they are understanding and honest, and are not afraid to tell you the truth.

Then pray in words like these —

> O my God, I gladly confess that you know everything, and that you have a plan for me and my life. I now deliberately ask for your guidance in respect of... I honestly want to do your will, and I acknowledge that your will for me is best and is what I ought to do. Help me to choose, for your sake and the sake of others.

And when later on you look back on the increasingly numerous experiences of his guidance, all the 'coincidences' that have happened to you, you will be able to say 'I being in the way, the Lord led me' (Gn 24:27 AV).

Further reading: Pr 3:5-6.

SGB

November 2

Lebensraum

You have set my feet in a spacious place. Psalm 31:8 (NIV)

In this psalm, which contains some of the words of Christ on the cross (v5), the writer is affirming his trust in God, telling of the problems from which he has been delivered and relating some of his present afflictions. He was delivered out of the hand of the enemy, and his feet were set in a wide (broad) place. Enemies were all around him, yet his confidence was in God who had set him free from fears. This is something we can all experience however great the pressures upon us.

A more abundant life, or life in all its fullness (Jn 10:10 NEB), is what Jesus has promised his followers. When he sets our feet in a large place, life takes on a new dimension. He gives life with a plus and places us in a spacious mould which involves service for others as well as for his Kingdom.

At the end of a busy 'take in', many a junior hospital doctor may feel that the 'wide place' is almost too much; so may a general practitioner at the end of a long consulting or visiting session. Yet in what other professions could we be exposed to such a spectrum of human need and be given the opportunity of helping so many? The Christian can see drudgery as privilege, and a long queue of patients as individuals for whom Christ died.

The writer practises in what some may consider to be a 'narrow' specialty; yet even here there are enormous opportunities for patient care, for meeting people at times of great anxiety, emotional upset and pain, and for dealing literally with matters of life and death. Medical qualifications set one's feet in a broad place, and there are opportunities for service in all specialties to the one prepared to look for them.

Christian belief does not make the doctor technically more proficient, or capable of undertaking more work. It does not make up for lack of knowledge. But when we consider that our wide view of life comes from a loving God of whose grace and mercy we are the recipients, we can more fully understand, and give thanks for, the words of Frederick Faber's hymn.

> There's a wideness in God's mercy,
>   like the wideness of the sea;
> There's a kindness in his justice, which is more than liberty.
> For the love of God is broader
>   than the measure of man's mind;
> And the heart of the eternal is most wonderfully kind.

Further reading: Phil 1:3-18.

JWD

November 3

The Way (11) — Clouds on the Way

Jesus said: Let not your hearts be troubled; believe in God, believe also in me. John 14:1

Travelling the Way is no fair-weather jaunt. True, God's sun will shine magnificently at times, and we shall want to sing and step out enthusiastically. But there will also be clouds on the Way and perhaps storms and floods. The Master made this very clear to his disciples, especially as the coming cross began to cast its shadow over him. This was to be a real part of their experience, as of ours, even though we live in the light of his resurrection victory. He spoke to them not only of the clouds gathering over them, but also of reassurance and strength. He wanted them to be prepared for what lay ahead. Some were to face martyrdom (two at least, Peter and Andrew, according to tradition, on a cross). Some were to face persecution and daunting challenge and, in John's case, exile. 'In this world you will have trouble', Jesus said, 'But take heart! I have overcome the world' (Jn 16:33 NIV).

Still today some who follow the Way face opposition, persecution and even death. For some the pressure is not so hard, but no less real. All may be assured that nothing can separate them from the love of God in Christ Jesus our Lord (Rom 8:39). Those who know little of 'external' persecution and pressure may still experience the clouds that seem to come less from outside than from inside — doubts, depression, changing moods, spiritual dryness. We know that these often have a physical basis and may call for medical and/or psychiatric management. They may point to the need for honest spiritual re-thinking.

The vital thing is not to allow them to come between us and God. The Way can be rough, but it is The Way. It will surely get there. Despite feelings, which cannot always be lightly dismissed, faith depends on facts, especially the ultimate fact of the love of God in Christ Jesus our Lord.

The English poet, William Cowper, who died in 1800, had more than his share of clouds on the Way. His adult life was dogged by bouts of melancholic insanity. Yet he kept his faith. His hymn 'God moves in a mysterious way', written two centuries ago, still retains its appeal. One verse particularly, coming from deep personal experience, should encourage those burdened with clouds on the Way.

> Ye fearful saints, fresh courage take;
>   The clouds ye sometimes dread
> Are big with mercy, and shall break
>   In blessings on your head.

Further reading: Jn 15:18-27, 16:1-4, 20-33. Rom 8:28-39.

RRW

November 4

Obedience

Dearest friends, when I was there with you, you were always so careful to follow my instructions. And now that I am away you must be even more careful to do the good things that result from being saved, obeying God with deep reverence, shrinking back from all that might displease him. For God is at work within you, helping you want to obey him, and then helping you do what he wants. Philippians 2:12-13 (LB)

A common problem in medical practice is the failure of patients to comply with the advice given to them. This often occurs in relation to medications prescribed. With effective listening and good communications, the patient's anxieties and objections frequently can be overcome. Correction of faulty attitudes and misconceptions leads to more co-operative behaviour.

Doctors need to learn the same lesson in professional life. Careful discussion of diagnosis and management are essential, for both consultant and junior can fall into error by arrogantly adhering to their personal opinions. Instructions ignored will lead to consequences not in the patient's best interests.

In the same way doctors need to learn compliance with the direction of God in their lives. In a busy life of action and drama, of skillful surgery and of intensive care, it may not be difficult to see evidence of divine purpose. To the perceptive Christian, situations occur which are 'more than a coincidence'. Unimagined resources of courage, and freedom from anxiety appear just as they are needed, and there are moments of quiet assurance of God's presence and care. However, we should remember that the scenario for God's work is also to be found in the ordinary routine of the outpatient clinic and consulting room.

A preacher once entitled a sermon about Moses and the burning bush 'Any old bush will do'. In any and every situation, God will use the obedient follower to achieve his will.

> Help me to make more sacrifice,
>   To walk where Christ would lead,
> That in my life he may arise
>   To hallow every deed.*

Albert Orsborn

Further reading: Rom 12:1-16.

WBAS

* Reprinted by permision of the copyright holders, Salvationist Publishing and Supplies Ltd.

November 5

Misunderstanding

But if when you do right and suffer for it you take it patiently, you have God's approval. 1 Peter 2:20

Ever since I was a child, nothing would cause me to lose my temper more quickly than being accused of something of which I was totally innocent. Even today I find it hard to take such misunderstandings, especially when it is the spiritual dimension of my life that is under fire.

My postgraduate training in medicine has recently involved much close contact with a senior doctor who has been observing not only my clinical ability, but many other aspect of my life, and with whom I have had hours of both academic and social discussion. He is one unbeliever who has grown to know me fairly well, and I have been literally staggered by the misconceptions he has about Christian belief that come up in our conversations.

As we have considered the old problems of euthanasia, abortion and so on, I have realised why this man initially looked at me so askance on hearing that I was a follower of Jesus Christ.

To take just one point, he had always thought that Christians were rather 'anti-life' in their approach. They were so concerned with heavenly goals and aspirations that, compared with life hereafter, our three-score and ten on earth were completely overshadowed; so it didn't really matter too much what our values on human worth were like! It was both a painful discovery to realise that I was viewed in this way, but also a useful opportunity to try to correct this man's distorted vision of Christianity. However he is only one of many thousands who do not understand us. And I have come to see that being misconstrued in this way is part of the price that all Christians have to pay for their faith, and perhaps particularly those of us who are also doctors and who thus have our reputation with our patients at stake.

We can thank God that the Lord Jesus is our brother in this, as in all other areas of life. His reputation was something that he was prepared to hold very lightly indeed as he faced the misunderstanding and ridicule of the many, in order that he might bring the truth to those who were really ready to listen.

Are we willing to follow his example or are we over concerned about what the majority of our contemporaries in medicine will inevitably think?

Further reading: 1 Pet 2:18-25. Eph 6:5-8. Col 3:22-25.

TGS

November 6

The Slippery Slope

See to it, brothers, that none of you has a sinful, unbelieving heart that turns away from the living God. Hebrews 3:12 (NIV)

There is one thing we must constantly guard against — allowing our hearts to slide into sin and unbelief. There are a thousand subtle ways in which we may be enticed away from the living God. The pressures on our time, the constant drain on our physical and emotional energy, academic interest, the excitement of involvement in medical practice, all easily lead to our guard being dropped and our hearts wandering away from the path of righteousness, and our love for God grows cold.

It is comparatively easy to maintain an organised intellectual framework of belief, and to give the impression of a continuing godly life, but these are no substitutes for a heart that longs for communion with God. The first stage in that insidious slide is the turning of our heart away from him, for, as our Lord taught, sin is primarily a matter of the heart. A heart that is not right with God leads to a life that is 'dead' toward him, even though a facade of obedience remains. We cannot stay in this half-stage for long; either we fail in our obedience and openly indulge in sin, or by God's grace we are forgiven and restored to a living communion with him.

God's word here teaches us that ours is the responsibility of maintaining our heart's warmth towards him, 'See to it, brothers...' How are we to 'see to it'? The example of the apostolic church cannot be bettered. 'They devoted themselves to the apostles' teaching, and to the fellowship, to the breaking of bread and to prayer' (Acts 2:42). These are the means of maintaining a living faith, and we need them as much today as they needed them then.

> O God, preserve us from the deceitfulness of sin that subtly creeps into our lives and causes our hearts to become hardened towards you. Give us today hearts that are dead to sin but alive to God, delighting in your word and assured of your presence. Enable us to serve you with glad and joyful hearts for Jesus' sake.

Further reading: Rom 6:11-23. Heb 3:1-15.

JHCM

November 7

All the Time in the World — or is there?

Watch therefore, for you know neither the day nor the hour... Matthew 25:13

There are several lessons to learn from the parable of the wise and foolish virgins. The first and most obvious concerns the danger of being ultimately unprepared for the coming of the Lord — the Bridegroom — and finding ourselves shut out from the wedding feast as those he has never known (Mt 25:12). But the danger of putting things off is present throughout our everyday life.

In Ephesians 4:26-27 Paul warns us about unresolved disputes and the use the devil can make of them. Perhaps you are reading this at the end of a frustrating day in the wards when you have spoken hasty words. Don't go to bed without doing something about it. Jesus said that our worship is valueless if there is anger in our hearts. If others have reason to hold anything against us, then that must be sorted out between us before our service to him is acceptable (Mt 5:23-24). It may be too late today to find the staff who were on the receiving end of our sharp tongue, they may be off duty now, but we can confess our sin to God, and apologise at the earliest opportunity. We may feel that we were justified in what we said or did — 'for the good of the patient' — but Christ warns us that anger can lead to sin. The assumption that our demands are paramount is the antithesis of his humility, and we are told that we should forgive one another 'as God in Christ forgave you' (Eph 4:32), totally, unreservedly and without remembering the wrong.

If we go to bed tonight unrepentant and unforgiven, before we realise it we shall be on the wards again, facing the very people whom we wronged, or who, we imagine, wronged us. Bitterness festers, harboured grudges grow, and positions become entrenched. The devil has his chance. Start each day forgiven and cleansed before God. Right any wrongs between ourselves and others as soon as practicable after they have occurred. Never put off until tomorrow what you can — and should — do today!

> Heavenly Father, we thank you that your Son knew frustration, loneliness, disappointment and irritation during his earthly life. Forgive us when we wrong others, speak hastily and hurt our colleagues. May we be saved from the sin of procrastination and be humble enough to make amends quickly.

Further reading: Mt 25:1-13. Eph 4:25-32.

TAG

November 8

All that Matters

One thing have I asked of the Lord, that will I seek after; that I may dwell in the house of the Lord all the days of my life, to behold the beauty of the Lord, and to inquire in his temple. Psalm 27:4

Conflicting claims readily crowd out essential ones. A crowd of patients with trivial problems may cause us to neglect the seriously ill. It is easy to be too busy in medicine. The work is important, interesting and rewarding. It may be easy to justify doing the job that presents itself, to deal with the urgent at the expense of the important, and to overlook the doctor's own need for times of relaxation.

The achievers in any discipline are the single-minded, and the Christian is told to do whatever he does wholeheartedly. But in the possible tension between God's claims and those which are professional, the greater danger is that God may be crowded out.

Running through all the demands of today — all my plans for tomorrow in clinical work: further diplomas; job prospects; domestic cares; leisure pursuits — it should still be possible to step on one side to remind myself that one thing only really matters. All these other things are ephemeral. 'The things that are seen are transient, but the things that are not seen are eternal' (2 Cor 4:18).

Sir Thomas More, in the midst of his high affairs of state, protested 'I neither could nor would rule my king...but there's a little... little... area... where I must rule myself. It's a very little — less to him than a tennis court'.

Thomas Brooke has written:

> 'If God be thy portion, there is no condition that can make thee miserable: if God be not thy portion, there is no condition that can make thee happy. If God be not thy portion, in the midst of thy sufficiency thou will be in straits. O sirs, it is not absolutely necessary that you should have this or that earthly portion, but it is absolutely necessary that you should have God.'

Further reading: Ps 27:4-9. Lk 10:38-42.

DEBP

November 9

My Shepherd (11)

Goodness and mercy shall follow me all the days of my life. Psalm 23:6

Goodness and mercy (the heavenly sheepdogs!) are there faithfully to pursue me. If I fall they come to my rescue. If I stray they bring me back on course. In another psalm David asks, 'Whither shall I flee from thy presence?' (Ps 139:7). The answer is that I can never flee him; neither would I want to elude these heavenly hounds. It may sometimes seem that life has fallen about my ears in pieces, with dreams shattered and sorrow, failure or emptiness all that lie ahead. I can no longer see the track, or if I can, it looks far too lonely and forbidding to follow further. Then the goodness and loving-kindness of God have a way of making themselves known to me in some small way that I could easily have missed, perhaps in a letter or 'phone call. As gently as a dog may lick one's fingers as we walk along, so lightly may such reassurances first come. He is good, he does show mercy. As time goes on, all that I thought as lost may come back repaired and restored, or replaced by something more honouring to him. I may need to hold on for many more 'days' before I can see that he is changing apparent tragedy into an invaluable instrument for future service. Eventually I shall even thank him for the experiences which, at the time, I only wanted to throw back into his face.

The words goodness and mercy also contain echoes of Lord and Shepherd, rod and staff, righteousness and comfort.

> His love has no limit, His grace has no measure,
>   His power no boundary known unto man,
>   For out of His infinite riches in Jesus
>   He giveth and giveth and giveth again.

Annie Johnson Flint

Further reading: Ps 103.

JG

November 10

My Shepherd (11 cont'd)

Goodness and mercy shall follow me all the days of my life. Psalm 23:6

We have been thinking over the psalm in the very personal terms in which David wrote it, but even though the Shepherd does care for us as individual sheep, we must never forget that we are each only a part of his flock, heading for the same fold, following the same voice (Jn 10:16,27). Goodness and mercy work together to keep the flock moving ahead as one, following the Shepherd, and we are not to respond to one or the other of them only, but to both. Yet since the church began, divisions have arisen because believers have polarised, some equating goodness with a strict aiding by the law to the neglect of mercy, while others may put response to what is perceived as mercy ahead of doing what is admitted to be good and right. One group then labels the other either as smug or sentimental, and both lose balance. Many of our ethical dilemmas in Medicine arise as we try to discern the relative goodness of one choice when comparing two bad possibilities, or hope to select the one which seems to be the most merciful from two cruel alternatives.

Goodness and mercy are divine qualities acting together with the intention of keeping us aligned to the Shepherd's voice. His word is our guide and we have the promise that his Spirit will anoint our heads as we seek to know and act upon the mind of Christ. To butt and kick at each other delays progress and sheep do not need to walk exactly in each other's hoof prints to be moving in the same direction. His goodness and mercy must also characterise our dealings with those whose position in the flock may differ somewhat from our own yet who may still be genuinely following the Shepherd's voice.

For goodness and mercy to be said to follow believers may indicate, too, that we are intended to leave a trail of these qualities behind us — the overflow from the cup — both as we live and when we die. The middle years of life are notorious for bringing a slackening off of enthusiasm, just as the early years may be marked by rather intermittent discipleship as other priorities keep on intruding. When 'all the days of my life' have gone, to leave a final legacy which will bring glory to God means that I endure and follow faithfully now. To look ahead and see the Shepherd's wounds, to spend time hearing and responding to his call and to look around at so many evidences of his goodness and his mercy, these cannot fail to encourage each of us to keep on keeping on and help others to do the same, until at last the Chief Shepherd appears (1 Pet 5:4).

> And so through all the length of days
> Thy goodness faileth never.

H W Baker

Further reading: 1 Cor 12:12-13, 18-27. Rev 5:9-12.

JG

November 11

'I'm Sorry to Disturb You, But...'

And the peace of God,... will guard your hearts and your minds in Christ Jesus. Philippians 4:7 (NIV)

It's 3am. I have just undressed, lain down and put the light out when the phone rings. A cheerful casualty officer tells me he has a young woman with ten hours' history of abdominal pain, anorexia and diarrhoea. I remember he has slept all day, and will go off duty at nine just as our ward round starts — and feel envious.

> 'I look to the mountains; where will my help come from? My
> help will come from the Lord, who made heaven and earth.'

My temper is not improved with sleeplessness, and although I try my hardest, I cannot feel very sympathetic towards my patient who undoubtedly has an acute abdomen, which my registrar will want to open tonight.

> 'He will not let you fall; your protector is always awake.
> The protector of Israel never dozes or sleeps.'

The atmosphere is quite different at night; we busy ourselves in theatre while the city sleeps on, For a while, concentrating on assisting, I forget my own tiredness, but then I can no longer stifle a yawn, and I realise my feet are suddenly aching and I imagine climbing into bed between cool sheets, stretching out and closing my eyes, and my concentration fails and is rewarded by sarcasm from the registrar. I know I shall feel awful in the morning.

> 'The Lord will guard you, he is by your side to protect you.
> The sun will not hurt you by day nor the moon during the
> night.'

Walking back to the Mess later, the dawn is just breaking — beautiful, rich colours across the eastern sky, although the west is still a dark velvety blue. The morning star has arisen, and the birds are beginning their noisy chorus. No mountains in the city, but the awe of creation remind me again of the opening lines of the psalm. I cannot meditate on the words — I just have not the energy, and I shall probably get up as late as I dare. All I can do is let the words stay in my mind, and believe them.

> 'The Lord will protect you from all danger,
> he will keep you safe. He will protect you
> as you come and go now and forever.'

Ps 121 (GNB)

Further reading: Phil 4:4-13.

PIMA

November 12

The Yoke

Do you know that if you yield yourselves to anyone as obedient slaves you are slaves to the one you obey? Rom 6:16

We all have a tendency to get ourselves, sometimes inadvertently, into various kinds of bondage. We can become slaves to bad habits, to our natural desires, even to our work, to ambition, to money or status. Some may be good things in themselves, but, paradoxically as with Eve, it is usually in the pursuit of freedom that we come under their mastery.

There is no human influence stronger than that of friendship, and God constantly warns us against the foolishness and misery of unwise relationships and gives us guidelines to the lasting joy and strength of right ones.

The unequal yoke

We are told in 2 Corinthians 6:14 to refrain from harnessing ourselves to those with whom we have little in common. To put an ox and an ass into the same yoke is to court trouble. They differ in type, size, pace and mode of action. The yoke will inevitably chafe, and the chafing can only get worse with time. Pulling in different ways their effort is squandered, and the resulting furrow is unlikely to be straight. How foolish to commit ourselves to a marriage partnership, or indeed to any friendship in depth, with one differing from us in beliefs, values and loyalty, and even in very nature, direction and destiny!

The easy yoke

Forbidden to submit to one yoke we are invited to take another, the yoke of Christ himself. In a sense this is also an unequal yoke, since he is the 'senior partner' and must make the 'going'. Even his yoke can chafe if we persist in our own way, but with our wills aligned to his, the yoke is easy, its restraints do not chafe (1 Jn 5:3), the load we pull is no burden, and we find rest and invigoration even in work (Mt 11:29).

Yokefellows

Does this mean that human friendship in depth has no part in the Christian's experience? Far from it! Having submitted to Christ's yoke, we find ourselves true 'yokefellows' with those who are like minded and are committed in love and service to the same Master (Phil 4:3). Such partnerships enhance the life and work of each, and increase the fruitfulness of both.

We are all slaves. Whose slave are you?

> O Lord, grant me wisdom and discernment in my friendships. Guard me from foolish choices that will rob me

of my freedom to serve you. May I commit myself only to such as are committed to you that we may be 'yokefellows' in your service.

Further reading: Rom 6:11-18. 1 Cor 6:12,19-20. 2 Cor 6:14-16.

MC

November 13

The Eternal Triangle

The Lord is between thee and me for ever. 1 Sa 20:23

There are few friendships as deep, as fruitful and as honouring to God as that of David and Jonathan. It repays study. Their secret — 'The Lord between'. The Lord was between them —

As witness
In the context of 1 Samuel 20:23 and 42, he was witness to their vows of loyalty to each other. Would to God that we could ask him to witness every aspect of our friendships!

As restraint
All Christians are required to live within the clear limits of God's law. Whether man or woman, married or single, hetero- or homosexual, all are subject to moral pressures and temptations of some sort. Regardless of genetic make-up we are all equally handicapped by our fallen human nature and without exception are subject to the restraints of God's word. No-one has a monopoly of disadvantages, no-one can say, 'but I'm different'.

As uniting force
If our friendship is of God, the closer we are to him the closer we are to each other and the closer to each other the closer to him. This is no sentimental platitude but a searching and practical test. Does our friendship disturb, dull and detract from our spiritual life? or does it make prayer and Bible study more attractive and meaningful, and God's call to service more clear and insistent?

As first priority
'Whoever comes to me cannot be my disciple unless he loves me more than he loves... his wife, his brothers and sisters, and himself as well' (Lk 14:26 GNB). Real Christian friendship is a by-product of Christian commitment and not an end in itself. It is only possible to give ourselves wholly to someone who is given wholly to Jesus if we are not to be faced with divided loyalties.

As liberation
There may be times of enforced separation, perhaps during years of

hospital residence or in missionary service. Constant physical nearness is not essential to true Christian friendship. Jonathan was able to say to David, 'I will send you away', because he knew 'the Lord has sent you away' (1 Sa 20:13,22). 'The Lord between' frees us to serve and obey him. God will be Master of our emotional life whether by the restraints of singleness or by the 'crucible of marriage' (Stanley Baldwin, *What Jesus says about...*).

> Lord, I pray that earthly friendship may never separate me from you. Rather may you always be between me and my friends, drawing us closer to each other, as we grow up 'into you' in all things.

Further reading: 1 Cor 6:9-20

MC

November 14

Focus on Friendship

He loved him as he loved his own soul. 1 Sa 20:17

God's greatest gifts are always the most vulnerable. In the realm of friendship above all others it is easy to miss God's best.

Our friendships should be many, and our relationships open, warm and outgoing, but there is a rare God-given friendship at a deeper level that can only exist between kindred spirits. This may be in the context of marriage, which is indeed a 'commitment and not a contract' ('Monty' Barker), but such quality of friendship is open to all Christians, even though a physical component be precluded. Such was God's gift to David and Jonathan. In 2 Samuel 1:26, David described Jonathan's love as wonderful, passing (RSV), better even than (GNB), deeper than (LB), the love of women. Jonathan's friendship with David was —

At soul level

His soul was 'knit to', joined to, one with the soul of David (1 Sa 18:1). They were one with each other in their love for their Lord and in devotion to his cause. Not surprisingly their friendship sprang up in the path of service as they found common cause against the Philistines (1 Sa 14:6ff, 17:32).

Unselfish

The underlying desire in many friendships is for self-gratification, but Jonathan loved David as much as he loved himself (1 Sa 18:1, 20:17). He was practical in his help and advice (1 Sa 18:4, 20:12-13), and as loyal to him in his absence as in his presence, even to his own detriment and danger (1 Sa 20:30-34). In no sense did he use David's friendship for himself.

Primarily concerned for David's faithfulness to God

Our only right in friendship is to help the other person to be the best for God. Jonathan sought out David in hiding and 'strengthened his hand in God' (1 Sa 23:16). How would we have spent those precious moments with the person we loved?

Without self-prominence

Most of our day-dreaming has ourselves at the centre of the picture. Jonathan was content to slip into the background rather than hinder God's plan for David's life, and to play 'second fiddle' to him, even though he was himself the rightful heir to the throne (1 Sa 23:17).

Open and unashamed

Granted that in the early days some of our developing friendships may be clandestine to avoid the baiting of our peers, yet beware of friendship that is furtive and secretive, when we have to be scheming and devious in our meeting each other lest we are observed by those whose respect we most cherish. Remember that 'all are open and laid bare to the eyes of him with whom we have to do' (Heb 4:13). Never be in circumstances in which you would prefer not to be found when the Lord comes again.

> Blest be the tie that binds
>   Our hearts in mutual love
> The fellowship of kindred minds
>   Is like to that above.

John Fawcett

Further reading: study the passages quoted

MC

November 15

The Geometry of Friendship

Can two walk together except they be agreed? Am 3:3 (AV)

Emotional fulfilment at all costs is the order of the day. The pressure to conform is on, and it is easy for the Christian to make shipwreck of his life. To the pictorially minded Christian friendship can be geometrically defined. It is —

Vertical and not horizontal

God determined the rapport and affection between Daniel and the chief eunuch, indicating that Daniel's heart's love belonged in the first place to God (Dn 1:9). A Christian's love is firstly to God. It is for the Lord, who knows the end from the beginning, to dispose it as he wills and as he alone knows best, and will 'work out'. Friendship sought horizontally and for its own sake is a will o' the wisp that taunts, deceives and takes the seeker into dangerous terrain. 'He shall choose our inheritance for us' (Ps 47:4 AV).

Triangular

Its base is shared by each. Both sides are equal in value and meet at the apex. All our activities individually and together are for his glory. 'Thou art the Rock of my salvation' (Ps 89:26). 'Grow up into him in all things which is the head, even Christ' (Eph 4:15).

Within a defined circumference

Christian friendship lies within the circle of God's law. Its focal centre is Christ himself. The radius of the circle is at all points constant. No one can say: 'God's law does not apply to me, my circumstances are different'. 'If you love me you will keep my commandments' (Jn 14:15).

In parallel straight lines meeting in infinity

The lives of Christian friends lie in parallel. They go in the same direction, side by side, yet without preventing each other from running a straight course. They are destined for eternity, and they live in the light of that perspective. 'I press toward the goal for the prize of the upward call of God in Christ Jesus' (Phil 3:14).

In outgoing concentric circles

Friendship that faces inwards is exclusive, selfish and self-destructive. Friends who stand back to back, however closely, are out-looking and out-reaching. Their love and warmth is inclusive of others, and theirs is an expanding usefulness and an ever-widening circle of influence. 'God so loved the world that he gave...' (Jn 3:16).

> Lord, take and keep my heart's love, and as you know the end from the beginning dispose it only as you know best. Keep me and my friends within the circle of your love and teach us always to live in the perspective of eternity.

Further reading: Study the references quoted.

MC

November 16

Depression

Why are you downcast, O my soul? Why so disturbed within me? Ps 42:5 (NIV)

The writer of the 42nd and 43rd Psalms (which comprise one song) suffered from reactive depression and anxiety. He was one of the many Levites who were cut off from worship of the Lord in Jerusalem when the kingdom of Israel was divided after the death of Solomon. As he thought of his situation, he became depressed (his soul seemed to have 'sunk down') and anxious and disturbed. There are many people like this in the world today. Some are refugees, trying to find a new life in strange surroundings, often among people whose culture and language is different from their own. Is it any wonder that many of them become anxious and depressed, and exhibit all kinds of psychosomatic symptoms?

What is the answer? While anti-depressant and anxiolytic drugs may be useful 'first- aid treatment', we should be careful not to think they are a complete answer to the problem. We should look rather at the solution which this Levite found some 2900 years ago. It immediately follows the words we have quoted in each of the three refrains of this song.

> 'Hope in God, for I shall praise him
> For the help of his presence.'

Although his circumstances had changed dramatically, he knew that God had not changed. He was 'the living God', his rock, and his exceeding joy. He prayed to God to send out his light and his truth to lead him: and the final stanza of the Psalm ends on a note of praise: 'I will praise you, O God, my God'. Praise and thanksgiving are often the best antidote for depression and anxiety. Try it for yourself: then recommend it to your patients.

> Lord, when I feel depressed teach me to look up to you, and
> to praise and thank you for all that you are in yourself, and
> all you have done for me.

Further reading: Ps 42:1-43:5.

JWMcM

November 17

Keeping Fit

Take time and trouble to keep yourself spiritually fit. Bodily fitness has a certain value, but spiritual fitness is essential, both for this present life and for the life to come. 1 Tim 4:8 (JBP)

Young Timothy had 'frequent ailments' (1 Tim 5:23). Paul, who obviously had a great affection for him, did not hesitate to advise him about all aspects of his welfare in a fatherly fashion: to let no one despise his youth while yet treating his elders in the church with respect; to keep good order in the church; to take his share of suffering as a good soldier of Jesus Christ; to keep himself physically fit; more importantly to keep himself spiritually fit. It was kindly but demanding counsel.

Paul's priorities for Timothy would seem to be sound general rules for Christians. He does not downgrade physical fitness (the words of the King James Version, 'bodily exercise profiteth little', are ambiguous and can easily be taken in a misleading way), and elsewhere he stresses the care of the body as the temple of the Holy Spirit (1 Cor 6:19). On a number of occasions also he uses the figure of the athlete to urge fitness. While here his mind is primarily on spiritual fitness, he clearly recognises that physical toughness is needed in order to cope with the sort of things he himself had to cope with. We would be very unwise, while fully recognising Paul's priorities, to let ourselves neglect doing what we can to keep our bodies fit. Spiritual fitness still has first priority (3 Jn 2).

> Grant me, Lord, the grace and the self-discipline to keep
> myself both spiritually and physically fit.

Further reading: 1 Tim 4:6-10, 6:11-12. 1 Cor 6:12-20.

RRW

November 18

The Mind of Christ

Let this mind be in you. Phil 2:5 (AV) We have the mind of Christ. 1 Cor 2:16

In days crowded with routine, and nights broken by duty-calls, with turmoil of thought about all we have to do and conscious of the pressures upon us, our Christian faith may at times seem strangely remote, and familiar prayers empty and irrelevant. We find ourselves unable consciously to relate directly all that we have to do, say and decide to the word of God. We may be envious of those able always to quote a relevant scriptural verse, or who seem to be vividly aware of God's prompting at every turn. But important as the study of the written word is in transforming our thinking, and however reassuring an awareness of God's guidance may be, we can rejoice that if Christ, the living word, is dwelling in our hearts by faith (Eph 3:17), then he is himself renewing and controlling our thinking. As a result our attitudes and reactions are becoming like his, and our day to day decision-making is being influenced, albeit without our conscious awareness, by the 'mind of Christ'.

Those who know the love of Christ that surpasses knowledge (Eph 3:19) can make the words of the familiar hymn their daily prayer:

> May the mind of Christ my Saviour
> Live in me from day to day,
> By his love and power controlling
> All I do or say.

334

> May the word of God dwell richly
> In my heart from hour to hour...
>
> May the peace of God my Father
> Rule my life in everything.
> That I may be calm to comfort
> Sick and sorrowing.

Kate B Wilkinson

God grant that I may today think, feel, understand and act as one who has the mind of Christ.

Further reading: Col 3:12-17.

DFEN

November 19

Put to the Test

This is no accident — it happens to prove your faith, which is infinitely more valuable than gold, and gold as you know, even though it is ultimately perishable, must be purified by fire. 1 Pet 1:7 (JBP)

Many things today may turn out to be of academic interest. Whereas they may be true and interesting, they nevertheless do not involve us as people, and have no effect on our lives or on those of others. Protest may be like that, especially now that forms of protest have been developed into a fine art. It is, however, another thing to suffer for protestation's sake.

The Christian faith can be expressed in words and ideas. The New Testament is, in part, devoted to an affirmation and analysis of the faith. But this can so easily be an academic exercise on our part, no matter how orthodox our expression of it. Real faith has to be experienced before it can be expounded. The way in which it is experienced may be painful. We wish to be happy and, in general, Western Christianity is a comfortable affair. But regardless of what the future holds for us as a community, there is no doubt that the proof of our personal faith is its robustness under trial. In fact, when Jesus sought to cheer his disciples, he promised them trouble (Jn 16:33)!

This truth should not surprise us when we remember that Christ is our Saviour because, as a man, he suffered intensely and uniquely for us — a theme which is central to Peter's letter. He is not saying that 'your faith is more valuable than gold', but rather that its genuineness is. Suffering that proves this is of infinite value and, according to the Oxford Dictionary, to prove means not only to demonstrate it, but to subject it to a testing process in order to establish its validity.

Home of our hearts, lest we forget what our redemption
  meant to Thee,
Let our most reverent thoughts be set upon thy Calvary.
We, when we suffer, turn and toss and seek for ease, and
  seek again;
But thou upon thy bitter cross wast firmly fixed in pain.
We, in our lesser mystery of lingering ill, and winged death,
Would fain see clear; but could we see, what need would be
  for faith?

Amy Carmichael

Further reading: 1 Pet 1:3-9. Jn 15:15-20.

DEBP

November 20

Whose Credit?

Whatever gain I had, I counted as loss. Phil 3:7

Perhaps you are sufficiently recently qualified still to have a sense of achievement and of quite immense medical knowledge! Paul had had much the same feeling about his Jewish upbringing. He had risen to the top of his class. He had done all the right things. Yet when he became a Christian he said he counted all this as loss. It was not that his Jewish standing was not real; it was real and because of it he was able to meet the Jewish leaders on their own ground. But rather that he ceased to place any reliance on it and realised that it had no part to play in his spiritual status.

To take credit to ourselves, especially when others also accord it to us, is a very deeply ingrained tendency in most of us, and doctors are peculiarly susceptible; it is so easy to 'do good' in our work. In that sense medicine is an easy calling for a Christian, and it is worth a clear-sighted review from time to time lest we find ourselves beginning to think that we do God service as we minister to the sick.

We have constantly to remind ourselves that such talents and knowledge as we have, have been given to us by God, to be used for his glory and not primarily for our profit — save that the labourer is worthy of his hire. It would be well to bear this in mind when we become involved in discussions about salary structure and terms and conditions of service.

'What have you that you did not receive?'

1 Cor 4:7

Further reading: Lk 17:7-10. Phil 3:4-11

GAL

November 21

Faith

Jesus answered 'How little faith you have!' Mt 8:26 (GNB)

I used to feel puzzled and (I admit) resentful at times when Jesus rebuked his disciples for their lack of faith. After all (I thought) it is fair enough to be angry with them for their greed or selfishness, or their lack of care about others. But why be cross simply because they couldn't quite work up enough belief that he was going to do something fantastic? Later, it made more sense to me. I began to realise that if people won't trust Jesus, they simply pull out the power plug, and he can't do anything for them. Maybe his anger with them arose from a mixture of deep love and concern with frustration that they could not believe him.

However we look at it, we shan't achieve anything today without faith in Christ. The first two verses of Hebrews 11 tell us: 'To have faith is to be sure of the things we hope for, to be certain of the things we cannot see. It was by their faith that people of ancient times won God's approval' (GNB).

'But', we say, 'this is a real bind. I'm happy with patients and colleagues and text books and scalpels and needles: things I can see, and touch and handle. Why do I have to keep on thinking about things I can't see, and telling myself that my Best Friend is at my elbow when I can't see him?' There is no glib answer to that one. But it may help us to remember that the only alternative to faith is sight. If God, and all the eternal spiritual verities were visible and accessible, our pilgrimage on this earth would be over. And the other important point is that it brings a special pleasure to God when we can trust him without having to see him. Maybe this kind of trust is a small fragment of the worship of God for which we were created. Today, all kinds of things may happen which would suggest to us that we ought to give up our faith and that we have got everything wrong. But (paradoxically) this is exactly the moment when we must stand firm. We take the shield of faith — with which we are able to withstand all the fiery darts of Satan — and, having done all, we stand. And as we pause, soaked in the spiritual sweat of struggling to hold on to Jesus even though he seems a thousand miles away, we hear him whisper the encouraging words 'I am with you always to the close of the age'.

> Lord Jesus, I wish it were easier to trust you all the time.
> Please strengthen my faith today and help me to know you
> are always with me when I don't feel it.

Further reading: Jn 20:26-29. 2 Cor 4:16-18. Heb 11.

JT

November 22

Listening Demands Patience

... encourage the timid, help the weak and be very patient with all men. 1 Thes 5:14 (JBP)

It was just after midnight on the second night of the long air journey from London to Sydney. Only a few hours to go — a few hours to sleep or doze... 'If there's a doctor on the plane, will he please come to the rear cabin?' Oh, no! Not just now! Still, one must go. And three somewhat jaded doctors meet in the rear cabin. 'Sorry to trouble you, doctors, but a young man is disturbing other passengers, and we can't seem to manage him. Can you help?' We'll try.

The young man is pale, thin, smoking steadily, talking incessantly, on guard. Overtly hostile to the cabin crew and defiant to the Captain, he refuses to return to his seat. His speech is coherent, but extravagant, and he is suspicious of everyone — except, curiously, of doctors. Even from them he refuses sedatives. But anyway, let's talk to him — rather listen to him. Listening it is, and being seen to listen. The stream of problems, dreams, hopes, frustrations, fantasies, pours out. And again and again comes the appeal: 'You're doctors, you understand, don't you?' Yes, we understand — and go on listening, through the long night, in relays of one or two at a time. He is never left alone. It is wearisome, yet fascinating and sad, for a deeper unspoken appeal for help is there behind the words. We can't meet that in this passing encounter, but still we can listen. The hours pass as the floor becomes littered with cigarette butts (the doctors don't smoke) and tea cups (we share those).

As the plane comes into Sydney, somehow we are reluctant to leave him. The talking and the listening have made some sort of bond. One of the doctors, longing to do something more, shakes the young man's hand: 'good bye, mate. God bless you.' The young man turns his head to one side, sudden tears in his eyes, and something like a sob escapes. Then he is his garrulous self again. Emotionally labile? Yes, but momentarily responsive to a gesture. Perhaps it was not wasted.

Then the reception party, alerted by radio, takes over and he is gone. The cabin crew is grateful. We disembark. What had we done? Well, we had kept the peace on the plane and been patient with a troubled young man. We had listened. And one of us had whispered that God was there.

Grant us, Lord, the love that brings patience, and the patience to listen.

Further reading: 1 Cor 13:4-7

RRW

November 23

When I Myself am Ill

Blessed be the God and Father of our Lord Jesus Christ, the Father of mercies and God of all comfort, who comforts us in all our affliction, so that we may be able to comfort those who are in any affliction, with the comfort with which we ourselves are comforted by God. 2 Cor 1:3-4

Even doctors get ill! This admission can be a reluctant one for the doctor, and an embarrassing one for the patient! We may, as any other human being, be smitten by the acute and unexpected, or we may be among those who battle with more chronic forms of illness.

When I was a houseman I had had diabetes for about ten years and generally kept extremely well. Inevitably though, at times there were difficulties, such as a dropping blood sugar while assisting at a protracted operation or the weariness resulting from the combination of diabetic instability and long hours of medical work.

One of the 'hidden agendas' behind periods of illness that I have appreciated increasingly through the years is that of finding God's strengthening in order to help others at their points of need. John Job, in his devotional commentary on the book of Job, says that those who suffer, and thereby care for others who are afflicted, are 'missionaries of comfort'. It is not easy to accept this perspective when we are feeling unwell. But if illness is permitted in your life or mine, let us allow God's grace to comfort us, 'so that we may be able to comfort those who are in any affliction'.

> Lord, I do not like getting ill. Help me if illness should come my way to learn through it and to find your comfort in my hours of need, so that I can be a 'missionary of comfort' to others.

Further reading: 2 Cor 1:3-11. Rom 5:3-5.

RFH

November 24

One Dish is Enough

Lord, do you not care that my sister has left me to serve alone? Tell her then to help me. Lk 10:40

The anxious spirit spoils the party. Obviously, it spoiled the party for Martha. What had started out as an act of joyous service had turned sour. Having spoiled the party for herself, Martha spoiled it for everyone else.

She spoiled the party for her sister, Mary. When Martha summoned Mary to help, she didn't tap her on the shoulder and gently ask her to come to the kitchen. Instead, she turned the request into a public rebuke, and a sensitive soul like Mary must have shrivelled under the open scolding. Martha spoiled the party for the disciples. We don't know how the dinner ultimately turned out, but we can be confident that the disciples didn't enjoy it. Martha had covered it with the gravy of hostility. In fact, Martha spoiled the party for Jesus. 'Lord, don't you care that my sister has left me to serve alone?' That's what happens when we push beyond our limits and take on too much. We get angry at God.

'If a thing is worth doing, it is worth doing well' can drive us over the edge, and we do our loving deeds with an unloving attitude. Jesus rebuked Martha and said, 'One dish would have been enough'. In other words, Jesus says, 'If a thing is worth doing, it may be worth doing simply'. The disciples needed to be fed, but soup and sandwiches would have been sufficient. In fact, a simple meal would have been much more acceptable if it were served in an atmosphere of love free of anxiety and tension.

Certainly, there are times for excellence and the extra effort, but we have over-committed ourselves if what we do springs from an anxious and troubled spirit. One dish served in love is better than a dinner served in fretfulness and anger. For those of us who tend to take on too much and tell ourselves that we must do it well, we must be reminded that often 'one dish is enough'. That is a sensible lesson for spiritual survival: 'If a thing is worth doing, it is worth doing simply'.

> Better a little with the fear of the Lord
>   than great wealth with turmoil.
> Better a meal of vegetables
>   where there is love
> than a fattened calf with hatred.

Pr 15:16-17 (NIV)

Further reading: Lk 10:38-42

HWR

November 25

Courage — For What?

Be strong and of good courage; for the Lord thy God is with thee. Jos 1:9 (AV)

Joshua had probably one of the most difficult jobs ever — that of continuing where Moses left off. One of the greatest leaders of all time had, for 40 years or more, taken half a million people through the wanderings of the desert and to the promised land. The people had caused him endless problems and difficulties, so that at times he despaired. Yet he remained confident that God was with him through it all, despite the golden calf, despite the murmurings, despite their hankering to return to Egypt. Moses had taken the people as far as the eastern side of the Jordan when he died. To Joshua was given the commission to lead them across the river, to fight and oust the people of Canaan and to occupy their villages and towns, their lands and their homes. To do this with a well trained and equipped army would have required nerves of steel, to do it with a motley crowd of young and old men, women and children would have taxed the heart of the stoutest, but to follow on where Moses had left off must surely have been the greatest challenge of all. That is why, several times, Joshua was given the promise that he would be victorious, if only he for his part were to be strong and very courageous. He took God at his word and received the strength which he needed. The cities were overthrown, and the walls of Jericho fell down. Joshua was a man with a purpose.

We too as believers have a commission in life, and the command given to Joshua holds true for us. We are called not to lead an army but to heal the sick, cheer the weak, strengthen the faint-hearted, comfort those in trouble, 'by the comfort wherewith we ourselves are comforted of God' (2 Cor 1:4). The doctor has to do many a daunting thing in his life — to tell a wife that her husband has an incurable disease, to tell a newly delivered mother and her husband that their baby has Down's syndrome, to tell a man that he has a carcinoma, or to answer the question of a boy with muscular dystrophy — 'Am I going to die?' The temptation so often is to avoid the issue. But when the Christian doctor speaks to a patient or a relative, he is going at the command of the Lord, and he must ask for courage, strength and wisdom together with the compassion of the Saviour. His prayer beforehand doesn't take away his fear of the assignment, but it does give him an assurance of God's resources. These may indeed be consciously felt but they can only be measured in eternity.

> Lord, I know that it is part of my humanity to be afraid.
> May I learn, like the psalmist (Ps 56:3), when I am afraid to
> put my trust in thee, so that one day I shall be able to do
> something better, 'to trust and not be afraid!' (Is 12:2).

Further reading: Dn 1:17-20. Jas 1:5-8.

OPG

November 26

To Serve Them All My Days

Your attitude should be the same as that of Christ Jesus. Phil 2:5 (NIV)

As a houseman you often seem at the beck and call of everyone in the hospital, 'boss', registrars, ward sisters, technicians and, of course, patients. In addition an inordinate amount of time is spent doing things for which five fairly hard years of training seem to have no relevance, filling in forms, making 'phone calls, holding pieces of metal for hours in theatre, etc. It is easy to become resentful and to feel that, as a qualified doctor, you deserve a better lot.

We need then to be reminded of our Lord Jesus Christ's voluntary humiliation for our sakes: 'Who, being in very nature God...made himself nothing, taking the nature of a servant... he humbled himself and became obedient to death — even death on a Cross!' (Phil 2:6-8). For us, who deserved only his condemnation and wrath, the Son of God left the glory that he shared as an equal with the Father, laying aside the privileges that were his by sovereign right. The hands that set the stars in the heaven learnt to cut and shape wood under the tuition of an ordinary man. The one who lived a life of perfect love and godliness was insulted, despised and beaten by men he loved, as created in his own image. He left the glory of heaven, tasting the dust of earth, that we who are born of dust might share in heaven's glory. 'For you know the grace of our Lord Jesus Christ, that though he was rich, yet for your sakes he became poor, so that you through his poverty might become rich' (2 Cor 8:9).

Saved by his grace we are called to follow his example of humility and service, not resenting tasks that we feel are beneath us because of false pride and in our imagined status. Rather we should seek in his strength to demonstrate to an unbelieving world his spirit of willing service. It is to him that we shall ultimately answer for how we have done the work given to us. 'Whatever you do, work at it, with all your heart... It is the Lord Christ you are serving' (Col 3:23-24).

> O God, forgive us for the selfish pride that so often wells up in our hearts, and separates us from you and our fellow men. Help us to follow the example of our Lord Jesus Christ, who lived a life of perfect service and sacrifice. Fill us with your spirit, that we may show forth your character in our daily lives for Jesus' sake.

Further reading: Rom 12:1-3, 14-21. Mt 20:25-28.

JHCM

November 27

Ageing and Disability

None of us lives to himself alone and none of us dies to himself alone. If we live, we live to the Lord; if we die, we die to the Lord. So, whether we live or die, we belong to the Lord. For this very reason, Christ died and returned to life so that he might be the Lord of both the dead and the living. Romans 14:7-9 (NIV)

A rose is still a perfect rose whether it be in bud or full bloom. How beautiful is a carpet of fallen petals, while the hip, the seed of the maturing rose, is perfected to perpetuate life. All too easily we can become conformed to the world's measure of loveliness which is often superficial and transient. Our Creator and Father in Heaven does not see it in this way: ... 'you whom I have upheld since you were conceived, and have carried since your birth. Even to your old age and grey hairs I am he, I am he who will sustain you' (Is 46:3,4 NIV). We are designed to portray him through all the changing scenes of life and as we have lived in the Lord, we shall die in him, for there is nothing which can separate us from his care, whether in life or in death (Rom 8:38,39).

'Is not wisdom found among the aged? Does not long life bring understanding?' (Jb 12:12). Yes, if lived in relation to Christ, who has been made unto us wisdom. It is only the 'high-tech', instant-satisfaction-seeking society which by-passes advice born of pertinent experience. We are gifted with an amazing assortment of abilities, many of which only blossom through disability or passing years. Often the handicapped and the elderly outshine the physically robust in many aspects of real living, but they would not do so if 'disabled' by the stumbling blocks of health and youth.

Thankfully it is the Lord and no-one else who will take us in death and who decides when. He warns us to be ready for him at any time. Old age or physical limitations are no reason to cease striving to exalt Christ whether by living or by dying. Jesus indicated to Peter that the manner of his death would glorify God, adding 'Follow me!' (Jn 21:19). We are not to fear death, but rather fear not having the life which Christ gives and which will continue after we have discarded our 'tent' (2 Pet 1:13-15).

> God be in my head, and in my understanding;
> God be in my eyes, and in my looking;
> God be in my mouth, and in my speaking;
> God be in my heart, and in my thinking;
> God be in mine end, and at my departing.

H W Davies

Further reading: Phil 1:15-26. Mt 24:36-51.

RKMS

343

November 28

Biblical Case Histories: The Jonah Syndrome

Jonah ran away from the Lord... Jon 1:3 (NIV)

The Jonah syndrome is a curious and fairly common affliction. It has a severe crippling effect of quite early onset. Yet those who suffer from it do not always appreciate how serious and dangerous it is until it has reached an advanced stage. If treatment is to be effective at that advanced stage, it may need to be drastic and painful. It is better to deal with it when it first starts.

This syndrome is not described in modern textbooks of medicine, either under the name of the Jonah syndrome or under the alternative designation of Nineveh-phobia. However, a description is to be found in a very old but thoroughly reliable book which is still available in reputable book shops. In that Book the classical case history of the Jonah syndrome is recorded. This is it in brief:

> The word of the Lord came to Jonah: 'Go to the great city of Nineveh and preach against it, because its wickedness has come up before me'. But Jonah ran away from the Lord and sailed for Tarshish.

> The the Lord sent a great wind upon the sea, and such a violent storm arose that the ship threatened to break up. All the sailors were afraid... They cast lots and the lot fell to Jonah. So they asked him, 'Tell us, who is responsible for making all this trouble for us? What do you do? Where do you come from?...'

> He answered, 'I am a Hebrew and I worship the Lord, the God of heaven, who made the sea and the land'. This terrified them and they asked 'What have you done?... What should we do to you to make the sea calm down for us?'

> 'Pick me up and throw me into the sea', he replied, 'and it will become calm. I know that it is my fault that this great storm has come upon you'... Then they took Jonah and threw him overboard, and the raging sea grew calm...

> But the Lord provided a great fish to swallow Jonah, and Jonah was inside the fish three days and three nights.

> And the Lord commanded the fish, and it vomited Jonah on to dry land. Then the word of the Lord came to Jonah a second time: 'Go to the great city of Nineveh and proclaim to it the message I give you'. Jonah obeyed the word of the Lord and went to Nineveh...

The Ninevites believed God. They declared a fast and...put on sackcloth.

When God saw what they did and how they turned from their evil ways, he had compassion and did not bring on them the destruction he had threatened.

This is relevant for us all. How it is relevant for any one of us is between us and our Lord. But he does expect us to listen for his voice and not to make excuses. If we have problems, he can deal with them. It does not help to run away: there may well be a storm and a big fish waiting for us around the corner. Beware of the Jonah syndrome.

There is a well-known old English prayer that sums it up:

Lord God, when you set us a task,
grant us also to know that it is not the beginning,
but the continuing of it to the end,
until it is thoroughly finished,
which yields the true glory.

Further reading: The Book of Jonah.

RRW

November 29

Love as Fruit

But the fruit of the Spirit is love... Gal 5:22

We were returning home after a discouraging visit to an out-lying church when the pastor said: 'I have been thinking of that mango tree and the Arab boys throwing their sticks at it. No matter how violently they did so, the tree's only response was to yield its golden mangos. I saw no twig reach down to cane them, but only the falling fruit they wanted. How I wish my life was more like that tree! So often my reactions are those of anger or self-pity or resentment instead of yielding the fruit of love...'

Our Lord said, 'By their fruits ye shall know them', and there is no doubt that by our fruit men know us. But we can't manufacture it ourselves. The seed must first be planted, 'it bears much fruit'. In verse 24, Paul puts it like this, 'Those who belong to Christ Jesus have crucified the flesh with its passions and desires'. This is what he meant when he testified, 'I die daily', and what Christ meant when he spoke of taking up our Cross and denying self everyday. If I want to bear fruit today, then in every decision the 'I' must be crucified. Phillips translates verse 26, 'Let us not be ambitious for our own reputation', reminding us of the one who for our sakes made himself of no reputation.

Joy is Love exulting, and Peace is Love at rest;
Patience, Love enduring in every trial and test;
Gentleness, Love yielding to all that is not sin;
Goodness, Love in actions that flow from Christ within;
Faith is Love's eyes opened, the living Christ to see;
Meekness, Love not fighting but bowed at Calvary;
Temperance, Love in harness and under Christ's control;
For Christ is Love in Person, and Love, Christ in the soul.

Further reading: Gal 5:22-26. Lk 9:23-26

KM

November 30

Free to Serve

All things to all men... for the sake of the gospel. 1 Cor 9:22-23

The Christian must straddle two worlds. He is to live in this present world (Gal 1:4), yet he is to seek the things that are above (Col 3:1). To combine these two callings often seems difficult. In 1 Corinthians 9:19-23 Paul outlines three basic principles which facilitate this harmony. Such an equilibrium of temporal and spiritual values is seen to involve:

A sense of freedom
Paul saw himself as 'free from all men' (v 19). We need fear no one save him before whose judgment seat we shall all appear (2 Cor 5:10). But what prejudices and taboos can burden our Christian lives! We fear the opinions of men, Christians and non- Christians alike. How inhibiting this can be! Notice, however, that freedom from the fear of man is closely linked to a great sense of obligation towards them, 'a slave to all that I might win the more' (v 19). My freedom must never cause others to stumble (1 Cor 8:9).

A spirit of flexibility
Such a freedom leads inevitably to a genuine flexibility in our attitudes towards others. This is why Paul could 'become' a Jew (v 20), as one under the law (v 20), and indeed, as all things to all men (v 22). Fearing none, he could care for all. Do you know such freedom and flexibility? The only offence that we should cause is the offence of the Cross (1 Cor 1:23-24).

A source of faith.
The freedom and flexibility so highly prized by the apostle were intertwined with a still deeper motive. Everything in his life was 'for the sake of the gospel' (v 23), so that 'by all means' he might save some (v 22). Without this greater perspective we may become worldly. But with this aim the balance of Christian witness is perfectly centred. The source of our

freedom, the strength of our friendships, and the centre of our faith is Christ Jesus.

> O Lord Jesus, who grew in favour with God and man,
> help me to live moment by moment as in your sight,
> and grant that fearing no man, but caring for all men,
> I may so live that your beauty may be seen in me
> and your saving power may reach out to all with whom I associate.

Further reading: Rom 14:7-22. 1 Cor 10:31-32.

BW

December 1

Doctor, Be Still: The Need to Pause

For this reason I bow my knees before the Father. Eph 3:14

Sometimes we can become so busy that the pressures of the needs of the moment make us blind to the greater realities.

We need to pause from time to time to reflect on the greatness of God and his love in all its breadth and length and height and depth.

The phrase 'for this reason' is repeated in Ephesians 1:15, 3:1 and 3:14. To be aware in even a limited way of the magnitude and wonder of God's love can only result in heartfelt worship and provides the stimulus to living out that love in all our lives. Hence the importance of pausing to reflect on his word, to praise, to give thanks, and to pray for forgiveness and help for ourselves and others.

We need power to live like this, and the Holy Spirit can give us that power. As we trust Christ, so he lives in our hearts. As we are rooted and grounded in the love of Christ, so we can grasp something of its dimensions.

The love of Christ is wider than our limited acceptance of people. It includes all mankind, whatever our racial background, our cultural heritage, our socio-economic classification, our educational or professional achievement, our political freedom or lack of it, our age or our sex. He loves each of us as his own dear child. That colleague we find unbearable, Christ died for him. That patient who has neglected himself to the stage of degradation, God loves him too, just as much as he loves you!

The length of the love of Christ is eternal. He never stops loving, no matter what we do or what happens. There is no time when Christ does not love you or all of us.

His love is higher than any other. It ennobles and enriches us in ways beyond description. Indeed, it lifts us to heaven to the very presence of God.

And the love of Christ reaches down to the worst in all of us. No matter how you've failed or what you've done, he forgives and forgives and forgives. But of course we must accept that forgiveness, it is not automatic. Sadly, there are those who will reject the love of Christ. But they need not, indeed must not. Our calling is to demonstrate that love in our own lives in such a way that all will have every opportunity to know it for themselves.

To him who is able and continually does for us immeasurably more than we can ask or imagine — to him be glory forever.

Further reading: Eph 3:14-21.

RC

December 2

A Guiding Principle

Whatever you do, in word or deed, do all in the name of the Lord Jesus, giving thanks through him to God the Father. Col 3:17

In this verse the apostle Paul gives us a guiding principle for life. All that we say or do should be said or done 'in the name of the Lord Jesus'. Taking the patient's history, carrying out a physical examination, giving advice, prescribing and/or carrying out the treatment needed — this should all be done in the name of the Lord Jesus, remembering that he indeed is our Lord. It follows that if there is anything which we really cannot do in his Name, we should not be doing it. Adherence to this simple yet all-inclusive principle will mean that we shall always have the highest interests of our patients at heart, just as our Lord Jesus has. We shall treat them as people for whom Christ died, not just as 'patients'. We shall do our best for them, just as if the Lord Jesus were in the room supervising us — which indeed he is, for he has promised to be with us all the days, to the very end of the age.

> Lord Jesus, I ask today that all I say and do may be in your name. You are my Saviour, my Lord and my God. I acknowledge that all my abilities have come as gifts from your bountiful hands. Grant that today I might use them all in your Name, for your glory and so for the blessing of all with whom you bring me into contact. May I show something of your compassion, humbleness, kindness, gentleness, patience, forbearance, forgiveness and love to everyone I meet today, for your Name's sake.

Further reading: Col 3:12-17. 1 Cor 10:23-24, 31-33.

JWMcM

December 3

The Way (12) — The End of The Way

Now we see but a poor reflection; then we shall see face to face. Now I know in part; then I shall know fully, even as I am fully known. 1 Cor 13:12 (NIV)

Death, as we see it in hospital, in home or wherever, looks final and absolute. And it would seem to be the end of the Way. But for those who have walked the Way in faith it is no dead end. It is the beginning of something new, something certain and glorious.

Up to that point our trust has been in the unseen Christ. Through faith in him we know that we have eternal life (1 Jn 5:11-13), that we have already passed from death to life (Jn 5:24). We have walked with him through both the smooth and the rough patches of life, confident of reaching the goal. We have been able to echo Paul's words: 'I know whom I have believed, and am convinced that he is able to guard what I have entrusted to him for that Day' (2 Tim 1:12). He is close by us in the valley of the shadow of death. And as he goes with us, the seeming end, the death of the body, will be just another step on the Way — the step by which we come into the unveiled presence of the Lord, to be for ever 'with Christ, for that is far better' (Phil 1:23). 'Beloved', writes John, 'we are God's children now; it does not yet appear what we shall be, but we know that when he appears we shall be like him, for we shall see him as he is' (1 Jn 3:2). Well may Paul cry exultantly, 'O death, where is thy sting? O grave, where is thy victory?' (1 Cor 15:55 AV).

The end of the Way in this life is to be the beginning of the ultimate reality. God's saints have always known this. As a great and wonderful and sure truth it became clear in Christ, to be seen by all who are willing to see. But long before then, the Psalmist had glimpsed the vision saved up for the great awakening: 'I shall see thy face, and be blest with a vision of thee when I awake' (Ps 17:15 NEB).

> Yea thro' life, death, thro' sorrow and thro' sinning
>   He shall suffice me, for he hath sufficed:
> Christ is the end, for Christ was the beginning,
>   Christ the beginning, for the end is Christ.

F W H Meyer, St Paul

Further reading: The references in the text, but especially: 1 Cor 15:51-58. 2 Cor 4:16-5:9. 1 Jn 3:1-3.

RRW

December 4

The Bargaining Syndrome

If God will be with me... and will give me bread... and clothing... so that I come again to my father's house in peace, then the Lord shall be my God. Gn 28:20-21.

The instinct to make a good bargain is inherent in human nature, as is the attraction of getting something for nothing; hence our enthusiasm for cheap offers, free gifts and concessionary rates (whether we want the advertised goods or not).

Jacob was a past master at manipulating circumstances to his best advantage, and at Haran he did God the favour of allowing him to be his God in return for having his material needs met. He even went further and promised to give God a tenth of his earnings. True, he did admit that his possessions came from God (v 22), and he did keep his promise. Many of us, too, allow God a place in our lives in return for the gifts he gives.

In his love and mercy God often first accepts us on these terms. But, as with Jacob, it may take years, sometimes our best years, to find the misery of making a commercial contract of God's blessings. How often, when we should know better, are we guilty of saying that God is slow to give us all the things he promised to those who seek first his kingdom and right-eousness (Mt 6:33), or, like Peter, of asking 'What's in it for us then? After all we have left everything and followed you' (Mt 19:27)?

But God is never in a hurry. Read Genesis 32:6-12 and 24-31. It took Jacob a lifetime to find his own worthlessness. It was only when he had played his last scheming card that he realised how much he needed, and indeed longed to know for his own sake, the God he had used for so many years. He found a new kind of bargaining. Staking everything on the promises of a faithful God, he pleaded for deliverance from the murderous anger of his brother (vv 9-12). God did more — he delivered him from himself and 'blessed him there' (v 29).

From that unforgettable confrontation Jacob went on his way crippled as a successful business man (v 31), but with a new power with God (v 28). He was alive for the first time, knowing face to face the presence of the living God (v 30).

Pity it took so long! but whose fault was that?

Further reading: Gn 28:10-22. 32:6-32.

MC

December 5

Going Against the Stream

Be not conformed to this world: but be ye transformed by the renewing of your mind. Rom 12:2 (AV)

Do not conform yourselves to the standards of this world, but let God transform you inwardly by a complete change of your mind. Rom 12:2 (GNB)

We all should be nonconformists! J B Phillips paraphrased the idea: 'Don't let the world around you squeeze you into its own mould'. Constant pressures operate to squeeze us into the shape of our environment, so that we lose our distinctiveness as pilgrims and foreigners, whose citizenship is in heaven and whose standards are determined by the King of Kings. 'The world is too much within us...getting and spending we lay waste our powers', writes Wordsworth.

This is a battle for the mind. Unthinking reading, uncensored viewing, unwise companionships, may each poison our thinking. God's answer is the miracle of metamorphosis. As we expose our minds to the influence of the Holy Spirit by the reading of the Bible and obedience to its teaching, the inner man is renewed day by day. Pilgrim at the house of Interpreter did not understand the secret of the fire that always burned, until he was taken to the other side of the wall and saw the figure clothed in white pouring in a constant supply of oil.

Shall we lay our life in all its aspects before God and ask of our conduct:

> Does it glorify God?
> Does it promote my Christian life or endanger it?
> Does it help my weaker brother?
> Does it promote my witness or hinder it?
> Does it please the Holy Spirit or grieve him?
> Does it lead me into God's will or out of it?
> Does it adorn the doctrine?

Further reading: 2 Cor 3:18. Heb 11:13-16. Phil 4:8. Eph 1:15-23.

VW

December 6

Feeling Hard Done-by?

Martha, you are fretting and fussing about so many things. Lk 10:41 (NEB)

We must all have thought that Martha was justified in her complaint. After all, she was hostess to Jesus, who had arrived unexpectedly, and she was busy with 'elaborate preparations' (JBP) in a manner suitable for her Lord. Her only offence seemed to be that she resented being left to carry this burden alone. It had to be done — it would be done sooner if the work were shared — and there was her sister not lifting a finger to help!

Is not our situation sometimes very similar? There is often so much work to do that we wonder how we can ever get through it; if it is skimped, the patients may suffer. Furthermore, we feel we must, as Christians, be extra conscientious. Each patient represents Jesus, offering us a unique problem, demanding as much thought, care and service as we would give to him who said, 'Inasmuch as you do it for them you do it for me'. But it does seem hard, when there are others who could see our situation and give us a hand instead of saying 'it's not my job'. It is easy to become resentful and harassed, especially when our times of spiritual renewal are being crowded out, or are fading into torpor and sleep. But remember, this crowded life is what we expect as doctors and were promised as Christians.

Although it needs discipline and forethought, our life must be organised so that Mary's 'good part' gets its share of our active thought; so that in the rush we do not (like Martha) lose touch with him. In Mark 1:32-35 we read that Jesus had a busy, unexpected evening casualty session, but he was up early the next morning for prayer. The peace that he promised, unlike the world's peace, is beyond understanding because it garrisons our heart and mind in the middle of turmoil and care. It comes from contact with him who shares the burden and gives us strength (Jn 4:27).

> Take from our souls the strain and stress,
> And let out ordered lives confess
> The beauty of Thy peace —
> The peace of God

J G Whittier

Further reading: Lk 10:38-42. Phil 4:4-7.

SDVW

December 7

My Life for Him or His Life for Me?

I am the vine; you are the branches. If a man remains in me and I in him, he will bear much fruit; apart from me you can do nothing. Jn 15:5 (NIV)

Preparing to spend time working abroad, I received a letter from a missionary friend of mine. It made me stop to think. 'Remember', the letter went, 'that the Lord is putting you into this situation, not primarily for what you can do, but because of his plans for you. His first concern is the growth of your relationship with him.'

Here was a rather different perspective from my own thoughts along the lines of how much I could contribute, with my training, in the Lord's name, and how I would be able to demonstrate his love practically. But his plans for me concerned teaching me to depend on him, the truth attested to in the verse above, and seen in its practical reality in the biographies of many pioneers in missionary work.

Somehow things can seem so different in mundane hospital life: I have found it temptingly easy to rely heavily on my own resources. Does a basic trust in and dependence on the Lord underlie all my daily dealings at work with other people? Is my relationship with him growing? The lives of men and women who have pioneered the Lord's work overseas, and who found themselves again and again in total dependence on him, are beautiful examples of the truth of what he promised in this teaching of his. May our situations not blind us to this truth.

> Lord Jesus, teach me to have in my life the perspective your word speaks of. Help me to make sure my life is firmly based on you, so that you pervade all I do and say today.

Further reading: Ps 1:1-3. Col 2:6-7

JSdeC

December 8

Whose Life?

What have you done? The voice of your brother's blood is crying to me from the ground. And now you are cursed... Gn 4:10-11

God's disapproval and condemnation of taking another's life are clearly expressed in these words. God is the creator of life, and he entrusts it to us

— not freehold, to do what we like with it, but leasehold (and not always 99 years?), to use it under his direction in the service of man.

Human life is not in the same category as animal life. Because God made man for fellowship with himself, and because man is made 'in the image of God' — with a rational mind, a sense of moral values, and the ability to perceive the love of God and respond to it — man's life is unique. He is of particular value in God's sight — of sufficient worth for Christ to endure the Cross. The Cross is the measure of man's worth to God, who sees every man potentially as a son.

Here is a patient who is a drain on us; his disease is unpleasant, and he is useless to society. So was Lazarus, the sick man at the gate of Dives — and yet God judged him worthy of eternal life (Lk 16:22). Or here is a victim of prolonged suffering. If he were an animal, compassion would compel us to 'put him down'. But he is a man, so our principle must be to relieve his suffering by every other available means. Among these are modern drugs, human friendship and the message of the love of God.

> I believe in one God... The Lord and giver of life.

Further reading: Gn 4:1-10. Mt 22:36-40

DMcGJ

December 9

Remember the Sabbath Day

Remember the Sabbath day by keeping it holy. Six days you shall labour and do all your work... Ex 20:8-9 (NIV)

The writer was one of a medical delegation which visited the People's Republic of China, spending 17 days in five provincial capitals. Beijing (formerly Peking) is divided into seven zones, each of which has its own day of rest. Moving from centre to centre, visiting hospitals and being involved in scientific exchanges as well as sight-seeing, left us with no break at all. By the end of the second week we were all convinced that one does not need to believe in the Jewish Sabbath, or its present day equivalent of the Christian Sunday, to be aware of the need of a regular day of rest. When France was decimalized after the revolution, it was suggested that there should be one day of rest in ten. God has made us in such a way as to need one day in seven kept apart from the routine of everyday work.

Insistence on time off to attend worship each Sunday is unrealistic, particularly during a residency. It is important for the young Christian doctor to think through the meaning of the word 'holy' and on this to base his attitude to 'Sabbath observance'. Christ healed on the Sabbath (Mt 12:9-13) and thereby sanctified the work of our profession: any necessary work done to help others must be considered holy.

The 'charging of our spiritual batteries' and a 'time of mental rest' are phrases commonly used to describe the need for worship. It is only too easy to excuse ourselves from regular worship. Perhaps we are so tired that we shall sleep through the service, and after all, we can spend a time alone with God without going out. Do not too readily give up the discipline of church attendance when opportunity arises.

Thinking through the problems of Sunday worship in relation to medical duties, remember three things:

- Jesus attended the synagogue on the Sabbath (Mk 6:1-2).
- Our Christian Sunday has replaced the Jewish Sabbath (Acts 20:7) and is the day when we commemorate the resurrection of our Lord — a cornerstone of our faith.
- The Sabbath was made for man and not man for the Sabbath (Mk 2:27).

Further reading: Mk 6:30-44.

JWD

December 10

Beatitudes (1) — Povery that is Rich

Happy are they who know they are spiritually poor; the Kingdom of God belong to them. Mt 5:3 (GNB)

Everyone seeks for happiness. Jesus reveals its secret. He turns the values of the world upside down. Here he tells us that the poor are the ones who are really rich for they possess the kingdom of heaven.

But the poverty of which he speaks is not financial. It is independent too of temperament, even of those who are diffident, shy and self-effacing by nature. It is irrespective of professional status and even of our conscientious service for others. The number of admissions we have checked today, the overtime we have uncomplainingly put in, these contribute nothing to bridge the gap between us and the kingdom of God. Nor does even what we may regard as our spiritual status — the Christian 'stable' we have come from, or the church duties we have undertaken — qualify us to possess the kingdom.

Poverty of spirit comes from a recognition of who we are and what we are like in the sight of a holy God, our Creator and Redeemer, and a realisation of our utter spiritual bankruptcy and total dependence on his mercy and grace towards us. It is a poverty that drives us day to day in repentance to the cross of our Saviour, who died and rose again to make the worthless worthy of his kingdom (Rom 3:23,24).

To such his kingdom belongs now, as daily we experience the riches of his grace, on the wards, in the mess, in the theatre. But there is more to come. Ours is an assured eternal inheritance, imperishable, undefiled and unfading, reserved in heaven for those who are kept by God's power (1 Pet 1:4-5). We shall come fully into that inheritance when Christ calls us or comes to take us to be in his presence for ever. The kingdom of God belongs to the spiritually poor solely because of the cross of our Lord Jesus Christ. When we come to that cross of Jesus with the words —

> 'Nothing in my hand I bring,
> simply to the cross I cling'

we have the certainty and security of his assurance that the kingdom of God does indeed belong to us now and for ever.

> 'Look at him, keep looking at him. You cannot truly look at him without feeling your absolute poverty and emptiness. But he is the all-sufficient one.'

D Martyn Lloyd-Jones,
Studies in the Sermon on the Mount

> 'Yea, all I need in thee to find,
> O Lamb of God, I come.'

Further reading: 1 Pet 1:3-9. Rev 3:17-21.

JABA

December 11

Beatitudes (2) — Sorrow that is Joy

Happy are those that mourn; God will comfort them. Mt 5:4 (GNB)

This beatitude follows logically from the first. It is impossible to treat a patient who has never admitted to any symptoms, and one who recognises no need certainly does not come for help (Mt 9:12). But while diagnosis is essential to cure, it is not of itself a cure. It is one thing to see our spiritual poverty before God; it is another to do something about it. A moment's thought about our impatience with people, our tactless statements to relatives or our idle gossip to the ward staff can make us regret bitterly what we have said or done, but it is only a deep sorrow about what we are like in God's sight that can bring the blessing of his comfort. In Romans 7:24 Paul cries: 'Wretched man that I am! Who will deliver me from this body of death?' This is no mere remorse. He is in mental torment about the state of his own heart. But as he 'mourns' he finds God's comfort; 'Thanks be to God who does this (delivers me) through our Lord Jesus Christ' (v25). God is the God of all comfort. He alone can and does meet our need at this point.

> 'It is when a man sees himself in this unutterable hopelessness that the Holy Spirit reveals unto him the Lord Jesus Christ as his perfect satisfaction. He sees in him the perfect provision that God has made and is immediately comforted.'
>
> D Martyn Lloyd-Jones,
Studies in the Sermon on the Mount

Again, the promise of God's comfort is not only for the here and now of hospital life, it is for the future too. As the Christian 'mourns' at the state of the world and the burden of its sin, he is comforted. He looks for a new heaven and a new earth wherein dwells righteousness, when God 'will wipe away all tears from their eyes, there will be no more grief, or crying or pain. The old things will have disappeared' (Rev 21:4 GNB).

> Lord, grant that I may never be flippant or superficial in my beliefs. Rather give me the joy unspeakable and full of glory that comes from an understanding of the seriousness of my sin and the perfection of your provision for my salvation here and hereafter.

Further reading: Lk 18:10-14. Lk 10:17-20.

JABA

December 12

Beatitudes (3) — Gentleness that is Strength Controlled

Blessed are the meek: for they shall inherit the earth. Mt 5:5 (AV)

The word *meekness* in the AV is variously translated as *humility* (GNB), and *gentleness* (RSV). A similar interchange is found in Galatians 5:23 referring to the fruit of the Spirit. This is helpful, since in the world's parlance meekness is equated with weakness, and aggressiveness, self-confidence and self-assertion are preferred to humility and a gentle spirit.

In the first two beatitudes Jesus shows how much we need a realistic view of ourselves, as spiritually bankrupt, and needing to mourn over our state in God's sight. Here he shows the change in attitude that such a realisation brings. There is place in the Christian life neither for arrogance toward God nor superiority toward others. Stephen Winward in *Fruit of the Spirit* defines meekness as humility before God and the gentleness of controlled strength toward others. Jesus showed this combination of humility and strength when he laid aside the insignia of godhead and for our sakes took the form of a servant, becoming obedient to the death of the Cross. This surely challenges us in all our relationships — with patients, cleaners, nurses, colleagues and our families.

The promised reward for meekness may puzzle us. How can the meek inherit the earth? We may have sensed the frustration and disappointment of some who have succeeded in their exclusive aim to reach the top but at tremendous cost. They have lost far more than they have gained. Jesus refocuses our ambition into paths of service. Jim Eliott, subsequently murdered by Auca Indians, said, 'He is no fool who loses what he cannot keep to gain what he cannot lose', and Jesus promises the meek, his co-heirs, an immense inheritance. Paul knew this truth in experience: 'we seem to have nothing, yet we really possess everything' (2 Cor 6:10 GNB).

> 'How blest are those of a gentle spirit;
> they shall have the earth for their possession.'

Mt 5:5 (NEB)

> The gentle don't conquer the earth: they inherit it... They may own very little of it but they do possess it...in part already. But only in part, for the realised hope is deferred until the kingdom of Christ is established and fulfilled on earth.'

Stephen Winward

> God grant that such an inheritance may be ours.

Further reading: Phil 2:5-11. Rom 8:16-23

JABA

December 13

Beatitudes (4) — Hungry yet Full, Thirsty yet Satisfied

Blessed are those who hunger and thirst after righteousness: for they shall be filled. Mt 5:6 (AV)

The first three beatitudes showed us the more negative aspects of our situation — the bankruptcy, poverty and arrogant selfishness of our hearts, and our desperate need of God's grace. Here Jesus encourages us to seek the positive righteousness which God has made available to us in the Lord Jesus Christ.

The righteousness is firstly that which is 'of God by faith' (Rom 3:22) — Christ's righteousness imputed to us when we trust in him and in his perfect work for us on the Cross (2 Cor 5:21). But there is another right-eousness we are to seek, equally of his grace alone — the righteousness of heart and life produced in us by his sanctifying Holy Spirit, freeing us from the power of sin, from the very desire to sin, and emancipating us from self and self-concern, in other words, a longing to be like Jesus. As J I Packer points out in *Keep in step with the Spirit*, the pursuit of holiness, though a Christian priority, is commonly neglected by Christians today 'as evidenced by the man-centredness of our godliness and our insensitivity to the holiness of God himself'. God intends us to be holy in thought, motive, speech and action.

And what of our concern for God's just and righteous reign in his world? in our homes, our hospitals, our churches, our cities? to say nothing of the wider world, be it in the favoured west or in developing countries? How much do we hunger and thirst for righteousness there? Do we care enough to pray, to give, to go?

God's promise is that those who hunger and thirst shall be satisfied and filled. Why then do we know so little of his fullness? Perhaps it is, as Martyn Lloyd-Jones points out in *Studies in the Sermon on the Mount*, that we often seek the wrong thing, happiness and blessing rather than right-eousness. Happiness sought directly, like a will-o'-the-wisp, will always elude us. We are to seek righteousness, not happiness. Or perhaps our desire to be righteous is but transient and superficial; 'to be hungry is not enough; I must be really starving to know what is in his heart towards me' (J N Darby).

Paradoxically, 'the Christian is one who at one and the same time is hungering and thirsting, and yet he is filled. And the more he is filled the more he hungers and thirsts' (D Martyn Lloyd-Jones).

> O Lord, you have been made sin for me that I might be made righteous. Give me a hunger for true holiness, that I may know your fullness here and hereafter.

Further reading: 1 Cor 1:26-31. Eph 3:14-21.

JABA

December 14

Beatitudes (5) — The Quality of Mercy...

Blessed are the merciful, for they shall obtain mercy. Mt 5:7

Mercy is one of the qualities apparent in those whom God is filling with his righteousness. Jesus himself showed us what it meant to be merciful. He relieved suffering and dealt with the results of sin. He spent time with the social outcasts, healed the sick, and comforted those in distress. He told the parable of the Good Samaritan as an illustration of mercy in action. The injured man had no claim on the Samaritan, who yet saw his need, pitied him and took spontaneous and costly action to bring relief.

Mercy is not a natural human quality, nor is a forgiving spirit. Our natural reaction is often to be vindictive, retaliatory and intolerant toward others, leaving them to suffer the results of their own stupidity or obstinacy. But that was not the way of Jesus. It was not that he was easy-going, ignoring or condoning sin. In fact it was just because he could not overlook it that he paid its penalty for us, and he asks us to show the same mercy, even to those to whom we have no contractual obligation. We should be prepared to spend time with the difficult patient or the terminally ill. We should be ready to see where there is a need and how best we can meet it, even beyond the call of duty.

In this beatitude at first it appears as if God's mercy towards us is a reward for our mercy toward others. That is not so. Rather the motive for our mercy is that we have seen our need and have found God's mercy for ourselves. The more we know his mercy in experience, the more our lives will show this characteristic of our heavenly Father.

> If I am not merciful there is only one explanation; I have never understood the grace and the mercy of God.

D Martyn Lloyd-Jones

Further reading: Lk 10:30-37. Titus 3:4-8. 1 Jn 4:19-21.

JABA

December 15

Beatitudes (6) — The Heart of Every Problem is the Problem of the Heart

Blessed are the pure in heart, for they shall see God. Mt 5:8

Jesus here gives us another of the results of hungering and thirsting after righteousness. He reaches the very core of the Christian faith with this beatitude, for the heart is the centre of our being and includes mind, emotions and will. The state of our heart determines all that we think, say and do. The Pharisees were concerned with the 'outside' — in what they were seen to do, and this may have seemed above reproach. But their hearts were not right, and their attitude was often bitter and resentful. It was just 'whitewash', and Christ's comments about them were far from complimentary (Mt 23:23-28). But might he not have been equally disappointed with us? Correct words and behaviour can often hide a twisted outlook. In our dealings with patients and colleagues we can become skilled at hiding our insincerity behind a convincing facade. Do we really mean all that we say? Are we really as honest and noble as we make out? Do we really care as much as we appear to do?

A pure heart is a united heart (Ps 86:11) — with an undivided love and loyalty. It is a heart cleansed by the indwelling Holy Spirit (Ps 51:10). The blessing that follows is the privilege of 'seeing God' — not with our physical eyes, since no man can see him and live (Ex 3:20). The invisible God is made visible as he reveals himself to our spiritual eyes by the Lord Jesus, who said 'He that hath seen me hath seen the Father' (Col 1:15. Jn 14:9).

But a day is coming when we shall no longer see 'through a glass darkly' but face to face (1 Cor 13:12), for 'we know that when Christ appears, we shall be like him, because we shall see him as he really is. Everyone who has this hope in Christ keeps himself pure, just as Christ is pure' (1 Jn 3:2-3 GNB).

> Oh for a heart to praise my God,
>   A heart from sin set free...
> A humble, lowly, contrite heart,
>   Believing, true and clean...
> A heart in every thought renewed,
>   And filled with love divine,
> Perfect, and right, and pure, and good,
>   A copy, Lord of Thine!

Charles Wesley

Further reading: Ps 51.

JABA

December 16

Beatitudes (7) — Peace at a Price

Blessed are the peacemakers, for they shall be called the sons of God. Mt 5:9

There is plenty of scope for peacemakers in our hospitals! Living at close quarters with those of differing personalities, outlook, and levels of intelligence and competence can be very difficult, and breeds minor irritations and frustrations easily worsened by thoughtless talk and malicious gossip. Differences of opinion strongly held, competition for advancement or credit, the hint of a smouldering sense of injustice are all made almost intolerable by over-tiredness and the strain of crisis situations.

And we as Christians are called to be peacemakers! Not just those avoiding trouble, but going out of our way to produce peace. Jesus wants us to do something more than 'patch up' differences. He wants us so to live as to be bringers of peace and reconciliation, and this involves a change of heart and attitude that must surely begin with us. He has reconciled us to God 'making peace by the blood of his Cross' (Col 1:20), and we know the keeping power of a peace of heart which is beyond human understanding (Phil 4:7). He asks us to be his followers in spreading his Gospel of peace, to be communicators or 'diffusors' of peace, and this we can only do if we are prepared to lose our concern for ourselves and our own interests.

Our work, our lives and our witness must point to Jesus the Peacemaker, through whom alone we can be at peace with each other, for 'Christ came and preached the Good News of peace to all — to you Gentiles who were far away from God, and to the Jews who were near to him. It is through Christ that all of us...are able to come in the one Spirit into the presence of the Father' (Eph 2:17-18 GNB).

> God promises to own as his children those who are peacemakers. Perhaps, too, those among whom we live and work will recognise that we are, indeed, sons of God.

Further reading: Eph 2:13-22.

JABA

December 17

Beatitudes (8) — With Persecutions

Blessed are those who are persecuted for righteousness' sake for theirs is the kingdom of heaven. Mt 5:10

It may seem strange that a beatitude about peacemakers should be followed by one about persecution. But God's peace is not peace at any price. He made peace with us and within us at immense cost — even the price of the life blood of his own Son. Our role as makers of peace will be costly too.

It is important to notice why the Christian will be persecuted. It is for righteousness' sake, and for Christ's sake (v11). It is possible to be persecuted because we are objectionable or tactless, fanatical or over-zealous, so bringing unnecessary suffering on ourselves. We can be persecuted for our championship of a cause, our campaigning against some social evil. This may not be a bad thing, but it is not what Jesus refers to here. He is speaking of persecution because we are like him: 'If the world hates you, know that it has hated me before it hated you' (Jn 15:19).

The world hated him because he was different. It will hate us for the same reason; 'If you were of the world, the world would love its own; but because you are not of the world, but I chose you out of the world, therefore the world hates you' (Jn 5:19).

Those who show the qualities described in the beatitudes cannot expect to be popular. In fact the lifestyle of the Christian should challenge the pagans round him: no lies, no insults, no 'fiddling', no 'pinching'; integrity and scrupulous honesty are the hallmarks of his character. Such behaviour may be respected, but it will not be popular. Without a word being spoken, it condemns the man of the world and makes him uneasy and unhappy, resentful and spiteful. Persecution is the inevitable consequence of a righteous life (2 Tim 3:12). If we suffer no persecution we should do well to ask ourselves 'why'? (Lk 6:26).

But if we are truly righteous in the sight of God, if we display the characteristics of the new nature described in the beatitudes, God tells us to rejoice, for ours is a reward beyond description. The Kingdom of God, with all its benefits belongs to us. We are part of God's purpose here and now, and we can look forward with expectancy to the future reign of Christ and our eternal inheritance (Mk 10:30). This extends our horizon beyond the bounds of hospital life to eternity, and gives a new perspective to all our relationships. Each quality brings its own blessing. Christ expects each of us to manifest all the qualities. He promises all the blessings.

Jesus ends the beatitudes where he began — Ours is the Kingdom of God (Mt 5:3,10).

Further reading: Mt 5:1-12. 1 Pet 4:12-16.

JABA

December 18

Brotherly Love or Homosexuality?

Love one another warmly as brothers in Christ, and be eager to show respect for one another. Rom 12:10 (GNB)

Nearly every verse in Romans 12 repays meditation, and application to ourselves. In verse 10 we meet one of Paul's favourite phrases 'brotherly love' (AV). This indicates that we should really love all our fellow Christians in every walk of life. We should find out their problems, pray for them and pray with them.

The other side of the coin was experienced by Paul when he went for only three weeks to the town of Thessalonica. In 1 Thessalonians 4:3, he tells them to abstain from sexual immorality (*akatharsia*). Paul uses this Greek word in Romans 1:24, when he describes homosexuality, and on other occasions when it can also be seen to mean homosexuality. In the New Testament adultery and fornication and homosexuality are all equally condemned, and we should be crystal clear in our Christian witness to this. None of these activities is acceptable to God.

When Paul came to Thessalonica he urged his converts not only to abstain from homosexuality, but also to continue in their 'brotherly love' for each other (1 Thes 4:9).

Jesus wanted Christians to be known by their love for fellow Christians. Do I as a Christian doctor show the kind of love — brotherly love — that my Saviour wants me to?

> Lord, help me to recognise my fellow Christians, to show brotherly love to them, and to be eager to show respect for them.

Further reading: 1 Thes 4:1-12

CSG

December 19

Bartimaeus on your Ward

As Jesus was leaving Jericho with his disciples and a large crowd, a beggar named Bartimaeus... sitting by the road... heard that it was Jesus. He began to shout 'Jesus! Son of David! Take pity on me!' Many of the people scolded him and told him to be quiet. But he shouted even more loudly 'Son of David, take pity on me!' Mk 10:46-48 (GNB)

It was a great procession. The crowd was hoping that Jesus would fulfil their expectations as the King of Glory. Many lined the route, and Jesus was the centre of attention. The blind man at the fringe of it all and sitting on the ground was excluded by the mass of shuffling feet. How could he attract attention? He shouted out, but his cry was ignored, even rebuked — they had other things to think about just now, the request for help was ill-timed, and the interruption was a nuisance. But Jesus heard. He stopped and asked to talk to him. He gave his whole attention to the one who wanted him, as though there was no one else there and nothing else to do. He met his need then and there.

I am reminded of a typical ward round; the consultant and his retinue proceed from bed to bed, with house officer, sister and the patients' notes at the centre of the party. The house officer is keen to impress with his memory of blood results, and his knowledge of the small print footnotes of Bailey and Love (a much-loved surgical textbook in UK). Does he hear the faint cry coming from outside the circle? So often a quiet 'Doctor...?' can be heard from a patient with a simple question to ask about his progress. But it is ignored. He is too late, and the 'round' has progressed further down the ward. Sometimes it is an anxious wife who raises her eyebrows as if to speak, hoping to be acknowledged and spoken to, or a nurse trying to get a word in, knowing that a need has been overlooked.

Try to notice the Bartimaeus on your ward today. Stop and listen or, with a quick nod of understanding and a word of promise to return later, calm his fears and anxieties.

> Lord make me sensitive to the spoken and unspoken needs of my patients. May I be quick to hear and respond to the plea for help, or to see the mute appeal in the eyes that follow me down the ward. May I never be too preoccupied to notice, or too busy to stop. Grant that I may comfort those in trouble with the comfort with which I myself am comforted of God.

Further reading: Mk 10:46-52.

HMKB

December 20

Don't Fence Me In

He who loses his life for my sake will find it. Mt 10:39

Most people hate to have their style cramped. It goes right against human nature. A popular song of a few years ago had the recurring refrain 'Don't fence me in'. It had no great merit as a song, but doubtless the thought in it appealed to people. Nobody wants to be fenced in.

Yet no one with a serious job to learn would imagine that training was possible without some surrender of freedom. Medical students know they must discipline themselves to observe and think and study. Young doctors in hospital know they must discipline themselves to work and to go on learning. And so it continues through the years of medical life. The going can be tough, but the result is worth the effort. We must give before we can receive.

This is a basic principle of Nature. Jesus Christ said: 'Unless a grain of wheat falls into the earth and dies, it remains alone; but if it dies , it bears much fruit' (Jn 12:24).

This is the secret that brings life. The abundant life that Jesus Christ speaks of comes only when we surrender our pride to him and admit that his sacrifice for us, not our goodness, fits us for God's presence.

This is the way of living. The Christian who clings to 'freedom', the right to live his own life, does so to his own loss. He has not yet learned that it is only those who, with the apostle Paul, rejoice to be the bond-slaves of Christ, who at the same time come to know the glorious liberty of the children of God.

This is God's own way. The Almighty Father gave his only begotten Son to be the propitiation for our sins. The Eternal Son accepted the limitations of our human nature and gave his life to redeem us. The Holy Spirit comes and dwells among us, so that with graciousness and patience he may turn us from stupidity and waywardness to life and joy and peace.

'Don't fence me in' is the natural cry of the rebellious human heart. It is not God's way. We need then to remember that 'a servant is not greater than his master' (Jn 13:16).

> Lord, help me to know and accept the truth that your service is perfect freedom.

Further reading: Mt 10:34-39. Jn 12:20-26.

RRW

December 21

Sharing the Gospel

And how are they to hear without a preacher? Rom 10:14

The importance of sharing the gospel is obvious. If people are never told about Christ Jesus, how can they believe in him and be saved? When Christ departed this earth he left us, his disciples, with this responsibility. He said, 'Go into all the world and preach the gospel to all creation' (Mk 16:15). Let us ask ourselves this question, 'Is my light shining before men or does it remain hidden?'

As medical practitioners we have intimate dealings with a multitude of people, many of whose needs require much more than a purely physical remedy. Hence we have a marvellous opportunity to witness. Unfortunately, however, our conventional medical education fails to recognise man's spirituality and has no answers for the management of spiritual problems.

As our calling is to be witnesses, how are we then to be effective witnesses? If we look to ourselves and our own strength, seeking answers in worldly resources, all will be darkness. But as we deny ourselves and our own works and instead look to Jesus — to the fullness, to the perfect provision of our needs that is in him — we move from darkness into light. And as the Apostle John says, 'if we walk in the light, as he is in the light, we have fellowship with one another' (1 Jn 1:7).

Walking in the light is a prerequisite for effective fellowship. Our ability to witness is not a natural gift, nor is it learned from literature or experience. The twelve disciples were taught and trained by Jesus himself for three years prior to going out and preaching the gospel. We, too, have to be educated and motivated to be effective witnesses. This is achieved through the activities of the Holy Spirit working within us. We can trust the Holy Spirit to show us when and how to speak freely about Christ and to minister to the spiritual needs of those we meet and treat.

> Heavenly Father, I thank you for the example of Jesus Christ and the early Christians in their work of building up your Kingdom here on earth. Lord, enable me to be an effective witness, through your Spirit working in me, that I may glorify your Name.

Further reading: Col 2:1-7

GB

December 22

Beautiful Feet

How beautiful are the feet of those who preach good news! Rom 10:15

We often have the privilege of passing on good news to our patients. Whether it's reporting that a newborn baby is normal or that a screening test for a fearful disease is negative, our words can trigger enthusiastic and happy responses. Occasionally, we can provide good news in tense situations. Gasping to pull air in past a swollen epiglottis, a young girl looked at her mother with panic in her eyes. Shortly after arriving at the hospital, the child slumped over, apnoeic. The mother ran from the room screaming, 'my baby's dead!' A few minutes later, however, I had the privilege of telling that mother that an airway had been established and that the child should be home and fully normal within days. It was a thrill to me to be able to proclaim the good news, to be able to report peace to a woman whose world seemed to be tumbling in on her. I still remember the grateful smiles as the girl left hospital a few days later.

Millennia ago oppressed Israelites knew this mother's feeling of relief. How lovely it was for them to see a young man, with dust trailing his feet, running on a distant mountain. And how glorious it was for people waiting at the city gate to hear the runner shout news of victory as he completed his run from a distant battlefield.

Twice in the biblical record before Christ, we are presented with a description of a messenger's beautiful feet. In each case, the courier was returning to afflicted people. Spiritually, politically, and economically, the Hebrew people faced difficult times. Having turned away from God, the nation had lost the freedom and stability that God offered. To people nearly buried in their distress, God's prophets told of coming messengers who would bring good news. There was promise for the near future and for times far off.

We wait today with godly men of old for the final revelation of God's victory over disease, sin and death. But we also have a promise that God will work now in all circumstances to bring about good for his people. This is good news for us and for our patients. Even though we may not see the beginning of the age free from sorrow and death in our physical lifetimes, God promises to bring about good from the bad situations that we, his people, face. With our patients, we shall face sorrow. Nonetheless, good can come. This truth encourages me.

I am thankful that I have the privilege of bearing good news. But I am challenged, too, to take some of the responsibility of the biblical messengers. Their messages did not end with news of victory at war. Isaiah's messenger told his people, 'Your God reigns!' I, too, must point to God as I provide good news, for every good and perfect gift is from above. And in hardship, I can look with my patients for the good that God will bring now and in the coming age.

> Get you up to a high mountain,
>   O Zion, herald of good tidings;
> lift up your voice with strength,
>   O Jerusalem, herald of good tidings.
>   lift it up, fear not;
> say to the cities of Judah,
>   'Behold your God!'

Is 40:9

Further reading: Is 52:7. Rom 8:28-39. Jas 1:17.

PRF

December 23

Retirement

... they shall sit every man under his vine and under his fig tree. Mi 4:4

Doctors and others contemplating retirement tend to think of it in terms of these words of the prophet Micah — admittedly taken somewhat out of context. I certainly did. When I retired from regular work some years ago, I was looking forward to a leisurely life of catching up on things I would love to do but had not found time for. I had heard about 'growing old gracefully', and it sounded good. Micah had the right idea: every man sitting under his own vine and under his own fig tree.

Maybe for me it would be a gum tree instead of a fig tree (in Australia the ratio of gum trees to fig trees is many millions to one). But that was a detail. It would just be good to put my feet up and relax.

It did not happen that way at all. A successful outcome from an operation made it clear that another chapter was ready to be written in the book of my life. Rashly I said to the Lord: 'What do you want me to do now? I am ready'. He took me at my word, and I have hardly stopped since.

In particular, my involvement in ICCP (now ICMDA) has brought much doing and travelling; so much so that a good friend of mine has referred in a letter to my 'going up and down upon the earth, like a distinguished predecessor'. I was not too keen about the 'distinguished predecessor' bit (see Jb 1:7, 2:2). But the 'going up and down' bit was fair enough.

The fact is that going up and down on the earth is rather more demanding than putting up my feet under my own gum tree. I have had many attacks of the Jonah syndrome, which is another way of saying that I've done my level best to wriggle out of going somewhere that I did not want to go to although I knew I should. I have hoped that circumstances would stop me from going. But again and again my hopes were dashed. God refused to give me an excuse for not going. And he knew best. Always I have been glad in the long run that I went and grateful for having been sent.

We humans can be very stupid at times — or at least I can be. It takes hard experience to get it into our heads that we cannot know the joy in living that God wants us to have unless we venture to grasp the opportunities he offers us. And that goes for retirement as much as for any other part of life — provided of course that we reach retirement. Some don't (Lk 12:20).

> Lord, teach me to number my days that I may at all stages
> of life apply my heart to wisdom.

Further reading: Mi 4:1-5. Lk 12:13-21.

RRW

December 24

The Woman Who Found Favour With God

... The angel said to her, 'Do not be afraid, Mary, you have found favour with God'. Lk 1:30 (NIV)

Many obstetricians and others who take part in midwifery never quite lose their sense of the wonder of childbirth. Every time it is new, a new event, a new person made in the image of God. And if it brings a sense of wonder to them, no word is adequate to describe the thoughts and feelings of the mother cuddling and beginning to feed this new little bit of life that has been part of her.

Have you ever thought of the mixture of wonder, bewilderment and love in Mary's mind and heart as she cuddled and began to feed the infant Jesus? This little bit of life that had been part of her was to save his people from their sins. He was Emmanuel ('God with us'). And he was her little son.

At the Reformation the excessive devotion and frank worship of Mary in the mediaeval church brought an excessive reaction of indifference in much of Protestant thought about Mary. But the record in Scripture both by Matthew and especially by our medical colleague Luke is clear. 'The Lord is with you', the angel Gabriel had said to Mary, 'you have found favour with God. You will be with child and give birth to a son, and you are to give him the name Jesus. He will be great and will be called the Son of the Most High' (Lk 1:28-32 NIV).

The birth of Jesus adds in infinite degree to the wonder of childbirth. The woman whom God chose for this, the most momentous birth in the world's history, was one who could say simply to God's messenger: 'I am the Lord's servant. May it be as you have said' (Lk 1:38 NIV). That must make us think.

> Not to the rich he came and to the ruling,
>   (men full of meat, whom wholly he abhors),
> Not to the fools grown insolent in fooling
>   Most, when the lost are dying at the doors;
>
> Nay but to her who with a sweet thanksgiving
>   Took in tranquillity what God might bring,
> Blessed him and waited, and within her living
>   Felt the arousal of a Holy Thing.
>
> Ay for her infinite and endless honour
>   Found the Almighty in this flesh a tomb,
> Pouring with power the Holy Ghost upon her,
>   Nothing disdainful of the Virgin's womb.

F W H Meyer, St Paul

Further reading: Mt 1:18-25. Lk 1:26-38.

RRW

December 25

No Ordinary Baby

... to you is born this day in the city of David a Saviour, who is Christ the Lord. Lk 2:11

It is nearly 2000 years since Jesus Christ was born in Bethlehem: at a point in history identifiable because of a census and tax levy ordered by Caesar Augustus at the time: at a location established within a few yards — a rock cave stable beneath the Bethlehem inn; at a time known within hours because the night shift of shepherds had gone on watch.

The scene was one of Spartan simplicity: a manger; a bed of hay; a flickering oil lamp; and their bundle of clothes. No tinsel; no trappings. We do not know if there was so much as a midwife present; the record suggests Joseph was alone to help with the delivery, tie the cord and assist with the third stage.

Such was the birth of Jesus.

This was no ordinary baby. It was the one foretold over the centuries by Abraham, Moses, David and all the prophets. This was he of whom it was said: 'For unto us a child is born, to us a son is given; and his name shall be called Wonderful Counsellor, Mighty God, Everlasting Father, Prince of Peace' (Is 9:6).

His life had been foretold throughout the centuries, often in extraordinary detail, as was revealed as his life progressed. This was he who was to reveal the person of God to mankind and to redeem us to himself.

This concept should not be surprising to us who have seen a baby born, seen the perfection of fingers and toes, face, features and body. We too have seen the microscopic perfection of every cell of every variety, of a million red corpuscles; and perhaps we alone can appreciate that all this was patterned on the nucleus of one cell, one fertilised ovum.

If all this amazing care was lavished on the formation of each one of us we scarcely should be surprised that the Creator does not then leave us but shows a continuing interest in our wellbeing, our needs and our troubles.

This is the marvellous message of Christmas: that God so cared for us — his creatures — that he came to live among us to reveal his nature and later to die for our salvation. Our colleague Luke has described this with great attention to detail. To read his description in the third gospel, perhaps in a modern translation, could make this Christmas the most meaningful we have had.

God has reached out to man; to us.

> Gracious God, we thank you that you have reached out to
> us in Jesus. Grant us grace to respond to you and use us to
> reach out to others with your love.

Further reading: Lk 2:1-22

NB

Reprinted by permission from: *Australian Family Physician*.

December 26

New Every Morning

The steadfast love of the Lord never ceases, his mercies never come to an end; they are new every morning; great is thy faithfulness. La 3:22-23

Anyone reading the book of Lamentations must be struck with the author's deep sense of bitterness at his own people's disobedience, and sadness at the consequent destruction of Jerusalem. Yet equally striking is his affirmation, in the midst of much bitter disappointment, of God's faithfulness and constancy notwithstanding the unfaithfulness of his people.

There are undoubtedly times when a sense of failure looms large — failure to control temper, a lack of patience, or simply a feeling of the inadequacy of my own ability to cope as a doctor (or indeed as a person). Neglecting to spend time with the Lord can make such a sense of guilt more marked. If there is any verse I find particularly encouraging, it is this one, reminding me of God's unshakeable constancy of attitude towards me. As if it is not enough to remind me that God's mercy is infinite, knowing no limits, he reminds me that each morning his mercies to me are new, regardless of the past. If my God can be so accepting of me, and patient with me, he certainly doesn't feel about me or regard me as I regard myself.

> Father, thank you that in your unchanging and yet daily renewed attitude to me you restore my own self-esteem. Help me never to forget the fact of your love and daily given new mercies to me.

Further reading: Ps 89:30-37. 1 Pet 5:7.

JSdeC

December 27

Jesus Cures Leprosy

Jesus... stretched out his hand, and touched him, saying 'Be clean'. And immediately the leprosy left him. Lk 5:13

It remains one of the sad facts about society today that the medical truth that leprosy is not one of the really contagious diseases has not 'got through' to ordinary people. Leprosy sufferers are still shunned in many 'civilisations' and in some parts of the world are still made to live in isolated communities. Indeed, to the shame of 'Christians', there have been 'Christian' hospitals that would not admit leprosy patients, for fear of what their respectable patients might think. Sad to say, the loose way in which the word 'leper' is still used in current English contributes to the perpetuation of this unhealthy view of the disease. Prominent politicians have referred to those they considered moral outcasts as 'the lepers of our society'. Perhaps as a start we as Christian doctors should never allow such usage of the word to go unchallenged. Certainly we should erase the word 'leper' from our personal vocabulary.

Did Jesus know the medical facts about leprosy when he healed the man? When he 'emptied himself' to become a man, did he allow himself in some respects to share the limited information available to those around him, and to share their real fear of contagion? We do not know. If he did, then his action showed courage. But even if he knew that leprosy does not pass itself on by a mere touch, he would still have had to overcome that initial revulsion that even we with our reassuring knowledge have to overcome when we first touch one of those patients more hideously affected by the disease.

But for Jesus there was another aspect. He touched the man, despite the fact that there was no need (Lk 7:10, Mt 8:13); he could heal at a distance. In doing so, he shared the man's ceremonial uncleanness (Lv 22:5-6) and would then himself run the risk of being an outcast. But that was so like him. Not the easy way, but, if necessary, the costly sacrificial way. The same attitude took him to the Cross.

> Help me, Lord, always to see the other person's need, as you did. And in seeking to help, grant me grace to forget myself.

Further reading: Lk 5:12-16. Is 53:4-6. Mt 27:45-46.

PCB

December 28

Christ Will Come Again

Never lose sight of this fact, that time is not the same with the Lord as it is with us — to him a day may be a thousand years, and a thousand years only a day. It is not that he is dilatory about keeping his own Promise... the fact is that he is very patient toward you... Yet, the Day of the Lord will come. 2 Pet 3:8-10 (JBP)

With life as it is we tend to oscillate between hope and despair. Individuals face sickness, suffering and insecurity or tragedy of one sort or another. Society flounders from one crisis to the next. The Christian gospel does indeed bring hope, joy and peace into men's lives now, but we must admit that it is not a panacea for all our current problems.

The Christian hope is an eternal one. Dismiss this as 'pie in the sky', and there is little left. Christians are right when they stress the qualitative and present nature of eternal life, but the Bible never does this at the expense of our future expectation. Jesus said 'I will come again' (Jn 14:3).

Peter has written at length on how to live as a Christian in this present age. He does so in the setting of God's eternal purpose and programme: his purpose — to give all men a chance to repent; his programme — the dissolution of the universe and the establishment of new heavens and a new earth, the home of righteousness (2 Pet 3:10-13).

God kept literally to his promise regarding Christ's first coming. It is not presumptuous to believe that he will do the same with respect to the second.

Peter says that there are two possible reactions to God's love and patience toward us. Men can ignore and spurn them, bringing on themselves a judgment as literal as that which fell on those who perished in the flood: or they can repent and believe, living in holiness and hope, in the light of his coming.

> Thank you for that blest hope of glory,
>   Great day when Christ shall come again,
> Day when, in perfect peace and justice,
>   He in his mercy shall reign.

J E Seddon

Further reading: 2 Pet 3. 1 Thes 4:13-18.

DEBP

December 29

A Life in Retrospect

And Israel blessed Joseph, and said, 'God before whom my fathers Abraham and Isaac did walk, the God which fed me all my life long unto this day, the Angel which redeemed me from all evil, bless the lads...' Gn 48:15-16 (AV)

Hebrews 11:21 tells us that by faith Jacob blessed both the sons of Joseph and worshipped, leaning on top of his staff. To a Jewish reader each of these phrases would carry a wealth of history and meaning. The blessing of Ephraim and Manasseh was remarkable for many things, including the way Jacob spoke of God. He uses a three-fold invocation and addresses the God of his fathers, the God who had fed (shepherded) him and the God who had redeemed him. He dwells on these aspects and stresses that God had shepherded him — all his life long — even when he had been wayward and careless! God had redeemed him — from all evil — even he, who had so greatly wronged and deceived others!

These are both new concepts of God. Of course Abraham, Isaac and others had known God as Shepherd and as Redeemer. But how appropriate that Jacob, the most rebellious of the patriarchs, is the first to speak of God in just these ways.

And what about the staff on which Jacob leaned while blessing the sons of Joseph (Heb 11:21)? Jacob's staff is symbolic of three things. Firstly, it indicated the fact that he was a pilgrim, 'seeking a city with foundations' (Heb 11:10) — that is, seeking the government of God. Secondly, it will have reminded Jacob constantly of his encounter with God, the time when, utterly alone and about to face his wronged brother, he had wrestled with God. He had emerged from that mysterious incident a broken man, but blessed and renamed — and he had limped ever since (Gn 32:24-32). Thirdly, his staff will have spoken to Jacob of his dependence on God. Immediately before he had had that encounter with God at Penuel, he had, as was usual for him, used all his guile and displayed all his resources with utmost skill (Gn 32:1-23). But his past had caught up with him at Penuel (the Face of God), and he had limped to the meeting with Esau, utterly inadequate. Yet God had been sufficient, and he had been preserved.

So an aged pilgrim, who has had dealings with God and who has learnt to depend on him, leans on his staff, worships God his Shepherd and his redeemer, and speaks with confidence of the future...

> Lord it belongs not to my care,
>   Whether I die or live.
> To love and serve thee is my share
>   And this thy grace must give.
> Christ leads me through no darker rooms
>   Than he went through before.
> He that into God's kingdom comes
>   Must enter through this door.

Richard Baxter

Further reading: as indicated in the text.

PCE

December 30

My Shepherd (12)

I shall dwell in the house of the Lord for ever. Ps 23:6

Shepherds sometimes keep a hand-reared lamb or a favourite old sheep close to their own home. The Good Shepherd himself wants us to be with him, where he is (Jn 17:24), and is preparing a 'house' for us 'that where I am, there you may be also' (Jn 14:3). In his revelation John saw the Lord Jesus as a lamb slain, adding: 'The lamb in the midst of the throne will be their Shepherd, and will guide them' (Rev 7:17). While earth-bound, we shall still be prone to wander, but the ultimate fold, our final goal, is to be in his chosen presence for ever.

Yet 'for ever' starts now: we can be very much aware of the enfolding of the Lord in some of the earthly 'homes' that are in a real way 'the house of the Lord'. Some tell thrilling stories of his provision, even of bricks and mortar. Many believers world wide, however, have no home of their own, yet they gather in worship and witness as 'his people and the sheep of his pasture'. We must not neglect such opportunities of fellowship (Heb 10:24-25). Particularly in their junior years, doctors may find it difficult to maintain connection with local churches, but hospital fellowships (though not to be neglected either) do not replace them. We need the mixed fellowship of families and the wider church to keep our outlook and understanding balanced. On the other hand we must beware being so immersed in local church activities as to neglect the particular territory that the Shepherd has given us in the hospital. 'Be shepherds of God's flock that is under your care' (1 Pet 5:2 NIV). To help a lost sheep to head for home is a privilege not to be missed.

Those who have known the Shepherd's faithfulness in this world have absolute confidence on entering the homeward run, that they are heading for the everlasting 'house of the Lord'. We look to our meeting with the Chief Shepherd in humble hope, trusting to his goodness and mercy, not to our own efforts. None of us knows when that will be, but let us echo the prayer in Hebrews 13:20-21 (AV), of one who loved the Shepherd and sought to be his faithful follower:

The God of peace, that brought again from the dead our Lord Jesus, that great Shepherd of the sheep, through the blood of the everlasting covenant, make you perfect in every good work to do his will, working in you that which is well-pleasing in his sight, through Jesus Christ; to whom be glory for ever and ever.

Good Shepherd, may I sing Thy praise
Within Thy house for ever.

H W Baker

Further reading: Ps 100. Jn 10:27-30

JG

December 31

My Shepherd (13) — Into the Fold

Jesus said 'I am the door; if any one enters by me, he will be saved, and will go in and out and find pasture'. Jn 10:9

In early June 1936 a five year old repeated to her mother the allotted memory verses for that day's Sunday School. The selected passage was Psalm 23. After the recital, her mother asked if she had understood what it meant to speak of the Lord as her Shepherd and had she ever asked him to become hers. That Easter had been spent in the Lake District where flocks of sheep and lambs had added interest to the holiday and although too young to understand parables, she could readily grasp the idea of a devoted shepherd seeking lost lambs and wanting to care for them, even at great personal risk. The realisation that the Lord Jesus had given his life to save her and now lived again to take care of her came home in a new way. She and her mother both went up and knelt at her bedside to commit her life into the Good Shepherd's safekeeping, wherever he might lead her. In years to come, he was to lead her to take care of other young children and her own experience was an assurance (sometimes to be shared with grieving parents) that there are none too young to come to Jesus. For her, the 23rd Psalm has never become hackneyed and it has seemed that the path of life pursued since that memorable Sunday has led her steadily through each verse in turn.

There have been many times of undoubted leading (often seen even more clearly in retrospect) yet times of hesitancy and doubt, too. There have been valleys, the darkest one being found in Africa when living at Cottage 23, Kitante Valley: imagine the wry surprise to find that 'Kitante' meant the place for slaughtering the cattle! Even though it felt like a verse 4 experience, it was an assurance to realise that verse 5 would follow — and so it did. Times and events have only served to enhance the psalm's meaning. Theory is now backed by practical experience, leading to increasing thankfulness for the never failing goodness and mercy of God, to be relied upon for the rest of the days to come.

The Lord is, indeed, her Shepherd. Is he yours? Then, come follow.

Further reading: Jos 21:43-45. Jn 4:39-42.

JG

List of Contributors

with Medical Specialty at time of writing and Country of origin

A and AE	Alfredo and Asunta Espinoza. Friends of Israel Gospel Ministry, Argentina
AMB	Allan M Bryson. Ear, Nose and Throat Surgeon, Australia
ASW	Andrew S Wilson. Anatomist, Australia
BH	Bernard Harnik. Psychiatrist, Switzerland
BP	Bruce Peterson. Psychiatrist, Australia
BW	Brian Webster. Research Assistant, Imperial Cancer Research Fund, UK
CDA	Charles D Anderson. Physician, UK retired
CGS	C Gordon Scorer. Surgeon, UK
CSG	C Stewart Goodwin. Associate Professor of Microbiology, Australia
DAB	David A Blaiklock. General Practitioner, New Zealand
DMC	Derek C Macallan. Senior House Officer, UK
DCT	David C Turk. Microbiologist, UK
DEBP	David E B Powell. Pathologist, UK
DEW	Doc E Wheeler. Physician, USA
DFEN	Denis F E Nash. Surgeon, UK
DJB	Donald J Boon. Specialist in Allergy, New Mexico, USA
DMcGJ	Douglas McG Jackson. Surgeon, Medical Research Council Burns Unit, UK
DPB	Denis P Burkitt. Formerly Member, External Staff, Medical Research Council, UK. Formerly Surgeon, Uganda
DPC	Denis Pells Cocks. Obstetrician and Gynaecologist, UK
EC	Ernesto Contreras. Director, a Medical Centre, Mexico
EPF	Ernest P Fritschi. Swiss Orthopaedic Surgeon, S India
FMJ	Fiona M Jameson. General Practitioner, UK
GAL	Gordon A Lavy. Surgeon, UK
GB	Graeme Bennie. General Practitioner with Paediatric Specialty, Australia
GJH	Geoffrey J Hall. General Practitioner, Australia
GKGL	Graeme K G Lim. Ear, Nose and Throat Surgeon, Australia
GNG	Gerald N Golden. Orthopaedic Surgeon, UK
GS	Gordon Stokes. Physician, Australia. Formerly Thailand
HMKB	Helen M K Brown. Senior House Officer, UK
HMW	Hugh Morgan Williams. General Practitioner, UK
HWR	Haddon W Robinson. Formerly General Director, Christian Medical Society, USA
JA	Jahja Adidjaja. Dental Surgeon, Jakarta, Indonesia
JABA	James A B Andrews. Trainee in General Practice, UK
JEL-J	John E Lennard-Jones. Professor of Gastroenterology, UK
JG	Janet Goodall. Paediatrician, UK
JHCM	J Huw C Morgan. General Practitioner, UK
JHEB	John H E Bergin. Radiologist, UK
JSdeC	John S de Caesteker. Medical Registrar in Therapeutics, UK

JT	John Townsend. Medical and Health Consultant, Tear Fund. Formerly Surgeon, Thailand
JWD	John W Dundee. Professor of Anaesthetics, UK
JWMcM	James W McMillan. General Practitioner, Australia. Formerly in India
KFC	Ken F Cabrera. Surgeon, Australia
KM	Kenneth Moynagh. Student Health Officer, City University of London, UK
KOT	Khoo Oon Teik. Formerly Professor of Clinical Medicine, University of Singapore
LMN	Lee-Moy Ng. Senior House Officer, UK. Born in Mauritius
LS	Laurence Simpson. Thoracic Surgeon, Australia
LT	Louis Tay. Dental Graduate. Anglian Minister, Singapore
MC	Muriel Crouch. Surgeon, UK Retired
ME	Micheline Escobar. Resident 2 in Psychiatry, Philippines
NB	Neville Babbage. General Practitioner, Australia
OPG	O Peter Gray. Professor of Child Health, UK
OMY	Ong Meng Yi. General Practitioner, Singapore
PCB	Peter C Bewes. Accident and Emergency Surgeon, UK
PCE	Peter C Elwood. Director, Medical Research Council Epidemiology Unit, UK
PDC	Peter D Campion. Lecturer in General Practice, UK
PIMA	Patricia I M Allen. Senior House Officer, UK
PJ	Peter Jensen. Principal, Moore Theological College, Australia
PMC	Patricia M Chipping. Haematologist, UK
PRF	Philip R Fischer. Paediatrician, USA. Leaving for Zaire
PV	Peter Vos. General Practitioner, New Zealand
RC	Robert Claxton. Surgeon, Australia
RFH	Roger F Hurding. University Medical Officer, UK
RKMS	R Keith M Sanders. General Secretary, ICMDA
RMJ	Robin M Jameson. Formerly Urologist, UK
ROS	Robert O Stephens. Family Physician, Canada
RRW	Ronald R Winton. Formerly Editor, Medical Journal of Australia
SDVW	Stanley D V Weller. Paediatrician, UK. Formerly Professor of Child Health, Uganda
SGB	Stanley G Browne. Chairman, WHO Expert Committee on Leprosy. Consultant Adviser on Leprosy, Department of Health, UK
S-IY	Shun-Ichi Yamamoto. Vice-Director, Tokyo Metropolitan Institute of Gerontology, Japan
S-KT	Siew-Kiong Tham. Surgeon, Australia
SMT	Sydney M Thornton. General Practitioner, Australia
TAG	Trevor A Gray. Registrar in Pathology, UK
TGS	Trevor G Stammers. Trainee in General Practice, UK
VW	Verna Wright. Professor of Medicine, Rheumatologist, UK
WBAS	W Bramwell A Southwell. General Practitioner, Australia
WGB	William G Benson. Industrial Health Officer, UK

Glossary of Terms

Casualty Department
Accident and Emergency Department of General Hospital.

Casualty Officer
Doctor in Casualty Department.

Final clinical year (student)
Year before graduation.

General practice (vocational) training
General practice trainee. Comparable to training of hospital specialists. Recognized rotation of junior hospital appointments with specified period in an approved general practice.

General Practitioner
Primary health care doctor; family physician.

Houseman, House Officer, House Physician, House Surgeon, Resident House 'job'
Terms applied to first year after graduation, during which residence in hospital is obligatory before registration as a doctor.

Intravenous (IV)
Intravenous drip or infusion.

Junior Hospital Doctor
General term for all hospital training grades.

Mess
Doctors' common room.

Primary FRCS
Part One of higher qualification in surgery.

Registrar
First step on 'specialist' ladder.

Senior House Officer
Hospital appointment, second or third year after graduation.

Senior Registrar

With higher qualifications than Registrar. Final training/preparation for recognized specialist appointment.

Unit Administrator

Lay Hospital Administrator.

Personal Notes